First Contigent of Fulton County Boys Ready to Leave for Training Camps

FULTON COUNTY
in the
WORLD WAR

▫▫

Reviewed Under the Direction and Censorship of the
FULTON COUNTY
COUNCIL *of* DEFENSE

▫▫

Edited by
HAROLD VAN TRUMP

"Honor to Whom Honor is Due"

PREFACE

As Chairman of the County Council of Defense, it is a privilege for me to dedicate this volume as a permanent record of the splendid co-operation of the people of Fulton county in the winning of the world war. To the boys who answered their country's call, and to the men, women and children at home who stood solidly behind them in every effort tending to bring the great struggle to a victorious conclusion, the record of Fulton county is one in which we can all take just pride.

By reason of my work as head of the County Council of Defense, none know better than I of the loyal, patriotic spirit of the people of Fulton county which manifested itself in unselfish devotion to the common cause. No work was too arduous, no hours too long, no personal sacrifice too great, but that among our people were found more volunteers for service than could be assigned to work. The county stood as a cohesive mass behind the government, ready to carry out, without question, every order from our leaders. We can all take pride in the fact that Fulton county was known far and near as one of the best organized counties in the state, and that it answered every call, of every nature, promptly and efficiently.

This spendid record of our people deserves to be preserved in permanent form that it may be handed down from generation to generation, not only as a record of a duty well performed, but as an inspiration to those who follow us. For this very reason, it is a matter of sincere regret that this history is not as complete as it should be. Many names are omitted from the following pages which have a proper place there. Among them are soldiers who served in foreign fields, men and women who gave unselfishly of time and money. It must not be intimated that those whose names were omitted were disployal or undeserving of recognition, because there was no blot upon Fulton county's war record. The omissions are due to modesty, indifference and other causes wholly beyond the control of the compilers of the history. Every effort was made and a great amount of time consumed in order to give proper recognition for all service, but the knowledge remains that the history is, at best, only a partial chronicle of the patriotism of Fulton county. However, as such it is a record of loyalty and devotion worth preserving and cherishing.

WILLIAM H. DENISTON,
Chairman County Council of Defense.

THE WORLD WAR

That the assassination of Archduke Ferdinand, heir to the throne of Austria-Hungary, and his morganatic wife at Sarajevo, in Bosnia, June 28th, 1914, was an event which would vitally affect the daily life of every citizen of Fulton county would have seemed preposterous had such a prediction been made when this news was flashed around the world on that memorable day.

That the fanatical youth who slew the royal pair should involve the whole world in war and bring death to over five million men; that his act should have to do with the peace and prosperity of Fulton county; that it should take the best of our young men from the fields, the stores, the factories, and send them beyond the seas to fight and die, if need be; that it should have to do with the food we ate, the clothes we wore, the money we spent or saved; that it should mobilize the thought and energy of practically every mind in Fulton county and bring us to stand united in a single purpose, was wholly unbelievable when the newspapers carried the story of his crime.

The death of the Archduke Ferdinand on June 28, 1914 was the beginning of the war so far as dates go. Yet, plans for the war on the part of Germany had been made many years in advance of this date by extensive preparation employing men, money and science in a mad dream of world domination. The assassination was only the spark which started the general conflagration.

For a time it appeared that the assasination of the royal couple would pass as an incident common to Europe. So far as outward manifestations were concerned the matter had almost dropped from the minds of average men and women when, on the 23rd of July, the Austrian government delivered to Servia an ultimatum which practically deprived that country of its sovereignty and put Austrian officials in charge of its affairs. Forty-eight hours was given for an answer and at the end of that period Austria, backed by Germany, began the bombardment of Belgrade.

The war had started.

Peace-loving men and nations made every endeavor to avert war, but all over Europe the mobilization of armies began. On August

1st, Germany formally declared war on Russia upon the pretext that the mobilization of the Russian army was a menace to Germany. Automatically France became involved as a part of the Triple Entente—England, France and Russia. England, utterly unprepared for war except at sea and with a people strongly wedded to peaceful pursuits, made every effort to avert war. The determination of Germany to attack France, by striking through the neutral territories of Belgium and the Duchy of Luxemburg on August 2nd, 1914, brought vigorous protests from Great Britain. The Germans followed by making formal request to King Albert of Belgium for permission to move troops through his territory, and offered guarantees of protection of life and property. The reply, "Belgium is a nation, not a highway," stamped King Albert as one of the most courageous figures of the war and marked the entry of Belgium into the struggle. A day later German troops entered Belgium, and as the invasion continued evidence of the complete lawlessness and total depravity of the German troops and the German high command became so convincing that those who hoped and prayed that peace might still be maintained gave up that hope and faced the stern reality of war. August 4th, the German army of the Meuse, the very flower of the perfectly equipped, highly efficient German army came into conflict with the Belgian forces, and on the same date Great Britain formally declared war on Germany. In the German Reichstag, Minister von Jagow said: "We are now in a state of necessity and necessity knows no law. We are compelled to override the just protests of the Luxemburg and Belgian governments. The wrong—I speak openly—that we are committing we will endeavor to make good as soon as our military goal is reached." And later in a personal letter to President Wilson, transmitted through Ambassador Gergard, Kaiser William declared that "Belgian neutrality had to be violated by Germany of strategic grounds, news having been received that France was already preparing to enter Belgium." But the untruth of this statement is proven from the fact that when the German army came rushing through Belgium, the French army was facing the Germany frontier and it took days for them to reach the point of attack. Thus Germany disregarded the treaty of 1839, and reaffirmed in 1870, by which Great Britain, Russia and Prussia—the German Empire not having been in existence at that time— agreed to defend the neutrality of Belgium. This treaty was the one which was afterward contemptously referred to as a "scrap of paper" by the German Emperor. Following the invasion of Belgium, the whole of Europe faced the fact that war was inevitable and Germany and Austria were faced by France, Great Britain, Russia, Serbia and Japan. The numerical superirity of the allied countries and the vast resources of men and money made it appear as an unequal contest with the odds favoring the allies, but against this apparent advantage was the most perfect war machine in the history of the world—a huge standing army, drilled to perfection and an accumulation of munitions such as the world had never seen before.

At the outset of the war the task of stopping the German tide fell mostly upon France and Belgium. England, like the United States, had never believed in a large standing army, and its 150,000 men in arms were scattered over the various British possessions all over the world. She at once began recruiting men, and in eight months General Kitchener had 750,000 men equipped and ready for service. The Belgian Army of 100,000 men attempted to hold the 200,000 Germans who demanded free passage into France. The great German howitzers, litterally smashed their way into Belgium, proved the utter uselessness of forts and demonstrated that the war was to be fought under new rules. In every town and village in Belgium, atrocities were practiced which, at the outset of the war, were unbelievable. Stories of the murder of innocent civilians, of the destruction of private property, the maiming of little children and wholesale crimes against women, were received with skepticism all over the civilized world, but subsequent proof of the guilt of the invaders left no room for doubt and showed that a well defined plan of "terrorism" was to be a part of German warfare.

On Thursday, August 10th, the German army had massed in heavy numbers before Namur, where the English and French awaited their attack, confident that they could hold their position by reason of their strategic position at the junction of the Meuse and Sambre rivers and the strength of the Namur forts. The British forces numbered approximately 70,000 men under Gen John French and General Joffre had approximately 120,000 French soldiers in his command. But the Germans with 700,000 men and powerful long range guns, pounded the Namur forts into powder and surged on relentlessly. The allied forces, surprised by the numbers of the German army and the superiority of their field guns, broke in retreat and for a time it appeared the retreat would become a rout, but the skill of the allied commanders saved the day and an orderly retreat was engineered which demanded the maximum toll of German lives for a minimum loss to the Allied forces. On August 21st a fierce German assault drove the allies back to Mauberge. On the 22nd the British lines were just inside the Belgian boundary at Mons. A week later they were at LaFere, only eight-five miles from Paris. At Rheims, the famous cathedral became a target for the German howitzers and the French lost the town, 410 guns and 12,000 men. The Army of the Crown Prince was advancing through Luxembourg, menacing Paris from that direction. Germany was wild with joy and it appeared that nothing could stop the successful advance on Paris.

September 1st, the Germans crossed the Marne into France, and the famous battle of the Marne began and lasted until the 9th, when the German line was pierced and the German retreat began. The forces engaged in this gigantic battle are said to have numbered nearly two-and-a-half million men, a million-and-a-half of allied troops pitted against a million of the Kaiser's fighters. The numerical strength of the allies was nullified to a certain extent from the fact that a large part of the forces were men of peaceful pursuits and of but little military training, while the Germany army was made up of seasoned soldiers equipped with better munitions of war. By the 11th the entire Germany army was in retreat, and the Von Kluck command at the extreme right was threatened with complete obliteration. Whole regiments were cut off and captured, cannon and munitions were left on the field, and only the remarkable strategy of the German commander enabled him to bring the torn remnants of this army back in safety. The battle of the Marne marked the first check in the German advance and ended the prospect of "Christmas dinner in Paris" for the Germany Army.

By September 12th, 1914, the battle of the Marne became the battle of the Ainse. The German retreat hand stopped, and here ensued fighting which ranged along a front from Lille to Nancy and lasted for eighteen months. Towns and villages were taken and retaken, shelled and reshelled until historic edifices became but piles of broken brick and mortar. The front seemed to be dead-locked, but never did the fighting cease. All Belgium, except 35 square miles in the extreme corner, was in German hands. Poison gas became an instrument of warfare in German hands. Ypres twice became a battle ground, and in the second defense the Canadian troops fighting under the British flag, showed a courage which made the new world proud. Hundreds of thousands of men were sacrificed in attack and counter attack along the western battle line without appreciable results.

Fighting in the East

The overwhelming ferocity of the attack of Belgium and France centered public attention on the western front and made important events of the war in the east seem of comparatively small importance. The apparent intention of the German war lords to strike France quickly and decisively in the hope of taking Paris, and to give attention to the war in the east after triumphing over France, left only three army corps for the defense of East Prussia and Galicia. The Czar's forces were striking the eastern border of Prussia almost immediately following the declaration of war. A Russian army of three-quarters of a million men was in possession of East Prussia the small German army was hardly a stumbling block to their advance. To stop this advance it became necessary for Germany to withdraw men from Belgium and France for the defense of her own territory.

General Von Hindenburg with a force of 350,000 men was placed in command of the eastern army and within a week had stopped the Russian army's advance. This feat was accomplished, against heavy odds, by taking advantage of Von Hindenburg's intimate knowledge and study, from a military point of view, of the Masurian Lake district. It illustrates too, the boasted German efficiency and the complete preparation for war. The Masurian Lake district was a region of bogy, marshy lands. What appeared to be solid ground changed into sink holes when heavy traffic attempted to cross it. The Germans had built narrow roads through these marshes and had mapped and studied the physical aspects of the territory as a means of defense in case of invasion. It was natural, therefore, that Von Hindenburg's small army should make a stand in this territory and await the onrush of the larger body of victorious Russians. A portion of the Russian forces were caught in this trap and it is estimated that near a hundred thousand men lost their lives in this quagmire, together with immense stores and munitions, and almost an equal number were captured. By October 1st the whole eastern front had been cleared of the Russians and a large part of the German forces could again be used in France. The superior strategy of the German commanders enabled them, with a comparatively small force of German and Austrian soldiers to invade Russian territory and the world watched with wonder the continued retreat of the stronger Russian army, until it was learned that Russia's small supply of muntions was practically exhausted and that treachery on the part Russian officials was sending food and munitions through the Russian lines into Germany.

It was months before the armies of the Czar were again suitably equipped for war and in the meantime the Germans had pushed on until Warsaw was threatened. On October 4th a force of more than half a million Germans and Austrians were at the very door of Warsaw where the Grand Duke Nicholas with an army of approximately a million men, met the enemy, and drove them back into Germany again encroaching upon German territory in East Prussia and Galicia. The Russians had come back and turned victory for the Germans into disaster. A long, bitter struggle for Warasw ensued with losses exceeding a million men, killed and captured, by the contending armies, and ended in August 1915 with the evacuation of Warsaw.

The fall of Warsaw started the third Russian retreat and again East Prussia was sept clear of the invaders. On June 1st, 1916, the Russian army, a million and a half strong, swept forward again for an attack upon the Germans. The line of battle extended from Riga on the Baltic sea to Czera now within Austria-Hungary. The success of the Russians along the southern end of the line, where they were fighting the Austrians, was overwhelming and it appeared that Russia was again to be the decisive factor in winning an allied victory. Czernowith, Dubno and Lutsk had been taken and a quarter of a million prisoners, and great stores of supplies, had been passed back through the Czar's lines..In the north, Kuropatkin was pushing back Von Hindenburg as succesfully as Brussilov was operating in the south. The Austrian losses in men and supplies had been enormous. There was talk of Austria-Hungary suing for a separate peace.

In spite of the success of her arms, the bravery of the Russian soldiery and the competence of most of the officers, it was soon apparent that the dash and vim had gone from the Russian attack. The slightest set-back was followed by long spells of inactivity. The most trivial defeat was followed by a retreat. Interest in the accomplishment of the Russian arms turned to the government and politicians. Stories of treachery and German influence gained prominence. The assasination of Rasputin, a monk who had gained an influence over the royal household, followed and was credited to those who endeavored to check the pro-German tendencies of the ruling classes. The force of the great Russian army was being crippled and made ineffective by treachery in high places. German intrigue and German propaganda was turning an effective weapon of warfare into a harmless mob. Russian and German soldiers fraternized in the trenches.

As the war progressed Germany's strength became apparent. The unity of purpose, the careful working out of a long-thought-out plan revealed the Kaiser's dream of world empire and "Mittel Europa" as a Teutonic nation. The object of the Kaiser's friendliness to Turkey, of the German training of the "young Turks" in military matters became obvious when Turkish troops, commanded by German officers entered the war. The Turks brought an effective fighting force of a million men to the Teutonic allies. Another addition of 600,000 fighters came when Bulgaria, in October 1915, went over to the Germans. Greece became a bone of contention between the warring factions. King Constance was pro-German, but the Prime Minister Venizelos had sufficient hold on the people to elect a cabinet favorable to the allied cause and give the Allies the use of her railways, telegraph lines and harbors. The king became an exile from his own capital and abdicated in favor of his son Alexander. The Grecian port of Saloniki became the headquarters of the French and English armies in Greece and in course of time more than 300,000 men were gathered here and rushed into Macedonia to join the remnant of the Serbian Army, but the union was made too late to be of much benefit to Serbia because early in October a great German force under Makensen had entered Serbia and practically obliterated the army and drove the civil population beyond the boundaries of their own land. On August 27, 1916 Roumania declared war on Austria-Hungary and on the same day Italy entered the war on the side of Allies. This action on the part of Roumania ended disasterously for her as her small army was powerless against the enemy after Russia became a negligent factor in the strife. The British expedition against the Dardanelles—characterized as the greatest blunder of the war—started in March 1915 and ended in failure in the following January. The British figures of the losses were reported as 112,921 killed and 96,683 admitted to the Allies' hospitals. The only extraordinary thing about the expedition as the withdrawal of the troops without losses of any consequence, when the hopelessness of the situation was realized.

Meanwhile, south of the Dardanelles the Turkish Empire was threatened by different forces. The Rusians had taken Erzerum, a Turkish stronghold. From there a part of the army of Grand Duke Nicholas was dispatched to take Trebizond, the chief port on the

Black Sea. On April 18th, Trebizond had fallen to the army cooperating with the fleet in the Black Sea. The British were fighting their way up the River Tigris toward Jerusalem, encountering stiff resistance and meeting with disheartening defeats. But the perseverance of the British forces finally won and December 1917 Jerusalem was taken by the Britsh under command of General Sir Edmund Allenby. This year closed with the British in full control of Syria, Palestine and Mesopotamia, but the Rusian operations, essential to complete Allied success were held in check by the conditions of anarchy prevailing in Petrograd.

The War at Sea and In the Air

The supremacy of England on the seas practically tied up the German battle ships, as well as all German merchant ships at home and in neutral waters, at the very beginning of the war. British destroyers promptly sunk practically every German vessel which attempted to run the blockade, while merchant ships flying the British flag supplied her people with food, transported her armies from the colonies and kept them supplied with munitions of war. The Allied plan was to control the seas and by enforcing a food blockade, eventually starve Germany into submission. At the outset of the war, the ultimate success of this plan seemed certain, however, on September 22nd, 1914, three British cruisers the Aboukr, Cressy and Hougue were quickly sunk by the German submarine U-9, in charge of Captain Otto Weddigen with 26 men aboard. Twelve hundred men, materials of immense value and three fine crusiers were totally destroyed by a handful of men. This marked the entrance of the submarine as an instrument of war.

The effectiveness of the submarines became more and more apparent as the war progressed, and despite the protests of neutral nations, merchant ships, bearing food and supplies, were sunk regardless as to whether they were armed or unarmed. On May 7th, 1915 occurred the sinking of the Lusitania, a passenger ship carrying more than 2000 people, including many women and children as well as a number of distinguished Americans. 1,198 lives were lost, including 114 Americans. This act, more than any one thing aroused the ire of the Aemrican people, and made it apparent that sooner or later the United States must enter the war on the side of the Allies. President Wilson made vigorous protest to the German government, and it appeared that the United States was on the verge of war, but Germany practiced a diplomatic deceit which temporarily lulled suspicion and postponed the American entry.

The air, like land and sea, was a battle ground. When the war opened there was a little difference between the air power of the belligerents, Germany had a considerable fleet of Zeppelins, which proved a disappointment when placed in operation. France had something near 2000 military planes at the beginning of the war, England 800, and the Central powers had, perhaps, as many planes and dirigibles as the Allies. The utility of these "eyes of the army" became more and more of importance as the war progressed and thousands of planes were in daily use in the conflict.

The West Front

September 15th, 1915 brings us again to the war on the west front when the French offensive in the Champaigne started with rush which drove the firmly-entrenched Germans from their front line trenches and swept them back two and one-half miles along a fifteen mile front in a single day. Simultaneously the French and British, under General Foch, were fiighting to the northward along Vimy Ridge. The battle started in September and lasted until January 1916, with losses of approximately 165,000 to the Allies and 200,000 for the Central Powers, when the active fighting shifted to the eastward and the historic battle of Verdun was begun. The Crown Prince was in command of the German forces, and the French determination crystallized in the cry "They shall not pass" resulted in effectually breaking the offensive of the German army and placing them on the defensive for the first time since the beginning of the war. The tremendous preparations of the Germans, the massing of huge armies relieved from service on the Eastern front by the collapse of the Russians, the wealth of big guns and munitions, were gathered together for breaking the Allied lines and continuing the march to Paris. It was the supreme effort of Germany to break the French, but after six weeks of fighting, Germany had sacrificed a quarter of a million men while the Allied losses were estimated at 100,000 men. The fighting continued until June 23, 1916, when the last great German effort was made against Verdun and the Crown Prince again threw the flower of the German army upon the Allied lines. The battle raged for months and ended in demonstrating the futility of forcing the Allied defense.

Italy entered the war on May 23rd, 1915 by declaration of war against Austria. Long a member of the Triple Alliance—Germany, Austria and Italy—which bound her to the Central Powers in a defensive war, it required many stormy arguments in the Italian parliment to bring that country into the conflict. The Russians were in full retreat from Galicia when Italy came to the aid of the Allies with aproximately a million men, ready for service. By the end of July Italy was in possession of most of Trentino and her troops were attacking along a front of seventy-five miles from Tarvis to the Adriatic. By December 1915, Italy had established herself within Austria's borders and made an Austrian invasion of her own country appear well nigh impossible.

In May 1916 the Austrians launched an attack which, in ten days, reclaimed practically all of the territory gained by the Italians and left the Austrians in possession of 300 square miles of Italy. The disaster resulted in an overthrow of the Italian ministry, and a stiffening of the Italian defense turned the advance into a deadlock. Soon, another Italian offensive was launched and on August 9th, King Victor Emanuel and the Duke of Acosta rode into the captured city of Goriza. Here Italy paused to recuperate her powers, and Germany, long apparently indifferent to the losses Italy had inflicted upon the Austrians, turned her attention to the menace of Italy. She withdrew great bodies of troops from the Russian front and in connection with the Austrians prepared for a decisive attack. Italy was without proper munitions and food, German propaganda had worked dissatisfaction in the ranks of the army and with the socialistic party in Italy. The Allies had been slow in appreciating the dire necessity of Italy for food and munitions. Austrian and Italian troops fraternized and mutual promises of no more killing were pledged. Then, the Austrian troops were withdrawn and replaced by German shock troops who smashed through the Italian lines, almost unopposed. The gap opened by this treachery was big enough to disorganize the whole Italian line and in three days the entire army was in retreat. By February 1918 the Italian army had fallen back to the River Piave, and only then did they succeed in reorganizing their forces and stopping the German advance. The Piave became to Italy what Verdun meant to the French.

The Russian Collapse

On March 16, 1917, the Czar's train was located on a siding at the little town of Pskov. Guchkoff and Shulgni came down from Petrograd and demanded the Czar's abdication in favor of his son. He declined to be separated from his son and signed an abdication in favor of his brother, the Grand Duke Michael. When the news of the abdication was reported to the Duma, a storm of protest broke and the Grand Duke rejected the proffered regency and the power passed into the hands of a Provisional Government, the members of which were appointed by the Duma. So passed the oldest autocracy in Europe and the real troubles of Russia began. The Duma was the legal instrument of government in Russia but its powers were immediately usurped by the "Council of Workmen's and Soldier's Deputies," known more briefly as the soviet. Alexander Kerensky, a member of both the Duma and the council, became the head of the government. He made a heroic effort to stem the tide of revolt and to hold Russia in line with the Allies. Nicolai Lenine and Leon Trotzky, leaders of the Soviet, overthrew the Kerensky government, obliterated the Duma and the Provisional Government, and established a reign of anarchy in Russia that continues until the present time. The overthrow of the Kerensky government ended the participation of Russia in the war.

The United States Enters the War

From the very outset of the war there was a "war party" in the United States, however small in number. The great mass of the American people viewed the struggle as an European muddle in which we had no interest, and in which we would be very foolish to interfere. The invasion of Belgium, and the almost unbelievable atrocities visited by the Germans upon civilians in that country and northern France, added vastly to the war sentiment in this country The war party clamored wildly for war, many American boys and men, roused by stories of the ravishing of women and maiming little children, enlisted in the French, English or Canadian troops, but the great majority of Americans were wedded to peace. A growing number favored military preparations on a large scale but wanted to cling to neutrality so long as such a course could be pursued with honor.

The sinking of the Italian liner Falaba, in which one American lost his life, and the attack upon the American ship, Gulflight, in which her captain lost his life, were followed by protests to the German government. By the sinking of the Lusitania, in which 1198 lives were lost, 114 of whom were Americans, Germany forced the United States into the war. On May 13, 1915 the President lodged a dignified and firmly worded protest against this murderous violation of the rights of neutrals and the German government replied with voluminous correspondence by which it sought to gain time. While this exchange of views was taking place, the White Star Liner Arabic was torpedoed without warning, on August 19, 1915. The Germans followed this act by giving orders that "liners will not be sunk without warning, and without insuring the safety of non-combatants." Time mellowed the Lusitania disaster, and the war party grew slowly—but surely. The President was re-elected in the fall of 1916 in a campaign in which the slogan "He kept us out of war," was a factor. The sentiment of the country was against war. William J. Bryan, a pronounced pacifist, resigned his portfolio as Secretary of State, following the diplomatic exchanges of opinion over the sinking of the Lusitania. The pacific tendency of the United States, the tenacity with which we clung to neutrality, convinced the German government that the United States could not be dragged into the world conflict. A large population of Germans and citizens of German ancestry, was an added reason for the Teutonic belief that the United States would not enter the war on the side of the Allies. Here Germany made an error in judgment which ended her dreams of world supremacy. Other submarine sinkings continued, the Tubabtia and Palembang—Dutch liners were sunk without warning. In March 1916 the channel steamer Sussex was torpedoed with great loss of life, including many American citizens. The Sussex incident caused the President, in a message to Congress, delivered on April 19th, to declare that "Unless the Imperial German Government should now immediately declare and effect an abandonment of its present methods of warfare against passenger and freight vessels, the Government can have no choice but to sever diplomatic relations with the Government of the German Empire altogether."

Further attempts on the part of Germany to continue diplomatic correspondence only showed the futility of attempting to remain neutral. On the 1st of February, Ambassador von Bernsdorff was handed his passports after delivering the ultimatum that Germany would continue sinking both neutral and belligerent ships found in the war zones. Following this additional sinkings were chronicled and Congres was called in special session on April 2nd, when the President read his message, which ended with these impressive words:

"It is a fearful thing to lead this great, peaceful people into war, into the most terrible and disasterous of all wars, civilization itself seems to be in the balance. But the right is more precious than peace, and we shall fight for the things which we have always carried nearest our hearts—for democracy, for the right of those who submit to authority to have a voice in their own governments, for the rights and liberties of small nations, for a universal dominion of right by such concert of free peoples as shall bring peace and safety to all nations and make the world itself at last free.

"To such a task we can dedicate our lives and our fortunes, everything that we are and everything that we have, the the pride of those who know that the day has come when America is privileged to spend her blood and her might for the principles that gave her birth and happiness and the peace which she has treasured.

"God helping her, she can do no other."

Congress was not slow in granting all the President asked. The Joint Resolutions declaring a state of war to exist was passed by the Senate April 4th and by the House April 5th. The same date the President issued a proclamation to all the world and the United States had entered the war.

But the United States was not prepared for war. Always a peace-loving nation, our Army and Navy was negligible when judged by European standards. Like England, we faced the problem of building an effective war machine from the ground up. At the beginning of 1916 our army numbered 5,016 officers and 92,973 men including 5,733 in the Phillipines. Our Navy had but 58,000 men. We were without transports, munitions, food and clothing. The tremendous task of financing the war, getting together the men and munitions, was not accomplished without blunders, waste and acrimonious debate. Delays that were criminal as well as heart-breaking resulted, but the United States moved forward, slowly but surely, in the building of a war machine. Twenty-eight days after the United States entered the war, an American fleet under Admiral William S. Sims reached the shores of Great Britain and joined the British navy to patrol the sea. In June 1917, an American Expeditionary Force under Gen. John Pershing was co-operating with the Allies on the fields of France. American factories were building ships, making airplanes, munitions, clothing and other supplies on a magnificent scale. The draft was mobilizing the man power of the country. The registration of June 5th, 1917 enrolled the names of nine and a half million men, from whom nearly 700,000 were selected for service and placed in training camps. The National Guard of nearly half a million men were either in camps or on their way over seas. By the end of 1917 more than 1000 ships were in service with almost that many more in course of construction. The food supply of the country had been placed in the hands of Herbert Hoover, who had saved Belgium from starvation during and after the German invasion, and men above military age, women and children were exerting every effort to raise, and conserve, foodstuffs for feeding our soldiers and their Allies. In France, American soldiers built harbors and docks and railroads, preparatory to landing and handling the great American forces in Europe. Camps and training quarters, both in this country and Europe, were built. The first of the American contingent to land in France and England were received with shouts of joy and tremendous demonstrations by the French and English. The Allies, war worn and deadlocked, took heart with the first coming of the American troops. The morale of the Allied Army was vastly improved even though the force of the Americans was numerically small. However, the extensives preparations of the United States for war was convincing evidence that America as in to stay until the finish, and there was little doubt among the Allies as to the ultimate result.

On March 1918 the Germans launched a drive which for more

than a month seemed able to sweep everything before it. General Ludendorf, with a force of 1,800,000 men, launched a ferocious attack on the Allied line from Lens to Rheims. For three months, the French and English, fighting heroically were forced to give ground until the German line stood within less than fifty miles of Paris. The German plan was to crush the Allies before help from the United States could arrive in sufficient numbers to stem the tide. Shells, hurled by a monster German gun, were falling hourly in the streets of Paris.

July 15th, the fifth—and last—German drive was launched. Forty-two German divisions, went into action on a front extending from Chateau Thierry, past Rheims almost to the forests of Argonne. At the former point the Americans faced the German line, and among them were battalions of the United States Marine Corps. The first terrific onslaught of the Germans drove the Americans back and the enemy crossed the Marne at two points. At the Soissons-Rheims salient the British and French were pushed back. But the next day, the line stiffened and the small detachment of marines held Chateau Thierry against the German horde and convinced the world that America could fight. The last German drive was stopped. General Foch, in command of the Allied forces believed that the time had come for an offensive against the Germans. By early August practically all of the territory taken by Germany between Lens and Rheims had been restored. Then came the most spectacular and, to the Americans at least, the most satisfactory operation of the campaign. American forces had been operating in conjunction with the British and French in various sectors of the front, but now, sufficient Americans were on the battlefields to form a great American army and this force under General Pershing, made its first great stroke at St. Mihiel, where four years before the Germans had made a great bend into French territory and held it against all attacks. But the Americans drove them out in two days, and pushed on until American guns were in range of Metz, the German stronghold in Lorraine. Late in August the Americans advanced far up the valley of the Meuse west of Verdun. Late in November the railroad over which the Germans received their supplies and munitions was cut by the American forces at Sedan.

Prior to this, Bulgaria had surrendered. In Palestine the British army under, Sir Edmund Allenby, was sweeping all before it, capturing great Turkish armies. Turkey surrendered during the last week in October and the English fleet, unopposed passed the Dardanelles and took possession of Constantinople. Italy had roused herself, and under the leadership of General Diaz, had pounded the demoralized forces of Austria-Hungary until an armistice was agreed to on November 4th, which put Austria out of the war for good.

The hope of Germany for world empire was dead.

November 8th, German officers, blindfolded and under the white flag, came humbly to General Foch's headquarters to learn upon what terms their surrender would be accepted. On the following day the Kaiser abdicated and Germany became a republic. November 11th, 1918, the armistice was signed and 11 o'clock of the same day the war had ended so far as battles went.

Arrayed against the Central Powers, made up of Germany, Austria-Hungary, Bulgaria and Turkey, were the United States, Belgium, Brazil, China, Costa Rica, Cuba, France, Guatamala, Great Britain, Greece, Haiti, Honduras, Itay, Japan, Siberia, Montenegro, Nicaragua, Panama, Portugal, Roumania, Russia, San Marino, Serbia and Siam. Of the Allies, Russia alone, is a changed nation and will be years in righting her internal troubles.

Germany lost all she hoped to gain. The Kaiser lost his throne and had to take refuge in Holland and may eventually be called upon to face a tribunal to answer for the terror he visited upon the world. Millions of his men are dead or crippled and the country faces a war debt which will be a burden to children yet unborn. The country has lost Alsace and Lorraine, Poland and all colonies.

The old Austrian Emperor is dead and the new one had to give up his throne and seek refuge in Switzerland. The empire is broken into many bits from which will spring new nations. The Bulgarian throne crumbled, Turkey is shorn of her power.

The peace treaty was drawn up after many months of work with President Wilson representing America, Premier Clemanceau for France, Premier Lloyd George for Great Britain and Premier Nitti for Italy taking the chief parts. Briefly sketched, the main points of the treaty are: Germany must pay for the property ruined in the war; she must give Alsace and Loraine to France, and Poland to the Poles; she must not form a large army or navy and Allied soldiers will occupy parts of her territory until she has paid in full.

Along with the peace treaty was drawn up the "Covenant of the League of Nations," designed to make future wars impossible, but the fate of this agreement still hangs in the balance as this is written.

General Pershing's Report of America's Part in the War

The following pages are from General John J. Pershing's official report to The Secretary of War, detailing the part America played on the western front:

COMBAT OPERATIONS

During our periods of training in the trenches some of our divisions had engaged the enemy in local combats, the most important of which was Seicheprey by the 26th on April 20th, in the Toul sector, but none had participated in action as a unit. The 1st Division, which had passed through the preliminary stages of training, had gone to the trenches for its first period of instruction at the end of October, and by March 21st, when the German offensive in Picardy began, we had four divisions with experience in the trenches, all of which were equal to any demands of battle action. The crisis which this offensive developed was such that our occupation of an American sector must be postponed.

On March 28th I placed at the disposal of Marshal Foch, who had been agreed upon as Commander in Chief of the Allied Armies, all of our forces, to be used as he might decide. At his request the 1st Division was transferred from the Toul sector to a position in reserve at Chaumont-en-Vexin. As German superiority in numbers required prompt action, an agreemnet was reached at the Abbeville conference of the Allied Premiers and Commanders and myself on May 2nd by which British shipping was to transport ten American divisions to the British army area, where they were to be trained and equipped, and additional British shipping was to be provided for as many divisions as possible for use elsewhere.

On April 26th the 1st Division had gone into the line in the Montdidier salient on the Picardy battle front. Tactics had been suddenly revolutionized to those of open warfare, and our men confident of the results of their training were eager for the test. On the morning of May 28th this division attacked the commanding German position in its front, taking with splendid dash the town of Cantigny and all other objectives which were organized, and held steadfastly

General Pershing's Headquarters in France

Aeroplane View of General Headquarters A. E. F. in France

against vicious counter-attacks and galling artillery fire. Although local, this brilliant action had an electrical effect, as it demonstrated our fighting qualities under extreme battle conditions, and also that the enemy's troops were not altogether invincible.

The German's Aisne offensive, which began on May 27th, had advanced rapidly toward the River Marne and Paris, and the Allies faced a crisis equally as grave as that of the Picardy offensive in March. Again every available man was placed at Marshal Foch's disposal, and the 3rd Division, which had just come from its preliminary training area, was hurried to the Marne. Its motorized machine gun battalion preceded the other units, and successfully held the bridgehead at the Marne opposite Chateau-Thierry. The 2nd Division, in reserve near Montididier, was sent by motor trucks and other available transport to check the progress of the enemy toward Paris. The division attacked and retook the town and railroad station at Bouresches and sturdily held its ground against the enemy's best Guard divisions. In the battle of Belleau Wood which followed our men proved their superiority, and gained a strong tactical position with far greater loss to the enemy than to ourselves. On July 1st, before the 2nd was relieved, it captured the village of Vaux with most splendid precision.

Meanwhile, our Second Corps, under Major General George W. Read, had been organized for the command of our divisions with the British which were held back in training areas or assigned to second line defenses. Five of the ten divisions were withdrawn from the British area in June, three to relieve divisions in Lorraine and the Vosges, and two to the Paris area to join the group of American divisions which stood between the city and any further advance of the enemy in that direction.

The great June-July troop movement from the States was well under way, and, although these troops were to be given some preliminary training before being put into action, their very presence warranted the use of all the older divisions in the confidence that we did not lack reserves. Elements of the 42nd Division were in the line east of Rheims against the German offensive of July 15th, and held their ground unflinchingly. On the right flank of this offensive four companies of the 28th Division were in position in face of the German infantry. The 3rd Division was holding the bank of the Marne from the bend east of the mouth of the Surmelin to the west of Mezy, opposite Chateau-Thierry, where a large force of German infantry sought to force a passage under suport of powerful artillery concentrations and under cover of smoke screens. A single regiment of the 3rd wrote one of the most brilliant pages in our military annals on this occasion. It prevented the crossing at certain points on its front, while, on either flank, the Germans who had gained a footing pressed forward. Our men firing in three directions met the German attacks with counter-attacks at critical points, and succeeded in throwing two German divisions into complete confusion, capturing six hundred prisoners.

The great force of the German Chateau-Thierry offensive established the deep Marne salient, but the enemy was taking chances, and the vulnerability of this pocket to attack might be turned to his disadvantage. Seizing the opportunity to support my conviction, every division with any sort of training was made available for use in a counter offensive. The place of honor in the thrust toward Soissons on July 18th was given to our 1st and 2nd divisions, in company with chosen French divisions. Without the usual brief warning of a preliminary bombardment, the massed French and American artillery, firing by the map, laid down its rolling barrage at dawn while the infantry began its charge. The tactical handling of our troops under these trying conditions was excellent throughout the action. The enemy brought up large numbers of reserves and made a stubborn defense both with machine guns and artillery, but through five days' fighting the 1st Division continued to advance until it had gained the heights above Soissons and captured the village of Berzy-le-Sec. The 2nd Division took Beaurepaire farm and Vierzy in a very rapid advance and reached a position in front to Tigny at the end of its second day. These two divisions captured 7,000 prisoners and over 100 pieces of artillery.

The 26th Division, which with a French division was under command of our First Corps, acted as a pivot of the movement toward Soissons. On the 18th it took the village of Torcy, while the 3rd Division was crossing the Marne in pursuit of the retiring enemy. The 26th attacked again on the 21st, and the enemy withdrew past the Chateau-Thierry-Soissons road. The 3rd Division continuing its progress took the heights of Mont St. Pere and the villages of Charteves and Jaulgonne in the face of both machine gun and artillery fire.

On the 24th, after the Germans had fallen back from Trugny and Epiede, our 42nd Division, which had been brought over from the Champagne, relieved the 26th, and, fighting it way through the Forest de Fere, overwhelmed the nests of machine guns in its path. By the 27th it had reached the Ourcq, whence the 3rd and 4th divisions were already advancing, while the French divisions with which we were co-operating were moving forward at other points.

The 3rd Division had made its advance into Roncherees Wood on the 29th, and was relieved for rest by a brigade of the 32nd. The 42nd and 32nd undertook the task of conquering the heights beyond Cierges, the 42nd capturing Sergy and the 32 nd capturing Hill 230, both American divisions joining in rapids pursuit of the enemy to the Vesle, and thus the operation of reducing the salient was finished. Meanwhile the 42nd was relieved by the 4th at Chery-Chartreuve, and the 32nd by the 28th, while the 77th Division took up a position on the Vesle. The operations of these divisions on the Vesle were under the Third Corps, Major General Robert L. Bullard commanding.

BATTLE OF ST. MIHIEL

With the reduction of the Marne salient we could look forward to the concentration of our divisions in our own zone. In view of the forthcoming operation against the St. Mihiel salient, which had long been planned as our first offensive action on a large scale, the First Army was organized on August 10th under my personal command. While American units had held different divisional and corps sectors all along the western front, there had not been up to this time, for obvious reasons, a distinct American sector; but in view of the important part the American forces were now to play it was necessary to take over a permanent portion of the line. Accordingly on August 30th the line beginning at Port-sur-Seille, east of the Moselle and extending to the west through St. Mihiel, thence north to a point opposite Verdun, was placed under my command. The American sector was afterward extended across the Meuse to the western edge of the Argonne Forest, and included the 2nd Colonial French Corps which held the point of the salient, and the 17th French Corps which occupied the heights above Verdun.

The preparation for a complicated operation against the formidable defenses in front of us included the assembling of divisions, and of corps and army artillery, transport, air craft, tanks, ambulances, the location of hospitals, and the moulding together of all the elements of a great modern army, with its own railheads, supplied directly by our own Service of Supply. The concentration for this operation, which was to be a surprise, involved the movement mostly at night of approximately 600,000 troops and required for its success the most careful attention to every detail.

The French were generous in giving us assistance in corps and army artillery, with its personnel, and we were confident from the start of our superiority over the enemy in guns of all calibres. Our heavy guns were able to reach Metz and to interfere seriously with German rail movement. The French independent air force was placed under my command, which, together with the British bombing squadrons and our own forces, gave us the largest assembly of aviation that had ever been engaged in one operation on the western front.

From Les Eparges around the nose of the salient of St. Mihiel to the Moselle River the line was roughly forty miles long and situated on commanding ground, greatly strengthened by artificial defenses. Our First Corps (82nd, 90th, 5th and 2nd divisions), under command of Major General Hunter Liggett, resting its right on Pont-a-Mousson, with its left joining our Fourth Corps (the 89th, 42nd and 1st divisions), under Major General Joseph T. Dickman, in line to Xivray, were to swing in toward Vigneulles on the pivot of the Moselle River for the initial assault. From Xivray to Mouilly the Second Colonial French Corps was in line in the center, and our Fifth Corps, under command of Major General George H. Cameron, with the 26th and 4th U. S. divisions and a French division at the western base of the salient, were to attack three difficult hills, Les Eparges, Combres and Amaranthe. Our First Corps had in reserve the 78th Division, our Fourth Corps the 3rd Division, and our First Army the 35th and 91st divisions, with the 80th and 33rd available. It should be understood that our corps organizations are very elastic, and that we have at no time had permanent assignments of divisions to corps.

After four hours' artillery preparation the seven American divisions in the front line advanced at 5 A. M. on September 12th, assisted by a limited number of tanks, manned partly by Americans and partly by the French. These divisions, accompanied by groups of wire cutters and and other armed with bangalore torpedoes, went through the successive bands of barbed wire that protected the enemy's front line and support trenches in irresistible waves on schedule time, breaking down all defense of an enemy demoralized by the great volume of our artillery fire and our sudden appearance out of the fog.

Our First Corps took Thiaucourt, while our Fourth Corps curved back to the southwest through Nonsard. The Second Colonial French Corps made the slight advance required of it on very difficult ground, and the Fifth Corps took its three ridges and repulsed a counter attack. A rapid march brought reserve regiments of a division of the Fifth Corps into Vigneulles in the early morning, where it linked up with patrols of our fourth Corps, closing the salient and forming a new line west of Thiaucourt to Vigneulles and beyond Fresnes-en-Woevre. At the cost of only 7,000 casualties, mostly light, we had taken 16,000 prisoners and 443 guns, a great quantity of material, released the inhabitants of many villages from enemy domination and established our lines in a position to threaten Metz. The signal success of the new American First Army in its first offensive was of prime importance. The Allies found they had a formidable army to aid them, and the enemy learned finally that he had one to reckon with.

MEUSE-ARGONNE OFFENSIVE—FIRST PHASE

On the day after we had taken the St. Mihiel salient, much of our corps and army artillery which had operated at St. Mihiel, and our divisions in reserve at other points, were already on the move toward the area back of the line between the Meuse River and the western edge of the Forest of Argonne. With the exception of St. Mihiel, the German front line from Switzerland to the east of Rheims was still intact. In the general attack planned all along the line, the operation assigned the American Army as the hinge of this allied offensive was directed toward the important railroad communications of the German armies through Mezieres and Sedan. The enemy must hold fast to this part of his lines or the withdrawal of his forces with four years' accumulation of plants and material would be dangerously imperiled.

The German Army had as yet shown no demoralization, and, while the mass of its troops had suffered in morale, its first class divisions and notably its machine gun defense were exhibiting remarkable tactical efficiency as well as courage. The German General Staff was fully aware of the consequences of a success on the Meuse-Argonne line. Certain that he would do everything in his power to oppose us, the action was planned with as much secrecy as possible, and was undertaken with the determination to use all our divisions in forcing a decision. We expected to draw the best German divisions to our front and consume them, while the enemy was held under grave apprehension lest our attack should break his line which it was our firm purpose to do.

Our right flank was protected by the Meuse, while our left embraced the Argonne Forest, whose ravines, hills and elaborate defenses screened by dense thickets had been generally considered impregnable. Our order of battle from right to left was the Third Corps from Malancourt to Vauquois, with the 70th, 37th and 91st divisions in line and the 32nd Division in corps reserve; and the First Corps, from Vauquois to Vienne-le-Chatueau, with the 35th, 28th and 77th divisions in line and the 92nd in corps reserve. The army reserve consisted of the 1st, 29th and 82nd divisions.

On the night of September 25th our troops quietly took the place of the French who thinly held the line in this sector, which had long been inactive. In the attack which began on the 26th we drove through the barbed wire entanglements and the sea of shell craters across No Man's Land, mastering all the first line defenses. Continuing on the 27th and 28th, against machine guns and artillery of an increasing number of enemy reserve divsions, we penetrated to a depth of from three to seven miles and took the village of Montfaucon and its commanding hill, and Exermont, Gercourt, Cuisy, Septsarges, Malancourt, Ivoiry, Epinonville, Charpentry, Very and other villages. East of the Meuse, one of our divisions which captured Marcheville and Rievelle, giving further protection to the flank of our main body. We had taken 10,000 prisoners; we had gained our point of forcing the battle into the open, and were prepared for the enemy's reaction which was bound to come, as he had good roads and ample railroad facilities for bringing up his artillery and reserves.

In the chill rain of dark nights our engineers had to build new roads across spongy, shell torn areas, repair broken roads beyond No Man's Land, and build bridges Our gunners, with no thought of sleep, put their shoulders to wheels and drag-ropes to bring their guns through the mire in support of the infantry now under the increasing fire of the enemy's artillery. Our attack had taken the enemy by surprise, but, quickly recovering himself, he began fierce counter attacks in strong force, supported by heavy bombardments with large quantities of gas. From September 28th until October 4th we maintained the offensive against patches of woods defended by snipers and continuous lines of machines guns, and pushed forward our guns and transport, seizing strategical points in preparation for further attacks.

OTHER UNITS WITH ALLIES

Other divisions attached to the Allied armies were doing their part. It was the fortune of our Second Corps, composed of the 27th and 30th divisions, which had remained with the British, to have a place of honor, in co-operation with the Australian Crops, on September 29th and October 1st, in the assault upon the Hindenburg line, where the St. Quentin Canal passes through a tunnel under a ridge. The 30th Division speedily broke through the main line of defense for all its objectives, while the 27th pushed on impetuously through the main line until some of its elements reached Guoy. In the midst of the maze of trenches and shell craters, and under cross fire from machine guns, the other elements fought desperately against odds. In this and in later actions, from October 6th to October 19th, our Second Corps captured over 6,000 prisoners and advanced over 13 miles. The spirit and aggressiveness of these divisions have been highly praised by the British Army Commander under whom they served.

On October 2nd-9th our 2nd and 36th divisions were sent to assist the French in an important attack against the old German positions before Rheims. The 2nd conquered the complicated defense works on their front against a persistent defense worthy of the grimmest period of trench warfare and attacked the strongly held wooded hill of Blanc Mont, which they captured in a second assault, sweeping over it with consummate dash and skill. This division then repulsed strong counter attacks before the village and cemetery of St. Etienne, and took the town, forcing the Germans to fall back before Rheims and yield positions they had held since September, 1914. On October 9th the 36th Division relieved the 2nd, and, in its first experience under fire, withstood very severe artillery bombardment, and rapidly took up the pursuit of the enemy now retiring behind the Aisne.

MEUSE-ARGONNE OFFENSIVE—SECOND PHASE

The Allied progress elsewhere cheered the efforts of our men in this crucial contest as the German command threw in more and more first class troops to stop our advance. We made steady headway in the almost impenetrable and strongly held Argonne Forest, for, despite his reinforcements, it was our Army that was doing the driving. Our aircraft was increasing in skill and numbers and forcing the issue, and our infantry and artillery were improving rapidly with each new experience. The replacements fresh from home were put into exhausted divisions with little time for training, but they had the advantage of serving beside men who knew their business and who had almost become veterans over night. The enemy had taken every advantage of the terrain, which especially favored the defense, by a prodigal use of machine guns manned by highly trained veterans and by using his artillery at short ranges. In the face of such strong frontal positions we should have been unable to accomplish any progress according to previously accepted standards, but I had every confidence in our aggressive tactics and the courage of our troops.

On October 4th, the attack was renewed all along our front. The Third Corps tilting to the left followed the Brieulles-Cunel road; our Fifth Corps took Gesnes, while along the irregular valley of the Aire River and in the wooded hills of the Argonne that border the river, used by the enemy with all his art and weapons of defense, the First Corps advanced for over two miles. This sort of fighting continued against an enemy striving to hold every foot of ground and whose very strong counter attacks challenged us at every point. On the 7th, the First Corps captured Chatel-Chehery and continued along the river to Cornay. On the east of the Meuse sector, one of the two divisions co-operating with the French captured Consenvoys and the Haumont Woods. On the 9th, the Fifth Corps, in its progress up the Aire, took Fleville, and the Third Corps, which had continuous fighting against odds, was working its way through Brieulles and Cunel. On the 10th we had cleared the Argonne Forest of the enemy.

It was now necessary to constitute a Second Army and on October 10th, the immediate command of the First Amry was turned over to Lieutenant General Hunter Liggett. The command of the Second Army, whose divisions occupied a sector in the Woevre, was given to Lieutenant General Robert L. Bullard, who had been commander of the 1st Division and then of the Third Corps. Major General Dickman was transferred to the command of the First Corps, while the Fifth Corps was placed under Major General Charles P. Summerall, who had recently commanded the 1st Division. Major General John L. Hines, who had gone rapidly up from regimental to division commander, was assigned to the Third Corps. These four officers had been in France from early days of the Expedition and had learned their lessons in the school of practical warfare.

Our constant pressure against the enemy brought day by day more prisoners, mostly survivors from machine gun nests captured in fighting at close quarters. On 18th there was very fierce fighting in the Caures Woods, east of the Meuse, and in the Ormont Wood. On the 14th the First Corps took Saint Juvin, and the Ffith Corps, by hand to hand encounters, entered the formidable Kriemhilde line, where the enemy had hoped to check us indefinitely. Later the Fifth Corps penetrated further the Kriemhilde line, and the First Corps took Champigneulles and the important town of Grand Pre. Our dogged offensive was wearing down the enemy, who continued desperately to throw his best troops against us, thus weakening his line in front of our Allies and making their advances less difficult.

DIVISIONS IN BELGIUM

Meanwhile, we were not only able to continue the battle, but our 37th and 91st divisions were hastily withdrawn from our front and dispatched to help the French Army in Belgium. Detraining in the neighborhood of Ypres, these divisions advanced by rapid stages to the fighting line and were assigned to adjacent French Corps. On

October 31st, in continuation of the Flanders offensive, they attacked and methodically broken down all enemy resistance. On November 3rd the 37th had completed its mission in driving the enemy across the Escant River and firmly established itself along the east bank included in the division zone of action. By a clever flanking movement, troops of the 91st Division captured Spitaals Bosschen, a difficult wood extending across the central part of the division sector, reached the Scheldt and penetrated into the town of Audenarde. These divisions received the high commendation from the corps commanders for their dash and energy.

MEUSE-ARGONNE—LAST PHASE

On the 23rd, the Third and Fifth Corps pushed northward to the level of Bantheville. While we continued to press forward and throw back the enemy's violent counter attacks with great loss to him, a regrouping of our forces was under way for the final assault. Evidences of loss of morale by the enemy gave our men more confidence in attack and more fortitude in enduring the fatigue of incessant effort and the hardships of very inclement weather.

With comparatively well rested divisions the final advance in the Meuse-Argonne front was begun on November 1st. Our increased artillery force acquitted itself magnificently in support of the advance, and the enemy broke before the determined infantry, which by its persistent fighting of the past weeks and the dash of this attack, had overcome his will to resist. The Third Corps took Aincreville, Doulon and Andevanne, and the Fifth Corps took Landres-et-St. Georges and pressed through successive lines of resistance to Bayonville and Chennery. On the 2nd, the First Corps joined in the movement which now became an impetuous onslaught that could not be stayed.

On the 3rd, advance troops were hurried forward in pursuit, some by motor trucks, while the artillery pressed along the county roads close behind. The First Corps reached Authe and Chatillon-sur-Bar, the Fifth Corps, Fosse and Nouart, and the Third Corps Halles penetrating the enemy's line to a depth of twelve miles. Our large calibre guns had advanced and were skillfully brought into position to fire upon the important railroad line at Montmedy, Longuyon and Conflans. Our Third Corps crossed the Meuse on the 5th, and the other corps in the full confidence that the day was their, eagerly cleared the way of machine guns as they swept northward, maintaining complete co-ordination throughout. On the 6th, a division of the First Corps reached a point on the Meuse opposite Sedan, twenty-five miles from our line of departure. The strategical goal which was our highest hope was gained. We had cut the enemy's main line of communications, and nothing but surrender or an armistice could save his army from complete disaster.

In all, forty-four enemy divisions had been used against us in Meuse-Argonne battle. Between September 26th and November 6th we took 16,059 prisoners and 468 guns on this front. Our divisions engaged were the 1st, 2nd, 3rd, 4th, 5th, 26th, 28th, 29th, 32nd, 33rd, 35th, 37th, 42nd, 77th, 78th, 79th, 80th, 82nd, 89th, 90th and 91st. Many of our divisions remained in line for a length of time that required nerves of steel, while others were sent in again after only a few days' rest. The 1st, 2nd, 5th, 26th, 42nd, 77th, 79th, 80th, 89th and 90th were in the line twice. Although some of the divisions were fighting their first battle, they soon became equal to the best.

OPERATIONS EAST OF THE MEUSE

On the three days preceding November 10th, the 3rd Corps and the 2nd Colonial and 17th French Corps fought a difficult struggle through the Meuse hills south of Stenay and forced the enemy into the plain. Meanwhile my plans for further use of the American forces contemplated an advance between the Meuse and the Moselle in the direction of Longwy by the 1st Army, while at the same time the 2nd Army should assume the offensive toward the rich iron fields of Briey. These operations were to be followed by an offensive toward Chateau-Salins east of the Moselle, thus isolating Metz. Accordingly, attacks on the American front had been ordered, and that of the 2nd Army was in progress on the morning of November 11th when instructions were received that hostilities should cease at 11 o'clock a. m.

At this moment the American sector from right to left began at Port-sur-Seille, thence across the Moselle to Vandieres and through the Woevre to Bezonvaux in the foothills of the Meuse, thence along the foothills and through the northern edge of the Woevre forests to the Meuse at Mouzay, thence along the Meuse connecting with the French near Sedan.

RELATIONS WITH THE ALLIES

Co-operation among the Allies has at all times been most cordial. A far greater effort has been put forth by the allied armies and staffs to assist us than could have been expected. The French government and army have always stood ready to furnish us with supplies, equipment and transportation and to aid us in every way. In the towns and hamlets wherever our troops have been stationed or billeted, the French people have everywhere received them more as relatives and intimate friends than as soldiers of a foreign army. For these things, words are quite inadequate to express our gratitude. There can be no doubt that the relations growing out of our associations here assure the permanent friendship between the two peoples Although we have not been so intimately associated with the people of Great Britain, yet their troops and ours when thrown together have always warmly fraternized. The reception of those of our forces who have passed through England and of those who have been stationed there has always been enthusiastic. Altogether it has been deeply impressed upon us that the ties of language and blood bring the British and ourselves together completely and inseparably.

STRENGTH

There are in Europe altogether, including a regiment and some sanitary units with the Italian army and the organizations at Murmansk, also including those en route from the States, approximately 2,053,347 men, less our losses. Of this total there are in France 1,338,169 combatant troops. Forty divisions have arrived, of which the infantry personnel of 10 have been used as replacements, leaving 30 divisions now in France, organized into three armies of three corps each.

The losses of the American army up to November 18th are: Killed and died of wounds, 36,154; died of disease, 14,811; deaths unclassified, 2,204; wounded, 179,625; prisoners, 2,163; missing, 11,660. We have captured altogether about 44,000 prisoners and 1,400 guns, howitzers and trench mortars.

COMMENDATION

The duties of the general staff, as well as those of the army and corps staffs, have been very ably performed. Especially is this true when we consider the new and difficult problems with which they have been confronted. This body of officers, both as individuals and as an organization, have, I believe, no superiors in professional ability, in efficiency, or in loyalty.

Nothing that we have in France better reflects the efficiency and devotion to duty of Americans in general than the Service of Supply, whose personnel is thoroughly imbued with a patriotic desire to do its full duty. They have at all times fully appreciated their responsibility to the rest of the army, and the results produced have been most gratifying.

Our Medical Corps is especially entitled to praise for the general effectiveness of its work both both in hospitals and at the front. Embracing men of high professional attainments, and splendid women devoted to their calling and untiring in their efforts, this department has made a new record for medical and sanitary proficiency.

The Quartermaster Department has had a difficult and varied task, but it has more than met all demands that have been made upon it. Its management and its personnel have been exceptionally efficient and deserve every possible commendation.

As to the more technical services, the able personnel of the Ordnance Department in France has splendidly fulfilled its functions both in procurment and in forwarding the immense quantities of ordnance required. The officers and men and the young women of the Signal Corps have performed their duties with a large conception of the problem and with a devoted and patriotic spirit to which the perfection of our communications daily testifies. While the Engineer Corps has been referred to in another part of this report it should be further stated that their work has required large vision and high professional skill, and great credit is due their personnel for the high efficiency that they have constantly maintained.

Our aviators have no equals in daring or in fighting ability, and have left a record of courageous deeds that will ever remain a brilliant page in the annals of our army. While the Tank Corps has had limited opportunity its personnel has responded gallantly on every possible occasion and has shown courage of the highest order.

The Adjutant General's Department has been directed with a systematic thoroughness and excellence that surpasses any previous work of its kind. The Inspector General's Department has risen to the highest standards, and throughout has ably assisted commanders in the enforcement of discipline. The able personnel of the Judge Advocate General's Department has solved with judgment and wisdom the multitude of difficult legal problems, many of them involving questions of great international importance.

It would be impossible in this brief preliminary report to do justice to the personnel of all the different branches of this organization which I shall cover in detail in a later report.

The Navy in European waters has at all times most cordially aided the Army, and it is most gratifying to report that there has never before been such perfect co-operation between these two branches of the service.

As to Americans in Europe not in the military services, it is the greatest pleasure to say that, both in official and in private life they are intensely patriotic and loyal, and have been invariably sympathetic and helpful to the Army.

Finally, I pay the supreme tribute to our officers and soldiers of the line. When I think of their heroism, their patience under hardship, their unflinching spirit of offensive action, I am filled with emotion which I am unable to express. Their deeds are immortal and they have earned the eternal gratitude of our country.

JOHN J. PERSHING,
Commander-in-Chief A. E. F.
November 20, 1918.

A FEW MISCELLANEOUS STATISTICS

If all the railroads constructed by the A. E. F., were laid in a continuous straight line the track would reach from St. Nazaire on the Atlantic Ocean, across France and Germany, to the Russian frontier. If fall the building construction were consolidated into one building having the width of our standard barrack, it would extend from St. Nazaire across France and into Germany as far as the River Elbe. If all the fire-wood produced by the A. E. F. were piled in a row, one meter high and one meter wide, it would extend one thousand three hundred and twenty-five (1,325) miles, enough to form an unbroken wall around three sides of the Republic of France. The Transportation Corps has erected and placed in operation in France 18,543 American railroad cars and 1,496 locomotives. If all of these were made up into a single train they would reach from St. Nazaire to Tours, a distance of 157 miles. On the day the armistice was signed the A. E. F. was operating 2,240 kilometers of light railways, of which 1740 kilometers had been taken from the Germans, and the balance newly constructed or rebuilt. Up to February 1st, 1919, our light railways had handled a total of 860,652 tons of material of which a total of 166,202 tons was ammunition. The Division of Construction and Forestry of the Engineers Corps had 81 saw-mills in operation in October, 1918, and had produced, up to December 1, 1918, 189,564,000 ft. b. m. of lumber, 2, 728,000 standard gauge railroad ties, 923,560 narrow gauge ties, 1,739,000 poles and pit props, besides fuel wood and other miscellaneous forestry products. On November 11, 1918, the Quartermaster Corps had 844 activities functioning in the A. E. F., distributed over a total of 267 localities. If all motor vehicles were placed end to end on a straight road they would extend over 290 miles forming a continuous convoy from Paris to The Hague, in Holland. Statistics similar to the foregoing could be given almost indefinitely, but these will suffice to impress the extent of the A. E. F., supply achievements in France.

Fulton County in the War

Prior to our formal entry into the war, by act of Congress, on April 6th, 1917, Fulton county, like many other counties over the country, was divided in opinion on the matter of our participation in the great conflict. We had our conscientious objectors, pacifists, those who imagined that Germany was not a menace to the United States and those who, by reason of German ancestry, gave no credence to the tales of German brutality and terriorism, but when the United Statse actually entered the war the people of Fulton county rallied to the call of country and accepted the judgment of the President and Congress. Whatever opposition was expressed to our participation in the war vanished almost at once and the whole population of the county soon became a united body in patriotic endeavor.

Long before our actual entry into the war many of our boys had enlisted in the regular army, hoping for a chance at the Boches, others had already entered the fight with the French, British or Canadian forces. Many of our citizens had volunteered for some sort of war service on the side of the Allies.

The first step taken officially in this county was made when it became apparent that conscription would be necessary to raise a large army with the least possible delay and Governor Goodrich, acting upon advices from Washington, appointed a conscription board in each county and called these boards to Indianapolis in order to explain the plans of the government, and to quickly and effectually organize Indiana for war work. The board thus appointed in this county consisted of Sheriff Lewis Clay Sheets, County Clerk Andrew E. Babcock and Harold Van Trump, and they met in Indianapolis on Monday, April 30th, 1917, with other men similarly called by the Governor, to receive instruction for carrying out the conscription law, yet to be enacted. It was the plan of Governor Goodrich to so thoroughly organize Indiana that by the time the draft law was passed, this state would be ready to act immediately.

The board returned home and appointed the following men to act as conscription registrars in their various townships: John L. Hoesel for Aubbeenaubbee, John D. Heighway and Fred G. Rowe for Henry, George A. Black for Liberty, Charles T. Jones for Newcastle, William Foster for Richland, Dell Kessler, Mahlon Bell and William K. Stevenson for Rochester, Geo. W. Garman for Union and Frank Douglas for Wayne. It became apparent that a physician was needed on the board and Dr. M. O. King replaced Harold Van Trump on May 17, 1917.

This organization began organizing Fulton county for War work, but the completion of the government plans centered the various war activities in the County Council of Defense which was created on Monday, June 4th, 1917, by Judge Smith N. Stevens, of the Fulton Circuit Court, acting on the request of Governor Goodrich. Judge Stevens named the following persons to serve for Fulton county: William H. Deniston, Rochester; Mrs. Perry Heath, Rochester; James H. Moore, Fulton; Austin O. Farry, Akron; Andrew A. Gast, Akron; L. M. Shoemaker, Kewanna and Dr. B. F. Overmyer, Leiters Ford, the purpose of the Council was defined as to "co-operate with the Federal and State governments in organizing the resources of the state in men and materials. The council was further instructed to meet on Monday, June 11th, 1917, to elect one of its members as chairman and another as secretary. This meeting resulted in the selection of William H. Deniston as Chairman and Mrs. Perry Heath as Secretary. As the work progressed J. Howard Reed, of Liberty township, and Asa J. Murray, of Wayne township, were added to the membership of the council, and upon this body devolved the gigantic task of unifying the sentiment of Fulton county for the winning of the war, of carrying out the many orders from the State and National Councils of defense and of completely organizing the county as a defensive unit.

To say that the duties were arduous and continuous is only emphasizing an obvious fact and it is but faint praise to say that they were performed with a fine patriotism and a uniform devotion to duty on the part of every member of the council.

It was a fortunate thing for Fulton county that we numbered among our citizens at this time, Mr. Grosvenor Dawe, a man of large experience as an organizer and in community work. Mr. Dawe was serving as secretary of the Farmers and Merchants Association of Fulton county and his services were requisitioned by the County Council of Defense. Co-operating with the council, Mr. Dawe speedily built up an organization which placed one man and one woman in each square mile of the county's area, ready and willing to carry out the work assigned and to stand responsible for the square mile. The organization proved efficient to a remarkable degree.

The personnel of the County Organization as effected by the County Council of Defense and other agencies of the government will be found on the following pages. The untiring efforts of these men and women, their unselfish devotion to the common cause and their practical patriotism was responsible for the fine record made by Fulton county in all forms of war work.

FULTON COUNTY COUNCIL OF DEFENSE—Chairman, W. H. Deniston, Rochester, Ind. Secretary, Mrs. Perry Heath, Rochester, Ind. A. A. Gast, Akron, Ind. A. O. Farry, Rochester, Ind. L. M. Shoemaker, Kewanna, Ind. Dr. B. F. Overmyer, Leiters Ford, Ind. James H. Moore Fulton, Ind. J. H. Reed, Rochester, Ind. A. J. Murray, Grass Creek, Ind.

PUBLICITY COMMITTEE—Earle Miller. Dean L. Barnhart. Pete Van Trump. S. N. Shesler, Akron News. F. C. Gould, Kewanna Herald. J. H. Moore, Fulton Leader.

EXECUTIVE COMMITTEE—Arthur Metzler. A. L. Deniston. Henry Bibler. Chas. Emmons. Maurice Shelton.

FINANCE COMMITEE—A. J. Haimbaugh. J. E. Beyer. F. E. Bryant. O. B. Smith. Will Biddinger. A. A. Gast. J. H. Reed. A. O. Ferry.

PUBLIC POLICY COMMITTEE—George W. Holman. Enoch Myers. Otto McMahan. H. G. Miller. Grosvenor Dawe.

MEDICAL—Dr. B. F. Overmyer, Leiters Ford.
WOMEN'S ACTIVITIES—Mrs. Perry Heath.
SHIPPING INTERESTS—A. L. Deniston.
LEGAL—Enoch Myers.
LABOR—H. G. Miller.
MILITARY AFFAIRS—Cyrus M. Davis.
PUBLIC MORALS—Rev. George Pullman. Rev. Geo. Chandler.
EDUCATIONAL—A. L. Whitmer.
EMPLOYER'S COOPERATION—Alfred Goodrich.
PROTECTIVE—A. A. Gast.
ORGANIZATION—Edward E. Murphy.
EXECUTIVE—Arthur Metzler.
CONTROL OF SOLICITATION—J. F. Dysert.
SPEAKERS—E. H. Sutherland.
WAR CONFERENCE—Charles E. Emmons.
HONOR ROLL—Mrs. Frank N. Hoffman.
LIBERTY GUARD ORGANIZER—Martin A. Irvine.
R. R. TRANSPORTATION—J. E. Beyer.

WAR WORKERS

U. S. SPECIAL APPOINTMENTS

FEDERAL EXPLOSIVE INSPECTOR—Norman R. Stoner.
BOYS WORKING RESERVE—T. F. Berry.
U. S. PUBLIC SERVICE—E. E. Murphy.
SURVEY OF MAN POWER—Otto McMahan.
U. S. COMMUNITY LABOR BOARD—Judge Harry Bernetha, Chairman. Harold Van Trump. Arthur W. Brubaker.
FOUR MINUTE MEN—C. K. Plank. Enoch Myers. F. J. Mattice.
CHAIRMAN—FOURTEEN MINUTE WOMEN—Mrs. Arthur Metzler.
EXPLOSIVE INSPECTION—Norman R. Stoner.
WAR INDUSTRIAL—Howard DuBois.
MERCHANT'S ECONOMY—Ike M. Wile.
COUNTY AGENT—L. R. Binding.

FOOD ADMINISTRATION—John R. Barr, County Administrator. Emerson Felder, Fulton—Liberty. Fletcher Stoner, Akron—Henry. Omer Montgomery, Talma—Newcastle. Dr. Saunders, Grass Creek—Wayne. Dr. Gilbert, Kewanna—Union. O. Brugh, Leiters Ford—Aubbeenaubbee. Harrison Wynn, Tiosa—Richland.

TOWNSHIP WORKERS

WAYNE TOWNSHIP COUNCIL OF DEFENSE—Chairman, Harold Hendrickson. Secretary, Miss Dessie Buchanan. Dr. Saunders. Roy Kumler, Treasurer. A. J. Murray. John McLaughlin. E. E. Murphy, Director.

WAYNE TOWNSHIP SQUARE MILE MEN—Carl Brewer. Harry Mogle. C. S. Callahan. Melvin Moore. Guy Nellans. Chas. Caton. Sherman Marsh. Earl Marsh. Leonard Carr. W. K. Costello. Samuel Hower. Harry Barnett. George Koenig. John Calvin. Thomas Search. James Barnett. Carrie Walsch. John Feidner. Chas. Dukes. Freemont Philips. E. J. Urbin. Chas. Nickels. Paul Costello. Frank Roberts. Ed Costello. Henry Ware. Albert Kerschner. William Walsch, Jr. Florence Hendrickson. John Shankley. Virgil Graffis. Emett Burns. Ed Kumler. John Herold. Otto Applegate. Henry Lease. Ed Gill. M. E. Jones. Roy Geyer. A. J. Murray. Melvin Sommers. Lawrence Funk. William King. I. R. Burns. Roy Todd. Odie Wills. Lyman Hill. Edgar Hill.

WAYNE TOWNSHIP SQUARE MILE WOMEN—Mrs. Carl Brewer. Mrs. Harry Mogle. Mrs. Melvin Moore. Mrs. C. S. Callahan. Mrs. Lloyd Rouch. Mrs. Chas. Caton. Mrs. Sherman Marsh. Mrs. Earl Marsh. Mrs. Leonard Carr. Mrs. William K. Costello. Mrs. Samuel Hower. Mrs. Harry Barney. Mrs. George Koenig. Mrs. Edna Comer. Mrs. Zella Horton. Mrs. James Barnett. Mrs. Carrie Walsh. Mrs. John Feidner. Mrs. William Allen. Mrs. Carrie Calvin. Mrs. G. J. Urbin Mrs. Chas. Nickels. Mrs. Pat

Sinnott. Mrs Frank Roberts. Mrs. Ed Costello. Mrs. Ella Sinnott. Mrs. Albert Kerschner. Mrs. William Walsh Jr. Mrs. Roy Benham. Miss Alice Shanley. Mrs. Virgil Graffis. Miss Carrie Burns. Mrs. Ed Kumler. Mrs. John Herold. Mrs. Otto Applegate. Mrs. Mazelle Brown. Mrs. Ed Gill. Mrs. M. E. Jones. Mrs. Roy Geier. Mrs. A. J. Murray. Mrs. Melvin Sommers. Mrs. Lawrence Funk. Mrs. Willam King. Mrs. L R Burns. Mrs. Roy Todd. Mrs. Emma Herrold. Mrs. Lyman Hill. Mrs Edgar Hill.

UNION TOWNSHIP COUNCIL OF DEFENSE—Chairman, George M. Calvin.

EXECUTIVE COMMITTEE—Rev. G. S. Reedy. Rev. J. H. Ferris. Thos. Willoughby. Dr. A. J. Gilbert. W. H. Gohl. H. D. Snepp. L. M. Shoemaker. David Hudkins, Secretary. Guy Barr, Director.

UNION TOWNSHIP COUNCIL OF DEFENSE SQUARE MILE MEN—George Morris. Chas. Mathias. S. S. Collins. Otto Morrow. John Herr. Howard Mutchler. David Brooker. Ray Lough. Alvah Lebo. Jesse Wentzel. Jesse Stamn. Link Overmyer. John Baker. Steven Bruce. William Shine. U. E. Dukes. Thos. Neff. Bert Talbott. Clifford Felder. Leroy Garman. Frank Miller. Geo. Pratt. W. W. McBeth. Frank Smith. Cline Sales. William Gray. Jacob Kreamer. Frank Hudkins. Howard Zellars. L. J. Hudkins. Vere Calvin. Jester Sparks. D. H. Snepp. Thos. Graffis. Frank Lamborn. David Keeney. Don Wagoner. Frank Hendrickson. Fred Gillespie. Forest Willoughby. William Calvin. William Collins. Frank Moon. Lester Stubbs.

UNION TOWNSHIP COUNCIL OF DEFENSE SQUARE MILE WOMEN—Mrs. George Mathias. Mrs. S. S. Collins. Mrs. Otto Morrow. Mrs. John Herr. Mrs. Howard Mutchler. Mrs. David Brooker. Mrs. Ray Lowe. Mrs. Alvah Lebo. Mrs. Jesse Wentzel. Mrs. Jesse Stamm. Mrs. Lincoln Overmyer. Mrs. John Baker. Mrs. Steven Bruce. Mrs. William Shine. Mrs. Locke. Mrs. Thomas Neff. Mrs. Bert Talbot. Mrs. Clifford Felder. Mrs. Margaret Garman. Mrs. Frank Miller. Mrs. George Pratt. Mrs. W. M. McBeth. Mrs. Frank Smith. Mrs. Cline Sales. Mrs. Will Gray. Mrs. Jacob Kreamer. Mrs. Frank Hudkins. Mrs. Howard Zellars. Mrs. L. J. Hudkins. Mrs. Bere Calvin. Mrs. Justin Sparks. Mrs. D. H. Snepp. Mrs. Tom Graffis. Mrs. Ed McVay. Mrs. Davis Keeney. Mrs. Belle Ayers. Mrs. Frank Hendrickson. Mrs. Samuel Woods. Mrs. Forest Willoughby. Mrs. Will Calvin. Mrs. Will Collins.

AUBBEENAUBEE TOWNSHIP COUNCIL OF DEFENSE—A. J. Ginther, Chairman. B. F. Overmyer. L. Luckenbill. Charley Kreichbaum. John D. Holman, Director.

EXECUTIVE COMMITTEE—B. F. Overmyer, L. Luckenbill. P. A. Guise. Samuel Kelley. George Brugh.

AUBBEENAUBBEE TOWNSHIP COUNCIL OF DEFENSE SQUARE MILE MEN—Elta Davis. Elsworth Edgington. Samuel Munvers. Simon Kaley. Emanuel Ditmire. Henry Fox. Richard Frey. Samuel Kelley. Edward Cavender. William Fernbaugh. Frank Kurtz. William Mehrling. Lester Mahler. K. J. Wagoner. Albert Faulstich. Simon Lahman. Ben

Overmyer. E. S. Ullom. Dean Ginther. John Van kirk. T. J. Bridegroom. J. J. Beerwart. George Brugh B. B. Campbell. Abraham Ginther. W. A. Baldwin. Samuel McKee. Joseph Guise. Leroy Guise. Henry Wentzel. Frank Freece. H. H. Moore. Henry Brugh.

AUBBEENAUBEE TOWNSHIP COUNCIL OF DEFENSE SQUARE MILE WOMEN—Mrs. Elta Davis. Mrs. Elsworth Edgington. Mrs. George Wilson. Mrs. Simon Kaley Mrs. Henry Fox. Mrs. Sam Kelley. Mrs. Alvin Hartle. Mrs. William Baldwin. Mrs. John Barger. Miss Florence Mahler. Mrs. Jessie Toner. Mrs. Albert Faulstich Mrs. Simon Lahman. Mrs. Ben Overmyer. Mrs. E. S. Ullom. Mrs. Nellie Cunningham. Mrs Omar Southall. Mrs. Thomas Bridegroom. Mrs. Maude Sales. Mrs. Chloe Hackett. Mrs. Rhoda Campbell. Mrs. Pearl Hiatt. Mrs. Walter Myers. Mrs. Wm. Yelton. Mrs. Pearl Milliser. Mrs. Sam McKee. Mrs. Edna Guise. Mrs. Perry Guise. Mrs. Harry Wentzel. Mrs. Omar Reichard. Mrs. Edith Moon. Mrs. Lou Bailey. Mrs. Harry Brugh. Mrs. Myrtle Luckenbill.

RICHLAND TOWNSHIP COUNCIL OF DEFENSE—Chairman, Robt. W. Shafer. Melvidore Briney, Sec. Bert Sausaman. Chauncey Overmyer. Albert Bunn. Perry Walters. Albertus Runnells. Bert Leedy. Robert Mowe. John Beck. A. J. Riddle. Byron Smith. Jake Reed. Arthur L. Deniston, Director.

RICHLAND TOWNSHIP COUNCIL OF DEFENSE SQUARE MILE MEN—David Carey. Bert Leedy. Chas. Leedy. Ben Halterman. Robert Mowe. Ezra Leedy. Byron Smith. Ed Smith. Mahlon Baer. A. J. Riddle. John Beck. Dean Nellans. Joe Thompson. Mel Briney. R. W. Shafer. Bert Sausaman. Milo Anderson. Hugh Guise. Irvin Walters. Bert Bunn. Mart Jackson. William Burkett. Bert Runnells. Orville Miller. Jake Reed. Perry Walters. Russel Warren. Clarence Castleman. Alvin Hiatt. Harry Overmyer. C. D. Overmyer. Del Anderson. Leo Rhinesmith. Howard Reed. Ed McGriff. George Adams.

RICHLAND TOWNSHIP COUNCIL OF DEFENSE SQUARE MILE WOMEN—Mrs. David Carey. Mrs. Bert Leedy. Mrs. Chas. Safford. Mrs. Ben Halterman. Mrs. Robert Mowe. Mrs. Ezra Leedy. Mrs. Mil Wynn. Mrs. George Wright. Mrs. Mae Wynn. Mrs. Samuel Arnold. Miss Rosa Hisey. Mrs. Edna Conrad. Mrs. Bertha Conrad. Mrs. Clar Nellans. Mrs. R. W. Shafer. Mrs. Bert Sausaman. Mrs. Milo Anderson. Mrs. Hugh Guise. Mrs. Irvin Walters. Mrs. Bert Bunn. Mrs. Bessie Walters. Mrs. William Burkett. Mrs. Bert Runnells. Mrs. Mary Drew. Mrs. Tena Beehler. Mrs. Oss Burkett. Mrs. Ambrose Overmyer. Mrs. Clarence Castleman. Mrs. Estella Hiatt. Mrs. Harry Overmyer. Mrs. Chas. Cunningham. Mrs. Del Anderson. Miss Anna Kerler. Mrs. Estella Hassenplug. Mrs. Ed McGriff. Mrs. Lee Mowe.

LIBERTY TOWNSHIP COUNCIL OF DEFENSE—Chairman, George A. Black, Fulton, Indiana. Ass't. Chairman, Lawrence Hendrickson. Sec'y. & Treas., Mrs. R. A. Johnson. Milton Henderson. Andrew Oliver. Ancil Gray. Otto McMahan, Director.

LIBERTY TOWNSHIP COUNCIL OF DEFENSE SQUARE MILE MEN—George Black. Lawrence Hendrickson. Ora Hudson. Chas. Horton. Andrew Oliver. Ancil Gray. Ray Mortz. Herbert Peffers. Henry Heckathorn. Chas. Cornell. Chas. Brown. Truman Ward. Leonard Cool. Lee Pownall. V. J. Pownall. Clyde Champ. Thos. Reed. Wm. Pownall. Wm. Gray. Chas. Mathias. John Dewald. John Shields. Thos. Enyart. Ernest Green. J. A. Large. Ben Dewald. Wm. Cunningham. Lee Davidson. Chas. Horton. Edgar McCarter. Dell Calloway. John Smith. Chester Whybrew. Thos. DuBois. Noble Goodner. Alfred Showley. Nelson Trout. Chas. Fry. Floyd Wildermuth. Nelson Rouch. Deo Rannells. George Surface. Andrew Rentschler. John Leavell. L. G. Armstrong. John Moss. Elmer Eytcheson. Town of Fulton (North Half)—Bowen and Zook. (South Half)—Deilman and Redmond.

LIBERTY TOWNSHIP COUNCIL OF DEFENSE SQUARE MILE WOMEN—Mrs. George Black. Mrs. Lawrence Hendrickson. Mrs. Ora Hudson. Mrs. M. Henderson. Mrs. Andrew Oliver. Mrs. Ancil Gray. Mrs. Ray Mortz. Mrs. Robert Peffers. Mrs. H. Heckathorn. Mrs. Chas. Cornell. Mrs. Chas. Brown. Mrs. Truman Ward. Mrs. Leonard Cool. Mrs. Lee Pownall. Mrs. V. J. Pownall. Mrs. Clyde Champ. Mrs. Thos. Reed. Mrs. Wm. Pownall. Mrs. Wm. Gray. Mrs. Chas. Mathias. Mrs. John Dewald. Mrs. John Shields. Mrs. Thos. Enyart. Mrs. Ernest Gohn. Mrs. J. A. Large. Mrs. Ben Dewald. Mrs. Wm. Cunningham. Mrs. Lee Davidson. Mrs. Chas. Horton. Mrs. Edgar McCarter. Mrs. Del Calloway. Mrs. John Smith. Mrs. Chester Whybrew. Miss Ethel DuBois. Mrs. C. B. Apt. Mrs. Noble Goodner. Mrs. Alfred Showley. Mrs. Wilson Trout. Miss Mable Easterday. Mrs. F. Wildermuth. Mrs. Nelson Rouch. Mrs. Deo Rannells. Mrs. George Surface. Mrs. Andrew Rentschler. Miss Garnett Leavell. Mrs. L. G. Armstrong. Mrs. John Moss. Mrs. Elmer Eytcheson.

HENRY TOWNSHIP COUNCIL OF DEFENSE—Chairman, Ivan R. Godwin. V. Chairman, W. C. Miller. E. I. Scott. W. C. Hossman. Dr. Hossman. Robert Burns. S. N. Shesler. W. D. Shewman, Sec'y. Frank Pressnall, Treas. Norman R. Stoner, Director. Executive Comittee—John Heighway. Robert Burns. Jake King. Chas. Flohr. A. A. Gast. Frank Dickey. Dr. Hosman.

HENRY TOWNSHIP COUNCIL OF DEFENSE SQUARE MILE MEN—S. C. Reeder. Reuben Royer. Allen Craft. George King. Chas. Miller. U. S. Croft. Chas. Hoffman. Hugh Miller. E. Burkholder. William Gerard. Frank Dielman. Otto Groninger. Alvah Clinker. Ora Leech. Oscar Heeter. Alvin Kuhn. Joe Barnett. G. H. Hutchinson. Dave Clevenger. Chas. Swartzlander. R. J. Maddox. Earl Barr. Ernest Bright. John Orr. Merrill Whittenberger. Lawrence Townsend. D. R. Sifert. John Funk. C. B. Wilhoit. Alfred Foor. Willis Ward. Chas. McMahan. Chas. Smoker. L. F. Merley. Justin Curtis. E. L. Scott. Frank Thompson. Mason Grogg. Ira Putman. Harry Yarlan. Selah Maby. Vern Miller. Ray Wildermuth. Nelson Bowen. Albert Bowen. Harvey Long. Jacob King. Clarence Pontius.

WAR WORKERS

HENRY TOWNSHIP COUNCIL OF DEFENSE SQUARE MILE WOMEN—Mrs. S. C. Reeder. Mrs. Elbridge Carpenter. Mrs. Ruth Lynch. Mrs. John Kreamer. Mrs. U. S. Croft. Mrs. Chas. Hoffman. Mrs. Ralph Trout. Mrs. Joe Dickerhoff. Mrs. Alice Dickerhoff. Mrs. Chas. Floor. Mrs. Roy Groninger. Mrs. Frank Dickey. Miss Delta Halderman. Mrs. Will Leininger. Mrs. Frank Peterson. Mrs. James H. Hutchinson. Mrs. John D. Heighway. Mrs. Irvin Bryant. Mrs. Oliver Utter. Mrs. Earl Barr. Mrs. Chas. Kreig. Mrs. Jesse Klise. Mrs. Daisy Slaybaugh. Mrs. Herbert Harter. Mrs. Daisy Merley. Mrs. Marion Moore. Mrs. Clifford Wilhoit. Mrs. Clark Foor. Mrs. Willis Ward. Mrs. Gilbert Nye. Mrs. Bert Wilhoit. Mrs. Viola Huling. Mrs. Minnie Curtis. Mrs. Chas. Day. Mrs. C. E. Smith. Mrs. Winfield Kuhn. Mrs. Ira Putman. Mrs. Henry Yarian. Mrs. Orville Moore. Mrs. Harry Mastellar. Mrs. Ray Wildermuth. Mrs. Nelson Bowen. Mrs. Perry Zartman. Mrs. Harvey Long. Miss Gertrude Givler. Mrs. Voris Davis. Mrs. W. C. Miller. Mrs. Roy Jones. Mrs. B. F. Dawson. Mrs. Dr. Ferry. Mrs. Amy Walton. Mrs. Albert Scott. Mrs. S. Thompson. Mrs. Geo. Kinder. Miss Dessie Sayger. Mrs. Dr. Stinson. Mrs. A. A. Gast.

ROCHESTER TOWNSHIP COUNCIL OF DEFENSE SQUARE MILE MEN—Carl Miller. Wm. Wagoner. Chas. Darr. Alvin Good. Del Kessler. Bert Cole. Ed Hagan. Elijah Wilson. Frank Carrithers. A. G. Neerman. Milton Smiley. Bert Myers. Charles Holden. William Ball. James Downs. Charles Stahl. John Wolf. William Hanna. Harry Estabrook. Calder Alspach. Fin C. Wiser. Chas. Woods. Wm. H. King. John McClung. Oscar Tatman. Omar Camerer. P. W. Lowe. Joel Brubaker. Carl Newcomb. Geo. Tobey. John W. Conrad. Ed Fishback. Steve Pyle. William Clay. Dee Berrier. Will Kennell. Fred Moore. Lloyd Castleman. John Cessna. Warren Gohn. Clarence Graffis. L. E. Crabbs. Charles Pyle. Herman Cleland. Jake Crabill. Web Beattie. William Clayburn. Jacob Eisenman. David Wolf. Delno Crabill. John Hayes. John DeVore. George Newman. James Westwood. Ray Woodcox. Ray Beattie. Charles Finney. Alex Black. Robert Miller. John McKinney. Daniel Kline. Stephen Bloom. Frank Davidson. J. W. Evans. Cora Vandegrift. Harley Kochenderfer. Abner McKay. H. E. Barkman. Lon Rogers. Oliver Ewing. Frank Marriot. Ulysses Personett. Levi Leiter. Wm. Anderson. J. W. Rhinehart. Milton Poffenberger. Ben Noftsger. Amos Sanders. J. C. Berry. Chas. Wiley.

ROCHESTER TOWNSHIP COUNCIL OF DEFENSE SQUARE MILE WOMEN—Mrs. Milton Smiley. Mrs. B. F. Carr. Mrs. Elmer Henderson. Mrs. Toughman. Mrs. Dell Kessler. Mrs. Bert Cole. Mrs. Nellie Hagan. Miss Louise Wilson. Mrs. Pierce Wilson. Mrs. A. G. Neerman. Miss Gladys Smiley. Mrs. William Zellars. Mrs. Henry Becker. Mrs. Kent Sibert. Mrs. Ezra Alspach. Mrs. Fred Mercer. Mrs. Charles Stahl. Mrs. Clippinger. Mrs. William Hanna. Mrs. Calder Alspach. Mrs. A. C. Nixon. Mrs. John B. Bush. Mrs. Madge Snyder. Mrs. John L. McClung. Mrs. Elmer Oliver. Mrs. William Brubaker. Mrs. Ben Lowe. Miss Etta Blacketor. Mrs. O. M. Miller. Mrs. George Tobey. Mrs. Roscoe Conrad. Mrs.

Ethel Fishback. Mrs. Dora Pyle. Mrs. Ida Clay. Mrs. Eula Berrier. Mrs. Gertie Kennell. Mrs. John Fultz. Mrs. Ruth Castleman. Mrs. Nellie Zegafuse. Mrs. Hannah I. Gohn. Mrs. Lelah Graffis. Mrs. L. E. Crabbs.. Mrs. Gresham Bearss. Mrs. Herman Cleland. Mrs. Jake Crabill. Mrs. Web Beattie. Mrs. Allen. Mrs. Jake Eisenman. Mrs. Clay Greer. Mrs. Delno Crabill. Mrs. John Werner. Mrs. Sam Phoebus. Mrs. George Newman. Miss Harriett King. Mrs. Ray Woodcox. Mrs. William Stone. Mrs. George Finney. Mrs. Alex Black. Mrs. James Charters. Mrs. Carrie McKinney. Mrs. Mel Hayes. Mrs. Martindale. Mrs. J. W .Evans. Mrs. Pat McMahan. Mrs. Nora Fultz. Mrs Leondias Rogers. Mrs. Oliver Ewing. Miss Gladys Garner. Mrs. Clem Miller. Mrs. Levi Leiter. Mrs. William Hetzner. Mrs. Lon Sheets. Mrs. Ben Noftsger. Mrs. Amos Sanders. Mrs. Hugh McMahan. Mrs. Chas. Wiley.

NEWCASTLE TOWNSHIP COUNCIL OF DEFENSE—Chairman—Chas. T. Jones, Secretary—Mrs. M. Deemer. Milton Kessler. Obe Haimbaugh. Clint Walburn. Will Mickie. Colfax Heighway. Carey Zolman. Meade Haimbaugh. Director—Chas. E. Emmons.

NEWCASTLE TOWNSHIP COUNCIL OF DEFENSE SQUARE MILE MEN—Obe Haimbaugh. Will Foor. Verdie Brockey. William Severns. Fred Busenburg. Roy Maxwell. Joseph Bybee. Milt Kessler. John A. Rouch. Ancil Jefferies. Vinson Meredith. Loren Busenburg. John Norris. Charles Peterson. F. C. Mickey. S. P. Zolman. C. C. Heighway. W. H Sheets. Samuel Nelson. Isaac Batz. George Stockberger. John Long. Miles Perschbacher. Meade Haimbaugh. Clinton Walburn. Mainan Deemer. Will Mickey. Mondo Barkman. John B. Haimbaugh. F. C. Montgomery. Alonzo Long. Carey Zolman. Joseph Kochenderfer. Charles Dalton. F. A. Rogers.

NEWCASTLE TOWNSHIP COUNCIL OF DEFENSE SQUARE MILE WOMEN—Mrs. Obe Haimbaugh. Mrs. William Foor. Mrs. Verd Brockey. Mrs. Ora E. Horn. Mrs. Fred Busenburg. Mrs. Roy Maxwell. Mrs. Joseph Bybee. Mrs. Milton Kessler. Mrs. John A. Rouch. Mrs. Ancil Jefferies. Mrs. Vinson Meredith. Mrs. Loren Busenburg. Mrs. John R. Norris. Mrs. Charles Peterson. Mrs. F. C. Mickey. Mrs. Colfax Heighway. Mrs. W. H. Sheets. Mrs. Sam Nelson. Mrs. Isaac Batz. Mrs. G. A. Stockberger Mrs. J. D. Long. Mrs. Miles Perschbacher. Mrs. Meade Haimbaugh. Mrs. C. L. Walburn. Mrs. M. F. Deemer. Mrs. Will Mickey. Mrs. Mondo Barkman. Mrs. J. B. Haimbaugh. Miss Belle Montgomery. Mrs. Alonzo Long. Mrs. Carey Zolman. Mrs. Jos. Kochenderfer. Mrs. Charles Dalton. Mrs. F. A. Rogers.

CHAIRMAN SQUARE MILE WOMEN—Rochester—Mrs. Wylie Bonine. Union—Mrs. Una Wilson. Newcastle—Mrs. M .F. Deemer. Richland—Mrs. J. H. Reed. Henry—Mrs. A. A. Gast. Aubbeenaubbee—Mrs. S. T. Kelley. Wayne—Mrs. Floyd Leasure. Liberty—Mrs. R. A. Johnson.

WAR WORKERS

CITY ORGANIZATION

In April, 1917, the Women's Committee was organizedby Mrs. Perry Heath, Secretary for the "Fulton County Council of Defense."

Mrs. Charles Emmons was appointed City Chairman, with four vice-chairman, or "Quarter Town Women", with one woman for every two blocks, or "Two Block Women".

The "Quarters Town Women" were:

Mrs. B. F. Fretz—Southeast Quarter.

Mrs. Charles Davis—Northeast Quarter.

Mrs. J. D. Bonine—Northwest Quarter.

Miss Ruth Sutherland—Southwest Quarter.

In October, 1918, it became necessary to make some changes in the Women's Committee." Mrs. J. D. Bonine was appointed City Chairman, with

Mrs. B. F. Fretz—Chairman, S. E. Q.

Mrs. F. R. Burns—Chairman, N. E. Q.

Mrs. I. N. Good—Chairman, N. W. Q.

Mrs. Frank Tracy—Chairman, S. W. Q.

Mrs. B. F. Fretz' TWO BLOCK WOMEN—Mrs. J. F. Dysert. Mrs. Stephen Parcel. Mrs. E. D. Gordon. Mrs. Ray B. Fretz. Mrs. Leslie Richter. Mrs. Charles Mogle. Mrs. Clara Rhodes. Mrs. Margaret Ewing. Miss Agnes McKee. Mrs. Walter House. Mrs. P. J. Stingley. Mrs. Fred Tipton. Mrs. K. W. Hartung. Mrs. Milo Coplen (dec.) Mrs. Gertrude Madary. Mrs. Ella Mogle. Mrs. Bessie Hurst. Mrs. Elsie Green. Miss Louise Bailey.

Mrs. F. R. Burn's TWO BLOCK WOMEN—Mrs. Harry Louderback. Mrs. Ed Smith. Mrs. Fred Perschbacher. Mrs. Merl Craig. Mrs. Alvah McCarter. Mrs. Loy Ross. Mrs. Frank Sheward. Miss Myrtle Ross. Miss Maude Clayton. Mrs. Roscoe Pontius. Mrs. Charles Raymer. Mrs. Ray Myers. Mrs. James V. Coplen. Mrs. Omar Wagoner. Mrs. Harry Young. Miss Rosella Stoner. Miss Marie Clayton. Miss Sue Thompson.

Mrs. I. N. Good's TWO BLOCK WOMEN—Mrs. Arthur Shore. Mrs. Heber Dunlap. Mrs. Earle Shore. Mrs. Sam Wenger. Mrs. L. K. Brower. Mrs. Ralph Arnold. Mrs. Clarence Viers. Mrs. Charles Appleman. Mrs. Atwell Seigfried. Mrs. Martha Ginther. Mrs. Scott Bowen. Miss Olive Hardin. Mrs. Al. Fenstermacher. Mrs. Charles Stahl. Mrs. Charles Brackett. Mrs. M. O. Shipley. Mrs. L. G. Holtz. Mrs. Fred Rannells. Mrs. L. G. Zimmerman. Mrs. John Hoover. Mrs. Ielda Thornburg. Miss Mae Leiter. Miss Mary Stacey. Miss Magdalene Stegemann.

Mrs. Frank Tracy's TWO BLOCK WOMEN—Mrs. Charles Robbins. Mrs. Thurston Young. Mrs. Marion Reiter. Mrs. Raymond McElwee. Mrs. Alex. Ruh. Mrs. Effie Brackett. Miss Florence White. Miss Edith Bitters. Miss Ruth Wallace. Miss Margaret Keeley. Mrs. Roy Deniston. Mrs. Frank Bryant. Mrs. Charles Gould. Mrs. George Dawson. Mrs. Warren Davis. Miss Rose Wile. Miss Edna Bitters. Miss Flavilla Tracy. Miss Ruth Coplen. Miss Myra Paramore.

The women of Rochester, being so thoroughly organized, made it possible to go over the top in every drive. They responded quickly and worked systematically. In the Fifth Liberty Loan Drive they sold $12,350 in bonds.

(Signed) MRS. J. D. BONINE

WOMAN'S EXECUTIVE COMMITTEES

REGISTRATION—County—Mrs. Chas. Emmons. Union—Mrs. Una Wilson. Newcastle—Mrs. M. F. Deemer. Richland—Mrs. Byron Smith. Aubbeenaubbee—Mrs. S. T. Kelley. Henry—Mrs. Minnie Curtis. Liberty—Mrs. R. A. Johnson. Rochester—Mrs. F. S. Tracy. Wayne—Miss Margaret Hines.

HOME ECONOMICS—County—Mrs. H. G. Miller. Union—Maude Conrad. Newcastle—Mrs. Meade Haimbaugh. Richland—Miss Bessie Walter. Aubbeenaubbee—Miss Evelyn Robinson. Henry—Mrs. W. C. Miller. Liberty—Mrs. R. A. Johnson. Rochester—Mrs. J. D. Bonine. Wayne—Mrs. A. J. Murray.

FOOD CONSERVATION—County—Mrs. Perry Heath. Union—Florence Buchanan. Newcastle—Mrs. Colfax Heighway. Richland—Mrs. Lon Jackson. Aubbeenaubbee—Mrs. Thos. Bridegroom. Henry—Mrs. A. A. Gast. Liberty—Mrs. Frank Bowen. Rochester—Mrs. John McClung. Wayne Mrs. Mollie Moore.

FOOD PRODUCTION—County—Mrs. O. L. Walter. Union—Mrs. Wm. Miller. Newcastle—Mrs. O. A. Farry. Richland—Mrs. Lewis Metzger. Aubbeenaubbee—Mrs. Nellie Cunningham. Henry—Mrs. Geo. Kinder. Liberty—Mrs. Milton Henderson. Rochester—Mrs. Hannah Gohn. Wayne—Mrs. Floyd Leasure.

PUBLICITY—County—Mrs. D. L. Barnhart. Union—Mrs. F. P. Gould. Newcastle—Miss Fern Arter. Richland—Miss Esther Burket. Aubbeenaubbee—Mrs. Martha Rouch. Henry—Mrs. Amy Walton. Liberty—Mrs. J. H. Moore. Rochester—Miss Ruth Sutherland. Wayne—Miss Nora Hines.

CHILD WELFARE—County—Mrs. Enoch Myers. Union—Mrs. E. B. Devault. Newcastle—Miss Edna King. Richland—Miss Ruth Foster. Aubbeenaubbee—Mrs. Elta Barr. Henry—Mrs. T. L. Ferry. Liberty—Mrs. Claudia Studebaker. Rochester—Mrs. B. F. Fretz. Wayne—Mrs. Janet Albro.

RED CROSS—County—Mrs. O. M. Hendrickson. Union—Pearl Shoemaker. Newcastle—Mrs. Chas. T. Jones. Richland—Mrs. A. E. Babcock. Aubbeenaubbee—Mrs. Joseph Harris. Henry—Mrs. Maude Jones. Liberty—Mrs. W. E. Redmond. Rochester—Mrs. C. A. Davis. Wayne—Miss Dessie Buchanan.

WAR WORKERS

HOME AND ALLIED RELIEF—County—Mrs. Fred Paramore. Union—Georgia Scott. Newcastle—Miss Eva Grass. Richland—Mrs. E. C. Trimble. Aubbeenaubbee—Mrs. A. D. Toner. Henry—Mrs. Frank Presnall. Liberty—Mrs. Wm. Gray. Rochester—Mrs. A. J. Haimbaugh. Wayne—Miss Dessie Buchanan.

MAINTAINING S. S. AIDS—County—Mrs. A. E. Babcock. Union—Nannie Sparks. Newcastle—Miss Edith Haimbaugh. Richland—Mrs. Caroline Herbic. Aubbeenaubbee—Mrs. John Campbell. Henry—Mrs. B. F. Dawson. Liberty—Mrs. Wm. Patterson. Rochester—Mrs. William Hanna. Wayne—Mrs. Ella C. Hines.

LIBERTY LOAN—County—Mrs. Lucile Leonard. Union—Jessie Slick. Newcastle—Mrs. Ancil Jefferies. Richland—Mrs. Myrtle Bunn. Aubbeenaubbee—Mrs. Myrtle Luckenbill. Henry—Mrs. Albert Scott. Liberty—Mrs. Redmond. Rochester—Mrs. Milton Smiley. Wayne—Mrs. Ed Costello.

HEALTH AND RECREATION—County—Miss Rose Wile. Union—Minnie Finlay. Newcastle—Mrs. Estil Bryant. Richland—Mrs. Chanc Overmyer. Aubbeenaubbee—Miss Grace Cook. Henry—Mrs. A. E. Stinson. Liberty—Mrs. Andrew Oliver. Rochester—Mrs. Robt. Miller. Wayne—Mrs. Con O'Hare.

EDUCATIONAL PROPAGANDA—County—Mrs. Arthur Metzler. Union—Plaudia Enyart. Newcastle—Mrs. Lloyd Eherman. Richland—Miss Carmen Palmer. Aubbeenaubbee—Mrs. Wm. Yelton. Henry—Miss Dessie Sayger. Liberty—Mrs. Robert Heath. Rochester—Mrs. Levi Leiter. Wayne—Miss Opal Spotts.

THOSE APPOINTED FOR THE PROTECTION OF SOLDIERS, ETC.—ATTORNEYS—Harry Bernetha, Rochester. M. A. Baker, Rochester. P. M. Buchanan, Rochester. J. H. Bibler, Rochester—Chairman. C. K. Bitters, Rochester. F. E. Bryant, Rochester. S. J. Brown, Rochester. C. C. Campbell, Rochester. R. R. Carr, Akron. O. A. Davis, Rochester. E. B. Devault, Kewanna. C. E. Emmons, Rochester. B. F. Fretz, Rochester. G. W. Holman, Rochester. M. W. Ivey, Rochester, Arthur Metzler, Rochester. Enoch Myers, Rochester. E. E. Murphy, Rochester. F. J. Mattice, Rochester. Julius Rowley, Rochester. Oliver Ewing, Rochester. Geo. Douglas, G. C., Wayne. Harley Davis, Leiters—Richland. Dr. Ferry, Akron, Henry. George Rentschler, Fulton, Liberty. Dr. B. F. Overmyer, Leiters, Aubbeenaubbee. F. C. Montgomery, Rochester, Newcastle.

WOMEN TOWNSHIP CHAIRMEN FOR GENERAL WAR WORK—Henry—Mrs. A. A. Gast, Akron. Liberty—Mrs. R. A. Johnson, Fulton. Aubbeenaubee—Mrs. Samuel Kelley, Delong. Wayne—Mrs. Floyd Leasure, Grass Creek. Union—Mrs. Una Wilson, Kewanna. Richland—Mrs. J. H. Reed, Rochester. Newcastle—Mrs. M. F. Deemer, Rochester. Rochester—Mrs. Chas. E. Emmons, City.

CHAIRMEN WOMAN'S LIBERTY LOAN—Rochester—Mrs. Milton Smiley, Rochester. Liberty—Mrs. W. E. Redmond, Fulton. Union—Miss Jessie Slick, Kewanna. Richland—Mrs. Myrtle Bunn, LeitersFord. Newcastle—Mrs. Ancil Jefferies, Rochester. Aubbeenaubbee—Mrs. Myrtle Luckenbill, Leiters. Henry—Mrs. Everett Strong, Akron. Wayne—Mrs. Mable Costello, Grass Creek.

THE WORLD WAR

MISCELLANEOUS COMMITTEES

MEN'S LIBERTY LOAN COMMITTEE—Chairmen—Omar B. Smith, First. Frank E. Bryant, Second-Third-Fourth. H. G. Miller, Fifth.

DIRECTORS—A. L. Deniston. A. E. Babcock. Omar B. Smith. E. E. Murphy. Chas. E. Emmons. Norman R. Stoner. Otto McMahan. John D. Holman. J. F. Dysert. Guy R. Barr. Ike M. Wile.

PUBLICITY—Dean L. Barnhart. Harold Van Trump.

SPEAKERS—Arthur Metzler. George W. Holman.

FOURTEEN MINUTE WOMEN—Mrs. Lillian Babcock. Mrs. Faye Van Trump. Mrs. B. F. Dawson, Akron. Mrs. Una Wilson, Kewanna. Mrs. Maude Emmons. Mrs. Myrtle Young. Miss Jessie McMahan. Miss Clara Mae Robbins. Mrs. Evangeline Holman. Miss Belle Montgomery. Mrs. Cynthia Deemer. Mrs. W. A. Patterson, Akron. Mrs. Imogene Hendrickson. Mrs. Glendolyn Heath. Mrs. Lucile Leonard. Mrs. Arthur Metzler, Chairman.

HONOR ROLL FOR ROCHESTER TOWNSHIP—Mrs. Milton Smiley. Mrs. John McClung. Mrs. Warren Gohn. Mr. Tom Toughman. Mr. Wm Wagoner.

HONOR ROLL FOR UNION TOWNSHIP—Mrs. L. M. Shoemaker, Chairman. Frank P. Gould. Geo. W. Ralston. Mrs. John Barnett Jr. Mrs. J. R. McCarsdyha.

HONOR ROLL FOR NEWCASTLE TOWNSHIP—Mrs. Mainan Deemer, Rochester. Mrs. F. C. Mickey, Rochester. 'Mrs. Frank Montgomery.

HONOR ROLL FOR HENRY TOWNSHIP—Mrs. W. H. Patterson, Chairman. Mrs. Roy Jones. Mrs. A. E. Scott. Cecil Kuhn. S. N. Shesler.

HONOR ROLL FOR AUBBEENAUBBEE TOWNSHIP—F. L. Beery, Chairman. Mrs. Pearth Hiath, LeitersFord. Mrs. Samuel Kelley, Delong.

HONOR ROLL FOR LIBERTY TOWNSHIP—Prof W. E. Nickels. W. E. Nickels. W. E. Redmond. Lawrence Hendrickson. Wm. Gray. Miss Mabel Easterday.

HONOR ROLL FOR RICHLAND TOWNSHIP—J. Howard Reed, Rochester—Chairman. Dr. Meek. Mrs. Harrison Wynn.

HONOR ROLL FOR WAYNE TOWNSHIP—Miss Ella Costello, Kewanna—Chairman. Mrs. Rhoda Burns, Grass Creek. Mrs. Warren Pensinger, Grass Creek.

GOOD ROAD COMMITTEE—W. H. Deniston. J. R. Barr. A. E. Babcock. Mr. Binding. Alvin Oliver.

WAR INDUSTRIAL COMMITTEE—Howard Dubois—Chairman. M. A. Baker. Henry Pfeiffer. Joel Stockberger. Alvin V. Oliver.

MAINTAINING AN HONOR ROLL—Mrs. F. N. Hoffman—Chairman. Mrs. C. E. Emmons. Mrs. Lucile Leonard. Mrs. H. G. Miller. Mrs. Omar Smith.

MERCHANTS ECONOMY COMMITTEE—Ike Wile—Chairman. Earl Leininger, Akron. George W. Ralston, Kewanna. John Fultz, Fulton.

WAR WORKERS

UNITED WAR WORKING ORGANIZATIONS—Y. M. C. A.—Dean L. Barnhart. Y. W. C. A.—Mrs. Hugh B. Holman. Knights of Columbus—H. G. Hirsch, Grass Creek. Jewish Welfare—Miss Rose Wile. War Camp Community Service—A. E. Babcock. American Liberty Association—Wm. Brinkman. Salvation Army.

CHAIRMAN OF UNITED WAR WORKERS DRIVE—Dean L. Barnhart.

SPEAKERS' BUREAU—Dr. E. H. Sutherland—Chairman. C. C. Campbell. C. K. Bitters. L. M. Brackett. F. N. Hoffman. Mrs. Arthur Metzler.

TRANSPORTATION COMMITTEE—Guy Alspach—Chairman. Geo. V. Dawson. J. D. Holman. Guy Barr. H. A. Fristoe. James V. Coplen. Norman R. Stoner. John E. Troutman. Fulton—Chas Becker. Akron—E. L. Scott. Kewanna—D. W. Sibert Talma—Frank Arter. Tiosa—Earl Wynn. Leiters—I. Luckenbill.

VOLUNTEER SPEAKERS—M. A. Baker. Mahlon Bell. J. H. Bibler. C. K. Bitters. Frank E. Bryant. Dean L. Barnhart. Harry Bernetha. L. R. Binding. A. W. Bitters. Rev. Geo. Crane. Vere S. Calvin—Kewanna. C. B. Carlton. C. C. Campbell. Rev. H. A. Davis—Leiters. Lloyd Ehernman—Talma. Chas. E. Emmons. E. B. DeVault—Kewanna. Rev. W. I. Eiler. Rev. I. H. Ferris—Kewanna. B. F. Fretz. Rev. Ivan Godwin—Akron. Rev. H. G. Gaige. Rev. Jos. B. Harris—Leiters. G. W. Holman. John D. Heighway—Akron. M. W. Ivey. R. C. Johnson. Roy Jones—Fulton. C. J. Loring. F. J. Mattice. Arthur Metzler. H. G. Miller. Archie B. Miller. James R. Moore. Fred Moore. James H. Moore—Fulton. E. E. Murphy. Enoch Myers. Otto McMahan. Hugh McMahan. Henry Pfeiffer. Rev. Geo. C. Pullman. J. H. Reed. Rev. G. S. Reedy—Kewanna. M. C. Shelton. S. N. Shesler—Akron. W. D. Shewman—Akron. Omar B. Smith. F. M. Sterner. Dr. E. H. Sutherland. Dr. H. W. Taylor. Rev. A. W. Warriner. Carl Van Trump. Prof. A. L. Whitmer. Dr. Wilson A. Smith. Rev. Geoge J. Nixen.

COUNTY THRESHING COMMITTEE—John R. Barr—Chairman. L. Binding—Secretary. Chas. Coplen. Perry Hill. W. H. Deniston. Henry Thompson, General Superintendent.

THRESHERMEN IN FULTON COUNTY—Charles Mauser. Martin Werner. Chas. E. Rader. Daniel Smith. Joe Mohler. Chas. Baird. W. S. Overmyer. William Blackburn. H. O. R ans. A. T. Coplen. Albert Bowen. B. Davis. Jake Eisenman. Nate O'Blenis. Virl Zartman. Edward Martin. Oliver Grier. William Baird. Charles Kimball. J. P. O'Connell. Edward Myers. Joseph Slaybaugh. Ezra Leedy. William Mahler. Ray Smith. George Deck. Fred Ault. Vernon Zartman. Lon Lowe. Vernon Runkle. Virgil Baker. L. L. Sheets. Charles Fry. Chas. Holloway. William Bright. Charles Coplen. J. P. Hill. Chas. O'Connell. Wliiam Saygers. Thomas Dubois. Philip Mikesell. Sherman Overmyer. Ben Harpster. J. B. Sheets.

SHEEP COMMITTEE—A. J. Haimbaugh, Chairman. J. H. Reed. A. O. Farry. Dr. B. F. Overmyer. A. A. Gast. A. J. Murray. L. M. Shoemaker. J. H. Moore.

COMMITTEE ON ARRANGEMENTS—William Brinkman. Grosvenor Dawe. Maurice Shelton. Dean L. Barnhart.

National, State and County Councils of Defense

When it became evident that the United States of America, much against her will, tradition and teachings, would eventually be forced into the war, Congress passed an Act creating what is known as the Council of National Defense, said Council to consist of the Secretary of War, the Secretary of the Navy, the Secretary of the Interior, the Secretary of Agriculture, the Secretary of Commerce and the Secretary of Labor.

The law in brief says that the Council of National Defense is established for the coordination of industries and resources for national security and welfare. That the Council shall nominate to the President, and the President shall appoint an advisory commission, consisting of not more than seven persons each of whom shall have special knowledge of some industry or be otherwise specially qualified, in the opinion of the Council, for the performance of their duties which were many and varied, having to do with every phase of the war work.

In compliance with the law the Council of National Defense early in March, 1917 nominated and the President appointed as an advisory commission the following named men, to-wit: Daniel Williard president B. & O. Railroad; Howard E. Coffin, vice president Hudson Motor Co.; Julius Rosenwald, president Sears, Roebuck & Co.; Bernard M. Baruch, banker; Dr. Hollis Godfrey, president Drexel Institute; Samuel Gompers, president American Federation of Labor and Dr. Franklin Martin, secretary General American College of Surgeons, Chicago, and they together with those named in the Act assumed the duties and responsibilities of their office.

Newton Baker, secretary of War, was elected chairman of the Council and on May 2nd, 1917, there was called in Washington, D. C. a conference of all the states, and from this meeting, which was addressed by many of the great men of the nation, sprang the council of defense system as we know it.

The Council of National Defense suggested that the Governor of each state appoint for their respective states, a State Council of Defense, and Governor James P. Goodrich of Indiana, appointed as members of the Indiana State Council the following well known persons of Indiana, to-wit: Will H. Hays, Frank Wampler, George Ade, A. W. Brady, Mrs. Carolyn Fairbank, Dr. Charles P. Emerson, Charles W. Fairbanks, Charles Fox, Will J. Freeman, Wm. G. Irwin, J. L.

Keach, H. R. Kurrie, A. E. Reynolds, N. E. Squibb, Rev. A. B. Storms, Isaac D. Straus, Thomas Taggart, E. M. Wilson and Evans Woolen. On May 19th, 1917 they met for organization and Will H. Hays was elected chairman and Frank Wampler secretary. Since that time the pressure of business affairs necessitated the retirement of Mr. Hays as chairman and Michael Foley was selected to succeed Mr. Hays to the office of chairman, and for the same reason Frank Wampler retired as secretary, and was suceeded in office by Frank C. Daily. Mrs. Anne Studebaker Carlisle was appointed as a member of the Council to replace Mrs. Carolyn Fairbank who was compelled to retire from active work on account of ill health.

At the first meeting of the State Council of Defense, in order to reach every county in the State of Indiana, the Council requested the various judges of the Circuit Court, to nominate a County Council of Defense, in each county of their judicial district, to consist of seven members, one of whom was to be a woman and another to be a representative of labor. The judge of the Fulton circuit court on the 4th day of June, 1917, appointed as members of the Fulton County Council of Defense the following well known residents of Fulton county, to-wit: William H. Deniston, Andrew A. Gast, Austin O. Farry, Mrs. Perry Heath, L. M. Shoemaker, Dr. B. F. Overmyer and James H. Moore. At a later date it was thought best to enlarge the committee, and J. H. Reed and A. J. Murray were appointed as additional members thereto.

On the 11th day of June, 1917, they met and William H. Deniston was elected chairman and Mrs. Perry Heath secretary. These three Councils worked together as a unit, in perfect harmony in mobilizing our resources and materials, and it awakened the National conscience to the many problems necessary to the winning of the war. So thoroughly was the United States organized that the council of defense system had 184,400 different units, made up of state, county, municipal and community councils of defense, and the most of this work was accomplished voluntarily. Indiana and Fulton county can always look back with pride to the part they played in helping to organize the resources and materials of the state and county. It was said by John Winterbotham of Chicago, chairman of the Western Division Section on State Councils, Council of National Defense, that Indiana was known and recognized as the model State Council of Defense, and the writer was told by one high in authority that Fulton county had one of the best organizations in the state, due to its County Council of Defense.

While it is true that practically every man, woman and child in Fulton county was loyal, patriotic and true and never faltered, but always went over the top when called upon and did well and nobly their part in helping to bring to a successful termination the world's greatest conflict, yet the burden fell heaviest upon your County Council of Defense. These eight men and one woman for nearly two years were in the front ranks giving freely of their time, energy and ability.

I know the people of Fulton county fully appreciate and feel grateful to each member of the County Council of Defense for the unusual amount of work, time and energy so graciously given in their behalf, and while their work was difficult and hard, and at times unpleasant, yet like good soldiers they never faltered but did their work faithfully and well.

JUDGE. S. N. STEVENS.

Fulton County's Policy

One of the interesting acts of the County Council of Defense was the preparation, in January 1918, of a "Statement of Public Policy" which was prepared for reading in churches, lodges, schools and other public gatherings. The statement was printed and posted in various public places and attracted much attention.

The statement read as follows:

"In order that every responsible person in Fulton County may reach an understanding of each individual's part in the war between the United States and the Central Powers of Europe, the Committee on Public Policy has prepared, by the authority of the County Council of Defense, a brief statement which will be left in charge of the officers of each Church and of each assemblage before whom members or representatives of the Committee may appear.

The United States, and therefore each citizen in Fulton County, is in a state of war with the German Empire and with the dual monarchy of Austria-Hungary. It is probable that it will soon be in a state of war with Turkey and Bulgaria. These four nations are spoken of as the Central Powers of Europe.

Alien Residents

By the fact that the United States and therefore each citizen in Fulton County is at war with the Central Powers it follows that every resident of Fulton County who has come here from Germany or Austria-Hungary, and is not a naturalized citizen of the United States, is from an enemy nation and is therefore an enemy of the United States, and of each citizen of Fulton County, unless he expresses his purpose among his neighbors to be loyal to the United States, even though not now able to become a citizen.

Loyal Citizenship

Each citizen of Fulton County, whether born in the United States or in a foreign country, has become an enemy of the Central Powers, and is therefore bound by his citizenship to support the government of the United States against the enemies of the United States, and of Fulton County. Consequently, if any of a citizen's acts can be interpreted as giving aid to the Central Powers he, by such acts, becomes a traitor to the United States.

Treason

The Constitution of the United States says 'Treason against the United States consists in adhering to their enemies; giving them aid and comfort.' The penalty is death, or at the discretion of the court, imprisonment at hard labor for not less than five years and a fine of not less than $10,000. Knowledge of treason, not revealed is a crime and is defined, with penalty as follows:

Knowledge of Treason

"Every person owing allegiance to the United States and having knowledge of the commission of any treason against the United States, who conceals and does not, as soom as may be, disclose and make known the same to the President, or some judge of the United States, (or others named in the law) is guilty of mis-prison of treason, the penalty for which is imprisonment for not more than seven years and a fine of not more than one thousand dollars.

Our Associates in the War

The Central Powers are at war with England, France, Japan, Italy, Brazil, China, and the majority of all smaller countries of the world—eighteen in all Beside those at war eleven other countries have broken off relations with Germany because of her ruthless warfare and disregard of the rights of small nations. The fact that we are at war with the Central Powers therefore brings us into friendly relations with all other nations opposed to the Central Powers. Consequently, it is the duty of every citizen of Fulton County, not only to safeguard the rights of the United States in this struggle, but to uphold our associates in the war—commonly known as our allies—against all criticism or aspersion that might weaken Fulton County's sense of loyalty to the joint effort these great nations are making.

The Causes of War

The causes which have brought us into war with the Central Powers are of such a nature that if the United States, and therefore Fulton County, had not met force with force we should have been regarded forever as a craven nation and people. These causes can best be summed up by quoting from the President's message to the Congress, December 4th, 1917.

> "The purposes of the Central Powers strike straight at the very heart of everything we believe in; their method of warfare outrages every principle of humanity and of knightly honor; their intrigue has corrupted the very thought and spirit of many of our people; their sinister and secret diplomacy has sought to take our very territory away from us and disrupt the Union of the States. Our safety would be at end, our honor forever sullied and brought into contempt were we to permit their triumph. They are striking at the very existence of democracy and liberty."

Our war with the Central Powers is therefore a defensive war.

Victory in Europe Essential

As confirming the causes mentioned by the President, we remind our fellow citizens of Fulton County that since 1914, when the World War broke out, documentary evidence has been secured showing that the German Empire expected to destroy the power of France and of England, then to destroy the great Monroe Doctrine of the Western Hemisphere, and later to bring the United States into subjection. It will thus be evident to our fellow citizens that unless the United States, and therefore Fulton County, stand with our associates in the war—our allies—to win the battle in Europe the fight will be transferred to the United States; and our homes, our loved ones, our property and our sacred honor as men will be subjected to the brutality of the German government's thought in conquest.

Evil Let Loose

To indicate what we may expect from the brutalized views of the German government, we quote what an authority said on his recent return from that part of France cleared of Germans forces.

"You have been told that our women and our girls have been protected by the British navy from the fate that befell the women of France and Belgium. Men, believe it; it is absolutely true. It is more than true: I have been in the hospital in the Department of Lamerk, of France, where there are nearly a thousand girls; not one is eighteen years of age, and all will be mothers. And 61 per cent. are in addition afflicted with the most filthy, unspeakable malady that we know of, and 11 per cent. in addition are stark mad. I have seen the boys that will never be men; I have seen the boys who have been cruelly mutilated."

There are thousands of photographs and tens of thousands of affidavits as to the ruthless destruction of innocent people and their possessions by German soldiers, under orders from their rulers. Our war with the Central Powers is therefore a righteous war.

A War to Free All People

Our President in his great message at the entrance of the United States into the World War used the words "To make the world safe for democracy." We wish to make the meaning of this clear to each one present. To make the world safe for democracy means "to make the world safe for all the people." Under such a form of government as the German Empire is trying to fasten on the world the people would have no freedom unless they carried out orders from powers above. Under our idea of government all the people select their own authorities, and set them up to govern; and change them by their votes or by other procedure in law.

Restriction By Free Will

In order to reach the minds of all hearers in this gathering with a further truth we shall turn President Wilson's words around and say that the great test in the United States, and therefore Fulton County, just now is this, "Is democracy—government by the whole people—safe for the world?" Will you, the people of Fulton County of your own free will, put yourselves under restriction in food, in fuel, in self-gratification for the sake of saving the constitution under which we live? If you will not, then the dream of our fathers relative to a free people was only a dream and we deserve to have the heel of German Militarism rest upon our necks.

We Must Win or Perish

It happens that this stupendous struggle comes in the life time of those assembled in this gathering. Consequently it is impossible for any one to close the eyes and say that this struggle has nothing to do with us. It has everything to do with us, with our children, with our property, with all our rights; for if the German idea should conquer in the field of battle not a single person or property or right would remain as before. Being alive in this moment of history makes each individual responsible for the outcome, otherwise we are in the position of the selfish, unthinking person who accepts all benefits from the past but will do nothing to pass those benefits on to his children.

Question All Must Answer

We have been left free for fifty years to pursue our individual aims, as if the nation and its past or its future were not our personal responsibility. But the trumpet of war's alarms has been blowing among us and we, just like preceding generations, are face to face with three questions: (1) whether in all our affairs we will acquit us like men for the glory that is yet to be the United States; or (2) whether softness, ease, pleasure have destroyed our merit to be inheritors of greatness; or (3) whether we, of Fulton County, permit our minds and acts to oppose the government of the United States and are thus traitors—shooting our soldiers and our leaders in the rear.

Small Self-Denials

We ask all households in Fulton County to understand that the requests from the United States Food Administrator to reduce consumption of meat, wheat, sugar and fats are requests based upon the urgent needs of our associates in the war—our allies—for these necessities; to understand that every particle of saving in beef, mutton, pork, wheat, sugar and fats is to give support to the nations that are carrying at the present time the heaviest burden of the war for American freedom and have carried it uncomplainingly since 1914. Our self-denial on their behalf is nothing compared with their sacrifices and the sacrifices our boys are yet to make.

Each at His Task

We call upon each fellow citizen to be cheerful and industrious and to be loyal in every thought and act; and to put into his daily labor a feeling of devotion, so that his task may be glorified as a small but essential part in winning new glory for that nation whose boast has been that it is the greatest republic on the face of the earth.

Our Pledge of Loyalty

We now call upon every one who hears this message to pledge support to requests coming from our government concerning increased production, the prevention of waste, the taxing of industries, the taxing of incomes; and without reserve to give his co-operation to the government in raising whatever funds may be needed for the successful progress of this supreme struggle of the ages between the divine rights of humanity and the supposed divine rights of autocrats.

Our Judgment is Near

The Hebrew Scriptures record that a divine hand wrote words on the wall of a banquet room in ancient Babylon meaning "weighed in the balance and found wanting," and a mighty force entered the city that night and destroyed the Babylonian civilization. The same divine hand is near each heart in Fulton County to write thereon "Worthy of Freedom" or "Unworthy of Freedom." None can escape the measuring of our personal merit which this moment in history has brought to us. We are either worthy or unworthy of the fights made by the Pilgrim Fathers for freedom to worship God; or by the Revolutionary soldiers for political freedom; or by the heroes of the War between the States for freedom from the disgrace of human slavery.

The Summing Up

This Statement of Public Policy has made clear in brief form, 1—Who are enemies:—2—The dangers of treason:—3—The causes of the war with the Central Powers:—4—The dangers that lurk in defeat:—5—The test of our value as citizens:—6—The personal task of each citizen in Fulton County.

Nine-tenths of all the inhabitants of the world agree that the German purpose is wrong. Each citizen of Fulton County must, therefore, align himself with right as against wrong.

We repeat that all who know of treasonable utterances or acts must report them. We earnestly hope no treason may be found or heard in Fulton County, but to avoid any excuses of ignorance, this statement is being made in all assemblages over the County."

The statement was signed by William H. Deniston, as chairman, and Glendolyn Myers Heath, as secretary of the County Council of Defense, and by George W. Holman, Enoch Myers, Otto McMahan, Hiram G. Miller and Grosvenor Dawe, for the Committee of Public Policy.

The statement received wide attention over the country and was reproduced, with flattering comment, in Leslie's Weekly which resulted in a deluge of letters asking for copies of the statement and in letters of a congratulatory nature from many prominent men, including Theodore Roosevelt, William H. Taft and other distinguished citizens. The statement was used as a model for similar statements in many counties over the country and many letters were received from industrial plants and public buildings, asking for copies of the statement for hanging on bulletin boards and in gathering places in these institutions.

Financing the War

The Liberty Loan Drives

The expression of patriotism through money loaned to the government gave an opportunity to those who could serve in no other way to "do their bit" in winning the war. Fulton county responded nobly to every call for funds and in the five Liberty Loan drives subscribed for nearly two million dollars worth of government bonds. After the county was once organized every drive went over with an over-subscription of the quota set for us and went over promptly. When one stops to consider that Fulton county has a population of only 16,879 people, and is not regarded as a rich county, the loyalty of our people is splendidly expressed in the results of the various drives.

First Liberty Loan

The First Liberty Loan was handled through the banks of the county without the extensive preparation and effective organization which was built up for the succeeding loans. Mr. Omar B. Smith was made chairman of the loan. The public was educated through publicity donated by the newspapers and underwritten by the business men. No quota was set for the county and subscriptions were opened at the banks on June 2, 1917 and continued to June 13. In this effort $72,300.00 worth of bonds were sold and the per capita subscription was $4.28.

Second Liberty Loan.

Frank E. Bryant, president of the Indiana Bank & Trust Company, Rochester, Indiana, was chosen county chairman for the second loan.

The second loan was called for October 15, 1917, at a time when the country was not yet aroused to the great need and importance of individual effort.

No tangible county organization had been effected, and the only channel through which to work quickly and directly, was the banks of the county. A strong effort was made by the banks to place these bonds with their customers. In some localities, the people had awakened to the importance of the hour and bought quite liberally, but for the most part, the banks obligated themselves to the county chairman to take all they could themselves.

Our quota was set at $342,270, which made the per capita subscription $20.30. $229,400 of this issue was sold, the captia subscription being $13.60.

Third Liberty Loan

The third loan was called for April 12, 1918.

The people throughout the entire country had become intensely aroused by this time, and every county in Indiana had a working organization of some kind. In Fulton county, the organization of the Square Mile Men under the auspices of the County Council of Defense, was a great boost for victory in all succeeding calls of the nation. Fulton county has the distinction of having been organized down to the smallest unit, viz: The Square Mile, of any couty in the state.

Frank E. Bryant was again appointed county chairman by Will H. Wade, chairman of the State Liberty Loan Committee, Indianapolis, Indiana.

A Central Committee was appointed by the county chairman, consisting of nine members, representing and becoming responsible for their respective township in the county and the city of Rochester, as individual units in the drive. These members were to serve for the duration of the war.

John D. Holman, working with Aubbeenaubbee township; Norman R. Stoner, working with Henry township; Otto McMahan, working with Liberty township; Charles E. Emmons, working with Newcastle township; A. L. Deniston, working with Richland township; Joseph F. Dysert, working with Rochester township; Andrew E. Babcock, working with Union township; Edward E. Murphy, working with Wayne township; Omar B. Smith, working with Rochester city; Dean L. Barnhart, chairman of publicity; and Arthur Metzler, chairman of speakers' Bureau.

This committee worked with the county and township chairmen of the County Council of Defense, the Square Mile Men of the townships and the Two-Block Women of the cities.

As a crowning result of the splendid work of these war organizations, the Third Liberty Loan was oversubscribed by $126,750, $456,750 being the total subscription, with a per capita of $27.06.

Fourth Liberty Loan

For the third time, Frank E. Bryant was appointed county chairman by Will H. Wade, Federal Director of Sales for Indiana, for the fourth loan which was launched October 1, 1918. The work fell upon the same leaders who handled the previous loan except Ike M. Wile replaced Joseph F. Dysert as chairman for Rochester township, and Rev. J. W. Niven replaced Andrew E. Babcock as chairman for Union township.

The largest quota of all the loans was set for us in this effort, $575,000 or a per capita of $34.07, being asked. Fulton county responded promptly with an over-subscription of $67,950.00, or a total of $642,850 and a per capita subscription of $38.09.

Victory Liberty Loan

On March 15, 1919, Will H. Wade appointed Mayor Hiram G. Miller as county chairman for the fifth, or Victory, Liberty Loan and the date of the drive was set for April 20, 1919. There was some apprehension that, the war being over, the money could not be raised as readily as formerly, but again Fulton county demonstrated her loyalty and patriotism by finishing the job with an over-subscription. The same organization which had been perfected by the County Council of Defense was again called upon to put the loan over and it responded with the same enthusiasm shown in the midst of the war.

Following are the members of the Central Committee for the Victory Loan: Hiram G. Miller, chairman; A. L. Deniston, vice-chairman; Harold Van Trump, publicity; George W. Holman, speakers; Omar B. Smith, Rochester city; Edward E. Murphy, Wayne; A. E. Babcock, Union; John D. Holman, Aubbeenaubbee; Guy R. Barr, Richland; Ike M. Wile, Rochester township; Otto McMahan, Liberty; Norman R. Stoner, Henry, and Charles E. Emmons, Newcastle.

The quota asked for the Victory Loan was $425,000.00, or a per capita of $25.18. The response was an oversubscription of $63,350.00, or a total of $488,530.00 and a per capita subscription of $28.93.

In each of the loans the newspapers of the county rendered valuable service by donating their space most liberally and by soliciting the merchants to use and pay for loan advertising.

Our Part in the War Savings Drive

Prior to our entrance into the world war the people of Fulton county, like all people of the United States, were exceptionally prosperous and as a result had grown extravagant. In December, of 1917, our government called upon all to encourage saving to the end that thrift would prevail. The plan was to sell Thrift Stamps and War Savings Stamps. A Thrift Stamp to sell for twenty-five cents and a War Savings Stamp to sell for $4.12 was placed on the market by the government. Thrift Stamps were to be redeemed for War Savings Stamps as War Savings Stamps were to bear interest at the rate of 4 per cent compounded quarterly. No individual could hold more than $1000.00 maturity value of this issue, the object in this limitation being to give the small investor an opportunity to assist the government, as the large investor had had an opportunity in the sale of Liberty Bonds.

After the plan had been launched it was necessary that an organization for the sale of the stamps be perfected. The Honorable J. D. Oliver of South Bend, Indiana, was chosen to head the state organization, with offices at South Bend, Indiana. He gave all his time and plenty of money to make the drive a success. The state was divided into districts to correspond to the congressional divisions, consequently we were in the Thirteenth. The Hon. Rome C. Stephenson of South Bend, a former Fulton County resident, was chosen to head the district organization, and Frank E. Bryant, president of the

WHIPPET TANK—A FEATURE OF THE VICTORY LOAN DRIVE

Indiana Bank and Trust Co., Rochester, Indiana, was chosen to head Fulton county's organization. Mr. Bryant at once chose the following men to assist in the work in our county. A central committee composed of the following: Frank Bryant, chairman; W. H. Deniston, chairman C. C. D.; Otto McMahan, postmaster, Rochester, Ind.; County Superintendent of Schools T. F. Berry; Omar B. Smith, President First National Bank, Rochester, Ind.; L. R. Binding, county agent, and Superintendent of City Schools A. L. Whitmer.

The following men were to head the respective townships of the county: Earl Rouch, Wayne township; Rev. Harley Davis, Richland township; Lloyd Eherenmann, Newcastle township; W. D. Shewman, Henry township; W. F. Nickols, Liberty township; A. L. Whitmer, Rochester township, and L. L. Lukenbill, Aubbeenaubbee township.

Under this organization Mr. Bryant was very successful in getting the schools of the county at work to the end that about $150,000.00 had been sold and pledged at the end of the first six months. At this time Mr. Bryant found that his duties as chairman of the various Liberty Loan drives were such that he could not longer act as chairman of the War Savings committee, so he tendered his resignation and Otto McMahan, postmaster, Rochester, Ind., was appointed to fill the vacancy. McMahan at once added all the postal employees of the county to the above organization and started an active drive through the postoffice of the county. The first drive of one week netted about $10,000.00. Great credit should be given the postal employees as some carriers sold as much as $11,000.00 worth in the week. The work of the postal employes during vacation of schools had accomplished so much that it was easy to place the county over the top with the assistance of the schools when convened again. Fulton county was the only county in her district to reach her quota. The quota was $337,500.00 and we sold more than $350,000.00 worth.

Work on the Farms

In this history of the deeds and accomplishments of various bodies and divisions of the citizens of Fulton county in their united efforts toward winning the great war, there is no brighter page than that written by the farmers of the county in their efforts to increase the production of foodstuffs. A volume might be written on this one subject, giving instances of individual effort and sacrifice, but as such a list of personal endeavor would need to include one for practically every farm family in the county, as all put forth the best effort of which they were capable, therefore we must content ourselves with presenting some general figures on the results accomplished.

The normal acreages of the leading food crops in Fulton county for the years preceding the war were about as follows:

Wheat—18000 to 19000 acres.

Corn—45000 to 55000 acres.

Oats—17000 to 20000 acres.

Rye—1500 to 2000 acres.

Hogs on hand Jan. 1st, 17000 to 19000.

Compare these figures with those of 1917, the first year we were in the war. The wheat crop for this year, being sown in the fall of 1916, before we were in the war is only normal, but all other products show large increases. The figures are as follows:

Wheat—18931 acres, a practically normal acreage.

Corn—62493 acres, increase above maximum normal acreage of 13%.

Oats—20506 acres, increase above maximum normal acreage of 2½%.

Rye—2972 acres, increase above maximum acreage of 48%.

Hogs on hand December 31st, 1917, 20976, an increase above maximum normal of over 10%.

This gives a total acreage for 1917 of 104,902, compared with the maximum normal of about 96000 acres.

The year 1918 shows still more remarkable results. The acreages for that year are:

Wheat—25392 acres, increase over 1917 of 34%.

Rye—6000 acres, increase over 1917 of 102%.

Oats—23000 acres, increase over 1917 of 12%.

Corn—53600 acres, decrease from 1917 of 16%.

Hogs on hand Jan. 1st, 1919, 28,070, an increase of 34% over Jan. 1, 1918.

Some of the increase in the small grain crop acreage was made up by decreasing the corn acreage, but the total acreage for 1918 was 107992, exceeding the 1917 acreage by 3090 acres.

But it was in 1919 when the farmers of the United States were all prepared to deal their heaviest blows to the Kaiser and win the war with food and in this effort the farmers of Fulton county were prepared to do their full share. The crop acreages for 1919 were:

Wheat—36064, increase over 1918 of 42%.

WORK ON FARMS

Rye—8600, increase over 1918 of 43%.
Oats—22700, decrease from 1918 of 1.3%.
Corn—50100, decrease from 1918 of 7%.

Again the acreage of corn and oats was decreased somewhat in order to increase the acreage of bread grains but the total acreage for 1919 shows the sum of 117464 acres, exceeding that of 1918 by 9472, and the maximum normal acreage of 96000 by 21464.

These achievements of Fulton county farmers appear the greater when it is remembered that about 400 of Fulton county's men were in the army. A large majority of these men were either farmer boys or lived in the small towns of the county and did a part of the work on the surrounding farms.

These great increases in the food producing acreages of Fulton county show that by the end of 1918 practically every acre of tillable land was under cultivation and producing its quota of foodstuffs. But it was not in increased acreage alone that the farming population of the county showed their eagerness and ability to help carry the load. In response to the appeals of the National Food Administration and the Indiana committee on Food Production and Conservation to make every acre produce at its maximum, largely increased quantities of commercial fertilizer were used, especially on wheat, in spite of the extremely high prices which prevailed for it. As a result, the reports sent in by the operators of threshing outfits in the county showed an average yield of wheat for the county of 21.4 bushels. Committees of farmers and threshers, acting with the County Council of Defense, undertook to see that none of this great wheat crop was wasted in harvesting and threshing, and were responsible for initiating such saving practices as spreading a canvas under the machine, using tight bottomed racks and wagon boxes, and being on the alert at all times to see that no wheat was being wasted in the manner of former years. As a result of this vigilance, an inspector from the United States Grain Corporation who was through the county at threshing time declared that conditions here were the best that he had seen in any of his inspection work. Great credit is also due the threshermen for their co-operation in this wheat saving, especially in the efficient operation of their machines to prevent grain being carried over into the straw, also for the willingness and promptness which they showed in making reports on yields and acreages of grain. Out of all the threshermen in the county, only three failed to report.

Another appeal for food conservation which met a ready response from farm owners was that for more silos. Believing that the thirty or forty per cent of the corn crop which goes back upon the ground when corn is picked should be saved in the war emergency, the Food Conservation Committee in the spring of 1918 sent out the word for a campaign in every county to increase the number of silos. Mr. Otto McMahan was appointed chairman of this campaign in this county and a series of township meetings were held. At the beginning of the campaign there were, according to the Indiana Year Book for 1918, 225 silos on the farms of Fulton county. During that summer 43 new ones were built, an increase of 19%. One township had a 100% increase in this line.

Throughout all the strenuous endeavors that they were making, and in the face of everything they were asked to do, the Fulton county farmers gladly did all that was asked of them. They did not, as the men in some other lines of industry did, take advantage of their position as the source of the food supply, to jeopardize the lives and comfort of our boys on the battlefields by striking, or threatening to strike in order to get more pay for the work they were doing. If some of them made money during the war it was not because they were receiving any unduly high prices for their produce, but because of the longer and harder hours they put in and the greater amount they produced. The prices that they received were not high compared with those in other lines. They went ahead and did their best, content to take whatever those at the helm allowed them, knowing that they were doing the best they knew for all concerned, feeling that nothing that was asked of them was too hard if it was of value in bringing victory to our side.

L. R. BINDING, County Agent.

The Food Administration

The conservation of food was a new thing to America. To have someone tell you how much or how little you could buy of the various necessities, regardless of how much money you had, was a radical departure from the existing order of things, and the food administration was not met with wild demonstrations of approval when it was first launched. The emergency of war which had taken thousands of producers out of the fields and the necessity of feeding millions of our allies combined to make strict conservation imperative. As the great need for economy of foodstuffs and increased production was pressed home to the people, they accepted the situation with good grace and co-operated in every possible way to make ends meet.

The food administrators were given broad powers. They fixed fair prices, limited the quantities of sugar and flour to be consumed in homes, bakeries, restaurants and hotels, and enforced the use of substitutes for flour. They had full authority to curb profiteering and to close any place of business which failed to observe the rules of the administration.

John R. Barr was appointed federal food administrator for Fulton county, December 5, 1917 and served until February 1919, and through his efforts and the efforts of his deputies splendid results were accomplished with very little friction and unpleasantness. As the people realized the necessity for the work they gave the food administration every support within their power. Mr. Barr and his deputies served without compensation. The county commissioners furnished a room in the court house for carrying on the work, and paid the salary of a stenographer, Mrs. Norabelle Bryant.

The personnel of the County Food Administration for Fulton county was as follows: John R. Barr, food administrator. Deputies: Dr. Saunders for Wayne township, Dr. Gilbert for Union township, Harry Brugh for Aubbeenaubbee township, Emerson Felder for Liberty township, Harrison Wynn for Richland township, F. M. Stoner for Henry township, with Doctor Hossman, of Akron and Dr. Stinson, of Athens, as assistants, Frank Arter for Newcastle township. O. M. Montgomery replaced Mr. Arter in Newcastle after his removal from the township in June 1918. Oren Karn, of Rochester, had charge of the bakery division and Wyle Bonine of the hotel and restaurant work. Henry Thompson, of Rochester, was chairman of the threshing division, and accomplished splendid work by preventing the waste of grain during the threshing season.

The Conscription Board

The declaration of war against Germany on April 5, 1917, found the country without a plan for raising an army commensurate with its needs, having in consideration the requirements of its industrial and agricultural means of support, until the enactment by Congress on May 18, 1917, of the Selective Service Regulations, which provided for the registration of the entire male population between certain prescribed ages, and their classification for military service in the order of the least possible disturbance to existing conditions. Civil war experiences with the canvassing method, bounty payments and the hiring of substitutes had not been satisfactory, and as it was early evident that the volunteer system would not prove sufficiently responsive to existing war demands, public opinion readily accepted the more equitable and business-like method of providing a National Army through the draft or conscription plan. In compliance with this law, and with the county as the principal unit, the people of the country responded with patriotic co-operation to the call for a census of its available man-power, and in less than a month after the law had been enacted, nearly 10,000,000 men were available for classification and the details of procedure that were prepared for the intricate processes of selecting an army. The assignment of this duty to civilians, aided by the moral support of voluntary war organizations, gave full opportunity for popular participation in the selective service, lent confidence to its success, and demonstrated an abiding faith in the American people and the solidarity of their institutions. The provisions of the first registration were that all male persons of the country, who had attained the age of 21 years and not yet reached the age of 31, should report on June 5, 1917, in their several designated places, and formally enroll their names for military service. This registration yielded 1173 names in Fulton county, and from its eligibles was to be selected the county's first quota for any call for general service men.

A brief review of the history and activities of the local board during the war with Germany shows that on June 29, 1917, Cyrus M. Davis, Dr. Harley W. Taylor and Frank H. Terry received notice from the War Department that they had been appointed members of the "Local Board for the County of Fulton." With full knowledge of the responsibilities involved, these men unhesitatingly accepted the trust, and were sworn in on the following day and on July 7th met at the court house at 9:00 a. m., and organized the board by selection of Cyrus M. Davis as chairman, Doctor Harley W. Taylor as medical director and Frank H. Terry as secretary. Each of the members named continued in active service until the resignation of Doctor Taylor was finally accepted by the War Department, that his unbounded spirit of patriotism might be better recognized by his enlistment on July 24, 1917, under the commission of first lieutenant in the Medical Corps.

His place was thereafter filled by appointment of Doctor Archibald Brown who took the oath of office and responded with the same unswerving integrity and zeal as his predecessor, serving until the final discharge of the board.

THE CONSCRIPTION BOARD 73

On July 17th notice was received that a net quota of 99 men had been apportioned to Fulton county to be furnished from the first draft, and on July 20th the first drawing of registrants was held in Washington to determine the order of call to the service, the first number drawn being 258—the serial number of George E. Warfield of Union township.

This drawing created widespread anxiety and the stern fact was forcibly brought to the people that the great war was on—and that America was preparing to strike.

The steady progress of preparation may be best realized by a brief reference to current events.

On August 3rd the board issued the first call for 196 registrants to appear for physical examination, on the 8th day of the same month the first meeting of the board was held for physical examination, with Doctor A. Brown also present as assistant examiner—and by some strange irony of fate the first man examined for physical ability in war was pre-eminently a man of peace—the Rev. George Conrad Pullman of the city of Rochester.

On August 15th the board was joined by Albert W. Bitters, who presented an appointment by Governor Goodrich as government appeal agent, and who did valiant service and gave valuable assistance to the board.

The first two men inducted by the board were George E. Warfield and James I. McMahan, entrained on September 5th to Camp Zachary Taylor, Ky., followed two days later by L. V. R. Louderback, James Stansbury and Omer Fennimore, and from this time on the calls for men grew steadily.

The insistent and increasing demands upon the time and energy of the local boards became so great that provision was finally made for assistance and in December, 1917, Joseph A. Myers was appointed chief clerk and continued to act as such during the war, relieving the board of much clerical work.

During the winter following, and the first few months of the year 1918, the calls for men were light by reason of severe weather and the impossibility of adequate provision for their comfort, but with the advent of spring preparations again became active, as shown by the record of young men sent to the front in the 60 days beginning with March 29th, 1918.

March 29th, 17 men were entrained to Camp Taylor, Ky.; April 3rd, 15 men to Fort Hamilton, N. Y.; April 26th, 30 men to Camp Taylor; April 27th, two men to Purdue Training School; May 2nd, four men to Ft. Thomas, Ky.; May 6th, two men to Ft. Ben Harrison,

Ind.; May 22nd, four men to Columbus Barracks, Ohio, and May 25th, 34 men to Camp Taylor—the latter entrainment being the largest contingent called for at any one time during the war.

Immediately following the Act of Congress of May 18th, 1917, a Board of Registration composed of A. E. Babcock, L. C. Sheets and Doctor M. O. King had been appointed for the purpose of taking the first registration of all male persons of the county, who had attained the age of 21 years and not yet reached the age of 31. This first registration of June 5th, 1917, was taken by the registration board which, on July 2nd following, turned the list of 1148 registrants over to the local board and was thereupon dissolved.

On June 5th, 1918—one year from the date of the first registration—a second registration was held, embracing those who had attained the age of 21 since the first registration and produced 118 men, followed on August 24th by a supplementary registration of those reaching the age of 21 since June 5th, and produced an additional 25 men.

These registrations of the youths just reaching manhood proved all too small to meet the ever increasing demands of the War Department and on September 12th, 1918, came the final registration, embracing all male citizens and declarants between the ages of 18 and 45, both inclusive, not already registered, and produced an additional 1810 men, making a total registration in this county to that date of 3101 and out of which a total of 310 of our vigorous young manhood were forwarded to the various training camps, inclusive of those received at the several student army training schools. This number does not include the large number of voluntary enlistments in the Regular Army and Navy, closely estimated at 75% of those forwarded by the local board, nor does it include our boys sent from other boards in the many large factory centers.

The last contingent sent to the colors were Dale Anderson and Alfred T. Butler, inducted and entrained for Camp Wadsworth, S. C., on November 11th, 1918, and stopped at Indianapolis and returned on receipt of wire announcing signing of armistice—and with the signing of this armistice the war closed, the active, exacting duties and strenuous labors of the local board ceased.

It is only fitting, closing a review of the activities of the Conscription Board, to give full credit to Frank H. Terry, the secretary, for the long hours and efficient service which he gave to the work. Mr. Terry, who furnished much of the information from which the above facts were written, modestly refrained from mention of himself, but his associates on the board, fully cognizant of his faithful and strenuous labors, his impartiality and fairness in a trying position, state that Mr. Terry did a lion's share of the work. Due credit should also be given to the attorneys of the county, all of whom labored many hours in giving free assistance in filling out the questionnaires of the registrants.

War Work in the Schools

Joint High School

In keeping with the spirit of the times, the Rochester Joint High school and Grades were glad to cooperate with the various agencies for war work in the county in doing their part to win the victory for world freedom from militarism.

Perhaps our most brilliant success in any line was the fact that every pupil in the city schools enrolled either in the Junior or Senior Red Cross and quite a number paid the fee in both organizations. The girls of the Domestic Art class made fifty petticoats for foreign children and some sixty-five Red Cross banners for the country schools.

As a result of the United War Work drive in the High school by Rev. W. J. Niven, the pupils pledged and paid $200.

The most active campaign and the one producing the greatest results was that for the sale of War stamps and Liberty bonds. The Columbia school sold approximately $5000 worth of stamps, the Lincoln, $5000 and the High school $2000. The bond sales by three schools totalled a good amount and reflected credit on both teachers and pupils. The teachers not only contributed their share in a financial way but kept up an active campaign which brought good results in more ways than one.

In addition, there was the work of the rake and the hoe. Most of the boys and many of the girls in the upper grades had their war gardens and thereby helped if only in a very small way to feed those in need. This work had a value not counted merely in dollars and cents. It meant larger visions of service and a broader spirit of altruism. Thus out of these hard and trying war times came many good and lasting results.

A. L. WHITMER.

Henry Township Schools

When school opened in the fall of 1917, the country was afire with the news of war and the preparation for war and, of course, the spirit aroused by this news permeated the school system from the old gray headed official to the youngest child who had just entered school for the first time.

During all that period of anxiety while the United States was actively engaged in war operations, the schools had a two-fold purpose, one to function in the ordinary way of preparing citizenship for the future and the other of assisting in every way possible in carrying on the war.

In pursuance of this two-fold ideal, every official, every teacher, and every pupil felt an individual responsibility and consecrated himself whole-heartedly to the task.

In its efforts to help win the war, there were two ways that the schools were able to assist; e. i.; in the spreading of information and government requests among the people and secondly in aiding in many ways directly. There was no factor more potent in disseminating federal information and regulations than the public schools. During the whole period of the struggle, our school walls were covered with posters and bulletins bringing the country's needs and requests to the pupils who in turn imparted the things learned at school to their parents at home. Not only did the school keep a continuous exhibit of patriotic pictures and literature but it was the central distributing point for a great many pamphlets to be sent to parents. Announcements of all important policies and all public war gatherings were made and speakers came in who brought added enthusiasm and patriotism to the community through the pupils. The schools were so organized that they were prepared to rearrange their regular schedule at a minute's notice in order to give time to any activity which would be of service to our country.

Our educational organizations were a very important factor in every effort of conservation, production, and finance made by Henry township during the war. The domestic science department so arranged its courses that a great deal of the work emphasized the conservation programme and so that the girls taking these courses could devote a part of their school times to aiding in the work of the local Red Cross society. All of the girls in the upper grades gave a definite amount of time each week to Red Cross work. These girls, inspired by their teachers and by a desire for service, not only aided during the school year but met at regular intervals during the summer of 1918 to sew for the Red Cross. Our boys worked diligently morning and evening and on Saturdays to increase farm production and a number joined the Boy's Working Reserve in the spring. They quit school a few weeks early to begin productive work but at the same time they made up their school work so that they would get their credits.

In order that each pupil could become identified personally with the wonderful service of the Red Cross, the Junior Red Cross was formed in the fall of 1917. An appeal came to the schools for the children to join the junior society. They responded quickly and almost the entire body of pupils, who were eligible, became members.

Not only did the pupils and teachers belong to the Red Cross and aid it in its service but the schools, in an organized way, aided the society financially. The graded schools dedicated an entertainment to its aid and the high school basketball team gave a benefit basketball game for the same purpose. In addition to these the Senior class of 1918 turned the net proceeds of their class play into the Red Cross treasury.

A number of pupils bought Liberty Loan Bonds and a preparation for each drive was made through the schools but the greatest financial effort of the war period, in which the school participated actively, was the buying of Thrift and War Savings Stamps and the solicitation of outsiders to buy these securities. The buying of stamps was stimulated in a variety of ways too numerous to record, but each school room had in it some device of honorable recognition, songs, competitions and games to encourage pupils in buying stamps and to make them understand the meaning of their investment. There were individual and collective efforts to raise money for this purpose. The schools gave entertainments and suppers, girls sold candy and popcorn, and the pupils industriously solicited adults for waste paper, old bottles, and anything that was salable. Children ransacked the home premises for old rags, old rubber, and old iron. Sometimes parents were irritated by the efforts of the pupils and yet they were serving with a consecration that probably few adults attained. These various activities of the children netted them between two and three thousand dollars' worth of War Savings Stamps during the school year 1917-18 in the grades alone. Perhaps the most spectacular single financial effort was made in March, 1918, when the girls of the high school competed with the boys for ten days to see which could dispose of the most War Savings Stamps by direct sale and pledge. The prize to the winners was to be a free moving picture show at the expense of the losers. During these ten days, parties from the two rival camps scoured the township of evenings and over the week end soliciting for War Savings Stamp sales. Absolute secrecy prevailed between the groups of competitors. The whole community was divided into factions, one supporting the girls and the other the boys. Sales and pledges from twenty-five cents to a thousand dollars were taken in this record drive. On the morning of the eleventh day, the rival organizations met in separate rooms to make an inventory of their sales. Intense excitement prevailed at these meetings. Pupils and teachers made talks urging others to pledge all they felt they could pay. After an hour of discussion, exhortation, cheering, and pledging, both sections returned to the assembly room where the results, totaling $20,400.00 and showing the girls to be the winners, were reported. The pupils were pitched to such high nervous tension that school was out of the question so a parade was held through town amid the shouting and singing of the pupils and the applause of the citizens. On the following afternoon, the boys took the girls to the show which was given by the owner with the understanding that the proceeds were to go to the Red Cross.

The per capita sales of War Savings Stamps in Henry township stood high among the units of the state of Indiana and this splendid record is certainly due, in no small way, to the work of the schools in buying, advertising and soliciting.

In every township drive: Liberty Bonds, Red Cross, Y. W. C. A., Y. M. C. A., United War Work fund, the records will show liberal support and devoted service on the part of school officials, teachers, and pupils.

Not only did the schools, as organized in 1917-18, bend every effort to their consecrated duty but the flower of the township's young manhood, no doubt influenced in many ways by their previous schooling, delivered themselves a living sacrifice in the training camps and on the field of battle. One former pupil of the schools, Adolph Merley, made the supreme sacrifice. Others were ready and willing to brave any danger when their country called them. Because of their former member and the thousands of other American boys who lie in France, the vision of the schools of Henry township will no longer be bounded on the east by the Atlantic but will ever reach beyond where our thousands fought and fell for an ideal.

The schools will go on, as before, with the steady purpose among patrons, officials, and teachers to prepare a future citizenship ever ready to sacrifice in service of country and fellow man and always prepared to trample down and throttle those theories which raise their heads in opposition to the ideals of true democracy as set up by our forefathers and tested by more than a century of prosperous history. The greatest problem of the schools is to instill the patriotism of peace and to be ready to assist if war comes. The Henry township schools have proven themselves equal to the task in the past and will always do so with the united support of the citizens of the community.

Victory Boys and Girls

Among the many notable features of the war work carried on at home was that of the boys and girls of our land. None were more loyal or more patriotic. In the United War Work Drive of the seven great welfare organizations, it was felt that our youngest citizens should be asked to help. They were vitally interested, for nearly every one had a brother or other relative in service. How well they responded can be seen by the hundreds and thousands whose united subscriptions amounted to several millions of dollars in the "Victory Boys and Girls" campaign. To become a "Victory Boy" or a "Victory Girl," it was necessary to make a pledge to earn and give five dollars in a specified length of time. Of all the millions given by the "Victory Boys and Girls", our own Fulton County gave its proportionate share. Rev. W. J. Niven, of Rochester, was chosen chairman for the County, organizing it into districts, with a chairman for each.

The work was done chiefly thru the schools, where the best opportunity was offered for the fullest explanation of the importance of the campaign. Two thousand dollars was pledged by the children of the county as follows:

Rochester City $720. Rochester tp. $234. Wayne tp. $350. Liberty tp. $243. Union tp. $140. Newcastle tp. $105. Henry tp. $100. Aubbeenaubbee tp. $85. Richland tp. $25.

Report of Fuel Administrator.

In obedience to an order from Indianapolis, the County Council of Defense, acting in conjunction with the Farmer's and Merchant's Association, recommended the appointment of Grosvenor Dawe, to act as Fuel Administrator during the critical coal famine period of 1917—1918. The position was an arduous one, inasmuch as the serious coal shortage was made more dangerous than it would otherwise have been, by an unusually cold winter.

Backed by the authority of a federal officer, Mr. Dawe apportioned the very small amounts of coal received by allotments, sometimes as small as fifty pounds, relieving actual need first, and others on the order of their urgency. During January, 1918, there was a terrific blizzard which effectually cut the county off from any outside communication, and the fuel situation was acutely dangerous; nothing but absolute organization could have handled it, and that organization was apparent in the office of the Fuel Administrator; men were sent into the country to cut wood, farmers were urged to use their fallen timber, citizens were compelled to conserve fuel, and by co-operation of the closest sort, the crisis was successfully passed, not, however, without the further inconvenience, entailed by the abandonment of public meetings, and the early closing of stores, with accompanying saving of fuel.

In July, 1918, Mr. Dawe resigned his position, which was filled during the remainder of the war by A. E. Babcock. In the early winter of 1918-19, there was a shortage of anthracite coal but no serious effects were felt, because there was an ample supply of Indiana coal for the whole county. Mr. Babcock received his discharge in February, 1919.

The Library Helped

During the whole period of the war the Rochester Public Library cooperated with national and local war organizations. One room in the basement was used by the Red Cross as a sewing room, and another was fitted up especially for a surgical-dressing room. Many meetings were held in the assembly room.

Hundreds of bulletins issued by various departments of the United States government on cooking, canning, saving fuel, etc. were distributed.

When the call was made by the American Library Association for books for the soldiers Rochester responded liberally. The library collected 1,215 books, which were sent to camps and hospitals at home and abroad. Posters of various drives were always given prominent places in the library.

Many books of interest in connection with the war were purchased. Some of the books gave the folks at home a better idea of the experiences of the boys at the front and what they had to endure, others were of value in that they expounded the views of noted men as to the cause and effect of the great war, together with documentary evidence, while still others gave help in practical ways in order that the war might be won

The Liberty Guards

On December 18, 1917, the 17th separate company of Liberty Guards was organized in Rochester with 162 members, all of whom were residents of Fulton county and ranged from 18 to 42 years of age. The company met on Monday nights of each week for drill and training and the attendance was good.

The first officers elected were Captain, Cyrus M. Davis; First Lieutenant, Harley McCarter; Second Lieutenant, Hector De Zias, and First Sergeant, Floyd J. Mattice.

On February 18th the company was newly organized and mustered into the service of the state of Indiana by Judge Stevens and new officers elected as follows: Captain, Cyrus M. Davis; First Lieutenant, Harley McCarter; Second Lieutenant, William Delp; First Sergeant, Harry Bitters; Second Sergeant, John Swartwood; Third Sergeant, Merle Ream; Fourth Sergeant, Edward Jones; Fifth Sergeant, Ayrton Howard; Sixth Sergeant, Walter House; First Corporal, Dean L. Barnhart; Second Corporal, Admiral Smith; Third Corporal, Earle L. Miller; Fourth Corporal, Milo Coplen; Fifth Corporal, Conrad Irvine; Sixth Corporal, Rev. H. G. Gaige. The company continued to drill under the above officers until the 9th of December, 1918, when they were mustered out of service by Capt. C. M. Davis.

The company was uniformed and equipped by the business men of Rochester and other citizens of the county who raised a fund for this purpose.

Following is the personnel of the Liberty Guard organization:

Barger, Guy
Bailey, Elliott
Ball, Omer
Barnhart, Dean, Corporal
Biddinger, William
Bitters, Harry, Sergeant
Braman, Milo
Braman, John
Butler, Jess
Byrley, Charles
Boulter, Otto
Coplen, George
Coplen, Milo
Davis, Cy, Captain
Delp, Wm., 2nd Lieut.
Dixon, Henry
Fields, Guy
Foglesong, Harry
Fretz, Ray
Gaige, Rev.
Garver, V. L.
Green, Dwight
Greek, Robert P.
Hetzner, Earl
Hiatt, Dee
House, Walter, Sergt.
Howard, Ayrton, Corp.
Irvine, Wilbert
Irvine, Conrad
Jackson, Willis
Jones, Ed., Sergt.
Kennell, Wm.
Lynch, B. B.
Louderback, Harry
Mathias, Earl
Mathias, J. W.
Marsh, Ora
Marsh, Marion
Manson, Fred
Mattice, F. J.
McCarter, Harley, 1st Lieut.
Miller, Earle, Corp.
Miller, Hugh
Miller, Otto
Montgomery, Ray
Myers, Ray

THE LIBERTY GUARDS

Newby, Fred
Oliver, Rue
Overmyer, Russell
Overmyer, Harley
Parker, J. C.
Pontius, Rosco, Bugler
Railsback, Don
Ream, Merle, Sergt.
Rouch, Dwight
Rouch, Eugene
Saunders, John
Saunders, Elza
Sherbondy, Bruce
Seigfried, P. A.
Snapp, Cecil
Slaybaugh, John
Snyder, Roy
Snyder, Willard
Smith, Admiral
Stanley, John
Swartwood, John, Sergt.
Swihart, Jerome C.
Tubbs, S. M.
Wagner, Omar
Wertz, L. I.
Wicks, Earl
Young, Thurston
Zimmerman, Emerson
Zimmerman, Leo

Red Cross Work

The Fulton County Chapter of the A. R. C. was organized June 2, 1917, with R. C. Johnson, chairman; Mrs. Imogene Hendrickson, vice-chairman; Omar B. Smith, treasurer, and Miss Edna Roth, secretary.

At the time of organization, 650 members were enrolled, but by 1919 the membership had increased to 3000.

Four thousand articles were turned out by ladies in the sewing room. Some of these workers also helped knit a part of the 1700 knitted articles sent out from the county. Surgical dressing classes made 24,786 articles of all kinds, for hospital use.

The expenditures for supplies for 1918 totalled $6,335.00

In 1917, the county quota asked for, was $7,000, but the amount given was $8,000. In 1918, the quota was $7,500, and our response was $11,000.

In December, 1918, the Fulton County Chapter furnished 225 Christmas boxes for the parents of soldiers and sailors to fill for the boys at war, and also undertook the transportation of the same.

The Comfort Kit Committee, throughout the county, gave a filled comfort kit to every boy who left the county for the service, so far as was known.

After the War, the attention of the chapter was given to needs of the returning soldiers; insurance was cared for, mileage and delayed checks were traced, and the care of the fighting men was not given over until they were safely placed in their own before-the-war conditions.

There was the promptest response from the county to every appeal made by the officers, throughout the war, and no work seemed too much, nor no amount too large, to be successfully and willingly handled.

Upon Mr. Johnson's resignation, because of other duties interfering, Mr. A. S. Warriner was appointed as chairman in 1918, and he held that position until the end of the War.

The Junior Red Cross

During the summer of 1917 when the American Red Cross was making plans for a greater work in helping win the war, it was suggested by some one in authority that a Junior Red Cross be formed, as to take in all the children in school in the United States.

In Fulton County, Thomas F. Berry, County Superintendent of Schools, was selected as the Junior Red Cross Chairman.

When school opened in September the county superintendent took up the question of securing Junior Red Cross members, with the teachers of all the schools in the county. The organization was greatly handicapped by the fact that no definite details of how to organize could be secured from Headquarters; but the splendid enthusiasm of teachers and pupils was so strong to do their part in winning the war, that it was impossible to hold them in check to await orders from the higher officials. By Thanksgiving many townships had enrolled every school child, and by Christmas every township, excepting one, had a 100 per cent enrollment and had sent in $500. After Christmas Rochester city enrolled 800 members and increased the Junior Fund to $700.00. Thus before final instructions were received Fulton County Junior Red Cross was over the top. The credit for this work is wholly due to the patriotic efforts of the teachers and pupils.

The demand for Junior Red Cross Buttons and Banners was so great that it was not possible for the sewing classes to make the banners fast enough. Many of the pupils from the High Schools of the county did a great deal of sewing and knitting and in many cases helped the Red Cross Chapters raise money for different enterprises.

In February of 1918 the county Chairman received a letter from the State Chairman of Indiana Junior Red Cross saying that Fulton County was the first county, so far as he knew in the United States to complete a 100 per cent enrollment. Thus the teachers and pupils were justly proud of the part they played. It was patriotism exemplified in doing.

Union Township Red Cross

The Kewanna and Union township Branch of the Fulton County chapter American Red Cross was organized June 12, 1917, with the following officers: Chairman, Mrs. L. M. Shoemaker; vice chairman, Mrs. C. B. Hiatt; secretary, Miss Jessie Slick; treasurer, E. J. Buchanan.

The first canvass for members resulted in a membership of two hundred.

The Red Cross drive for the War Relief Fund was made during the week beginning July 2 under direction of Dr. A. I. Gilbert who was appointed chairman of the drive. Union township's share, $560.00, was oversubscribed.

The membership was divided into units for work. Mrs. Shoemaker was appointed chairman and the inspectors were Mrs. Etta Teeter, Mrs. George Troutman, Mrs. A. I. Gilbert, Mrs. Etta Singer, Mrs. Una Wilson, Mrs. Fred Russell, Mrs. E. J. Buchanan and Mrs. Chas. Snepp.

Sewing machines and other equipment were provided in the library where the workers met on Tuesday, Wednesday, Thursday and Friday of each week. The sewing was carefully planned and inspected so that the garments sent out from this shop showed strictly high class work.

This branch made and sent to headquarters more than six hundred hospital garments, including pajamas, hospital bed shirts, surgeon's aprons, seventy-five sweaters, twenty pairs of wrislets, six scarfs, two hundred and five pairs of socks and one thousand surgical dressings. A comfort kit fully equipped was furnished to every soldier who went into service from Union township.

The Kewanna branch responded to every call including the old clothes drive, the linen shower, etc. During the week beginning May 20, 1918, Kewanna's quota for Red Cross money, $700.00, was oversubscribed. The Christmas roll call universal membership, 1918, was finished with 425 members.

Henry Township Red Cross

Authority to organize an Akron Branch of the Fulton County Chapter of the American Red Cross, with jurisdiction over Henry township, was granted June 28, 1917. The temporary committee on organization was made up of Roy Jones, A. A. Gast, S. N. Shesler, Miss Deborah V. Strong, John McCullough, E. L. Scott, E. O. Strong, Rev. I. R. Godwin, Mr. and Mrs. M. L. Patterson.

Mrs. M. L. Patterson was made temporary chairman and Miss Deborah V. Strong temporary secretary. The Chapter was organized with the same officers until November 6, 1917, when an election of officers was held and the following were elected for one year: Mrs. M. L. Patterson, chairman; Mrs. A. A. Kistler, vice-chairman; Mrs. W. A. Patterson, secretary; Mr. John McCullough, treasurer.

In the December Red Cross membership drive the Akron Branch enrolled 497 Seniors and seven Juniors. Besides these members, the Grade Schools of Akron gave an entertainment and used the proceeds to join the Junior Red Cross in a body. During the early spring, Miss Ruth Sutherland, of Rochester, held three classes daily in surgical dressings and thirty ladies completed the course. These in turn acted as instructors for the various classes under the supervision of Mrs. Roy Jones. Several hundred surgical dressings were completed and sent to headquarters at Rochester.

In October, 1918, new Red Cross officers were elected for one year, as follows: Mrs. M. L. Patterson, chairman; Mrs. F. M. Weaver, vice-chairman; Miss Elizabeth Morrett, recording secretary; Mrs. R. R. Carr, corresponding secretary; Mr. John McCullough, treasurer.

The Christmas membership drive gave the Chapter an enrollment of 572 Seniors and 229 Juniors. The Chapter has always been strong financially due to the loyal support of its members and friends. Several entertainments were given for the Red Cross, including a High School play, a two-day, all-star cast moving picture show, two entertainments by the graded schools and several suppers. A horse, a young heifer, a quilt and a hand-painting were donated and sold, making a total of $448.00. Besides these there were many smaller donations which added to the treasury.

The executive officers made an effort to expend the money wisely, viz. home-charities, pneumonia jackets for our sick during the flu epidemic and for two adopted French orphans whose father had given his life in the World's War. Liberal donations were also made to the Armenian and Syrian Relief Funds, Jewish Welfare and "Soldiers' and Sailors' Home Coming Day" held at Akron, Thursday, September 11, 1919. Considerable money was expended in buying materials for the Red Cross workers. It is impossible to give the exact number of knitters. Suffice it to say, that yarn was continually in demand. The Chapter and friends knit, in all, 229 pairs of socks, 111 sweaters, 15 pairs of wristlets, 32 scarfs, 34 helmets, three quilts and several dozen wash rags and wipes. The sewers were just as faithful. The first work they did was to make and fill a comfort kit for every Henry township service boy and 300 navy comfort kits for the Great Lakes Training Station, Chicago, Illinois. During the summer of 1918 the sewing groups were kept busy making up ready-cut operating gowns and underclothing, supplied by county headquarters. More than a dozen boxes and barrels, each, of old, as well as new clothing, besides several comforters made by the school children, were shipped to France. Two boxes were shipped to the "Battleship Indiana," as Christmas Greetings. Forty-seven Christmas boxes were sent to soldiers overseas, three marked to unknown. The Chapter had a faithful auxiliary body of workers at Athens, under the supervision of Mrs. Frank Pontious, who did their part of all the work required of the township Red Cross.

The fifth and sixth grades of Akron schools knit enough blocks to complete two quilts, the first going to France—the second to West Baden, Indiana. During the summer of 1918 the fifth and sixth grade girls met weekly at the Red Cross room and pieced comforter tops, also a class of older girls met and completed a comforter top and a quilt, all were sent to France. We had many Junior knitters in the grades and high school.

Report of the Women's Work

Immediately following the appointment of the woman member of the County Council of Defense, as chairman of Women's Activities in the county, a call came from the State Food Chairman, Dr. H. E. Barnard, of Indianapolis, to organize the county by having food conservation pledges signed by housewives. An organization to carry out this request was at once appointed, as follows: Union township: Chairman—Mrs. Una Wilson. Wayne township: Chairman—Miss Dessie Buchanan. Richland township: Chairman—Mrs. J. H. Reed. Newcastle township: Chairman—Mrs. M. F. Deemer. Rochester township: Chairman—Mrs. Chas. Emmons. Liberty township: Chairman—Mrs. R. O. Johnson. Aubbeenaubbee township: Chairman—Mrs. Sam. Kelley. Henry township: Chairman—Mrs. A. A. Gast. These women served as chairman of their townships for the entire period of the war, with the exception of Miss Buchanan, who resigned her chairmanship in order to give her entire time to the Red Cross Work, and was succeeded by Mrs. Floyd Leasure. To this group of women should be given the greater share of credit for the splendid record of the county.

In the Food Card drive, the chairmen organized their helpers, and undertook to obtain the signature of all the women in the county, but because of the haste necessary, which gave little time for the education of the women as to the necessity of this move, a very small percent of the women appealed to, took the matter in an interested way, and the drive was a failure from the point of numbers; however, the seed thus tediously planted bore much fruit, and in time, when the food conditions were understood, there were no more consistently conserving communities anywhere, than in Fulton county.

In January, 1918, in response to a request from Mrs. Anne S. Carlisle, state chairman of Women's Activities, a more intensive organization was undertaken, and twelve women were appointed in each township retaining the original chairman. These women were then each one given the chairmanship of one of the twelve departments, advised by headquarters, for her township. By this means, when there came a necessity for special emphasis on any one phase of war work, the entire township could be expected to work on that committee, the permanent chairman giving for the moment, her place to the department chairman. Futhermore, there was always a complete county committee on any department, for the county chairman to use, if occasion arose and finally all of these chairmen, with the county chairman, formed an executive committee, which was ready to act upon any necessary questions. This system seemed a trifle complex, at first, but it proved to be surprisingly effective, and it is a matter of county pride, that the women, thus organized, went over the top, in every drive, in the shortest possible time consistent with a complete canvass. When, at the time of the men's finger-tip organization, a square-mile woman was appointed to work with every square-mile man, it is safe to say that not a county in the union was more thoroughly prepared, or more fittingly represented for the most effective work in any crisis which might need to be faced.

The second drive which the women handled was the Registration drive, which was planned for April, 1918. The purpose of the drive was the registration of every woman in the state in regard to her fitness for some form of war work, at home or afield. The drive was preceded by an educative period, during which speeches were made by the Fourteen Minute Women in every locality in the county, explaining the use of the cards, and their necessity in case of a prolonged war. As a result of the clear understanding thus obtained, there was more than a 99% enrollment made, every woman except fifty, so far as was known, having signed in some capacity. This report, it may be interesting to note, was one of the ten best in the state. A tabulated report, showing the various departments in which the women enrolled, would be interesting, too, but unfortunately, it is not available.

Also in April, 1918, was undertaken the Child Welfare Drive for the physical examination of all children under five. Thanks to the generous co-operation of all the county physicians, this examination was completed and the report sent in, first of all the counties in the state and later it proved to be one of the most complete reports sent in. There were, so far as known, less than fifty babies unexamined, and this meant that for one whole week, every doctor's office was filled with a steady stream of mothers and babies—the latter being weighed, measured, and tested carefully for weakness, malnutrition, or disease. Too much appreciation cannot be expressed for the energy, time, and skill which the physicians gave so freely to this work. It is interesting to notice, in this connection, that, because of the information thus received, many parents have taken steps to correct the abnormal conditions pointed out changing diet, having tonsils and adenoids removed, etc., so that the net results of this drive was a distinct rise in the children's health rate for the county.

The women's organization helped in three Liberty Loan drives, the United War Work drive, the Y. W. C. A. drive, the book and magazine drive, the organization of food clubs, which was the only activity introduced into the county, not eagerly taken up, since there was but one successful food club (the Mt. Zion) in the county, and in many other places of equal importance, of less note. It is due the women, too, to add that the enthusiasm showed in the very last work was as keen and earnest as in the first; and no one showed any disposition to slow up, so long as there was any need for the organization to continue its war activities.

There were two different Domestic Science instructors sent to the county through the efforts of the Home Economics department, who gave demonstrations in the use of substitutes, and in cold-pack canning. These were only fairly well received, and the results, while gratifying to those in attendance, were not so far-reaching as had been hoped. But it is safe to say that as an echo of these visits, many canned who had never canned before, and many learned lessons of thrift in home cooking who had thought they had nothing in that line to learn.

The Fourteen Minute women, organized for the purpose of presenting the various requests of the committee at Indianapolis, and of explaining the need for concerted action in the many drives, were very successful in their efforts. They delivered about seventy-five speeches, some four minute, some fourteen and some longer than either. They were always heard with courtesy and interest. In conjunction with the recreation committee, they put on "Community Sings" at the lake hotels during the summer months.

The latter committee, too, put song leaflets into the churches, and with the co-operation of the pastors, introduced a fifteen minute "sing" before the Sunday evening service.

Women's Club Work

The past four years have been without precedent in the history of club work while the black shadows of the gigantic tragedy were lowering over our loved land. No club woman of Fulton county ever shirked her share of the great responsibility in aiding our government to win the war for humanity. When the President of the General Federation of Women's Clubs telegraphed to Washington within 24 hours after the declaration of war, saying that the club women of America stood loyally behind the government in the national crisis and offering their organization for service, the club women of Indiana and Fulton County interpreted that pledge literally and enlisted as soldiers, obedient to every command. There are fifteen clubs in Fulton county, not including the social clubs, with about three hundred members, and all answered their country's call.

Club programs were constructed on war service plans—to offer a plan not only patriotic in its intent but also in its effect—to emphasize the amazing scope of the war work—to prove that every phase of war activity could be made a potent factor in winning the war. The clubs took on a broader and greater scope and a larger view of causes and effects, looking into the future for great results. They interested themselves in the health laws, better legislation, home economics, good food, clothing and shelter, conservation, good roads, forestry, education, literature, music and art. Thus the clubs felt they were helping to make better citizens, better Americans, therefore "A Greater America."

The clubs of Fulton county were all concerned in these studies, all doing their part in every way possible. We realized that it was our patriotic duty to have healthy men and women and that childhood must be looked after to this end; that healthful and clean surroundings, good food and clothing are helpful to a citizen's patriotism. That in reducing the death rate we were working for the highest patriotism and for our country. We learned that good roads facilitated war transportation; that forest conservation related itself to ships and aeroplanes; that bird production meant crop production. Years ago we realized the great problem of Americanization and bent ourselves to help in every way to inspire American ideals. How civics helped to build our democracy and government; how art was used in the war in camouflage and various ways; how music helped to keep up the spirit and morale of our boys at the front; none of these subjects were new. The clubs only put more energy and stress on these old questions and while perhaps we could not see immediate results, it all counted for much and made conditions possible for the winning of the war.

The clubs of Fulton county played an important role in all war work of the county. There was a close co-operation between The Council of Defense and the club women, the latter assisting in every way possible to carry on the war work. The clubs furnished many of the square mile and two block women. Many of the 15 minute speakers were club women. They helped to make all the different drives, in the registration and distribution of food cards. They conserved food by using substitutes and many made war gardens to increase the food supply.

The Woman's Club of Rochester gave twenty-nine dollars to the Furlough Homes in France and twenty-four dollars to a Red Cross hospital outfit. This club also bought two fifty dollar Liberty Bonds and thirty of its members bought twenty thousand dollars worth of bonds.

Report of the Women's Liberty Loan Committee

The women were not represented in the First Liberty Loan, but for the Second, Mrs. Lucile Holman Leonard was recommended for the Woman's County Chairman, by Mrs. Perry Heath, secretary of the County Council of Defense. Mrs. Alice Foster McCulloch of Ft. Wayne, Woman's State Chairman for Liberty Loans.

The women were asked to help in the publicity end of the Drives, going into different parts of the county distributing literature and putting up posters at war meetings.

The Third Liberty Loan found the women organized—

Township Chairmen as follows: Rochester—Mrs. Milton Smiley. Henry—Mrs. Albert Scott. Liberty—Mrs. W. E. Redman. Wayne—Mrs. Ed. Costello. Union—Miss Jessie Slick. Aubbeenaubbee—Mrs. Myrtle Luckenbill. Richland—Mrs. Myrtle Bunn. Newcastle—Mrs. Ancil Jeffries.

Meetings were held in the different townships where speeches were made in behalf of the Liberty Loan. One at Delong was made especially enlightening by a little English girl, the young wife of a returned soldier. She had recently gone through the air raids over London. Her appeal for subscriptions was especially helpful to the Loan Committee. In Rochester, Akron, Kewanna and Fulton the two block women made a house to house canvass for subscriptions.

During the various drives, fourteen minute women attended all Woman's Clubs, Ladies' Aid and other meetings, picture shows etc., speaking in behalf of the Loan. Akron women at first were going to give their whole attention to Red Cross work but how they did work and raise quotas after they had a change of heart. Wayne township had to be shown but met the emergency nobly. Newcastle was always up and doing, and Liberty wanted no suggestions. They did things for themselves.

The same committee chairmen worked for War Savings, selling stamps and bonds and backing the movement through the schools.

The first day of the drive for the Fourth Liberty Loan came during the Fulton County Fair and a great parade marched through the streets of Rochester to the Fair Grounds. After much consultation, planning and work by the women, ever keeping in mind the publicity of the loan, each township brought in floats, representing Liberty and war work, to join the bands, the Red Cross, and all the organizations forming the line of march.

Woman's mission in each drive seemed to be to help the men. This they tried to do to the best of their ability. When the Victory Loan drive promised to start out badly, enthusiasm waning because of the signing of the armistice, the woman's county chairman attended the Seventh Federal Reserve Victory Loan Convention held in Chicago in March, 1919, hearing Carter Glass, the new Secretary of the Treasury, on the subject of the Loan. Five states represented two thousand strong, with drum corps and speakers and enthusiasm ran high. The slogan "Finish the Job" spread rapidly and the workers at the first call, jumped into harness.

Prizes of German helmets were offered to the school children of the county, for the best essay on "The Victory Loan." Columbia

School of Rochester, being the only school to respond to the invitation of the Committee and arrange such a contest, all four prizes were awarded to pupils of this school. Margaret Elizabeth Bryant received first prize, Jean Rannells second, George Hurst third and Dean McMahan fourth.

MRS. LUCILE H. LEONARD,
County Chairman Woman's Liberty Loan Committee.

Women's Activities in Newcastle Township.

The women of Newcastle township tried to follow out to the letter everything that was asked of them during the war. They organized with 34 square mile women, observed registration week with an almost 100% registration, observed Child Welfare week and saw that every child under school age was examined, placed food conservation cards in practically every home and held a Food Conservation Demonstration at Talma.

The Red Cross had three organizations in the township, the Bethlehem unit with Mrs. F. C. Mickey as manager, the Palestine unit with Mrs. Frank Collins and Mrs. Meade Haimbaugh as managers and the Talma unit with Mrs. Lou Grove and Mrs. Charles Jones as managers. Miss Fern Arter had charge of the knitting for the township. Mrs. Frank Montgomery knitted 104 pairs of sox and was first in the county to use the rainbow colors in the sox and the only one to knit the emblem of the Red Cross in them.

Bridge Workers Helped

In a large measure the plant of the Rocheser Bridge Company became a shipyard, where steel was fabricated for the American merchant marine. Early in the ship-building program of the government this plant was given small contracts for ship parts, and so successfully did the company handle the work that the plant was practically double and between one hundred and fifty and two hundred men were continuously employed in government work. Through many months, the men in the employ of the local bridge plant gave tireless support to the Nation in helping to build ships which went into the merchant marine and were used to carry food to the American army and the hungry people overseas. These workmen showed a fine loyalty to the government by their effort, and in every Liberty Bond drive and other fund-raising effort contributed liberally of their earnings.

Newspapers and Banks Loyal

In giving credit for loyalty and devotion to the common cause, not to mention the newspapers of the county would be to ignore one of the important factors in successfully uniting the sentiment of the county for effective war work. Without exception every newspaper of the county did heroic service in carrying government publicity, without charge, and in giving liberally of their space for every drive for funds. The Rochester Sentinel, Republican and Sun, the Akron News, the Kewanna Herald and the Fulton Leader carried columns of government publicity and aided in every possible way to give publicity to all war matters.

The banks of the county, without exception, and with an unselfish patriotism, aided in every financial effort. Without the wholehearted support of the banks of the county it would have been impossible to "go over the top" in every demand for funds.

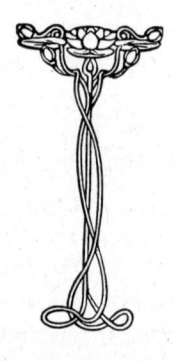

The Boys in Khaki

Fulton county had approximately 650 of her sons in some branch of the service. Every effort was made by the compilers of this history to secure the service record of every Fulton county boy who served Uncle Sam in the world war. Questionnaires were mailed, not once, but several times to the last known address of our boys in the service as well as to relatives, but in spite of the exhaustive effort made, the list is not nearly so complete as it should be. Modesty, indifference and probably still other motives unknown to the compilers, prevented the completion of the list after months of effort to make it complete. Neither is it as accurate as one would wish, but still it shows, unmistakably that Fulton county boys did their part in winning the war in many widely separated fields of endeavor.

ADAMSON, Arthur B., 30, Rochester, cook, son of Mr. and Mrs. Homer L. Adamson, entered service May 24, 1918 at Rochester, trained at Camp Taylor and West Point, Ky. 1st cook 325 Hdqrs. Co., F. A. Sailed Sept. 8, 1918 and served as cook in France. Mustered out March 1, 1919 at Camp Sherman.

ANDERSON, Lloyd Wilbur, 20, Kewanna, R. R. Clerk, son of William T. and Maude L. Anderson, entered service Oct. 1, 1918 at Chicago. Served as acting Corporal, Co. D., S. A. T. C. Detachment. Mustered out Dec. 11, 1918 at Chicago.

ARMSTRONG, Max Ray, 28, Kewanna, optician. Entered service Sept. 18, 1917. Trained at St. Paul, Minn., and assigned to air service. Mustered out Feb. 18, 1919 at Camp Grant.

ADAMSON, Edgar H., 20, Rochester, telephone work, son of Homer L. and Isabelle A. Adamson, entered service July 29, 1918, trained at Great Lakes, promoted to second class seaman, did coast patrol work. Mustered out Dec. 3, 1918 on U. S. S. Montana.

ANDERSON, Dale, 21, Rochester, railroad, son of William and Ella M. Anderson, entered service Nov. 10, 1918 at Rochester. Armistice was signed en route to Camp Taylor.

ANDERSON, Max, 18, Leiters Ford, railroader, son of J. W. and Adda Anderson, entered service April 24, 1918, at Logansport, trained at Jefferson Barracks, Ft. Totten, Eustis, Stuart, Ft. Hancock and Campt Grant. Private Battery C, 37th. Mustered out at Camp Grant, Dec. 19, 1918.

GLEN EMMONS	PERCY SMITH	WILLIAM SOWERS
HERBERT ROGERS	ERNEST H. McCALL	RAYMOND GOSS
JAMES A. BABCOCK	CLARENCE R. SNYDER	EDWARD K. GILLILAND

ANDERSON, Harley R., 22, Tiosa, teacher, son of Harmon and Malinda Anderson, entered service at Rochester, March 29, 1918, trained at Camp Taylor and Upton, made first class private Co. A., 111th Regt. Div. 28. Sailed May 5, 1918 and with 1st, 2nd, 3rd and 4th Army Corps in France. Mustered out May 13, 1919 at Camp Sherman.

AULT, William H., 22, Leiters Ford, farmer, son of John and Mary Ault, entered service Sept. 21, 1917, trained at Camp Knox, promoted from private to wagoner, Supply Co. 325 F. A. Sailed Sept. 8, 1918 and served as teamster. Mustered out April 9, 1919 at Camp Taylor.

ADAMS, Otis B., 23, Kewanna, athletic coach, son of Almer and Elizabeth Adams. Entered service March 2, 1917, at Ft. Benjamin Harrison, trained at Camp Taylor, Camp Gordon and Camp Sheridan. Promoted from private to 2nd Lt., 2nd to 1st Lt., 1st Lt. to Captain. Served as Regimental Adjutant and was instructor of bayonet. 5th Inft. Mustered out at Camp Benning. Sailed from U. S. Nov. 7th, 1918 and was recalled by wireless.

BAILEY, Garl Forrest, 21, Grass Creek, carpenter, son of James and Nettie Bailey, entered service May 22, 1918 at Logansport, Ind., trained at Jefferson Barracks and Ft. Caswell, private, Battery A., 75th Reg. Sailed Oct. 21, 1918, Battery D., 118 Field Artillery, 31st Division, 56th Brigade, training for Instrument Detail. Mustered out Jan. 14, 1919 at Camp Taylor.

BAGGERLY, Clifford, 21, Kewanna, farmer, son of Charles M. and Melissa Baggerly, entered service June 3, 1918 at Indianapolis, trained at Great Lakes and Ithica, N. Y. Seaman. Discharged June 9, 1919, at Great Lakes.

BECKER, Ernest Ferdinand, 26, Fulton, telephone lineman, son of Mrs. Mary M. Becker, entered service April 25, 1918, Rochester, trained at Camp Taylor and Washington Barracks, private Co. A., 314 Engineers, 89th Div. Sailed June 13, 1918, in battles of St. Mihiel, Sept. 12 and Meuse-Argonne, Nov. 1. Discharged June 4, 1919 at Camp Taylor

BRYAN, Clarence S., 21, Leiters Ford, electrician, married, son of Frank J. and Emma E. Bryan. Entered service at Niles, Ohio, Oct. 7, 1917, trained at Camps Sherman and Pike, promoted from private to corporal, Co. L., 348th Inf. Sailed Aug. 26, 1918, slightly gassed. Did convoy work. Mustered out March 22, 1919 at Camp Sherman.

RALPH HATFIELD
OMER H. MIKESELL
BOYD PETERSON

OMER DRUDGE
GROVER SMITH
RALPH BROUILLETTE

LOWELL E. SMITH
FRED ROBBINS
IVAN MURR PERSONNETTE

BAILEY, Clark, 29, Rochester, farmer, son of Lewis and Amanda Bailey, entered service June 15, 1918 at Rochester, trained at Camp McClellan, promoted from private to wagoner and did truck driving with Supply Co. 36th Regt., F. A. Mustered out Feb. 17, 1919 at Camp Taylor.

BENNETT, Forrest L., 28, Mishawaka, Ind., printer, son of N. E. and Margaret Bennett, Kewanna. Entered service May 20, 1918 at Mishawaka, Ind., trained at Columbus Barracks, Ft. Snelling, Camp Gordon, Camp Grant. Made 2nd Lt. U. S. A. 36th Inf. Co. E. Instructor of Infantry in Officers Training School. Mustered out Dec. 5, 1918 at Camp Grant.

BAKER, Ermal C., 24, Kentland, Ind., dentist, son of Mr. and Mrs. J. R. Baker, Union township, entered service June 1, 1918, at Marine Barracks, Paris Island, S. C. Private Marine Corps. Discharged Dec. 19, 1918 at Marine Barracks.

BRUCE, Earnest P., 21, Kewanna, railroad work, son of Richard F. and Minnie P. Bruce. Entered service Dec. 12, 1917, trained at Camps Taylor, Green and Hancock. Sailed June 21, 1917 and did motorcycle dispatch work for Headquarters Co., 3rd Air Service. Mustered out July 12, 1919 at Camp Sherman.

BYRER, Joel Frederick, 25, Kewanna, electrician, son of J. C. and Ida B. Byrer. Entered service April 2, 1918 at Rochester. Trained at Ft. Wadsworth. Made first class private, Battery D., 70th Artillery, C. A. C. Sailed July 15, 1918. Mustered out March 12, 1919, at Camp Sherman.

BABCOCK, James A., 28, married, Rochester, carpenter, son of Andrew O. and Sarah Babcock. Entered service Sept. 18, 1917, trained at Camps Pike and Dodge. Private Co. E., 313th Eng. Sailed March 5, 1918 with Co. A., 1st Gas Regt., 1st Army Corps. Participated in battles on Alsace-Loraine front, St. Mihiel and Argonne drives. Wounded by shrapnel at apex of right lung, Oct. 15, 1918 Mustered out Feb. 15, 1919 at Camp Taylor.

BACON, LeRoy H., 19, Rochester, clerk, son of Mr. and Mrs. Elmer Bacon, entered service Nov. 4, 1917 at Indianapolis, trained at Kelly Field and Ft. Thomas. Promoted from private to corporal to chauffeur, 73rd Aero Squadron. Sailed July 13, 1918 and served as chauffeur in 1st and 2nd Army. In battles of St. Mihiel and Argonne. Mustered out July 1, 1919 at Camp Sherman.

DEAN K. VICKERY DENNIS JAMES MAHONEY HARRY EARL BEATTIE
RALPH SHELTON LT. LYMAN E. BRACKETT LOTUS TROY THRUSH
DANIEL KOPP LEO S. HARTER EDGAR ADAMSON

BARNETT, Victor Fitzgerald, 24, Chicago, newspaper reporter, son of Philip A. and Nellie Barnett. Entered service Oct. 2, 1917 at Madison, Wis. Promoted from private to 2nd Lt. C. I., 341st Inf., Co. I., 230th Inf., Hdqrs. Co,, 360th Inf. Sailed May 6th, 1918, served as instructor R. O. T. C., A. E. F. In Somme offensive July 4th to Aug 12th. Discharged July 14, 1919.

BECK, Thomas William, 23, married, Rochester, farmer, son of John and Anna Beck, entered service May 24th, 1918 at Rochester, trained at Camps Taylor and Greenleaf, served as officer's cook and mess sergeant, 159th Depot Brigade, 17th Co. Discharged Jan. 10, 1919 at Camp Taylor.

BARR, Fred D., 19, Talma, lineman, son of Burr and Elizabeth Barr. Entered service April 14, 1917 at Columbus Barracks, Ohio, trained there and Ft. Andrews, Mass., promoted private to corporal, Bat. C,. 44th Artillery. Sailed Aug. 14, 1917 and served as gun pointer and lineman. In battles Weller, Alsace April 16 to May 25, 1918; Rammersmatt, Alsace, May 25 to July 29; Hagenback, Alsace, July 29 to Sept. 7; St. Mihiel drive Sept. 12 to 15; Bouillonville Sept. 17 to Nov. 11, A. E. F. to Feb. 4, 1919. Mustered out Feb. 20, 1919 at Camp Sherman.

BOWEN, Ray, 22, Leiters Ford, farmer, son of John P. and Rebecca Bowen, entered service July 29, 1917 at Ft. Thomas, Ky., trained at Kelley Field, Texas, and Garden City, L. I., made private first class and did carpenter work with 492nd Aero Squadron. Sailed Nov. 22, 1917. Mustered out Feb. 13, 1919 at Garden City, L. I.

BEATTIE, Harry Earl, 26, Rochester, horse trainer, son of Wilbur and Elizabeth Beattie, entered service Oct. 4, 1917 at Rochester, trained at Camp Taylor, promoted private to sergeant and served as stable sergeant Bat. E., 325th F. A. Sailed Sept. 7, 1918. Mustered out March 1, 1919 at Camp Sherman.

BROUILETTE, Ralph, 29, married, Rochester, farmer, son of Mr. and Mrs. Chas. Brouilette, entered service Sept. 20, 1917 at Rochester, trained at Camp Taylor, promoted private to saddler, Battery B. 325th F. A. Sailed Sept. 9th, 1918 with 84th Div. and served as saddler in France. Mustered out Feb. 13, 1919 at Camp Taylor.

BOWMAN, Sidney L., Akron, farmer, son of Edward L. and Minerva Bowman, entered service Sept. 21, 1917 at Rochester, trained at Taylor and Shelby. Made private 1st Class. Sailed Aug. 6, 1918 with Co. I., 83rd Div. and served as P. M. overseas.

DON BIDDINGER	ROBERT E. DANIEL	OTTO R. BEERY
JOHN W. COSTELLO	WALTER J. SWIHART	ROBERT GAULT
FORREST L. BENNETT	FRED CAMERER	FLORENCE HENDRICKSON

BURNS, Vernon L., 21, Akron, farmer, son of George A. and Mary E. Burns, entered service Oct. 5, 1917 at Rochester, trained at Taylor and Hamilton. Private C. A. C. Sailed July 15, 1918 and carried messages to front in Meuse-Argonne offensive. Mustered out April 4, 1919.

BURNS, Cecil R., 30, Akron, farmer, son of George A. and Mary E. Burns, entered service Oct. 4, 1917 at Rochester, trained at Camps Taylor and Shelby. Private Co. H., 152nd Inf. Mustered out Jan. 25th, 1919 at Camp Shelby.

BACON, Fred B., 27, Macy, electrician, married, son of Mr. and Mrs. Elmer Bacon, entered service August 15, 1918, trained at Ft. Wayne, Mich., corporal, 1st Aerial Recruit Squadron. Mustered out Jan. 22, 1919 at Ft. Wayne, Mich.

BRYANT, Wilbert Andrew, 28, mechanic, son of Rudy and Harriet Bryant, entered service June 28, 1918, trained at Camp Taylor, promoted from private to mechanic and sergeant, Bat. A., 6th Regt. Mustered out Dec. 14, 1918 at Camp Taylor.

BRUCE, George Franklin, 19, Rochester, barber, son of Richard F. and Harriett E. Bruce, entered service April 10, 1917, at Rochester, trained at Ft. Delaware, Ft. DuPont, Camp Eustis and Brinon Sur Soldare, Fr. Promoted from private to 1st Gunner and Acting Sgt., served as gun pointer and drilled recruits, 3rd Co. 8th, 6th, 48th and 74th, C. A. C. Sailed Oct. 7, 1918 with 48th and 92nd, C. A. C., Bat. B. Participated in battles of Chateau Thierry and Argonne. Gassed and bayonetted. Discharged March 29, 1919 at Camp Taylor.

BRICKEL, Harry A., 31, Rochester, lineman, son of Mrs. S. A. Wenger, entered service June 23, 1916 at Plymouth, Ind., trained at Ft. Benj. Harrison, private and telephone work Bat. A., 150th F. A. Sailed Oct. 16, 1917 with 42nd Div., 150th Regt. and did telephone work. In Battles of Champagne, Marne, Chateau Thierry, St. Mihiel, Meuse-Argonne. Wounded at Chateau Thierry. Discharged May 9, 1919 at Camp Taylor.

BROWER, George L., 24, Rochester, clerk, son of Louis K. and Kate Brower, entered service May 11, 1917 at Ft. Benj. Harrison, made 2nd Lt., promoted to Captain, 801st Pioneer Infantry. Sailed Sept. 8, 1918. Mustered out Aug. 28, 1919 at Camp Dix.

RAY BOWEN   ESTIL DEAN BRUGH   CLINTON HOWARD YEAZEL
JOSEPH BATT   FREDERICK P. CAMPBELL
R. E. HUDTWALCKER   WILLIAM EASTWOOD   FORREST W. HIGGINS

BRILES, Dale Morten, 29, married, Rochester, bookkeeper, son of Charles F. and Eva I. Briles, entered service Aug. 29, 1918 at Rochester, trained at Camp Gordon, Private Co. B., 6th Inf. Replacement Regt. Recommend for Sgt. when armistice was signed. Discharged Jan. 4, 1919 at Camp Gordon.

BRACKETT, Lyman E., 24, Rochester, wholesale grocer, son of Lyman M. Brackett, entered service May 12, 1917 at Ft. Benjamin Harrison, trained at Taylor, New Orleans, Jefferson Barracks and Overseas. Private to 2nd Lt. Aug. 15, 1917, to 1st Lt., Feb. 15, 1918. Administrative officers D. Q. M. and Purchasing Officer, D. Q. M., New Orleans Sailed Oct. 2, 1918, hospital patient. On British front near Mons, Belgium, Nov 5 to 10, 1918, returned to hospital at Dingfield, Eng,. Nov. 12. Assigned to duty Hdqrs. S. O. S. London, transferred to Windall Down Camp, Winchester and on duty there until Jan. 20, 1919. Discharged Feb. 24, 1919 at Camp Shelby.

BURNS, Robert Raymond, 19, Akron, railroader, son of S. N. and Mary B. Burns, entered service Oct. 1, 1918 at Logansport, train- at Ft. Thomas. Private Troop L., 7th Cavalry. Still in service at Ft. Bliss, Texas.

BRADWAY, Lee, 17, Akron, farmer, son of Frank E. and Rhoda E. Bradway, entered service May 6, 1917 at Raymond, S. D., trained on Mexican border, private Co. G., 109th Am. Train. Sailed Oct. 12, 1918. Mustered out Jan. 18, 1919.

BURNS, Irven R., 26, farmer, son of George A. and Mary E. Burns, entered service Sept. 21, 1917 at Peru, Ind., trained at Taylor, Shelby and Mills. Promoted private to wagoner, Supply Co., 152nd Inf. Sailed Oct. 6, 1918 with Cyclone Division. Discharged April 1919 at Camp Taylor.

BOWMAN, Ernest E., 28, Akron, electrician, son of William and Elizabeth Bowman, entered service March 10, 1918 at Wabash, Ind. trained at Vancouver, Wash. Promoted to Sgt. 1st class, 5th Aero Squadron.

BOWMAN, Samuel, 25, Akron, car inspector, son of William and Elizabeth Bowman, entered service July 26, 1917 at Elkhart, Ind., trained at Camp Wheeler, promoted private first class and served as car inspector with 167th Co. North Reserve Transportation Corps. Sailed March 27, 1918 and served as car inspector overseas.

LEROY MATTHEWS	LT. VICTOR BARNETT	CLARENCE CHAMBERLAIN
ROY BRYANT	HARRY (Mike) BRICKLE	RUSSELL B. RICHARD
HARLEY ZOLMAN	ROBERT FOSTER OWENS	JAMES F. JOHNSON

BABCOCK, Dean E., 24, married, Waterman, Ill., farmer, son of Andrew E. and Lillie Babcock, Richland tp., entered service May 28, 1918 at Sycamore, Ill., trained at Camp Gordon, promoted 1st class private, nurse and ward master, 70th Co., 6th Regt. Sailed July 28, 1918 with Medical Det., 163rd Inf. with which he worked overseas. Discharged Aug. 2, 1919 at Camp Mills, L. I.

BABCOCK, Otto Russell, 27, Waterman, Ill., merchant, married, entered service Jan. 12, 1918 as seaman and assigned to Great Lakes training station. Mustered out at Great Lakes, Dec. 17, 1918.

BRYANT, Ernest Ray, 25, married, Rochester, farmer, son of George S. and Mary Bryant, entered service April 25, 1918 at Rochester trained at Camp Taylor, promoted private to corporal to sergeant, 12th Co., 1st Regt., 159 D. B. Mustered out Camp Taylor, Dec. 10, 1918.

BAKER, Glenn Paul, 23, Pueblo, Colo., farmer, son of Mr. and Mrs. John Baker, Delong, entered service March 8, 1918 at Pueblo, trained at Ft. Logan and Ft. Caswell. Sailed June 10, 1918 with 6th Anti Air Craft Battery, C. A. C., in battles in St. Die sector Aug. 28th to Sept. 27th and in Toul sector Sept. 28th, to Nov. 11. Mustered out May 7, 1919 at Camp Custer.

BAUKE, Claude W., 32, Rochester, railroader, son of Charles and Cora Bauke, entered service May 10, 1917 at Detroit, Mich., trained there, private Co. B., 16th Regt. Sailed Aug. 1, 1917. In Lys defensive April 7 to 27, 1918 and Meuse-Argonne offensive Sept. 26 to Nov. 11. Mustered out May 7, 1919 at Camp Custer.

BECKER, Edward C., 27, Fulton, laborer, son of Mrs. Mary M. Becker, entered service Sept. 3, 1918 at Rochester, private 13th Co. 4th Tr. Bri., trained at Camp Taylor. Mustered out Dec. 5, 1918 at Camp Taylor.

BLACKETOR, Paul Shryock, 22, married, Rochester, laborer, son of Mr. and Mrs. Thomas B. Blacketor, entered service May 25, 1918, trained at Camps Taylor, Greenleaf and Gordon, promoted to first class private. 17th Co. 5th Bn., 157th Depot Brigade and Recorder Base Hospital, Camp Gordon. Discharged Feb. 21, 1918, at Camp Gordon.

DANIEL WILLARD GEORGE BRUCE GERALD WALTERS
GRANT GOCKING SGT. RALPH CLINGENPEEL ERNEST KOPP
ALBERT H. FOX HARRY HETZNER VERNON T. BURNS

BECKER, Omer, Russel, 17, Fulton, son of Chas. E. and Edith Becker, entered service April 16, 1917, private, truck driver, trained Fort Constitution, Motor transport Detch. No. 2, 3rd Bn. 42nd Artillery, C. A. C. Sailed Jan. 15, 1918, in battles of de Maseirgs and Butte de Mesniel. Mustered out March 10, 1919 at Camp Sherman.

BRUGH, Estal Dean, 20, Leiters Ford, farmer, son of John and Dora Brugh, entered service April 25, 1918 at Logansport, trained at Ft. Casey, Wash., and Camp Eustis, Va., served as wagoner with 48th Art., Bat. E. Sailed Oct. 7, 1918. Discharged March 29, 1919.

BIDDINGER, Charles, 23, Leiters, bookkeeper, son of Loren and Calar Biddinger, entered service May 18, 1917, at South Bend, trained at Ft. Benj. Harrison and Camp Shelby. Reg. Supply Sgt., Supply Co. 137th F. A. Sailed Oct. 6, 1918. Mustered out Jan 17, 1919 at Ft. Harrison.

BRIDEGROOM, Hugh Ginther, 18, Leiters Ford, farmer, son of Thomas and Jennie Bridegroom, entered service Oct. 1, 1918, trained at Camp Franklin. S. A. T. C. of Franklin College. Mustered out Dec. 21, 1918 at Camp Franklin.

BIDDINGER, Don Namon, 21, Rochester, teacher, son of Jesse and Elizabeth Biddinger, entered service March 15, 1915 at Vancouver Barracks, Wash. Private Co. H., 21st Regt. Inf. Promoted from private to Corporal to Sergeant to 2nd Lt. Philippine Scouts. Served in Philippines. Still in service.

BEERY, Otto R., 31, Chicago, traffic manager, married, son of Frank L. and Jennie Beery, Rochester. Entered service Aug. 27, 1917 at Ft. Sheridan, Ill., promoted to 2nd Lt. 23rd Cadet Officers Training Co. Sailed Jan. 21, 1918 and served as platoon commander, Co. L., 26th Inf., 1st Div. Participated in battles of Catigny, May 17, and Soissons, July 18. Received gun shot wound in left thigh. Discharged March 27, 1919.

BARKMAN, Irvin W., 20, Rochester, teacher, son of George M. and Sarah E. Barkman, entered service April 14, 1917 at Columbus Barracks, Ohio., promoted private to corporal to 1st Sgt., and served as plotter, mine company, 7th Co., C. A. C., 54th Art. Sailed Sept. 23, 1918. Mustered out July 29, 1919 at Camp Sherman.

BLAUSSER, Verne, 20, Kewanna, farmer, son of William and Melissa Blausser, entered service Dec. 19, 1917 at Decatur, Ind., trainer at Camp Eustis, private, powder detail Bat. A., 61st Art., C. A. C. Sailed July 30, 1918 with 33rd Brigade. Mustered out March 11, 1919 at Columbus Barracks.

LLOYD HAGAN WALTER McCOY OLIVER GROVE
ERNEST W. LONG CHARLES KISTLER CAPT. OTIS ADAMS
FRANK SWIHART MELVIN OTIS INGRAM ORVILLE M. SNYDER

BABCOCK, Charles C., 26, Rochester, salesman, son of Mrs. J. J. Hill, entered service May 25, 1918 at Rochester, trained at Ft. Oglethorpe, private 17th Co., 159th Depot Brigade. Discharged Jan. 22, 1918 at Ft. Oglethorpe.

BARNHART, Hugh A., 25, Rochester, advertising man, son of Henry A. and Louretta Barnhart, entered service May 14, 1917, at Ft. Benj. Harrison, trained at Ft. Russell, Camp Logan, Ft. Bliss. Commissioned at end of the first training Camp as 2nd Lt., promoted to 1st Lt. Cavl. 82nd F. A. Was Regimental Adjutant, 82nd F. A., and did border guard duty at El Paso, Texas. Mustered out May 16, 1919 at Ft. Bliss.

BARTIK, Joe M., 30, Rochester, electrician, son of Bohemian parents, both dead. Entered service Feb. 1917 at Rochester, trained at Ft. Riley and Camp Green. Promoted private to corporal. Sailed July 1, 1918, 7th Co. 3rd Rgt., Motor Mechanic Air Service. Still in service.

BATT, Joseph S., 27, Rochester, advertising, son of Martin and Fannie L. Batt, entered service May 13, 1917 at Boston, Mass., trained at Ft. Omaha, 2nd Lt. A. S. S. C. Organized Enlisted Specialists School for Cordage and Fabric Inspection (Balloon Div.) Camp John Wise, Commanding Officer 68th Balloon Div., Aerial Observer, Sherical Balloon Pilot. Mustered out March 14, 1919 at San Antonio, Tex.

BLACK, Thomas E., 21, Rochester, salesman, son of George and Mary Black, entered service Sept. 3, 1918, trained at Taylor, West Point and Knox. Made first class private, Bat. C., 72nd F. A. Mustered out Feb. 5, 1919 at Camp Knox.

CARR, Stanley Byron, 20, Rochester, student, son of Mr. and and Mrs. Benj. F. Carr, entered service Oct. 11, 1918 at Purdue University, private Co. 2, S. A. T. C. Mustered out Dec. 19, 1918 at Purdue.

CHAMP, Harry R., 22, Rochester, teacher, son of George and Clara Champ, entered service May 24, 1918 at Rochester, trained at Taylor, Oglethorpe, Eustis, Stuart, Mills, Dix and Sherman. Had charge of Regimental Surgeon's office and promoted from private to 1st. Sergt., Med. Div. 45th Regt., C. A. C. Sailed Oct. 1918 with Med. Div. 37th Brigade. Mustered out Feb. 27, 1919, at Camp Sherman.

CHAS. NOFTSGER   HARVEY F. HUNTER GUY PETERSON   ALBERT VAN KIRK
E. L. MORPHET C. CALLENTINE C. K. GARNER L. EMMONS   A. HUDKINS
AXEL L. ERICKSON M. E. PETERSON OREN S. KELLEY   C. E. EDGINGTON

COPLEN, Donald, 21, Rochester, farmer, son of H. L. and Gertrude McClure Coplen, entered service Oct. 1, 1918 at Bloomington, Ind., private Co. A, 41st Inf. S. A. T. C. Mustered out Dec. 21, 1918 at Bloomington.

CLAY, Roland Franklyn, 22, Rochester, farmer, son of William A. and Ida A. Clay, entered service Aug. 1917 at Rochester, trained at West Point, Musician 325th F. A. Sailed Sept. 1917 with 84th Div. Discharged March 1, 1919 at Camp Sherman.

CHARTERS, Gresham Omer, 22, Rochester, farmer, son of John D. and Clara Charters, entered service May 20, 1918 at Rochester, trained at Camp Taylor, promoted private to Corporal, 17th Co., 5th Bn., 159th Depot Brigade. Discharged Dec. 5, 1918 at Camp Taylor.

CAIN, James Homer, 28, Indianapolis, carpenter, entered service Aug. 1917 at Indianapolis, trained at Camp Shelby, private Co. H, 167th Inf. Sailed in spring of 1918 with Rainbow division. In battles of Chateau Thierry and Meuse-Argonne. Discharged May 1919.

CLAYBURN, Fred, Rochester, farmer, entered service April 20, 1917 at Jefferson Barracks, Mo., trained at Ft. Barrancas, Fla. Sailed with 64th Reg. Battery C, Artillery July 14, 1918. Discharged at Camp Grant April 3, 1919.

CARPENTER, Seth Clarence, 21, Akron, teacher, son of Elbridge and Della Carpenter, entered service Aug. 25, 1918 at Rochester, trained at Taylor, Greenleaf and Ft. Oglethorpe. Private Ambulance Co. 22, 7th Sanitary Tr., 7th Div. Sailed Aug. 14, 1918 with 6th Army Corps, 2nd Army. In Prevenelle sector Oct. 10 to Nov. 11. Mustered out July 9, 1919 at Camp Taylor.

CUFFEL, Charles, 27, Kelsey, Alberta, Can., mechanic, son of W. H. and Louisa Cuffel, served as private with Canadian Engineers overseas.

COOK, Willis W., 22, Akron, farmer, son of Mr. and Mrs. G. G. Cook, entered service Nov. 22, 1917 at Indianapolis, trained at Ft. Thomas and Kelley Field, promoted private to corporal to sergeant, Co. 20, 1st Regt., A. S. M. Sailed Feb. 8, 1918 and served as mechanic overseas. Was in Voges at date of armistice with 7th French Army Corps. Mustered out June 3, 1919 at Camp Mills.

NOBLE SMITH   WALTER WHITTAKER   OTTO R. BABCOCK
ERNEST M. HOGAN   ROBT. M. DELEHANTY
ROBERT P. BRUCE   FRED M. DAY

CLEVENGER, William Chester, 22, Rochester, railroader, son of Mr. and Mrs. David B. Clevenger, entered service March 29, 1918, trained at Camps Upton and Taylor, made first class private Co. C. 52nd Eng. 17th Div. Sailed June 11, 1918. Discharged Sept 9, 1919 at Camp Taylor.

CLAYTON, Bernard, 31, married, Akron, editor, son of George and Minnie Clayton, entered service June 1, 1918 at Rochester for Y. M. C. A. work. Trained in New York, sailed August 1, 1918 and did athletic work in France. Discharged Nov. 15, 1918 at Chicago.

COX, Henry, 23, Kewanna, railwayman. Entered service May 1, 1917 at Ft. Thomas, Ky., trained at Chickamauga, Ga. Promoted to Corporal, Co. C, 52nd Regt. Sailed July 6, 1918 from Hoboken, N. J. Served in the Gerordnier and Vosges sectors and participated in the Meuse-Argonne offensive. With the American army of occupation in Germany. Mustered out June 19, 1919 at Camp Sherman.

CAMPBELL, Paul Frederic, 21, Kewanna, farmer, son of James and Barbara Campbell. Entered service Nov. 30, 1917 at Ft. Thomas, Ky. Promoted to private of first class, Hospital Train 54. Sailed Feb. 10, 1918 and participated in the Champagne-Marne offensive July 15 to 18, the Ainse-Marne battles July 18 to August 6, and the Meuse-Argonne offensive Sept. 26 to Nov. 11. Mustered out July 28, 1919 at Camp Sherman.

COSTELLO, John William, 28, Chicago, Ill., lawyer, son of Mr. and Mrs. Jno. W. Costello, trained at Great Lakes Naval Training Station, seaman 2nd class, assigned to U. S. S. Gopher, Great Lakes Fleet, assigned to Municipal Pier, Chicago, Ill., Naval Reserve Unit, Cleveland, Ohio, Officers School, Pelham Bay, N. Y. Promoted from 2nd class seaman to ensign. Service on Naval Reserve Receiving Ship, N. Y. and Naval Reserve Receiving Ship, San Francisco, Cal. Released Feb. 28, 1919 at New York City.

COOPER, Russel B., 21, Fulton, mechanic, son of Mr. and Mrs. Wm. Cooper, entered service Sept. 3, 1918 at Fulton, trained at Camps Taylor and Jackson, private with 13th Co. 4th T. R. B. M. 159 Depot Brigade. Mustered out Jan. 2, 1919 at Camp Taylor.

JOSEPH I. CONDON　　　　OMER JOHN MEYER　　　　LEO. R. CLEMANS
Wm. POLEN, JR.　　ALFRED R. FLYNN　WHIT HEIMINGER　H. LESLIE GINTHER
DEWEY THOMAS　　　　CLARENCE OREN BENGE　　　JESSE H. JONES

COOK, Ray Dell, 29, Fulton, mechanic, son of George W. and Amanda L. Cook, entered service Sept. 4, 1918 at Detroit, Mich. Trained at Camp Custer, promoted from private to private 1st class, 33rd Co. 9th Bri. 160 Depot Bri. Sailed Oct. 26, 1918. Base Hospital No. 99, mechanical work. Mustered out June 26, 1919 at Camp Sherman.

CROWNOVER, LeRoy A., 26, married, Rochester, garage, son of Asbury Lee and Cleora Crownover, entered service May 2, 1918 at Rochester, trained at Ft. Thomas, Chattanooga and Camp Upton, private Signal Corps, 52nd Machine Gun Co. Sailed July 5, 1918, in the Argonne offensive. In Feb. 1919 sent to Germany to guard Russian Prisoner of War Camp, at Gardelegen. With Inter-Allied Military Commission at Berlin. Discharged Sept. 27, 1919 at Camp Taylor.

CRAIG, Merle M., 23, married, Rochester, truck driver, son of Bert and Leona Craig, entered service Sept. 3, 1918 at Rochester, trained at Taylor and Jackson, private 13th Co. 159th Depot Brigade and Bat. C, 18th Regt. Mustered out Dec. 23, 1918 at Camp Jackson.

COPLEN, Oscar O., 18, Rochester, student, entered service April 15, 1917 at Rochester, trained at Ft. Thomas and Ft. Delaware. Sent to Ft. Dupont as assistant sergeant in medical department. Discharged Dec. 20, 1918 at Camp Sherman.

COOK, Avery B., 35, Rochester, painter, son of George and Belle Cook, entered service May 1, 1917 at Rochester, trained at Ft. Thomas and Ft. Mott, promoted from private to corporal, Medical Dept., Regular Army. Nursing. Still in service.

CONDON, Joseph Irving, Rochester, freight clerk, son of H. C. and Martha S. Condon, entered service May 14, 1918 at Indianapolis, trained at Ft. Harrison, promoted from private to Sergeant, Prov. Post Hdqrs. Co. Discharged Dec. 18, 1918.

COLLINS, Robert William, 18, Rochester, auto mechanic, son of William and Jessie Collins, entered service Feb. 5, 1918 at Rochester, Ind., trained at Kelly Field and Indianapolis Speedway, promoted from private to corporal and served as aviator mechanic with 809th Aero Squadron. Mustered out March 18, 1919 at Indianapolis Speedway.

HUBERT MOGLE   EARL SISSON   ARTHUR R. HATFIELD
ARCHIE GROVE   LT. C. A. SCHIRM   ARTHUR ADAMSON
CHAS. G. IRVINE   VIRGIL K. MARIOTT   RAY E. KING

CLINGENPEEL, Ralph R., 25, Rochester, mechanic, son of William and Elizabeth Clingenpeel, entered service Dec. 11, 1917 at New Orleans, La., trained at Ft. Houston, promoted from Private to Sergeant, M. R. U. 309 M. T. C. Sailed Oct. 16th, 1918, Auto Repair. Mustered out Aug. 1, 1919, Camp Taylor.

CLEMANS, Leo R., 31, South Bend, Ind., married, pharmacist, son of Lincoln and Emma Clemans, entered service Dec. 3, 1917 at Elkhart, Ind., trained at Ft. Thomas, Ft. Wood, N. Y., promoted from Private to Sergeant, Sergt. Telephone Operator, Telephone work, Co. E, 419th Teleg. Bn. S. C. U. S. A. Sailed Sept 14, 1918. In battle of Meuse-Argonne, Verdun. Mustered out July 29, 1919 at Camp Sherman.

CLAYTON, Lewis Jay, 28, Rochester, baker, son of George and Minnie Clayton, entered service Dec. 13, 1917 at Indianapolis, trained at Jefferson Barracks and Ft. Riley, promoted from private to sergeant, Bakery Co. 351. Sailed Sept. 4, 1918 and did bakery work behind the lines and later for prison camp in France. Mustered out Oct. 1, 1919 at Camp Dix.

CLARY, Harvey Foy, 22, Rochester, merchant's delivery, son of Elbert E. and Nevada B. Clary, entered service March 28, 1918 at Rochester, trained at Camp Taylor. Private Co. A. 111th Inf. 28th Div. Sailed May 5, 1918. In second battle of the Marne, and Rohmaine Hill. Wounded Sept. 6th at Rohmaine Hill and sent to American Red Cross Hospital No. 5, Paris. Discharged May 13, 1919 at Camp Sherman.

CHANDLER, Harvey West, 26, Rochester, teacher, son of George C. and Emily M. Chandler, entered service July 1, 1917 and served as acting Bn. Sgt. Major, Personnel Dept., Valparaiso, Ind. Discharged Dec. 21, 1918 at Valparaiso.

CHAMBERLAIN, Clarence B., 20, Rochester, electrician, son of John E. and Elsie B. Chamberlain, entered service Jan. 31, 1918 at Columbus, Ohio, trained at Columbus Barracks and promoted from private to private of first class and radio operator with Headquarters Co., 39th Inf., 4th Div. Sailed May 10, 1918 and did radio and telephone work in the Aisne-Marne, St. Mihiel and Meuse-Argonne offensives. Now at Rolandseck, Germany, with Army of Occupation.

ELZA N. SCHIRM
LEVI THORTON ZOLMAN
ED. HETZNER

PAUL F. CAMPBELL
WILLIAM FANSLER
MAX HOOVER

WILLARD MELVIN FRYE
DALE ANDERSON
FRED D. BARR

CHAMBERLAIN, Chester Alexander, 18, Rochester, office work, son of William C. and Florence Chamberlain, entered service August August 27, 1917 at Tampa, Fla., trained at Camp Wheeler, promoted to private first class, served as cook. Sailed Oct. 6, 1918, Co. M, 107 Inf., 27th Div. 2nd Army Corps, and served as cook in France. Mustered out April 4, 1919 at Camp Sherman.

CAMPBELL, Paul Frederick, 22, Kewanna, farmer, entered service Nov. 30, 1917 at Ft. Thomas, Ky., trained at Camp Greenleaf and Ft. Oglethorpe, made first class private. Sailed Feb. 10, 1918 and served with Hospital Train Unit which removed wounded from all battle fronts on American sectors. Discharged July 28, 1919 at Camp Sherman.

CAMERER, Fred D., 18, Rochester, farmer, son of Henry E. and Emma B. Camerer, entered service April 9, 1917 in the west, trained at Douglas, Ariz., and Ft. Bliss, promoted from private to corporal, Troop C, 17th Cavl. Served as Army Post Master, and is still in service with troops guarding border near ElPaso, Tex.

CALLENTINE, Clarence W., 21, South Bend, painter, son of Mrs. Racheal Eisenman, Rochester, entered service Oct. 11, 1917 at Rochester, trained at Camp Shelby and Washington Barracks, private to wagoner, 465th Pontoon Train Engineers. Sailed Aug. 1, 1918, trained in Brookwood, England. Mustered out May 26, 1919 at Camp Sherman.

DAVIDSON, Robert H., 42, Delong, structural engineer, entered service August 5, 1917 at Denver, Colo., trained at Camp Kearney, promoted private to Master Engineer, senior grade, and did construction work with Hdqrs. Det. 115th Engineers. Sailed August 8, 1918 with 115th Engineers. In St. Mihiel and Meuse-Argonne offensives, wounded in Argonne Oct. 7. Discharged July 15, 1919 at Camp Taylor.

DILLON, Clarence Allen, 24, Rochester, son of William A. and Mary E. Dillon, entered service March 7, 1918 at Rochester, took photographic training at U. S. School of Aerial Photography, made private Photo Section 42 and took further training at Door Field, Fla. and ordered to port of embarkation when war was over. Mustered out Dec. 19, 1918 at Garden City, L. I.

Wm. F. JOHNSON	MAX ANDERSON	GERALD W. EBER
OMER RUSSELL BECKER	JEAN DITMIRE	LOYD G. POLLEY
CHARLES BIDDINGER	RALPH WALDO DITMIRE	ROBERT CLEON NYE

DITMIRE, Jean Edward, 22, Fulton, embalmer, entered service June 3, 1918 at Indianapolis, trained at Great Lakes Training Station and Philadelphia Navy Yard. Service on sea on U. S. S. Buffalo, repair and supply ship. Mustered out Jan. 20, 1919 at New York City.

DITMIRE, Ralph Waldo, 28, Detroit, Mich., factory hand, entered service May 28, 1918 at Detroit, Mich., trained at Camp Wheeler and Camp Jackson, promoted from private to 1st class private in Supply Co. 118th F. A. 31st Div. Sailed Oct. 21, 1918 trained at Rennes. Mustered out Jan. 13, 1919 at Newport News.

DUDGEON, Dewey G., 20, Rochester, student, son of H. and Mary E. Dudgeon, entered S. A. T. C., Oct. 12, 1918 at Purdue University, Lafayette, Ind. Private Co. 4, section A. Mustered out Dec. 19, 1918 at Lafayette.

DAVIS, Edwin A., 26, Rochester, laborer, son of Columbus and Margaret Davis, entered service March 3, 1918 at Rochester, trained at Camp Eustis and Ft. Monroe, promoted from private to corporal to sergeant, 5th Co., 57th Ammunition Train. Discharged Dec. 20, 1918 at Columbus, Ohio.

DAVISSON, Harold B., 23, married, Rochester, contractor, son of Mr. and Mrs. A. C. Davisson, entered service Sept. 1, 1918 at Culver Academy, candidate 20th Obs. Bat., Camp Taylor. Mustered out Dec 7, 1918 at Camp Taylor.

DRAKE, Fred T., 17, Rochester, mechanic, son of Benjamin and Mae Drake, entered service June 4, 1917 at Chicago, trained at Jefferson Barracks, Mo. Private Co. C, 8th U. S. Mounted Engineers. Made camp baker at ElPaso, Tex. Still in service.

DANIEL, Robert Earl, 23, Kewanna, telephone business. Son of L. E. and E. V. Daniel. Entered service May 1, 1918 at Indianapolis. Trained at Camp Forrest, Ga. Served as Regimental telephone operator, Headquarters Co. 52 Inf. 6th Div. Sailed July 6, 1918 and served with Headquarters Co. in Gerardmer sector, Vosges and in the Meuse-Argonne offensive. Mustered out June 18, 1919 at Camp Sherman.

DUKES, Lauren Andrew, Kewanna, 20, farmer, son of Ulysses E. Dukes, entered the service at Hoopeston, Ill. May 23, 1917. Entered service at Camp Logan, Texas, as a private. Promoted to Corporal and served as company clerk. Co. B, 129th Inf., 33rd Div. Saw service in the Meuse-Argonne offensive and at Verdun and St. Mihiel. Mustered out at Camp Grant, June 6, 1919.

CHAS. CLYDE MOW	CLARENCE O'CONNELL	ERMAL C. BAKER
VERNON NOYES	FRED BYRER	J. N. VAN CLEAVE
RALPH HAMILTON	PAUL DEAN HENDERSON	LOYD W. ANDERSON

DUKES, Paul L., 23, Kewanna, farmer, son of Ulysses and Rosa Dukes, entered service July 27, 1917 at Sioux City, Iowa, trained at Ft. Logan and Camp Douglass, promoted private to corporal Co. F, 20th Inf. Discharged March 27, 1919 at Nitro, W. Va.

DELEHANTY, Robert Emmitt, 35, Akron, farmer, son of James and Lida Delehanty, entered service Sept. 29, 1917, at Rochester trained at Camp Greene, N. C., private Co. K, 61st Inf. Sailed April 15, 1918. In St. Mihiel and Argonne offensives. Wounded Oct. 15, 1918, Argonne, by high explosive shell. In general Hospital 28 at Ft. Sheridan for nine months. Discharged July 5, 1919 at Ft. Sheridan.

DRUDGE, Omer, 24, Rochester, signalman, son of Amos and Maude Drudge, entered service July 27, 1917 at Ft. Wayne, trained Ft. Thomas, Kelly Field and Mineola, N. Y., promoted private to corporal, 492 Aero Squadron. Sailed Nov. 22, 1917 and did construction work. Mustered out Feb. 13, 1919, at Mineola, N. Y.

DRUDGE, Wilson Lee, 23, married, Rochester, farmer, son of Charles and Ella M. Drudge, entered service Sept. 3, 1918 at Rochester, trained at Taylor, Knox and West Point. Promoted private to wagoner Supply Co. 72 F. A. Discharged March 7, 1919 at Camp Knox.

DAY, Fred M., 24, Rochester, farmer, son of Edward and Ida Day, entered service Sept. 20, 1917 at Rochester, trained at Camp Taylor, private 1st class and teamster, Bat. A, 325th F. A., 84th Div. Sailed Sept. 9, 1918. Mustered out March 1, 1919 at Camp Sherman.

DIXON, Thomas W., 23, Rochester, farmer, son of J. A. and Wilhelmina L. Dixon, entered service July 11, 1918 at Beloit, Wis., trained at Ft. Hancock, promoted Sgt., trained machine Gunner and instructor. 5th Group, 52nd Co., M. G. T. C. Mustered out Jan. 12, 1919 at Camp Grant.

DIXON, Joseph E., 26, Rochester, farmer, son of John A. and Wilhelmina L. Dixon, entered service Sept. 20, 1917 at Rochester, trained at Taylor and Knox, promoted private to corporal, Bat. B, 325th F. A. Sailed Sept. 9, 1918 and trained as gunner on French 75 Mm. Guns. Mustered out Feb. 13, 1919 at Camp Taylor.

ROY SHELTON	DEWEY E. DUDGEON	STANLEY B. CARR
RUSSELL B. COOPER	CHARLES O. PACKER	GUY R. FREES
Wm. H. REISH	HUGH R. HENDERSON	WARREN DOWNS

DOWNS, Warren William, 19, Rochester, farmer, son of Mr. and Mrs. James Downs, entered service Jan. 11, 1917 at Rochester, trained at Ft. Bliss and Camp Green, private Bat. B, 13th F. A. Sailed May 22, 1918 with 4th Div. Participated in actions on Ainse-Marne, Vesle river, Toul sector, St. Mihiel, Meuse-Argonne and with A. of O. in Germany. Still in service.

DAVIS, Warren C., 21, married, electrician, Rochester, son of Mr. and Mrs. C. M. Davis, entered service June 20, 1916 at Warsaw, Ind., trained at Ft. Benjamin Harrison. Promoted private to corporal to 2nd Lt. Co. H, 32nd Inf., Battery D, F. A. Brigade. Served as Supply officer 21st F. A. Brigade. Mustered out Dec. 1, 1918 at Camp Sheridan.

EDGINGTON, William, 31, Rochester, farmer, son of George and Malinda Edgington, entered service May 24, 1918 at Rochester, trained at Camps Greenleaf and Gordon, private Unit 52, Base Hospital. Mustered out at Camp Gordon.

EBER, Gerald V., 19, Rochester, farmer, son of Charles and Maude Eber, entered service April 16, 1917, trained at Columbus Barracks, Fort Constitution and Fort Myers. Promoted from Private to 1st class Private, guard duty, with 12 F. A. Battery E. 2nd Div. Sailed Jan. 11, 1918, in battles of Chateau Thierry, Soisson, Pont A, Mousson, St. Mihiel, Mont Blanc and Argonne, transferred to Army of Occupation. Mustered out Aug. 14, 1919 at Camp Sherman.

EASTERDAY, Loris Everett, 22, Rochester, mechanic, son of George W. and Lavina Easterday, entered service March 29, 1918 at Rochester, trained at Camp Taylor, private Co. A, 111th Infantry. Sailed May 5, 1918. In Battle of Marne, wounded Aug. 10, 1918 at Fismes. Still in service.

EMMONS, William F., 26, Kewanna, lineman, son of Charles and Nezzie Emmons. Entered service Sept. 5, 1918, trained at Camp Taylor. 6th Co. 2nd Developing Battalion. Mustered out Dec. 4, 1918.

EMMONS, Grover B., 24, married, Logansport, barber, son of George and Sarah Emmons, Newcastle, entered service Sept 19, 1917 at Logansport, trained at Camp Taylor and West Point, private Supply Co., 325th F. A. 84th Div. Sailed Sept. 1918 with 84th Div. and served as barber. Mustered out March 1919 at Camp Sherman.

VANCE HARSH　　　　AMOS WAGONER　　　　FRANK H. UTTER
LESTER EBER　　　　ALVA N. THOMPSON　　　CHARLES FAULSTICH
SAMUEL BOWMAN　　　ROBERT C. MARSHALL　　　EARL J. SWASON

EDINGTON, Clarence Earl, 27, Rochester, farmer, son of Simon and Sarah Edington, entered service May 24, 1918, at Rochester, trained at Camp Greenleaf, private Mobile Hosp. No. 8. Sailed Aug. 23, 1918 and served as ambulance driver in France. Discharged July 22, 1919 at Mitchell Field, L. I.

EBER, Lester Albion, 18, Akron, farmer, son of Jacob and Waity Eber, entered service May 6, 1918 at Ft. Wayne, trained at Camp Humphreys, Va. Private 41st Div. 116th Regt. Co. A. Sailed Aug. 23, 1918 with 41st Engineers and did carpenter work overseas. Mustered out Jan. 9, 1919 at Camp Sherman.

ERICKSON, Axel Leonard, 26, Rochester, farmer, entered service Sept. 10, 1917 at Rochester. Trained at Camps Taylor and Mills. Private and dispatch carrier, Hdqrs. Co., 115th F. A. Sailed June 4, 1917. Saw service in Toul sector, St. Mihiel, Meuse-Argonne and Tryon Woerve. Mustered out April 8, 1919.

EISENMAN, Glen Louis, 23, Rochester, farmer, son of John and Della Eisenman, entered service July 31, 1918, trained at Valparaiso, Ind., Washington Barracks, Ft. Hamilton and Elmhurst, L. I., made wagoner Co. I, 71st Engrs., Sec. 12. Discharged at Camp Leach, Dec. 21, 1918.

EISENMAN, Fred Samuel, 18, Rochester, farmer, son of Mr. and Mrs. John W. Eisenman, entered service Dec. 11, 1917 at Ft. Wayne, trained at Ft. Thomas, Marfa and Glenn Springs, Tex. Promoted to sergeant and drill master Troop D, 8th Cavalry. Did guard duty along Mexican border and was in chase after Mexican bandits, May 16 to 20, 1918. Mustered out Feb. 5, 1919 at Marfa, Tex.

EASTWOOD, William Oscar, 19, Rochester, blacksmith, son of William and Flora Eastwood, entered service July 21, 1918 at Rochester, trained at Great Lakes Station, promoted from private to seamans Guard. Mustered out April 5, 1919 at Great Lakes.

FARRY, Charles Fulton, 22, Rochester, teacher, son of Austin O. and Annie M. Farry, entered service Oct. 4, 1917 at Rochester, trained at Camps Taylor and Jackson, promoted private to Sgt., to 2nd Lt., battery clerk, Battery B, 325th F. A. Sailed May 23, 1918 with Battery B., 8th, F. A. 7th Div. Mustered out Feb. 6, 1919 at Camp Meade.

FOSTER, Herbert William, 22, Tiosa, teacher, son of Mr. and Mrs. William Foster, entered service June 1, 1918 at Great Lakes, assigned to 1st Regt. Camp Dewey. In Great Lakes Band. Discharged March 26, 1919 at Great Lakes.

DEO FOOR	RUSSELL MURPHY	STANLEY CARR
CLAUDE W. BAUKE	KENNETH PERSONETTE	GLEN SMILEY
JUSTIN HALL	FRANK SWANGO	ROY O'BLENIS

FOOR, Osa Vern, 27, Rochester, machinist, son of Parlee E. and Essie M. Foor, entered service Feb. 27, 1918 at Kokomo, Ind., trained at Camp Greenleaf, made private of first class and did clerical work with Medical Detachment, Base Hospital, Camp Shelby, Miss. Still in service.

FOOR, James David, 21, Rochester, farmer, son of Parlee E. and Essie M. Foor, entered service May 7, 1918 at Jefferson Barracks, Mo. trained at Ft. Totten and Camp Eustis, made private first class in Battery E, 38th Art. Sailed Oct. 13, 1918 with Battery F, 47th Art. 1st Army, A. E. F. Mustered out at Camp Sherman March 21, 1919.

FOOR, Deo F., 26, Rochester, farmer, son of Parlee E. and Essie M. Foor, entered service March 12, 1918 at Columbus, Ohio, trained at Ft. Hancock, N. J. Sailed Aug. 17, 1918 as private with Battery D, 53rd C. A. C. and took part in Meuse-Argonne offensive. Mustered out at Camp Sherman, Ohio, April 4, 1919.

FERRY, Perry Lawson, 38, Akron, physician, son of John L. and Sophia Ferry, entered service June 26, 1918 at Akron, trained at Camp Greenleaf. Promoted 1st Lt. to Capt. M. R. C., Detachment Commander, Base Hospital 122, Camp Greene, N. C. Mustered out Dec. 11, 1918 at Camp Greene.

FLYNN, Alfred R., 23, Rochester, iron worker, son of Frank and Priscilla Flynn, entered service May 9, 1917, at Ft. Thomas, trained there and at Camps D. A. Russell and Jones, promoted to wagoner, Troop I, 1st Cav. Mustered out Sept. 4, 1919 at Douglass, Ariz.

FOKER, Elmer M., 29, married, Rochester, laborer, entered service March 21, 1918 at Camp Green, N. C. Private Co. M, 39th Regt., 4th Div. Inf. Sailed May 10, 1918 and participated in Battles of the Marne, July 18 to August 12, St. Mihiel Sept. 12 to 18, started in Meuse-Argonne offensive and was gassed in Argonne Forest Sept. 27th and taken to Base Hospital 117 for treatment. Mustered out May 17, 1919 at Camp Lee.

FOGLESONG, Harry E., 19, Rochester, student, son of Henry L. and Marcia E. Foglesong, entered service July 29, 1918 at Indianapolis, trained at Great Lakes and Hampton Roads. Fireman aboard ship Susquehanna. Sailed Nov. 12, 1918. Discharged Jan. 21, 1919 at Great Lakes.

HARLAN SHAW	OTIS JAY WRIGHT	GEORGE E. WARFIELD
HERBERT GOULD	R. W. GARMAN	MERLIN F. SNYDER
PERRY W. GILLESPIE	HERMAN MEYER	C. G. SAUSAMAN ELZA HOGAN

FIELDS, Francis Guy, 19, Rochester, iron worker, son of Charles and Carrie Fields, entered service Oct. 14, 1918 at Rochester, trained at Winona, Ind. Promoted from private to acting corporal and sergeant at Winona, Co. G. Mustered out Dec. 16, 1918.

FIELD, Ernest A., 23, Rochester, farmer, son of Walter and Jessie Field, entered service April 1918 at Douglas, Wyo., private Regular Army, 14th F. A. Supply Co. Discharged March 1919.

FELTY, Fred Wilson, 24, Rochester, barber, son of Henry M. and Indiana Felty, entered service Oct. 4, 1917 at Rochester, trained at Taylor, private 325th F. A. Hdqrs. Co. Mustered out Dec. 14, 1918 at Taylor.

FEIDNER, Arthur, 23, Grass Creek, farmer, son of William M. and Sarah E. Feidner, entered service Aug. 23, 1917 at Ft. Wayne, Ind., trained at Kelley Field, promoted private to sergeant, 98th Aero Squadron. Sailed Nov. 14, 1917 and served as airplane mechanic overseas. Mustered out April 8, 1919 at New York.

FANSLER, William Jacob, 20, Kewanna, farmer, son of Stephen and Lena Fansler, entered service Oct. 6, 1917 at Kokomo, trained at Laredo, Tex., promoted private to horse shoer for Troop H, 14th Cavalry. Mustered out Sept. 20, 1919 at Camp Grant.

FAULSTICH, Charles, 20, Delong, farmer, son of Albert and Elnora Faulstich, entered service Feb. 7, 1918 at Indianapolis, trained at Camp Sam Houston, Texas, promoted to Corporal and served as truck driver with 404th Transport Corps on Mexican border. Discharged May 26, 1919 at Camp Taylor.

FREESE, Guy Ralph, 22, Kewanna, farmer, entered service May 14, 1917 at Rochester, trained at Ft. Bliss, Ky., attached to medical department, 64th Inf. Sailed July 26, 1918 and was in fighting in Marbache and Purvenell Sectors. Discharged June 26, 1919 at Camp Sherman.

FRYE, Willard Melvin, 23, Delong, mechanic, son of Richard and Clara Fry, entered service Feb. 7, 1917 at Indianapolis, trained at Vancouver, engineering with Co. A., 318th Regt., 6th Div. Sailed May 1918 and was in battles of Argonne forest and on Alsace front. Mustered out June 21, 1919 at Camp Taylor.

FOX, Albert H., 26, Delong, farmer, son of Henry and Elizabeth Fox, entered service Dec. 11, 1917 at Hammond, trained at Camp Johnson, Fla. Sailed June 10, 1918 with Fire Truck and Hose Co. 322. Still in service.

SIDNEY BOWMAN
BENJAMIN MURPHY
ROBERT MITCHELL

HANFORD H. MILLER
EVERETTE D. MOGLE
IVAN R. BURNS

ROY RICHMOND (Left)
CHARLES ERNEST GOHN
JAMES M. WARE

FOSTER, Ora A., 23, Logansport, Funeral director, son of Mr. and Mrs. William Foster, Richland Tp., entered service March 29, 1918 at Rochester, trained at Camp Taylor, promoted private to corporal to sergeant, to Army Field Clerk, 11th Co., 1st Regt., 159th D. B. Mustered out May 1919 at Camp Taylor.

GOODRICH, Daniel, 32, married, Rochester, cigar maker, son of Alfred L. and Mary A. Goodrich, entered service April 26, 1918, trained at Camps Taylor and Custer, promoted private to Corporal. Discharged Dec. 21, 1918. Died at the home of his mother in Rochester, June 25, 1919.

GOHN, Charles Earnest, 22, Rochester, farmer, son of Charles and Kizzie Gohn, entered service March 12, 1918 at Rocheser, trained at Ft. Canby, Ft. Stevens, private Battery F, 69th Regt., C. A. C. Sailed Aug. 16, 1918. Discharged March 10, 1919 at Camp Sherman.

GINTHER, Merl, 18, Leiters Ford, carpenter, son of Adam R. and Lella Ginther. Entered service at South Bend, Ind., July 7, 1917, trained at Taylor, sailed Sept. 18, 1917 with 3rd Army Corps, 2nd Div., 9th Inf. Participated in battles in Verdun sector Sept. 18, 1917, St. Mihiel, Blanc Mont and Meuse-Argonne. Wounded at St. Mihiel, Sept. 11, 1917. Mustered out Aug. 14, 1919 at Camp Sherman.

GREEN, Sidney, 30, Delong, married, farmer, son of Samuel R. and Lydia Green, entered service at Rochester Sept. 20, 1917, trained at Camp Taylor, served as wagoner with 325th Supply Co., F. A. Mustered out Jan. 9, 1919 at Camp Taylor.

GAULT, Robert E., 21, Grass Creek, farmer, son of L. Allison and Annie E. Gault, entered service Sept. 3, 1918 at Rochester, trained at Camp Knox, private, Battery E. 70 F. A. Mustered out Feb. 3rd at Camp Knox.

GREENWOOD, Robert F., 18, Akron, machinist, son of L. R. and Fannie Greenwood, entered service June 4, 1918 at Indianapolis, trained at Ft. Caswell, N. C. Private Headquarters Co., 70th Art. C. A. C. Sailed Sept. 25, 1918. Mustered out March 12, 1919 at Camp Sherman.

GROVE, Oliver, 26, Talma, merchant, son of Simon Y. and Lizzie B. Grove, entered service June 14, 1918 at Rochester, trained 2nd Detachment, Chamber of Commerce, Indianapolis, promoted private to corporal, 9th Motor Supply Train, 9th Div. R. A. Mustered out at Camp Taylor March 28, 1919.

EMMET S. TRAMBARGER CLEM H. O'BLENNIS JAMES HOWARD WEIR
THOMAS WM. BECK WILLIAM H. OVERMYER WILLIAM MILLER
DEAN E. BABCOCK OSA FOOR WILLIAM H. AULT

GOULD, Herbert H., 19, Kewanna, reporter, son of Frank P. and Carrie Gould. Entered service April 17, 1917 at Rochester. Trained at Columbus, Ohio and San Antonio, Texas. Made Sergeant and promoted to Sgt. 1st class, 30th Aero Squadron. Sailed August 23, 1917 and was in first American air service to arrive in France, and was sent to aviation school in Paris for two months. Had fifty hours flying time in bombing planes. Founder of "Flights and Landings" the only official air service publication and served as editor of same for last ten months overseas. Went to France from Liverpool on H. M. S. Baltic, same ship Pershing went over on. Torpedoed by Germans off Irish coast and ordered to life boats but later arrived in Liverpool by using full steam ahead. Mustered out June 9, 1919 at Camp Sherman, Ohio.

GOULD, Francis B., Rochester, entered service at Jefferson Barracks, Mo., Nov. 14, 1907, assigned to Co. A., Signal Corps, stationed at Ft. Leavenworth, Kan. Promoted from private to corporal to sergeant. Discharged Nov. 13, 1910. Reenlisted Feb. 10, 1911, assigned to Coast Artillery, 35th Co., Ft. Monroe, Va. Promoted Corp to Sgt. to Q. M. and Mess Sgt. Discharged Feb. 9, 1914. Reenlisted Feb. 10, 1914, discharged to accept commission, May 10, 1918, when commissioned 2nd Lt., promoted to 1st Lt. Since 1916 served in Philippines. Commanded M. G. Co. 3rd Phil. Inf., Provost Officer, Casual Officer and Intelligence Officer, Ft. Wm. McKinley, P. I.

GOSS, Raymond M., 18, Rochester, chauffeur, son of John and Isabel Goss, entered service Feb. 2, 1918 at Indianapolis, trained at Rich Field, private 281 Aero Squadron. Sailed Aug. 13, 1918, and served with 281 Aero Squadron as a mechanic. In the Meuse-Argonne offensive. Discharged July 10, 1919 at Camp Sherman.

GROVE, Archie, 29, Talma, hardware merchant, son of Simon and Lizzie Grove, entered service March 28, 1918 at Rochester, trained at Camp Taylor and Washington Barracks, promoted private to corporal, 35th Engineers. Sailed Aug. 3, 1918 and did construction work with Co. F, 21 Grand Div. Discharged May 5, 1918 at Camp Dix.

GINTHER, Herbert Leslie, 23, Delong, laborer, son of Jacob O. and Mollie Ginther, entered service May 1917 at Rochester, trained at Kelly Field, Wilbur Wright's Field and Camp Mills, served as motorcycle rider with 19th Aero Squadron. Sailed Dec. 4, 1917. Mustered out May 5, 1919 at Camp Sherman.

MERL GINTHER	WILLIAM EDGINGTON	CLINT W. MILLER
HARRY CHAMP	HARVEY P. MARTIN	SIDNEY GREEN
CLARK BAILEY	CLARENCE G. STINGLEY	WALTER I. REDMOND

GINN, Irven, 24, Akron, clerk, son of Mr. and Mrs. S. C. Ginn, entered service Aug. 5, 1917 at Warsaw, Ind., trained at Camp Shelby, promoted private to corporal, Bat. D, 137 F. A. Sailed Oct. 6, 1918. Mustered out Jan. 14, 1919 at Ft. Harrison.

GINN, Harland Harrison, 28, Akron, barber, son of Sylvester C. and Mollie E. Ginn, entered service Sept. 20, 1917 at Rochester, trained at Camp Taylor. Private Bat. B, 325th F. A. Sailed April 8, 1918 with Bat. D, 321 F. A. 82nd Div. In St. Mihiel drive Sept. 12, and Meuse-Argonne offensive Sept. 26 to Oct. 8, when wounded by explosion. Mustered out May 29, 1919 at Camp Sherman.

GARMAN, Perry C., 27, Kewanna, Ind., dental student, son of Leroy and Harriet Garman. Entered service Nov. 16, 1917 at Ft. Benjamin Harrison. Trained at Camp Greenleaf, Ga. Served as assistant to dental surgeon, Dental Co. No. 1. Mustered out Jan. 26, 1919 at Camp Sherman.

GARMAN, Reed Waldo, 27, Bruce Lake, student. Entered service Feb. 26, 1918 at Lafayette, Ind. Private 1st class Eng. Trained at Camp Lee, Va., Camp Humphrey, Va., Camp Kearney, Cal., assigned to Co. D., 216th Engrs., 16th Div. Promoted to 2nd Lieutenant, July 30, 1918. Discharged Dec. 4, 1918 at Camp Kearney.

GILLISPIE, Perry Warren, 27, Kewanna, farmer, married. Entered service April 5, 1918, trained at Camp Taylor and Ft. Foot. Promoted to Corporal, Co. D, 306th Eng. Sailed Sept. 1, 1918 and did construction work overseas. In the Meuse-Argonne offensive. Mustered out June 24, 1919 at Camp Taylor.

GRAHAM, Frank P., 21, Lucerne, Ind., farmer, son of Mr. and Mrs. James Perry Graham, entered service Aug. 14, 1918 at Rochester, trained at Ft. Wayne, Mich. Private 607 Aero Squadron. Mustered out Feb. 22, 1919 at Ft. Wayne.

GOOD, Otto A., 28, South Bend, Ind., painter, son of Frank and Etta Good, Tiosa. Entered service May 5, 1918 at South Bend. Promoted from private to sergeant, Co. E, 22nd Eng. Sailed July 21, 1918 and operated narrow gauge railroad. In Meuse-Argonne and Toul offensives. Discharged July 11, 1919 at Camp Sherman.

GOCKING, Grant C., 28, married, Rochester, veterinary, son of George and Anna Gocking, entered service September 1917 at Rochester, trained at Camp Taylor, private, veterinary work, Bat. 1, 7th Regt., F. A. R. D. Mustered out Dec. 21, 1918.

ANDREW A. LARGE HUGH G. BRIDEGROOM CORP. VANCE E. HOFFMAN
LT. EVAN A. WHALLON EVERETT W. HAMMOND JOSEPH K. WILHOIT
CLIFFORD V. NYE CHARLES S. SANNS ROBERT RAYMOND BURNS

GOSS, Byron Cassius, 27, Rochester, teacher, son of Jonas and Mary Goss, entered service in August 1917, at Princeton, N. J. Assigned to General Headquarters, A. E. F. Promoted from 1st Lt. to Capt. Engrs., Feb. 20, 1918; Capt. Engrs. to Major C. W. S., July 27; Major C. W. S. to Lt. Col. Sept. 29. Sailed Aug. 29, 1917. Chemical Adviser to Chief of Gas Service, Oct. 15, 1917 to Feb. 20, 1918. Chief Gas Officer, 1st Army Corps, Feb. 20 to Oct. 20, 1918; Chief Gas Officer, 2nd Army, Oct. 20 to Nov. 20, 1918. Participated in second battle of the Marne, Belleau Wood, Chateau Thierry, Foret de Fere, St. Mihiel offensive, Argonne-Meuse attack, Apremont, Chene Tondu and Grand Pre. Slightly gassed, Feb. 25, 1918, severely gassed July 18, 1918 and in A. R. C. Hospital, Paris. Recommended by Commanding General, Chemical Warfare Service for Distinguished Service Medal. Discharged April 14, 1919 at Washington, D. C.

GINTHER, Silas, 23, married, Rochester, son of John D. and Agnes Ginther, entered service Oct. 20, 1917 at Rochester, trained at Camps Taylor and Knox. Promoted Private to Corp., to Sergeant, to 2nd Lt., Battery A, 325 F. A. Discharged Dec. 20, 1918 at Camp Knox.

GILLILAND, Edwin Keither, 24, Rochester, farmer, son of Arley and Emma Gilliland, entered service July 10, 1918 at Rochester, Great Lakes, Norfolk and Hampton Roads, promoted from private to fireman to seaman. Served on U. S. Ships Ohio, Santa Paula, Chattanooga. Landed in Africa, saw service in Asia, Russia, England and France. Still in service.

GARNER, Clarence K., 26, married, Rochester, farmer, entered service Oct. 4, 1917 at Rochester, trained at Taylor and West Point, Ky., promoted from private to sergeant and did blacksmithing for Battery B, 325 F. A. Sailed Sept. 8th, 1918 and continued blacksmithing. Mustered out July 11, 1919 at Camp Taylor.

HOLMAN, Hugh Brackett, 37, married, Rochester, contractor, son of George W. and Louise B. Holman, officers reserve corps called to service May 19, 1917, served as Capt. Q. M. Corps, served on construction of Camp Jackson, June 1 to Aug. 1, 1917 and on Camp Hancock, Aug. 1, 1917 to Feb. 1, 1918. Sailed March 4, 1918 and at Intermediate Q. M. Depot at Gievres, France, from May 26, 1918 to Sept. 7, 1918. Was railhead officer on advanced railheads on the Meuse-Argonne front Sept. 10 to Nov. 12, at Verdun railhead Nov. 12 to 22, at Battenburg, Luxenburg Nov. 23-30 with Army of Occupation. Was railhead officer at Treves, Germany from Dec. 1, 1918 to March 5, 1919. Discharged April 7, at Camp Lee.

CAPT. HUGH B. HOLMAN   EARNEST LANTZ   NEAL MOORE WEST
Unknown   Three Generations of Fulton County Fighters LOUIS E. EASTERDAY
Geo. Murray—World War.   O. M. Kumler—Spanish American War.   J. J. Kumler—Civil War.
GUY FREESE   P. A. SEIGFRIED

HILL, Clarence Franklin, 21, Rochester, student, son of John F. and Anna Hill, entered service at Lafayette, as apprentice seaman, trained at Purdue. Mustered out Dec. 20, 1918.

HETZNER, Harry, 40, Ft. Wayne, Ind., married, cement factory, son of Mr. and Mrs. M. H. Hetzner, entered service 1917, Texas. Sergeant, Cook. Sailed 1917, Rainbow Division.

HETZNER, Edward, 39, married, Rochester, policeman, son of Mr. and Mrs. Michael Hetzner, entered service at Ft. Wayne with regular army. Still in service.

HAGAN, Loyd, 17, Rochester, telegraph messenger, son of John and Rose Hagan, entered service March 12, 1914, trained at Great Lakes, promoted from private to Quartermaster for Admiral Andrews. Served on U. S. Destroyers Warrington and Kimberly and Scout Cruiser Chester. Did destroyer duty, convoy and patrol work. Engaged numerous enemy submaries in action. Sunk enemy submarine U-91 off Fastnet Light, south coast of Ireland, at night in September 1918. Member of Admiral Andrews staff on scout ship Chester, first American ship to enter German waters after signing of armistice. Still in service.

HALL, Elbert Lee, 22, Rochester, cigar maker, son of John and Catherine Hall, entered service May 24, 1918 at Rochester, trained at Taylor, Greenleaf and Oglethorpe, private Detached Service, Signal Corps and Hdqrs. Motor Units. Discharged Jan. 18, 1919 at Ft. Oglethorpe.

HENDRICKSON, Florence, 28, Kewanna, son of George P. and Agnes M. Hendrickson, entered service May 21, 1918 at Rochester. Trained at Ft. Snelling, Minn. and Devens, Mass. Promoted private to corporal Hdqrs. Co. 36th U. S. Inf. Mustered out Feb. 3, 1919 at Camp Taylor.

HENDRICKSON, Arthur W., 28, real estate, son of Isaac E. and Phila E. Hendrickson, entered service May 17, 1917 at Benj. Harrison, trained at Camps Taylor and Shelby. 2nd Lt. on special duty as commander of Co. 28, Detention Camp at Camp Shelby. Sailed Oct. 6, 1918 and served with Battery F., 137th F. A. Mustered out Jan. 21, 1919 at Ft. Harrison.

HENDRICKSON, Minden, 18, Grass Creek, farmer, son of George P. and Agnes M. Hendrickson, entered service Nov. 16, 1916 at St. Paul, Minn., trained at Paris Island, S. C. Private, promoted to Corporal June 1917, to Sgt., 1918, served as gas and bomb instructor. Sailed Oct. 1918 with U. S. Marines Corps. Still in service.

PERRY GARMAN   LT. E. L. WAITE   CLARENCE HILL
DAVID L. REITER   EARL PRESNALL   CHARLES SEARS
THOMAS E. BLACK   JAMES W. PENSINGER   MAX ARMSTRONG

HENDRICKSON, Milan, 22, Grass Creek, farmer, son of George P. and Agnes M. Hendrickson, entered service April 2, 1918 at Rochester, trained at Ft. Hamilton, N. Y., private 13th Co. Coast Artillery. Sailed July 15, 1918 with Battery F., 43rd Art. In St. Mihiel offensive Sept. 11 and 12, Argonne offensive Sept. 26 to 29 and Verdun, west of Meuse, Oct. 13 to Nov. 11. Mustered out Feb. 6, 1919 at Camp Sherman.

HENDERSON, Paul Dean, 19, Rochester, student, University Mich., son of Milton and Metta Henderson, entered service Oct. 1, 1918 at Ann Arbor, Mich., private, Students Army Training Corps of U. S. Army. Mustered out Dec. 12, 1918.

HENDERSON, Hugh Roberson, 19, Rochester, mechanic, son of Milton and Metta Henderson, entered service April 16, 1917, trained at Columbus Barracks, Syracuse, N. Y., Camps Shelby and Logan. Promoted from private to Battalion Sergeant Major, Headquarters Co. 4th F. A. Mustered out March 26, 1919 at Camp Logan. Re-enlisted March 27, 1919.

HUDTWALCKER, Rudolph Emil, 22, Rochester, printer, son of Emil and Elise Hudtwalcker, entered service April 14, 1917 at Columbus Barracks, Ohio, trained at Fort Warren, Mass. Promoted to Private 1st cl., 1st class gunner, 7th Co., Boston, C. A. C. Sailed Sept. 23, 1918 with 3rd Unit, Boston S. A. R. D. Transferred to 54th Art. and later to Battery C., 43rd Regt., Railway Artillery Reserves, (C. A. C.) Mustered out at Camp Sherman, Ohio, Jan. 23, 1919.

HUNTER, Rex, 25, Rochester, poultryman, son of Joseph and Effie Hunter, entered service March 12, 1918 at Rochester, trained at Ft. Hancock, N. J., promoted private to corporal. Mustered out Dec. 23, 1918.

HAMILTON, Ralph, 21, married, Kewanna, son of Samuel F. and Mary B. Hamilton, entered service Sept. 3, 1918 at Rochester, trained at Ft. Benj. Harrison and Camp Taylor. Private Co. B, 138th Engineers. Mustered out Dec. 4, 1918 at Ft. Benj. Harrison.

HARDING, Alphonso P., Jr., 23, Kewanna, student, son of A. P. Harding. Entered service March 28, 1919 at Rochester. Trained at Camp Shelby, Miss. Promoted from private to Corporal and Sergeant. Mustered out at Camp Taylor, Feb. 5, 1919.

CECIL S. BURNS LLOYD SNYDER GEORGE NICHOLS
CLARENCE C. PETERSON GEORGE PASSWATER VORIS D. ZARTMAN
JESSE LOWMAN RUSSELL RICHARDS JAMES HOMER CAIN

HEMINGER, Whitfield, 22, Kewanna, druggist, son of Amos C. and Maria Louisa Heminger. Entered service May 25, 1918 at Rochester, trained at Taylor and Beauregard. Corporal 126th Inf. 32nd Div. Instructor. Sailed Aug. 6, 1918 and served as instructor. Served in the Argonne, and out of line three weeks because of shrapnell wounds received October 3rd, 1918, caught in air raid on way to infirmary when ambulance was hit by piece of shell. With American Army of Occupation in Germany.

HOGAN, Earnest W., 20, Kewanna, farmer, son of William and Deama Hogan. Entered service May 10, 1916 at Logansport, Indiana. Trained at Ft. Bliss, Texas, promoted from private to Sergeant L Troop, 8th Cavl. Still in service on Mexican border.

HOGAN, Elra, 32, married, Kewanna, barber, son of William and Deama Hogan. Entered service Jan. 4, 1918 at Indianapolis. Trained at Ft. Thomas and Eagle Pass, Texas. Made private of 1st class, Co. E, 3rd U. S. Inf. Mustered out Jan. 31, 1919 at Ft. Sam Houston, Texas.

HARTER, Leo Sanford, 22, Akron, farmer, son of Clem and Clara Harter, entered service April 26, 1918 at Rochester, trained at Camp Taylor and Washington Barracks, Private 97th Co., 35th Regt., 21st Grand Div., Transportation Corps. Sailed Aug. 2, 1918. Mustered out May 10, 1919 at Camp Sherman.

HIGGINS, Forrest, 22, Akron, lumber dealer, son of Thomas and Esther Higgins, entered service Nov. 23, 1917 at Chicago, trained at Great Lakes, promoted apprentice seaman to seaman to coxswain, served on U. S. S. Frederick, doing convoy duty. Discharged June 23, 1919 at New York .

HOLLOWAY, Donald V., 18, Akron, mechanic, son of Benjamin F. and Eliza J. Holloway, entered service April 8, 1917 at Rochester, trained at Ft. Thomas and Ft. Hancock, promoted private to first class private, 3rd Co. C. A. C. Sailed Jan. 4, 1918 with Bat. A, 1st Bn., Trench Artillery, 1st Army Corps. Served as motorcycle orderly and participated in Second Battle of the Marne, July 19 to Aug. 2; St. Mihiel offensive, Sept. 5 to 12; Thiancourt, Sept. 23 to Oct. 18; Meuse- Argonne, Sept. 23 to Oct. 18. Mustered out March 15, 1919 at Camp Taylor.

HASLETT, Peter J., 19, Rochester, farmer, son of George and Ida Haslett, entered service Oct. 14, 1918 at Indianapolis. Private Indiana Dental College Branch. Mustered out Dec. 25, 1918.

WALTER D. ROSS NORMAN CLAIRE MOORE VAUSE POLEN
PAUL L. DUKES J. F. THOMPSON JOHN E. SCHIRM
HOWARD JACKSON JAY CLAYTON GEO. R. MURRAY

HATFIELD, Arthur R., 20, Rochester, salesman, son of Loren and Sarah Hatfield, entered service June 20, 1918 at Indianapolis, trained at Jefferson Barracks, Camp Crane and Ft. Ontario, promoted private to Corpl. to Sgt. Medical Dept., R. A., served as property Sergeant and Recruiting Officer. Still in service at General Hospital No. 5, Ft. Ontario, N. Y.

HATFIELD, Ralph, 22, Talma, merchant, son of L. W. and Ola Hatfield, entered service Sept. 3, 1918 at Rochester, trained at Taylor, West Point and Knox. Private, chauffeur, Hdqrs. Co., 70th F. A. Mustered out March 7, 1919 at Camp Knox.

HOOVER, Don C., 23, Rochester, farmer, son of Mr. and Mrs. F. P. Hoover, entered service Dec. 18, 1916 at Rochester, trained at Ft. Bliss and Douglass, Ariz., promoted private to sergeant, Co. L, 18th Inf. Sailed June 12, 1917, served for time as stenographer in Division Quartermasters Office; was with 18th Inf. in many actions and gassed in May 1918. With 1st Div. Q. M. Corps at Neuweid, Germany.

HOOVER, Ernest V., 24, Rochester, farmer, son of Mr. and Mrs. F. P. Hoover, entered service April 1918 at Rochester, trained at Ft. Foote, private Co. B, 1st Replacement Engineers. Sailed Sept. 1, 1918, Co. D, 103rd Engineers, 28th Div. In St. Mihiel drive. Discharged May 1, 1919 at Camp Taylor.

HORN, Robert M., 20, Tippecanoe, farmer, son of Orlando E. and Myrtle E. Horn, entered service Oct. 14, 1918 at Rochester, trained at Winona and Purdue, promoted private to sergeant, truckmaster, Co. D. Discharged Dec. 13, 1918 at LaFayette.

HUNTER, Harvey Fred, 21, Rochester, farmer, son of Alvin and Nora Hunter, entered service April 3, 1918, trained at Camp Eustis, Camp Lee, Ft. Tilden. Promoted private to corporal, Battery D, 38th Regt., C. A. C. Had charge of searchlight and run power plant. Sailed Oct. 8, 1918. Mustered out Dec. 18, 1918.

HUNTER, Otto, 24, Rochester, laborer, son of Lee and Tincy Hunter, entered service May 24, 1918 at Rochester, trained at Camp Sevier, private 148th Base Hospital. Mustered out Jan. 1, 1919 at Camp Taylor.

HAND, Floyd F., 19, married, steel worker, resident of Akron at time of entry into service, Oct. 18, 1917. Trained at Ft. Thomas. Ft. Riley and Camp Hampton, served as baker with Bakery Co. 342, Quartermaster's Dept. Mustered out Jan. 7, 1918 at Allentown, Pa.

WM. KESTNER   ERMAL H. SHINE   GLEN LOUIS EISENMAN
HEROLD ROSS   DAN COPLEN   ROBERT HORN
ROBERT P. MOORE   CLAUDE JAMISON   HUGH A. BARNHART

HOFFMAN, Vance Eber, 21, Akron, telephone work, son of Joseph and Emma K. Hoffman, entered service Sept. 20, 1917, trained at Camps Taylor, West Point, Mills and DeSouge, Fr., promoted private to corporal. Sailed Sept. 8, 1918 and did telephone work, Liason, in France. Mustered out Feb. 13, 1919 at Camp Taylor.

HENDRICKSON, Robert O., Rochester, railroad fireman, son of William and Myrtle Hendrickson, entered service July 4, 1917 at Ft. Thomas, Ky., Sgt. and machine gun instructor, Co. L, 46th Regt.

HAMMOND, Everett Walter, 23, Longmont, Col., brakeman, son of Clement H. and Mary J. Hammond, Henry tp., entered service May 15, 1917 at Chicago, trained at Paris Island, private and served as gunner, 3 inch piece, 91st Co., 10th Regt. U. S. M. C. Mustered out March 12, 1919 at Quatico, Va.

HARROLD, Willis L., 19, Miles, Mich.,-mechanic, son of Mr. and Mrs. Harlan Harrold, of Henry tp., entered service Sept 12, 1918 at Kalamazoo, Mich. Private Co. A., S. A. T. C. Discharged Dec. 15, 1918 at Kalamazoo.

HOFFMAN, Ralph W., 22, Akron, teacher, son of Ezra and Lydia Hoffman, entered service Dec. 15, 1917 at Indianapolis, trained at Great Lakes. Ensign, 1st Regt. Great Lakes. Discharged March 15, 1919 at Great Lakes.

HUDKINS, Alphonso, 21, Delong, farmer, son of B. F. and Harriet Hudkins, entered service Sept. 3, 1918, at Rochester, private 13th Co. 159th Depot Brigade. Discharged at Camp Taylor, Sept. 16, 1918.

HOOVER, Max J., 22, Akron, auto mechanic, son of Chas. C. and Grace B. Hoover, entered service Dec. 10, 1917 at Ft. Thomas, Ky., trained there and at Camp Hancock and Merritt, promoted private to corporal, 3rd Co. 2nd Regt. A. S. M. Sailed March 4, 1918. Mustered out June 24, 1919 at Camp Sherman.

HALL, Justin Leroy, 21, Rochester, farmer, son of Bert and Aurilla Hall, entered service Sept. 20, 1917 at Rochester, trained at Camp Taylor, promoted private to wagoner, Supply Co. 325th F. A. Sailed Sept. 8, 1918 with 84th Div. and did supply work overseas. Mustered out March 8, 1918 at Camp Sherman.

HAUSER, Albert William, 27, married, Gary, Ind., motorman, son of Charles and Frances Hauser, entered service Sept. 5, 1917 at Gary, trained at Taylor, promoted from Pvt. to Sgt., to Master Engineer, to 1st Lt., worked at roads and bridge building, sailed with Co. A, 602 Engineers, A. E. F. In battles of Chateau Thierry, St. Mihiel, Meuse-Argonne. With company of 250 built pontoon bridge across Meuse river in Meuse offensive. Each time the bridge was ready to connect with opposite shore it was blown up by German shells and five attempts were made before the bridge was laid, requiring more than three hours work in terrific shell fire. Wounded in foot. Still with A. E. F.

HAYWARD, Richard Gibbs, 22, Rochester, farmer, son of Calvin B. and Effie E. Hayward, entered service Dec. 11, 1917 at Toledo, O., trained at Kelly, Ellington and Mather aviation Fields, promoted private to corporal to Sgt. 1st Cl., and instructor of Aerial Gunnery, 283rd Aero Squadron. Discharged Feb. 10, 1919 at Columbus, Ohio.

HORN, Grover C., 30, married, Rochester, carpenter, son of S. M. and Mary Horn, entered service July 18, 1918 at Hammond, Ind., trained at Camps Taylor and McClellan, promoted private first class, Battery B, 25th Regt., 9th Brigade, on French 75 guns. Mustered out Feb. 10, 1919.

INGRAM, Melvin Otis, 26, Bruce Lake, laborer, entered service at Rochester, Ind., April 25, 1918. Trained at Camp Taylor, Ky., Fort Foot, Md., Washington Barracks, D. C. Assigned to Co. A, 73rd Engineers. Promoted from private to Supply Sergeant. Mustered out Dec. 4, 1918.

IVEY, Charles Robert, 18, Rochester, student, son of Martin W. and Minnie B. Ivey, entered service Oct. 12, 1918 at Purdue University, trained there with Co. 4, S. A. T. C. Discharged Dec. 19, 1919 at Purdue.

IRVINE, Charles Glendor, 21, Rochester, clerical, son of Martin A. and Elizabeth Irvine, entered service Dec. 4, 1917 at Indianapolis, trained at Taylor, Johnston, Merritt, cooked at Camp Johnston, later transferred to Clerical Company. Sailed May 10, 1918 and spent fifteen months at clerical work in various departments, promoted to sergeant 1st class. Mustered out Aug. 6, 1919 at Camp Sherman.

JOHNSON, Harry James, 19, R. F. D. 6, Rochester, Y. M. C. A. Secretary, entered service Jan. 2, 1918, at Indianapolis, as landsman for radio work, trained at Great Lakes. Served with Fuel organization under assistant to Aid for Supply at Hoboken, N. J. and on tugs in New York harbor. Discharged Jan. 1, 1919 at Hoboken, N. J.

JONES, Edgar Leroy, 40, Akron, teacher, married, son of Daniel and Amelia Holman Jones, entered service May 5, 1918 at Indianapolis for Y. M. C. A. Service, trained in New York, promoted to Divisional Athletic Director, with 76th Div., and 28 and 31 companies of 20th Engineers. Was delegate to the A. E. F. Athletic Conference held in Paris, Dec. 25 to Jan. 1 at which the A. E. F. and Inter-Allied Army Athletic Tournament was organized. Mustered out March 27, 1919 at New York.

JACKSON, Howard, 21, Kewanna, farmer, son of John and Ada Jackson. Entered service Sept. 3, 1918 at Rochester. Trained at Taylor and Knox. Mustered out Dec. 19, 1918.

JONES, Jesse Harold, 18, Rochester, student, son of Jesse Herbert and Etta S. Jones, entered service May 7, 1917 at Indianapolis, trained at Camp Shelby, promoted from private to Corporal, Co. C., 113th Engineers, 38th Div. Sailed Sept. 14, 1918, transferred to 7th Div. and with American Army of Occupation in Germany, near Trieves. Mustered out June 25, 1919 at Camp Sherman.

JOHNSON, John Byron, 22, Rochester, electrician, son of J. C. Johnson, entered service May 24, 1917, trained at Camp Grant, promoted from private to corporal, did electrical work with Co. A and B., 5th Limited Service Regt., 161st Depot Brigade. Mustered out Nov. 30, 1918.

JOHNSON, James F., 23, Rochester, machinist, son of Mrs. Annetta Ault Johnson, entered service Dec. 14, 1917 at Ft. Logan, Col., trained at Camps Merrill and Hancock, promoted from private to corporal and rated as Sgt., served as motor mechanic 20th Co., 2nd Regt., M. M. S. C. A. S. M. Sailed March 4, 1918 and served as air service and motor mechanic. After armistice served at Mantes, France collecting and repairing motor trucks. Received broken knee cap at Mantes in February 1919. Returned to United States June 18, 1919. Still in service.

JOHNSON, Alvin Lee, 21, Rochester, machinist, son of Wiley and Effie Johnson, entered service Sept. 1, 1918 at Rochester, trained at Purdue University, Port Clinton, Camp Hancock, private 7th Casual Co. 1st Prov. Regt., and served as engineer. Discharged March 1, 1919 at Pt. Clinton.

JAMISON, Claud, 27, married, Rochester, son of Lee and Ella Jamison, entered service April 25, 1918 at Rochester, trained at Washington Barracks, private Co. B., First Replacement Regiment. Sailed Sept. 1, 1918 and served at flash and sound ranging with Co. D, 29th U. S. Engineers, 2nd Army Corps. Discharged March 25, 1919 at Camp Taylor.

JOHNSON, William F., 20, Macy, farmer, son of Francis M. and Jane A. Johnson, entered service May 7, 1917 at Fort Wayne, Ind., trained at Fort Thomas and Camp Syracuse, private, Co. K., 30th Regt. of Infantry. Mustered out Sept. 17, 1917 at Camp Syracuse.

JENKINS, Hugh I., 19, Kewanna, farmer, son of Millard and Mary Jenkins, entered service July 23, 1918 at Logansport, Ind., trained at Jefferson Barracks and Ft. Barrancas, Fla., made corporal. Mustered out Dec. 29, 1918 at Camp Taylor.

KAMP, Estil, 21, Akron, farmer, son of Reuben and Alpha Kamp, entered service Sept. 20, 1917 at Rochester, trained at Camp Taylor, private Co. B, 325th F. A. Sailed April 8, 1918 with Co. B, 103rd Regt., 26th Div., 1st Army.

KINDIG, Roy Earl, 28, Tiosa, carpenter, son of C. V. and Hattie Kindig, entered service Sept. 20, 1917 at Rochester, trained at Taylor, Stanley, McArthur, private, Headquarters Co., 21st Regt., 5th Div. Sailed May 26, 1918. In Battles of Frapelle, St. Mihiel, Purvenelle and with Army of Occupation in Germany. Mustered out July 30, 1919.

KELLEY, Oran Samuel, 18, Delong, farmer, son of Samuel and Alma Kelly, entered service April 29, 1918 at South Bend. Sailed May 24, 1918 with 23rd Co. Camp Meade Replacement Unit, No. 5. Served in France and is now with Army of Occupation along the Rhine.

KING, Raymond E., 25, Rochester, hardware, son of Mr. and Mrs. John L. King, entered service June 15, 1918, at Indianapolis, trained at Camp Jackson, promoted to corporal, 339th M. T. C., served as instructor, automobile transportation dispatcher. Discharged June 18, 1919 at Camp Jackson.

KISTLER, Chas. S., 23, Chicago, Clerical, son of Mr. and Mrs. A. A. Kistler, Akron, entered service June 28, 1917 at Chicago. Promoted priate to corporal to Sgt. 1st Cl., Master Signal Electrician, Co. A, 314th Field Signal Battalion. Sailed June 11, 1918 with 89th Div. In St. Mihiel offensive and Meuse-Argonne. Mustered out June 12, 1919 at Camp Grant.

KINDIG, Vernon, 21, Akron, laborer, son of Orvil and Alfaretta Kindig, entered service June 20, 1917 at Warsaw, Ind., trained at Ft. Benj. Harrison and Camp Mills, promoted private to wagoner Supply Co., 150th F. A. Rainbow Div. Sailed Oct. 17, 1917 and participated in following actions: Lunneville Feb. 25 to May 22, 1918; Baccarat May 30 to June 30; Champagne-Marne defense July 10 to 18; Aisne-Marne offensive July 25 to Aug. 11; St. Mihiel Sept. 12 to 16; Argonne Sept. 30 to Nov. 11. Discharged May 9, 1919 at Camp Taylor.

KERN, Frank William, 21, Athens, prop. auto bus line, entered service Oct. 24, 1918, trained at Camps Polk and Greene, promoted private to Sgt., Co. B, 308th Bn., Tanks Corps, R. A. Discharged Jan. 6, 1919 at Camp Taylor.

KOPP, Ernest L., 17, Kewanna, student, son of Daniel and Sarah Kopp. Entered service April 12, 1917. Trained at Ft. Constitution, N. H. and Ft. Adams, R. I. Sailed July 17, 1918 and became part of Battery B, 66th Artillery, C. A. C. Mustered out March 21, 1919, at Camp Sherman, Ohio.

KOPP, Daniel, Jr., 19, Kewanna, hardware clerk, son of Daniel and Sarah Kopp. Entered service at Columbus, Ohio, April 17, 1917. Trained at Camp Kelly, Texas and becocme chauffeur in 496th Aero Squadron. Sailed Aug. 23, 1917 and served as automobile driver for 496th Aero Squadron. Discharged May 10, 1919 at Camp Sherman.

KISSINGER, Herschal, 25, Rochester, painter, son of Harry and Olive Kissinger, entered service July 6, 1917 at Toledo, O., trained at Camps Perry, Sheridan and Jackson. Made First Class private and served as supply accountant Co. C., 112th Field Signal Bn. Mustered out Feb. 11, 1919 at Camp Jackson.

KING, Milo S., 25, Rochester, farmer, son of Joseph V. and Anna S. King, entered service with the French Army April 1, 1917 at Paris, France and with the American Army, Oct. 3, 1917 at Vassney, France. Served with the 6th French Army in June on the Chemin des Dames, and with the French 66th Div. Chasseurs in the attack and counter attack on the Chemin des Dames in July. With the same in the attack on the Malmaison Fort, Oct. 17 to 26th, 1917. In 1918 working on all units during the retreat and advance on the Marne, lasting from May 1st to Sept. 30. With the 2nd Div. Marocaine Oct. 18th to 31st on the Champagne. Mustered out May 10, 1918.

KESTNER, George William, 31, Rochester, laborer, son of Henry and Matilda Kestner, entered service at Rochester, April 25, 1918, trained at Camps Forrest, Gordon, Merrick, Thomas and Oglethorpe. Private Co. A, 6th Regt., 52nd Inf. Sailed Oct. 27, 1918. Mustered out Feb. 13, 1919 at Camp Gordon.

KEEL, Carl Byron, 22, Rochester, auditor, son of Chas. B. and Mary E. Keel, entered service Jan. 16, 1918, at Rochester, trained at Camp Hancock, San Antonio Arsenal and Raritan Arsenal, Sergeant Ordinance, 6th Co. Discharged Dec. 13, 1918 at Camp Hancock.

LARGE, Andrew C., 18, Rochester, farmer, son of Mr. and Mrs. John A. Large, entered service April 14, 1917 at Rochester, trained at Forts Constitution and Adams, made private first class and served as assistant cook, 4th Co. Coast Defenses. Sailed July 19, 1918 with Bat. A, 66th C. A. C. Sent to hospital Oct. 17, 1918 with influenza and there when armistice was signed. Discharged March 21, 1919 at Camp Sherman.

LONG, Worth W., 19, Akron, student, son of John H. and Rosa A. Long, entered service Feb. 15, 1917 at Columbus, O., trained at Ft. Totten, N. Y., and Ft. Adams, N. J. Promoted private to corporal and served as observer. Sailed Aug. 15, 1917 with Bat. B, 44th C. A. C. Served as observer overseas. In Lorraine sector, Champagne, and St. Mihiel April 1918 to Nov. 11, 1918. Mustered out March 14, 1918 at Ft. Totten, N. Y.

LONG, Ernest W., 23, Akron, mechanic, son of Mrs. T. J. Burkett, entered service June 2, 1917 at Warsaw, Ind., trained at Camp Shelby, made first class private Bat. D, 137th F. A. Sailed Oct. 6, 1918. Mustered out Jan. 14, 1919 at Indianapolis.

LANTZ, Ernest, 25, Akron, railroad construction, son of Joseph H. and Ida L. Lantz, entered service Aug. 5, 1918 at Rochester, trained at Syracuse, N. Y. and Camp Stuart, made 1st cl. private, 59th Co. Inf., 15th Bn.

LOWMAN, Jesse L., 32, Patton, Cal., nurse, son of Richard and Mary Jane Lowman, Rochester. Entered service July 12, 1918, at St. Louis, trained at Ft. Hancock, promoted from private to corporal, served as gunner with 5th Trench Motor. Sailed Sept. 13, 1918. Mustered out Feb. 3, 1918 at Columbus, Ohio.

LOUDERBACK, L. V., 24, Rochester, student, entered service Sept. 1, 1917 at Rochester, trained at Taylor, assigned to Battery A, 325th F. A. Promoted private to Chief Mechanic to 2nd Lt., to 1st Lt. Asst. Adjutant, 1st Regt. F. A. R. D. Camp Jackson to Oct 24, 1918, Adjutant, to Feb. 5, 1919. Discharged Feb. 5, 1919 at Camp Jackson.

LACKEY, Hiram Silas, 31, Rochester, steel worker, son of Andrew and Angeline Lackey, entered service June 27, 1918 at Rochester, trained at Camp Taylor, promoted to corporal, Vocational Co. A, Indianapolis. Discharged Dec. 13, 1918 at Camp Taylor.

MARTIN, Floyd, 31, Hammond, Ind., teamster, son of James T. and Sarah C. Martin. Entered service May 24, 1918 at Hammond, trained at Camp Jackson, served as wagoner 314th Cavalry. Mustered out Jan. 4, 1919 at Camp Grant.

MYERS, August A., 22, Leiters Ford, herdsman, son of John J. and Lyda A. Myers. Entered service May 24, 1918 at Kentland, Ind., trained at Camp Taylor, promoted to first class private and served as bayonet instructor and runner, Co. I, 126th Inf. Sailed August 6, 1918, served as Leozoneman. In Meuse-Argonne offensive and with American Army of Occupation in Germany. Mustered out May 29, 1919 at Camp Sherman, Ohio.

MURPHY, Russel D., 20, Rochester, farmer, son of Alpheus and Clara Murphy, entered service Sept. 12, 1918 at Purdue University, Private 2nd Co. S. A. T. C. Mustered out Dec. 19, 1918 at Purdue.

MILLER, Hanford, 24, married, Rochester, laborer, son of Edward and Anna Miller, entered service Oct. 2, 1917 at Ft. Dodge, Iowa, trained at Camp Pike and Brooklyn, N. Y., private worked at guarding ships. Mustered out March 13, 1919.

McCLUNG, William P., 31, Rochester, farmer, entered service July 18, 1918 at Lewiston, Mont., trained San Francisco Presidio, Private 51st Co., C. A. C. Mustered out May 24, 1919 at Camp Fremont, Cal.

McCLUNG, Arthur, Rochester, entered service Sept. 20, 1917 at Rochester, trained at Camp McArthur and Camp Taylor, private Bat. C, 21st F. A., 5th Div. Mustered out April 27, 1919 at Camp McArthur, Texas.

MURPHY, Benjamin, 29, Rochester, motor adjuster, son of Alpheus and Clara Murphy, entered service March 12, 1918 at Rochester, trained at Columbus, O., and Portland, Me., promoted private to wagoner, Bat. D, 72nd Regt. Sailed Aug. 6, 1918 and did motor adjusting with 35th Brigade. Discharged April 17, 1919 at Camp Grant.

MOORE, Daniel M., 19, Athens, railroader, son of John and Flaura Moore, entered service Aug. 3, 1917 at Mankato, Minn., trained at Camp Jefferson, Ft. Bliss, Texas, and Columbus, N. M., Ist Cl. Private R. A., Sailed Jan. 4, 1918. Still in service.

MOORE, Benjamin Franklin, 26, married, Rochester, railroad, son John A. and Flaura Moore, entered service June 15, 1918 at Peru, Ind., trained at Camp Jackson, private 161 R. R. Transportation. Sailed Oct. 28, 1918 with 28th Automatic Replacement Regt. Discharged July 9, 1919 at Camp Sherman.

MILLER, Hanford H., 24, married, Rochester, laborer, son of Edwin and Anna Miller, entered service Oct. 2, 1917 at Sioux City, Iowa, trained at Camps Dodge and Pike, private Co. A, 350th Regt. Discharged March 13, 1919, at Brooklyn, N. Y.

MATTHEWS, Leroy Ellsworth, 22, Tiosa, farmer, son of Stephen D. and Julia A. Matthews, entered service March 29, 1918 at Rochester, trained at Camp Taylor and Washington Barracks, private Co. F, 108th Engineers. Sailed July 14, 1918. In action Villers-Buttenaug Aug. 8, 1918; Baes de Forges Sept. 26; Lonsivey Oct. 8, Bancourt Nov. 11. Mustered out June 4, 1919 at Camp Sherman.

MIKESELL, Omer Harrison, 24, married, Oak Park, Ill., postal clerk, son of Mr. and Mrs. John W. Mikesell, Newcastle, entered service July 31, 1918 at Oak Park, trained at Camp Jackson, made 1st cl. private and qualified as gunner 3 in. piece, Bat. B. 117th F. A. 56th Brigade. Sailed Oct. 13, 1918 with Dixie Division. Mustered out Jan. 14, 1919 at Camp Taylor.

MARSH, Marion A., 21, Athens, farmer, son of James A. and Henrietta Marsh, entered service Sept. 31, 1918 at Rochester, trained at Camp Knox, promoted to private 1st Cl., served as gun pointer and cannoneer, 72nd F. A. Mustered out Feb. 24, 1919 at Camp Knox.

MARRIOTT, Virgil K., 20, Rochester, farmer, son of Mr. and Mrs. Frank Marriott, entered service Oct. 11, 1918 at Purdue University, private Co. 3, S. A. T. C., did surveying and map drawing. Discharged Dec. 19, 1918 at Purdue.

MAHONEY, James Dennis, 21, Rochester, telephone lineman, son of William and Pearl Mahoney, entered service Aug. 14, 1918 at Rochester, trained at Cincinnatti, O., and Pittsburg, Pa., private. Mustered out Jan. 14, 1919.

MOW, Charles Clyde, 30, Rochester, farmer, son of M. L. and Eva L. Mow, entered service April 26, 1918, trained at Camp Taylor and Washington Barracks, made private 1st Cl., 28th Div. Engineers. Sailed Sept. 1, 1918 with Co. B, 103rd Reg. Engrs. In Battle of Thiacourt Oct. 10 to Nov. 11. Discharged May 19, 1919 at Camp Sherman.

MILLER, Wilhelm H. A., 24, Tiosa, farmer, son of Fred B. and Caroline Miller, entered service Sept. 20, 1917 at Rochester, trained at Camp Taylor and West Point. Private and first aid in hospital, 325th F. A. Sailed Sept. 9, 1918. Mustered out March 1, 1919 at Camp Sherman.

MEEK, James Harold, 25, Tiosa, mechanic, son of Loren and Jessie Meek, entered service July 31, 1918 at Rochester, trained at Syracuse, N. Y., Astoria, L. I., and Lake Hurst, N. J., promoted from private to sergeant and helped to test gasses. Co. A, First Gas Regt. Mustered out June 14, 1919, Lake Hurst, N. J.

MARSHALL, Robert Claude, 23, Rochester, farmer and teacher, son of George W. and Lydia L. Marshall, entered service March 13, 1918 at Rochester, trained at Ft. Moultrie and Camp Eustis, promoted to Corporal, 77th Co. C. A. C. Sailed Oct. 21, 1918 with Headquarters Co. 45th Regt. 1st Army. Mustered out April 10, 1919, at Camp Taylor.

MADLEM, Harland T., 24, Akron, farmer, son of Jacob T. and Martha Ann Madlem, entered service Dec. 2, 1917 at Indianapolis, trained at Camp Custer, Jefferson Barracks, Chanute Field, Hampstead Field and Cormack Field, promoted private to 1st Cl. Chauffeur, 268th Aero Squadron. Sailed July 16, 1918 and served as chauffeur overseas. Mustered out Dec. 22, 1918 at Camp Sherman.

MARTIN, Cloyd, 30, Leiters Ford, laborer, son of James T. and Sarah Martin, entered service March 15, 1918 at Rochester, trained at Camp Severn and at Edgewood, Md. Private, Ordnance Dept., Co. D., 1st Bat. Still in government service at Edgewood, Md.

MOORE, Norman Clair, 18, Akron, student, son of Lee and Cora Moore, entered service Oct. 1, 1918 at Indiana University. Trained there, private S. A. T. C. Mustered out Dec. 21, 1918.

MEREDITH, Russel Sage, 23, Akron, mechanic, son of Mr. and Mrs. Henry L. Meredith, entered service Sept. 20, 1917 at Rochester, trained at Camp Taylor, private Bat. B, 325th F. A., 89th Div. Discharged Aug. 19, 1918 at Camp Taylor.

MEREDITH, Donal D., 21, Akron, stenographer, son of Henry and Viola Meredith, entered service Nov. 12, 1917 at Denver, Colo., trained U. S. N. training station, San Francisco. Promoted apprentice seaman to quartermaster, 3rd class, to quartermaster, 2nd class. Still in service.

MILLS, Nathaniel Russell, 25, Kewanna, salesman, son of L. C. and Rachael Mills. Entered service June 3, 1917 at Ft. Wayne, Ind. Trained at Ft. Ogelthorpe, Camp Fremont and Ft. Sill. Served as Asst. Reg. Supply Sergeant, Troop G, 23rd Cav. U. S. A. Supply Co. 81st F. A. Mustered out Dec. 20, 1918 at Louisville, Ky.

McCOY, Walter A., 27, Dallas, Texas, machinist, son of James and Julia McCoy, Kewanna. Entered service March 25, 1918 at Detroit, Mich. Entered as private, 868th Aero Squadron, promoted to Sergeant April 1, 1918 and to 1st Class Sgt. June 11, 1918. Worked as machinist and at aviation repairs. Discharged Jan. 25, 1919.

MOGLE, Hubert Eldon, 27, Rochester, teacher, son of Charles W. and Iva L. Mogle, entered service May 25, 1918, trained at Camp Taylor, promoted from private to corporal to 2nd Lt., and did personnel work with 20th Co., 159th Regt., D. P. Brigade. Mustered out at Camp Gordon, Nov. 30, 1918.

MOORE, Robert Paul, 22, Rochester, accountant, son of Mr. and Mrs. Frank F. Moore, entered service Sept. 1, 1918, at Camp Gordon, Ga., assigned to 19th Co., Central Officers Training School, commissined 2nd Lt., Inf., Off. Reserve Corps Nov. 30, 1918, when he was discharged and placed on reserved list.

MOGLE, Everett Dale, 25, Rochester, miner, son of Charles and Iva Mogle, entered service April 12, 1918, trained at Ft. Monroe, Hampton Roads and Great Lakes. Promoted to fireman. Served as Engineer on Admiral's barge and on U. S. S. Missouri and Wisconsin. Still in service.

MITCHELL, Robert Corletus, 19, Rochester, plumber, son of Mrs. Charles Fulkerson, entered service June 17, 1917 at Warsaw, Ind., trained at Ft. Harrison and Camp Shelby. Did plumbing and line work with Battery F, 124th F. A. Sailed June 12, 1918. In battles at St. Mihiel, Argonne and Meuse-Argonne. Gassed at Mt. Foncone Oct. 2, and wounded at Verry Oct. 12. With A. of O. in Germany. Mustered out June 6, 1919 at Camp Sherman.

MILLER, Walter W., 22, Rochester, electrical inspector, son of Archie B. and Lydia A. Miller, entered service May 28, 1917 at Chicago, trained at U. S. Naval Academy, made ensign, served on U. S. Cruiser Vermont and U. S. Dreadnaught Arkansas. Still in service.

MILLER, Raymond Frederick, 20, Rochester, mail carrier, son of Vincent and Anna Miller, entered service Oct. 12, 1918, private Co. I, U. S. Inf., S. A. T. C. Purdue. Discharged Dec. 19, 1918 at Purdue University.

MILLER, Lucius C. E., 18, Rochester, electrical inspector, son of Archie B. and Lydia A. Miller, entered service May 28, 1917 at Chicago, trained at Great Lakes. Served on U. S. S. Louisiana, promoted from apprentice seaman to coxswain and gun pointer. Now on U. S. S. Edellyn.

METZ, Jack, 17, Rochester, cigar maker, son of Orton and Versa Metz, entered service May 15, 1916, trained at Marathon, Texas, promoted private to corporal Troop C, 8th Cavalry. Discharged June 1919.

McMAHAN, Patrick, 31, married, Rochester, farmer, son of John B. and Rebecca McMahan, entered service Oct. 16, 1918 at Rochester. Candidate Officers Training School, Camp Taylor. Mustered out Dec. 2, 1918 at Camp Taylor.

McMAHAN, John L., 25, Rochester, bank teller, son of John B. and Rebecca McMahan, entered service Sept. 27, 1918 at Rochester. Candidate and instructor O. T. C., 14th Observation Bn. 3rd Tr. Bn. Discharged Nov. 27, 1918 at Camp Taylor.

McMAHAN, James I., 21, Rochester, student, son of John B. and Rebecca McMahan, entered service Sept. 4, 1917, promoted private to 1st Lt., instructor O. T. C., head of fire discipline, Camp Taylor. Discharged Nov. 30, 1918 at Camp Taylor.

McKEE, Brant R., 25, Rochester, letter carrier, son of Mr. and Mrs. Albert McKee, entered service April 26, 1918 at Rochester, trained at Purdue University. Promoted from private to wagoner to corporal. Hdq. Det., Motor Bn., 315th Am. Tn. Sailed July 6, 1918 and served as chauffeur. Mustered out June 20, 1919, at Camp Taylor.

McINTIRE, Lowell B., 25, married, Rochester, cement worker, son of Daniel and Effie McIntire, entered service Sept. 1917 at Rochester, trained at Camp Taylor, promoted private to corporal to sergeant, Co. A, 325th Regt. Sailed Sept. 1918.

McCARTY, William Lee, 19, married, Rochester, farmer, entered service April 18, 1917 at Columbus, Ohio, trained on Mexican border, made first class private, Co. F, 30th Inf. Sailed Sept. 18, 1917. In battles on Toul sector March 17 to May 14, 1918; Chateau Thierry June 1 to July 19; Soissons July 24 to 28, Marbach sector Aug. 9 to 24; St. Mihiel Sept. 9 to 13; Champaigne Sept. 30 to Oct. 6. Wounded by shrapnel on Oct. 6, 1918, and removed to Base Hospital 15, Shaumount, France. Discharged March 18, 1919 at Camp Grant.

MASTERSON, Orange Lee, 22, Rochester, clerk, son of William and Anna Masterson, entered service May 29, 1918 at Rochester, trained at Taylor, Greenleaf and Sherman. Private. Sailed Oct. 29, 1918 with Medical Corps, Evac. Hosp. Hosp. 28. Still in service.

MASTERSON, Alvin McKinley, 23, Rochester, electrician, son of William and Anna Masterson, entered service April 23, 1917 at Ft. Wayne, Ind. Sailed Aug. 6, 1917, with 1st Trench Mortar Battery, 1st Div. Gassed Feb. 26, 1918.

MURTHA, George, 22, Kewanna, farmer, son of John and Julia Murtha, entered service Aug. 22, 1918 at Camp Dodge, Iowa. Private and served as teamster Co. 19, 163rd Depot Brigade. Mustered out June 27, 1919 at Camp Dodge.

MILLER, Chas. A., 31, Kewanna, farmer, son of Jacob E. and Mary T. Miller, entered service April 25, 1918 at Rochester, trained at Camps Taylor and Mills and at Washington Barracks, private Co. B, 103rd Engineers. Sailed August 29, 1918. Mustered out May 19, 1919, at Camp Sherman.

MARONEY, John T., 22, Kewanna, farmer, son of John and Marg Maroney, entered service Sept. 4, 1918 at Kewanna, trained at Camp Knox, private, 72nd F. A. Mustered out Jan. 30, 1919 at Camp Knox.

MURRAY, George R., 22, Grass Creek, student Purdue Uni., entered service June 4, 1918, recruit, Coast Artillery, trained at Fort Caswell, 11th Co., C. A. C., promoted from corporal to sergeant. Mustered out Dec. 17, 1918 at Camp Sherman.

MEYER, Herman Anthony, 22, Kewanna, farmer, son of Charles and Magdalena Meyer, entered service Sept. 3, 1918 at Rochester, trained at Camps Taylor and Jackson, Private, 13th Co., 4th Training Bn., 159th Depot Brigade. Mustered out Jan. 2, 1919 at Camp Taylor.

MURTHA, Joseph, 29, Stockton, Cal., son of John and Julia Murtha, Wayne tp., entered service April 6, 1918 at Stockton, Cal., trained at Great Lakes and Pelham Bay, N. Y. Promoted private to sergeant. Served on troop transport. Still in service.

MILLER, Earl, 26, Kewanna, farmer, son of Jacob E. and Mary T. Miller, entered service Sept. 20, 1917 at Rochester, trained at West Point, Ky. Private and mechanic Battery A, 325th F. A. Sailed Sept. 8, 1918 with Lincoln Division. Mustered out March 1, 1919 at Camp Sherman.

MORPHET, William L., 23, Grass Creek, student, son of Mr. and Mrs. William M. Morphet, entered service Aug. 14, 1918 at Camp Grant, Ill., trained at Ft. Benj. Harrison. In Y. M. C. A. work until May 1, 1919 when transferred to Medical Department U. S. Army as Reconstruction Aide. Mustered out Aug. 15, 1919.

MILLER, Calvert Roscoe, 20, Fulton, electrician, son of Clinton F. and Ida Miller, entered service June 4, 1917, trained at Ft. Thomas, promoted from Private to Non-Commissioned Officer, with Co. F. 3rd Engineers. Sailed July 20, 1917. Yet in service in Panama.

MARTIN, Harvey P., 27, Fulton, garage mechanic, son of Frank A. and Mary Ellen Martin, entered service May 24, 1919 at Rochester trained at Camps Taylor and Johnston, promoted from Private to Corporal, 415 M. S. T. 455 M. T. Co. (3rd corps.) Sailed Aug. 14, 1919, mechanic and truck driver, in battles of St. Mihiel and Meuse-Argonne. Mustered out Aug. 12, 1919 at Camp Sherman.

MEYER, Omer John, 22, Ft. Wayne, married, stock clerk, son of Mr. and Mrs. Henry Meyers, Fulton, entered service June 10, 1918 at Great Lakes, Ill., Musician, traveled with band on Liberty Loans, 11th Reg. Band. Mustered out Dec. 23, 1918 at Great Lakes, Illinois.

McCALL, Ernest Hazen, 20, Rochester, printer, son of Lewis B. and Elma F. McCall. Entered service Sept. 11, 1917, trained at Camp Greene and Camp Mills. Sailed Nov. 27, 1917 with Co. B, 116th Engineers, transferred after landing in France to Co. E, 1st Engineers. Private. In St. Mihiel, Soissons, Argonne-Meuse offensives. With Army of Occupation in Germany. Mustered out Sept. 11, 1919 at Tacoma, Wash.

NOYES, Lucius Vernon, 24, married, Rochester, butcher, entered service April 1918 at Warsaw, Ind., trained at Camp Shelby, made cook, Co. H, 3rd Ind. Inf. Sailed Sept. 28, 1918 and served as cook overseas. Discharged Jan. 15, 1919 at New York.

NELSON, Kenneth, Akron, entered service June 27, 1917 at Ft. Wayne, Ind., trained at Camp Custer, Camp Morse, Ft. Leavenworth, Kan. Made Sergeant, promoted to 2nd Lt., Signal Corps. Sailed July 15, 1918, transferred to 402nd Telegraph Battalion and on duty in charge of telegraph office at Nevers, France until Sept. 24, transferred to 416th Tr. Bn. and stationed at St. Nazaire, moved to Tours. Promoted to 1st Lt. Sept. 29 and was placed at LeMans on Oct. 6 as superintendent of telegraph and telephone of Tours-Brest railroad. Remained in this position until Jan. 23, 1919. Discharged April 6, 1919 at Camp Sherman.

NOFTSGER, Charles Benjamin, 18, Loyal, son of Bennie E. and Ida Noftsger, entered service Feb. 12, 1918 at Columbus, O., trained at Kelly Field and Camp Wise, promoted private to cook, 57th Balloon Co. Mustered out Dec. 17, 1918 at Camp Morrison, Va.

NYE, Clifford V., 21, Akron, farmer, married, son of Gilbert S. and Ida B. Nye, entered service July 17, 1918 at Rochester, trained at Camp Sheridan, promoted private to corporal and served as truck driver with Co. E, Motor Supply Train 429.

NYE, Robert C., Akron, farmer, son of Gilbert S. and Ida B. Nye, entered service Oct. 1918 at Chicago, trained at Camp Greene, promoted private to corporal Co. A, 307th Battalion, Tank Corps. Discharged Jan. 5, 1919 at Camp Taylor.

NEWELL, Manford A., 24, Athens, cook, son of Mr. and Mrs. Robert Newell, entered service Sept. 5, 1917 at Rochester. Trained at Camp Taylor, promoted to Sgt. Sailed Sept. 9, 1918 with Bat. B, 325th F. A. Mustered out Feb. 15, 1919.

NELLANS, Charles Thomas, 23, Rochester, physician, son of Ami B. and Amanda E. Nellans, entered service Oct. 1917 at Chicago, trained at Presbyterian Hospital, Chicago. Private. Mustered out Dec. 11, 1918 at Chicago.

NEHER, Truman V., 22, Rochester, farmer, son of Mr. and Mrs. John A. Neher, entered service April 25, 1918 at Rochester, trained at Camps Taylor and Foote, private Co. B, 1st Replacement Engineers. Sailed Sept. 1, 1918, Co. B., 103rd Engrs. 28th Div. In Thiacourt sector Oct. 15 to Nov. 11. Mustered out May 19, 1919 at Camp Sherman.

NEHER, Russel R., 24, Rochester, truck driver, son of John A. and Elizabeth Neher, entered service April 2, 1918, trained at Fort Wadsworth, promoted private to wagoner, Bat. A, 70th F. A. Sailed June 13, 1918, served as truck driver and was in American offensives for two months. Discharged March 12, 1919 at Camp Sherman.

NICKELS, George Herman, 21, Grass Creek, farmer, son of Walter F. and Alice E. Nichols, entered service Oct. 12, 1918, at Rochester, trained at Valparaiso, Ind., and Interlaken, promoted from Private to Corporal, Students Army Training Corps. Mustered out Dec. 11, 1918.

O'BLENIS, Clem Henry, 26, Rochester, farmer, son of William C. and Rosalba O'Blenis, entered service May 24, 1918 at Rochester, trained at Camp Taylor and Camp Devens, private 17th Co. 5th Depot Brigade. Mustered out Jan. 16, 1919 at Camp Taylor.

O'BLENIS, Milton Ray, 21, Rochester, farmer, son of William C. and Rosalba O'Blenis, entered service at Columbus Barracks, O., March 7, 1918, trained at Ft. Monroe. Private 12th Regt., C. A. C. Mustered out Jan. 21, 1919 at Camp Sherman.

O'CONNELL, Clarence E., 21, Leiters Ford, farmer, son of Mr. and Mrs. Jack O'Connell, entered service Sept. 3, 1918, trained at Camps Taylor and Knox. Promoted to first class private, Artillery, 24th Regt., 8th Div. Discharged Jan. 31, 1919 at Camp Knox.

O'DELL, John Gilbert, 23, Rochester, farmer, entered service Sept. 21, 1917 at Rochester, trained at West Point, Ky., promoted to Sgt., Bat. E, 325th F. A. Sailed Sept. 8, 1918 with Lincoln Division. Mustered out March 1, 1919 at Camp Sherman.

OVERMYER, Leroy, 23, Leiters Ford, farmer, son of Boyd and Rosa Overmyer, entered service Sept. 20, 1917 at Rochester, trained at Taylor, Seviere and Camp Jackson, private first class and did telephone work with Headquarters Co., 115th F. A. Sailed March 4, 1914, did telephone work and participated in all American drives overseas. Mustered out April 18, 1919 at Camp Taylor.

OVERMYER, William M., 21, married, Leiters Ford, teacher-farmer, son of Mr. and Mrs. A. B. Overmyer, entered service Sept. 21, 1917 at Rochester, trained at Camp Taylor, made horseshoer. Bat. A, 325th F. A. Sailed Sept. 9, 1918, and did horseshoeing overseas. Mustered out March 1, 1919 at Camp Sherman.

OWENS, Robert Foster, 29, Rochester, telephone lineman, son of Robert and Sarah Owens, entered service Feb. 22, 1916 at Columbus, O., with Company D, 16th Inf. On International Bridge between El Paso, Texas and Juarez, Mexico when war was declared. Embarked with 16th at Hoboken, N. J., June 11th, 1917, paraded with 2nd Battalion in Paris on 4th of July, went into training at Gondecourt on the Marne. Served in Toul sector through January and February 1918, with the French on Picardy front in April, received shell wound May 31, 1918, back on the Toul front on Sept. 12, and with the Meuse-Argonne offensive and with the American Army of Occupation in Germany. Returned to America Aug. 8, 1919 and participated in the Pershing parade in New York. Still in service.

PERSONETTE, Ivan Murr, 24, married, Rochester, cook, entered service April 21, 1917 at Great Lakes N. T. S. Served as 4th class cook. On Transport Virginian, U. S. S. Bushnell and Submarine L 9. Discharged Feb. 2, 1919 as 1st Cl. Ships Cook, at Chicago.

PETERSON, Clarence C., 28, Rochester, farmer, son of Mr. and Mrs. Charles J. Peterson, entered service Sept. 20, 1917 at Rochester, trained at Camp Taylor, promoted private to corporal, Battery B, 325th F. A. 84th Div. Sailed April 9, 1918 and assigned to 5th Battery, F. A. Replacement Regiment. Mustered out July 29, 1919 at Camp Taylor.

PETERSON, Boyd, 21, Rochester, farmer, son of Charles J and Katy M. Peterson, entered service Oct. 1, 1918 at Bloomington, private Co. B, 41st Inf. S. A. T. C. Mustered out Dec. 21, 1918 at Bloomington.

PETERSON, Marvin Earl, 27, Rochester, laborer, son of Oscar and Sarah Peterson, entered service Dec. 11, 1917 at South Bend, trained at Ft. Thomas and Camp Taylor, promoted private to corporal to motor mechanic, 3rd Co. 3rd Rgt. Sailed July 4, 1918 and served in air service in France. Discharged July 1919.

PETERSON, Guy, 28, Rochester, laborer, son of Oscar and Sarah Peterson, entered service March 1, 1918 at South Bend, trained at Ft. Thomas, promoted private to corporal to sergeant, served as photographer and connected with General Hospital 42. Still in service.

PERSONETT, Kenneth Vane, 23, Akron, electrician, son of Ulysses and Rose Personett, entered service June 27, 1917, trained at Camp Taylor, promoted private to cadet, 31st Training Battery, F. A. C. O. T. S. Mustered out Nov. 26, 1918 at Camp Taylor.

PETERSON, Marvin E., 26, Rochester, rubber worker, son of Oscar and Sarah Peterson, entered service Dec. 9, 1917 at South Bend, trained at Ft. Thomas, promoted private to corporal, 3rd Company Mechanic Aviation Section, Regular Army. Sailed July 4, 1918, served as an aviator in France and took part in many air raids over German lines. Still in service.

POLEN, William, Jr., 29, Kewanna, mechanic. Entered service October 4, 1917 at Rochester. Trained at Camp Taylor. Assigned to Battery B, 325th F. A. 84th Div. Embarked from Hoboken, N. J., Sept. 9, 1918. Discharged Feb. 13, 1919.

POLEN, Vause, 34, Kewanna, Mgr. Dept. Store, married, son of William and Maria Polen. Entered service June 21, 1917 at Harrisburg, Pa. Trained at Camp Taylor. Served as Cook and Acting Mess Sergeant. Headquarters Co. F. A. R. D. Discharged Feb. 14, 1919 at Camp Taylor.

PALMER, Oswald, 22 Tiosa, farmer. Entered service March 28, 1918 at Rochester, trained at Camp Taylor, private Co. A, 111th Regt. 28th Div. Sailed May 5, 1918, trained at Boovelingham, France. In battle of Chateau Thierry, wounded and in hospitals at Paris, St. Nazaire and Blois. Discharged Jan. 16, 1919 at Camp Sherman.

PHILLIPS, Thomas, Augustus, 26, Tiosa, tobacco moulder, son of John T. and Lucy A. Phillips, entered service July 18, 1917 at St. Louis, Mo., trained at Paris Island and Guantanamo Bay, Cuba. Private Co. E. 13th Marines. Sailed Sept. 13, 1918 for skirmish duty in Cuba and France. Mustered out August 13, 1919 at Hampton Roads, Va.

PASSWATER, George, 18, Kewanna, farmer, entered service March 4, 1917 at Ft. Thomas, Ky. Trained at Carlstrom Field, Fla. Promoted from private to Sergeant First Class, 118th Aero Squadron. Served as pilot on target ship. Still in service.

PATTON, Benjamin Harrison, 17, Rochester, son of William and Pearl Patton, entered service March 15, 1917 at Ft. Thomas, Ky., trained at Douglas, Ariz., Chickamauga, Ga., Camp Upton, N. Y. Promoted from private to corporal to sergeant, Co. G. 52nd Inf., 6th Div. Sailed July 6, 1918, did gas and bayonet work. In battles in Geradmer sector, Vosges, Alsace-Lorraine, Meuse-Argonne offensive. Returned to U. S. June 6, 1919 and still in service.

PENSINGER, James Walter, 21, Grass Creek, agriculturist, son of Warren and Delia Pensinger, entered service Aug. 24, 1917, trained at Ft. Thomas, Kelly Field, Garden City, promoted from Private to Sergeant, 109th Aero Squadron. Sailed Dec. 10, 1917, 803rd Aero Squadron and Hdqrs. Detachment, Military Police and Motor Transportation, in battle of Chateau Thierry. Mustered out May 24, 1919 at Camp Sherman.

PRESSNALL, Earl Halderman, 24, Akron, pharmacist, son of Frank and Emma Pressnall, entered service June 16, 1918 at Fort Wayne, Ind., trained at Ft. Thomas, Gordon, Taylor, Harrison and Sherman. Private and pharmacist Medical Dept., 46th U. S. Inf. Mustered out March 8, 1919 at Camp Taylor.

PICKENS, Charles Omer, 20, Delong, farmer, son of Mrs. Schuyler Johnson, entered service May 8, 1917 at Rochester, trained at Ft. Thomas and Ft. Bliss. Private Med. Dept., 18th F. A., 3rd Div. Sailed April 21, 1918. In battles of Marne, St. Mihiel, Meuse-Argonne. Wounded Oct. 19, 1918 in the Meuse-Argonne offensive. Mustered out Aug. 25, 1919 at Camp Sherman.

POLLEY, Lloyd G., 28, Leiters Ford, railroader, son of George W. and Cora M. Polley. Entered service April 25, 1918 at Rochester, trained at Taylor and Washington Barracks. Sailed July 14, 1918 with Co. E, Reg. 11 Engrs., Div. 36, 1st Army Corps Engineers. Was in St. Mihiel and Meuse-Argonne offensives. Discharged June 12, 1919 at Camp Sherman.

RODEN, Harold, 21, Kewanna, laborer, son of Rollie and Emma Roden. Entered service Sept. 4, 1918, trained at Camp Taylor, West Point and Camp Knox. 70th F. A. Battery E. Mustered out May 4, 1919 at Camp Knox.

RIDDLE, George M., 22, Tiosa, teacher, entered service May 24, 1918 at Rochester, trained at Taylor, Greenleaf, Cape May and Upton, private and ward master in Base 115. Sailed August 15, 1918 with Base 115 and did hospital work in France. Mustered out May 19, 1919 at Camp Sherman.

ROGERS, Lester Clement, 22, married, Rochester, farmer, son of M. O. and Myrtle Rogers, entered service June 15, 1918 at Rochester, trained at Indianapolis, private Co. C, 129th M. G. Bn., 35th Div. Truck driver. Sailed Sept. 2, 1918 and trained in France for machine gun work. Mustered out May, 19, 1919 at Camp Taylor.

ROGERS, Hobart, 20, Rochester, medical student, son of Jonathan P. and Susan A. Rogers, entered service March 18, 1918 at Indianapolis, private medical section reserve corps, U. S. A. Mustered out Dec. 14, 1918 at Indianapolis.

REISH, Willis H., 22, Leiters Ford, signalman, son of Calvin W. and Lizzie E. Reish, entered service Sept. 3, 1918 at Camp Taylor. Trained there and at Ft. Benjamin Harrison. Private Co. C, 120th Engineers. Mustered out Dec. 17, 1919 at Ft. Harrison.

RHODES, Sumner Jefferson, 31, Rochester, carpenter, entered service April 22, 1918 at Rochester, trained at Ft. Hamilton and Ft. Wadsworth, promoted private first class, Bat. D, 70th C. A. C. Sailed July 15, 1918. Mustered out Feb. 22, 1919 at Camp Sherman.

ROSS, Walter D., 21, Rochester, mechanic, son of William P. and Anna A. Ross, entered service Nov. 29, 1917 at Indianapolis, trained at Ft. Thomas and Kelly Field, private served as instructor Air Service, Mechanical School. Mustered out Feb. 18, 1919 at Camp Taylor.

ROSS, Herold T., 22, Rochester, student, son of Mr. and Mrs. Omer T. Ross, entered service Jan. 10, 1918 at Rochester, trained at Camps Jackson and Hancock. Promoted from private to Sgt. first class. Sailed Aug. 24, 1918. Headquarters First Army Corps, Office Chief Ordnance Officer. In Meuse-Argonne offensive. Mustered out Aug. 2, 1919 at Camp Mills.

RUH, Harold Oliver, 33, Cleveland, O., physician, son of Mr. and Mrs. Alex Ruh, Rochester, entered service May 1917 at Cleveland, trained at Allentown, Pa., and Camp Dix, N. J. Sailed May 20, 1918. Promoted to 1st Lt. to Capt. to Major. Did laboratory work Base Hospital 117. Married to Miss Edith Caldwell, Cleveland nurse of the Youngstown Unit, Jan. 8, 1919 at Orleans, France. First American couple married there. Still in service Central Lab., Hospital Center A. P. O. 731.

ROBBINS, Fred T., 22, Rochester, student, son of Mr. and Mrs. C. E. Robbins, entered service Oct. 15, 1917 at Indianapolis, trained at Boston, Mass., and made Ensign C. Q. M., in the aviation branch of the navy. Sailed Oct. 16, 1918 and did coast patrol and convoying from Killingholme, England, on the North Sea. Discharged March 26, 1919 at Great Lakes.

RICHMOND, Roy D., 19, Rochester, electrician, son of Charles and Lulu Richmond, entered service April 15, 1919 at Rochester, trained at Ft. Dupont, promoted to corporal, special positions of observer, plotter and reader, Battery D., 74th Artillery, C. A. C. Sailed Sept. 22, 1918. Mustered out Jan. 8, 1919, Camp Sherman, Ohio.

RICHARD, Russell B., 18, Rochester, laborer, son of Charles J. and M. E. Richard, entered service Dec. 13, 1917 at Jefferson Barracks, Mo., trained at Camp Johnston, made private of first class and did salvage work in 19th Salvage Squad. Sailed June 30, 1918. In Vosges defense and Somme drive. Discharged June 30, 1919 at Camp Taylor.

REITER, David Laurimer, 34, Rochester, auto mechanic, son of Marion C. and Estelle Reiter, entered service Sept. 21, 1918 at Rochester, trained at Camps Polk and Green, promoted from private to sergeant, Co. C, 308th Bn. Served as tank mechanic. Mustered out Jan. 5, 1919 at Camp Taylor.

REES, Myron T., 22, Rochester, student, son of Milton O. and Margaret Rees, entered service Oct. 23, 1918 at Camp Taylor. Candidate, 53rd Training Battery, F. A., C. O. T. S. Mustered out Dec. 2, 1918 at Camp Taylor.

REES, Charles C., 27, Rochester, horticulture, son of Milton O. and Margaret Rees, entered service May 11, 1917 at Ft. Benj. Harrison, after training made Capt. Field Artillery, commanding Battery B, 325th F. A. Sailed Sept. 9, 1918. Trained at Camp De Souge, France. Mustered out March 3, 1919 at Camp Taylor.

REDMOND, Walter I., 19, Fulton, son of Willis E. and Lillie W. Redmond, entered service June 1, 1914 at Monticello, Ind. Trained at Ft. Harrison and Newport News, Va., promoted from private to 1st class private and sergeant. Sailed Feb. 3, 1918, Battery A. Ind. 150 Field Artillery, 42nd Div. (Rainbow Division), in battles of Chateau Thierry, St. Mihiel and Meuse-Argonne. Discharged Nov. 14, 1919 at Camp Dix.

SWIHART, Frank, Akron, electrician, son of E. L. and Anna M. Swihart. Lieutenant. Overseas. No other information furnished.

SWIHART, Russell Everett, 23, Tiosa, laborer, son of Mrs. Della Markley, entered service July 23, 1918 at Plymouth, trained at Camp McClellen, private Co. C, 12th Ammunition Train, 12th Div. Discharged Feb. 20, 1919.

STATON, George Jefferson, 23, Brook, Ind., student, married, son of Frank and Elizabeth Staton, Rochester, entered service May 19, 1918 at Kentland, Ind., trained at Camp Johnston, promoted private to Sgt. to Sgt. Major, M. T. C. 441. Sailed with 1st Army Corps July 10, 1918 and served as convoy Sgt. and dispatcher. In action at Chateau Thierry, St. Mihiel and Argonne. Received seven machine gun bullets in right ankle, Aug. 9, 1918 and gassed Sept. 13, 1918. Still in service.

SNYDER, Jesse LeRoy, 21, Rochester, farmer, son of William and Elizabeth Snyder, entered service June 4, 1918 at Rochester, trained at Camp Taylor. Private, 13th Inf. R. A.

SMITH, Grover C., 25, Rochester, mechanic, son of Marshall and Anna Smith, entered service July 2, 1917 at Plymouth, trained at Ft. Harrison, promoted private to corporal and served as truck driver Co. B, 118th Ammunition Train. Sailed Sept. 1917 and served as truck driver. Discharged Aug. 8, 1919 at Camp Sherman.

SMITH, Lowell E., 23, Rochester, laborer, son of Julius E. and Louisa E. Smith, entered service March 29, 1918 at Kokomo, trained at Taylor, Greenleaf and Jackson, private 159th Depot Brigade, R. A. Mustered out June 27, 1919 at Camp Sherman.

SAWSON, Earl J., 22, Leiters Ford, farmer, son of Robert and Emma Sawson, entered service Sept. 20, 1917 at Rochester, trained at Camps Taylor and Shelby, private Hdqrs. Troop, 3rd Div. 3rd Army. Sailed June 4, 1918, participated in battles of Chemin Des Dames June 27 to July 5, 1918; Marne July 15 to 18; Aisne-Marne July 18 to August 6; H. P. Aug. 18 to Sept. 6; St. Mihiel Sept. 12 to 16; Meuse-Argonne Sept. 26 to Nov. 11. Mustered out Aug. 29, 1919 at Camp Sherman.

SWANGO, Frank, 26, Rochester, farmer, son of William and Harriet Swango, entered service March 12, 1918 at Rochester, trained at Ft. Hancock, Camp Eustis and Newport News, private Battery D, 50th Regt., C. A. C. Sailed Sept. 14, 1918. Mustered out March 5, 1919 at Camp Sherman.

SMITH, Noble, 18, Rochester, R. R. ticket agt., son of Marshall and Anna Smith, entered service Dec. 2, 1917 at Kokomo, trained at Camp Greene, promoted private to corporal to sergeant. Sailed June 27, 1918 and served as clerk in Hdqrs. Office, 3rd Motor Mechanic Air Service. Discharged July 12, 1919 at New York.

SMILEY, Glen, 23, Rochester, farmer, son of Mr. and Mrs. Milton Smiley, entered service April 8, 1917 at Rochester, trained at Ft. Thomas, Ft. Hancock, 3rd O. T. C., Camps Lee, Custer and Sherman, promoted private to Sgt., to 2nd Lt., to 1st Lt. Served as drill instructor. Mustered out Jan. 31, 1919 at Camp Sherman.

SHELTON, Ray, 23, Rochester, teacher, son of P. Eugene and Aletha Shelton, entered service March 28, 1918 at Rochester, trained at Camp Taylor, private Co. A, 111th Inf., 28th Div. Sailed May 5, 1918. In battle of Chateau Thierry. Gassed and removed to Hospital at Contrexville. Discharged April 14, 1919 at Camp Sherman.

SHELTON, Ralph, 22, Rochester, farmer, son of P. Eugene and Aletha Shelton, entered service June 23, 1918 at Rochester, trained at Camp McClellan, promoted private to wagoner Supply Co., 35th Regt., 12th Div. Mustered out March 8, 1919 at Camp Taylor.

SUTHERLAND, Harry Holden, 24, Rochester, electrician, son of Edward H. and Lola M. Sutherland, entered service April 21, 1917 at Gary, Ind., trained at Camps Jackson, Shelby, Meade and Merritt, promoted to corporal, Co. F, 151st Inf. Nat. Guard, trans. Co. A, 1st Eng. Sailed March 28, 1918 with 301st Heavy Tank Battalion. In Somme offensive Aug. 8, Canal Tunnel Bouey, Sept. 29, Brancourt Oct. 8, LaSalle river Oct. 17, Botse L'Eveque Oct. 23 to Nov. 4. Mustered out April 9, 1919 at Camp Sherman.

STOCKBERGER, Dennis D., 23, Rochester, hardware dealer, son of Joel and Alma A. Stockberger, entered service Sept. 20, 1917 at Rochester, trained at Camp Taylor, promoted private to sergeant. Had charge of plumbing and heating supply house, Utilities Constr. Div. Det. Q. M. C. Discharged March 7, 1919 at Camp Taylor.

STINSON, Max James, 27, Rochester, pipe fitter, son of Mrs. Almeda Stinson, entered service June 17, 1918 at Boston, Mass., made 1st Boatswains Mate and did convoy work. In August 1918 two boats in fleet were torpedoed on the same day in the Bay of Biscay, the Montana and Westbridge. Montana was sunk. Mustered out April 11, 1919 at Hoboken, N. J.

STETSON, Joia Ray, 20, Rochester, clerk, son of Frank M. and Myrtle C. Stetson, entered service Oct. 14, 1918 at Rochester, trained at Camp Purdue, Truck Driver Co. C. Discharged Dec. 14, 1918.

STERNER, Howard Stanton, 22, Rochester, student, son of Frank M. and Elizabeth E. Sterner, entered service Aug. 21, 1917 at Ft. Benjamin Harrison, made 1st Lt., Co. A, 335th Regt., 89th Div. Sailed June 4, 1918 and served as Assistant Division Adjutant. Mustered out August 4, 1919 at Camp Sherman.

STEFFEY, Ernest, 23, Rochester, barber, son of Frank and Almina Steffey, entered service Dec. 3, 1917 at Elkhart, Ind., trained at Ft. Thomas, Ft. Wood and Camp Gray. Promoted private to Sgt., Depot Co. H, Signal Corps. Discharged March 15, 1919 at Atlanta, Ga.

STANLEY, John Allen, 34, married, Rochester, truck driver, son of Frank and Ada Stanley, entered service June 22, 1918 at Rochester, trained at Jefferson Barracks, Ft. Totten, Ft. Monroe and Camp Eustis. Made Sgt., C. A. C., 41st Brigade. Served as instructor in auto school. Mustered out Dec. 22, 1918 at Camp Sherman.

STACY, Russell Maddux, 20, Rochester, student, son of William H. and Ida V. Stacy, entered service Oct. 12, 1918 at Purdue University. Private Co. 2, U. S. Inf. S. A. T C. Mustered out Dec. 19, 1918 at Purdue.

SOWERS, William H., 21, Rochester, electrician, son of Winfield S. and Nattie Sowers, entered service July 21, 1917 at Ft. Wayne, Ind., trained at Ft. Leavenworth, Kan. Private, promoted to corporal, to sergeant, Co. C., 5th Field Battalion, served as lineman in Signal Corps. Sailed Feb. 1, 1918, saw active service in battles of Chateau Thierry June 4 to July 30, St. Mihiel Sept. 10 to 14, Meuse-Argonne Sept. 6 to Oct. 29. On Nov. 16, started on march to Rhine and arrived Dec. 10, 1918. Mustered out August 30, 1919.

SNYDER, Arthur, 21, Rochester, locomotive fireman, son of Mr. and Mrs. Joseph Snyder, entered service Sept. 19, 1917 at Rochester, trained at Camp Taylor, promoted private to corporal, Bat. B, 120th F. A. Sailed April 8, 1918, participated in battles Haute-Alsace June 8 to July 10; Aisne-Marne, July 11 to Sept. 22; Oise-Aisne Sept. 23 to 31; Ourcq Sept. 31 to Oct. 10; Meuse-Argonne Oct. 10 to Nov. 7. Mustered out May 21, 1919 at Camp Taylor.

SMITH, Gerald Percy, 24, Rochester, banking, son of Omar B. and Lelia C. Smith, entered service at Ft. Benj. Harrison, May 13, 1917, trained at Camp Taylor, Camp Johnston and Zone Supply Office, Washington, D. C. Commissioned 2nd Lt., promoted to 1st Lt., Aug. 8, 1918, officer in charge of Sales and Issue Branch, Depot Quartermaster, Washington, D. C., charge of Washington Commissary and Commanding Officer, Detachment Q. M. Corps, 12th and E. streets, Washington, D. C. Mustered out March 7, 1919, Washington.

SHRIVER, Everett E., 27, married, Rochester, accountant, son of Oliver and Rose B. Shriver, entered service July 1, 1917, promoted private to corporal and did clerical work with Hdq. Det., 2nd Regt., 164th Depot Brigade. Mustered out Dec. 8, 1918, at Camp Funston, Kansas.

SHRIVER, Charles Edward, 17, Rochester, farmer, son of Mr. and Mrs. James W. Shriver, entered service Jan. 3, 1916 at Rochester, trained at Ft. Sam Houston and Eagle Pass, Texas. Private Headquarters Co., 26th Inf. Still in service.

SISSON, Earl LeRoy, 30, Rochester, telegrapher, son of Chas. D. and Jennie E. Sisson, entered service May 5, 1917 at Toledo, O., trained at Camps Sheridan and Perry, made 2nd Lt. Co. A, 112th Field Signal Bn. Sailed June 23, 1918. Participated in actions at Baccarat (Vosges) Aug. 1 to Sept. 15; Avacourt (Verdun) Sept. 21 to 25; Meuse-Argonne Sept. 26 to Oct. 1; St. Mihiel, Oct. 6 to 17; Ypres-Lys Oct. 31 to Nov. 11. Decorated with the French Croix de Guerre by Gen Petain at St. Mars Sous Ballon, France, Feb. 6, 1919 for maintenance of liason, Argonne-Meuse offensive. Personal citation by Maj. Gen. Farnsworth, Order No. 86, Headquarters 37th Div., at Chateau de Huysse, Belgium, Dec. 24, 1918, for meritorious service Ypres-Lys offensive. Part of Guard of Honor for the King and Queen of Belgium upon their return to Brussells, Nov. 1918. Mustered out April 12, 1919 at Camp Sherman.

SHRIVER, Charles E., 28, Rochester, son of James Shriver. Entered Regular Army Jan. 14, 1917 at Columbus, O., trained at Eagle Pass, Texas, Private B 3rd Inf., transferred to 26th Inf. 1st Div. Brigade Citation. Embarked from Hoboken, N. J. June 13, 1917. Participated in battles Luneville sector defenses Oct. 21 to Nov. 20, 1917; Toul sector March 2 to March 24, 1917; Mount St. Die June 9th to June 18th, 1918, Soissons July 18th to 23rd; St. Mihiel Sept. 12th to 16th; Meuse-Argonne Sept. 26th to Oct. 9th and on front when armistice was signed. Discharged Sept. 17, 1919.

SHIPLEY, Frank Wendell, 19, Rochester, student, son of Miller O. and Alice S. Shipley, entered service Oct. 12, 1918 at Purdue University, private Co. 4, U. S. Inf., S. A. T. C. Mustered out Dec. 19, 1918 at Purdue.

SEWELL, Guy E., 18, Rochester, son of Andrew and Jessie Sewell, entered service Jan. 26, 1918 at Indianapolis, promoted from private to corporal, 89th M. G. Co., Camp Sumner, D. C. Discharged March 1919.

SEIGFRIED, P. A., 31, married, Rochester salesman, son of Jos. F. and Mary B. Siegfried, entered service July 22, 1918, at Rochester, trained at Camp Taylor, made Battery Clerk 3rd Bat. F. A. Sailed Oct. 26, 1918. Mustered out May 15, 1919 at Camp Taylor.

SEE, Gordon Earle, 19, Rochester, laborer, son of Mr. and Mrs. Charles See, entered service April 19, 1917 at Rochester, trained at Columbus Barracks, Kelly Field, Ft. Totten, 1st Class Private, 31st Aero Squadron. Sailed Aug. 23, 1917. Chauffeur. Discharged June 8, 1919 at Camp Sherman.

STINGLEY, Clarence Grover, 30, Fulton, postmaster, son of Jacob and Sadie A. Stingley, entered service July 1, 1918 at Rochester, trained at Camps at Valparaiso, Ind. and Burlington, Vt., Private 46th Service Co. Signal Corps, transferred to 428 Telegraph R. R. Bn. Co. D Signal Corps. Mustered out Jan. 20, 1919 at Camp Taylor.

SHAW, Harland, 25, Grass Creek, farmer, son of Francis and Elizabeth Shaw, entered service Sept. 1, 1918 at Rochester, trained at Ft. Harrison, private, Co. D. Mustered out Dec. 16, 1918 at Ft. Harrison.

SNYDER, Clarence Ray, 27, Fulton, student, entered service September 20, 1917 at Rochester, private, Battery A. 325th F. A., trained at Camp Taylor, transferred to Air Service, Kelly Field, San Antonio, Texas, 256th Aero Squadron, Ward, Texas, Field No. 2, Garden City. Mustered out March 24, 1919 at Camp Sherman.

SHEETZ, Joseph, 27, Kewanna, farmer, son of John B. and Mary G. Sheetz, entered service Aug. 1918 at Camp Taylor. Private.

SNYDER, Merlin W., 18, Kewanna, farmer, son of Peter and Lucinda Snyder, entered service May 25, 1917 at Rochester, trained at Nogales, Ariz., and Camp Travis, Texas. Promoted private to corporal, Co. F, 35th U. S. Inf. Served on Mexican border duty and in Mexican skirmish at Nogales, Aug. 28, 1918. Mustered out Feb. 14, 1919 at Camp Grant.

STANLEY, Russell George, 26, Rochester, son of Frank and Ada Stanley of Liberty township, entered service April 25, 1918 at Rochester, trained at Camp Taylor and Washington, D. C., promoted private to wagoner Supply Co., 339th Inf., 85th Division. Sailed July 23, 1918. Discharged July 14, 1919 at Camp Taylor.

SCULL, James A., 50, Rochester, druggist, son of James A. and Emma Y. Scull, entered service Jan. 30, 1915 at Camp Meyer, Va. Promoted to 1st Lt. Aug. 22, 1917, to Captain Jan. 6, 1918, to Major March 3, 1919. Served as Supply Officer General Hospital No. 1, 1917, Medical Supply Officer, 1st Army, France, 1918, Medical Supply Officer, 3rd Army, 1919. In charge of Army Medical Supplies. Sailed June 30, 1918. In St. Mihiel and Argonne offensives. On duty in office of Surgeon General of the Army, Washington, D. C.

SNIDER, Byron, 19, Akron, student, son of A. R. and Mary Belle Snider, entered service Oct. 1, 1918 at Bloomington, Ind., Private Co. B., S. A. T. C. Mustered out Dec. 21, 1918 at Bloomington.

SAUSAMAN, Clifford Guy, 28, Hammond, Ind., railroad fireman, married, son of Thomas J. and Florence M. Sausaman, entered service July 23, 1918 at Valparaiso, Ind. Trained at Camp Taylor, promoted private to sergeant, 81st Engineers. Sailed but was returned on account of influenza. Mustered out Dec. 23, 1918 at Camp Taylor.

SWIHART Oren Melvin, 20, Tiosa, son of David C. and Mollie C. Swihart, entered service May 28, 1918 at Great Lakes, trained there with Co. L, 7th Regt. Mustered out June 31, 1919 at Great Lakes.

SWARTWOOD, Fred, 28, married, Rochester, machinist, son of Samuel and Susan Swartwood, entered service Dec. 11, 1917 at Ft. Thomas, trained at Taylor and Hancock, made private first class, 17th Co., 2nd Regt., A. S. M. Sailed March 14, 1918 with Air Service Mechanics and did camouflaging in France. Discharged June 8, 1919 at Camp Sherman.

SCHIRM, Charles Ammon, 21, Kewanna, Ind., farmer, son of John and Minnie Schirm. Entered service Oct. 14, 1914 by joining the C. A. C., assigned to 51st Co., promoted to corporal March 26, 1916. August 22, 1917 was ordered to Second Officers Training Camp at Plattsburg, N. Y., and on completion of three months course was commissioned 2nd Lt. of Infantry and assigned to 10th Co. 3rd Training Battalion, 153rd Depot Brigade, later to Co. M., 312th Inf. Sailed May 21, 1918, and trained with British. Was in battles of St. Mihiel, Sept. 16 to Oct. 5; Grand Pre, second phase of the Meuse-Argonne offensive Oct. 20 to 27, and last phase of the Meuse-Argonne offensive Nov. 1 to 11. Transferred to 81st Div. for further service, later to 5th Div. Army of Occupation, and still later to Co. M., 61st U. S. Inf. Discharged at Camp Taylor, Aug. 20, 1919.

SCHIRM, Elza Newton, 21, Kewanna, farmer, son of John and Minnie Schirm. Entered service Sept. 4, 1918 at Rochester. Trained at Camps Taylor and Knox. Served as cannoneer Battery C 72nd F. A. Mustered out at Camp Knox, Feb. 4, 1919.

SCHIRM, John Edward, 22, Kewanna, farmer, son of John and Minnie M. Schirm. Entered service at Rochester, Ind., May 24, 1918. Trained at Camp Taylor, Ky., Camp Greenleaf, Ga., Cape May, N. J., Camp Upton, N. Y. Did photography and nursing, Base Hospital 115, 2nd Army Corps. Went overseas August 16, 1918 and was connected with hospital work. Mustered out May 17, 1919 at Camp Sherman, Ohio.

SEARS, Charles, 31, Kewanna, laborer, son of Henry and Ella Sears, entered service Sept. 21, 1917 at Kewanna, trained at Camps Taylor and Sevier, private Hdqrs. Co. 115th F. A. Sailed June 4, 1918. In defensive north of Toul Aug. 28 to Sept. 10, 1918; St. Mihiel offensive Sept. 11 to 13; Argonne Sept. 25 to Oct. 5; Valley of Woevre Oct. 10 to Nov. 11. Mustered out April 18, 1919 at Camp Taylor.

SHINE, Ermal Neville, 24, Kewanna, farmer. Entered service April 25, 1918 at Rochester, trained at Camp Taylor and Washington Barracks. Made First Class Private. 11th Engineers. Sailed July 14, 1918, trained at Angers, France and assigned to Co. E, 1st Replacement Reg. Eng. Participated in battles on St. Mihiel sector; Meuse-Argonne offensive. In service.

SNYDER, Loyd Elmer, Blue Grass, Ind., 23, farmer, son of Jacob S. and Clara Snyder, entered service at Rochester, April 25, 1918, trained at Washington Barracks. Co. D, First Replacement Regiment of Engineers. Sailed September 1, 1918 and served in Co. A, 303rd Engineers, 78th Division, 1st Army Corps. Was in the Meuse-Argonne offensive from October 16 to November 5, 1918. Mustered out June 17, 1919 at Camp Sherman, Ohio.

SNYDER, Orville M., 22, Kewanna, farmer, son of Jacob S. and Clara Snyder. Entered service May 21, 1918. Trained at Columbus Barracks, Ohio, Ft. Snelling, Minn., and Camp Devens, Mass. Private Co. A, 36th Inf. Mustered out at Camp Taylor April 5, 1919.

STAMM, Charles Henry, 18, Kewanna, farmer, son of Jesse M. and Cora M. Stamm, entered service April 26, 1917 at Columbus Barracks, O., trained at Ft. Williams, promoted private to corporal Bat. F, 51st C. A. C. Sailed Aug. 14, 1917, served as chauffeur with Bat. C, 51st C. A. C. In St. Mihiel offensive, and bombardment of German positions on Bois de Grant Portion, Oct. 21 to 24. Mustered out Feb. 25, 1919 at Columbus Barracks.

SANNS, Charles J., 21, Akron, railroader, son of William and Mae Sanns, entered service June 25, 1917 at Ft. Wayne, Ind., trained at Ft. Thomas and Ft. Leavenworth, promoted private to corporal, Co. C, 5th Field Bn., Signal Corps, 38th Regt. Sailed Feb. 27, 1918. In second battle of the Marne, Jaulgonne, Vesle, St. Mihiel offensive and Argonne. Mustered out Feb. 28, 1919 at Camp Sherman.

SHIVELY, Noah, 29, Akron, farmer, son of William and Mary E. Shively, entered service Sept. 4, 1918 at Rochester, trained at Camps Taylor and Jackson, private Bat. B, 18th Regt., F. A. R. D. Discharged Dec. 23, 1918 at Camp Jackson.

SMITH, Gernie, E., 28, Akron, blacksmith, son of Irwin E. and Jannie Smith, entered service Sept. 4, 1917 at Rochester, trained at Camp Taylor, private 103rd Co., F. A., 35th Eng. Sailed March 30, 1918 with 13th, Grand, Div., worked at box car building in France. Discharged July 8, 1919 at Camp Sherman.

SANNS, James E., 30, Rochester, railroader, son of Mr. and Mrs. Peter Sanns. Entered service March 28, 1918 at Rochester, trained at Camp Taylor. Private Co. A. 111th Ind., 28th Div. Sailed April 25, 1918. In Chateau Thierry battle, wounded by shrapnel. Mustered out at Camp Grant, March 18, 1919.

THOMPSON, Jacob F., 30, Newcastle township, laborer, son of Samuel F. and Eliza Ann Thompson, entered service May 25, 1918 at Rochester, trained at Camps Taylor, Oglethorpe, Chattanooga, Tenn., and Newport News, Va. Served as hospital nurse and still in service. Ill as this is written (January 1920) at Camp Dix Base Hospital.

TONER, Albert Worth, 23, Delong, son of Albert D. and Jessie M. Toner. Entered service March 15, 1918 at Rochester, trained at Columbus Barracks and Ft. McKinley, Me., sailed August 1918 with Battery D, 72nd C. A. C. Served as instructor in auto school at Limogese, France. Mustered out April 1919, at Camp Grant.

THOMPSON, Alva Nathan, 24, Argos, farmer, son of Mr. and Mrs. Isaac H. Thompson, entered service at Rochester, Sept. 20, 1917, trained at Taylor, promoted to Corporal, Bat. E., 325th F. A. Sailed Sept. 8 1918 with 84th Div. Discharged March 1, 1919 at Camp Taylor.

TAYLOR, Frank, 28, Akron, born in Austria-Hungary, entered service Dec. 12, 1917 at Rochester, trained at Ft. Monroe, Camp Stuart, made 1st class private Co. F, 60th Coast Artillery. Sailed April 23, 1918, served as telephone lineman. Participated in St. Mihiel offensive Aug. 12 to 15, Verdun-Argonne Oct. 25 to Nov. 11. Wounded in left foot by high explosive at Somerance Oct. 28. Discharged March 19, 1919 at Camp Taylor.

THOMAS, Dewey, 18, Mentone, farmer, foster son of C. E. and E. E. King, entered service May 2, 1917, trained at Ft. Thomas, private Co. B, Military Police, Cristobel Canal Zone, Panama. Still in service.

THRUSH, Lotus Troy, 21, Kokomo, Ind., clerical, son of Mrs. Mary E. Foster, entered service Sept. 4, 1918 at Kokomo, private 15th Co. 4th Battalion 159th Depot Brigade. Mustered out Nov. 12, 1918 at Camp Taylor.

TRANBARGER, Emmett S., 21, Rochester, farmer, son of Dorus W. and Estella J. Tranbarger, entered service June 11, 1918 at Indianapolis, trained at Great Lakes, landsman, Machinist's Mate, Aviation Branch U. S. Naval Reserve Force. Discharged Feb. 16, 1919 at Great Lakes.

TYRELL, William E., 18, Rochester, farmer, son of Mr. and Mrs. Peter Redmond, entered service Sept. 12, 1917 at Lafayette, Ind., trained at Jefferson Barracks, Ft. Sheridan and Camp Greene. Private. Sailed May 1, 1918. Co. E., 16th Regt. Served as supply cab driver and in American offensives. Now with Army of Occupation at Kelberg, Germany.

TERRY, Lyon F., 26, Rochester, Civ. Eng., son of Frank H. and Gertrude Terry. Entered service June 5, 1918 at Rochester, Ind., trained at West Point, Ky., and Camp Taylor, promoted from private to 2nd Lt., 85th F. A. Discharged Dec. 11, 1918 at Camp Sheridan.

TAYLOR, Harley Wilbert, 41, married, Rochester, physician and surgeon, entered service July 25, 1918 at Ft. Benj. Harrison, trained at Camp Greenleaf, Ga. 1st Lt. Surgeon 429th Rev. Lab. Bn. Discharged Dec. 30, 1918 at Newport News, Va.

TAYLOR, Guy Hubert, 22, Rochester, student, son of Charles F. and Estelle Taylor, entered service April 3, 1918, trained at Fort Totten, promoted from private to 1st class private, 15th Co. C. A. C., Chauffeurs Training Detachment. Sailed July 14, 1918. Spent entire time in Base Hospital 27 at Angers. Discharged Feb. 20, 1919 at Camp Sherman.

UTTER, Franklin H., 31, married, Akron, farmer, son of David and Eliza Utter, entered service Aug. 29, 1918 at Warsaw, Ind., trained at Camp Custer, made 1st class private Co. B, 214th F. S. Bn. Discharged Jan. 19, 1919 at Camp Custer.

VAN KIRK, John Albert, 27, married, Leiters Ford, physician, son of John W. and Ellen Van Kirk, entered service at Watseka, Ill., June 8, 1917. 1st Lt., Battalion Surgeon, Commanding Officer Medical Detachment, 342nd Machine Gun Bat. Sailed June 3, 1918, served with Medical Detachment 89th Div. and 32nd French Corp. Participated in battles in Lucy sector Aug. 7 to Sept.11, St. Mihiel offensive Sept. 11 to 15, Eurezin sector Sept. 16 to Oct. 10, Meuse-Argonne offensive Oct. 19 to Nov. 11. Discharged June 10, 1919

VAN KIRK, George H., 29, married, Kentland, Ind., physician, son of J. W. and Ellen Van Kirk, Leiters Ford, entered service April 19, 1918 at Chicago, trained at Camps Greenleaf and Dix. Captain and Regimental Surgeon 807th P. Inf. Sailed Sept. 4, 1918 and served with Medical Division in Meuse-Argonne offensive. Mustered out August 7, 1919 at Camp Grant.

VICKERY, Dean K., 21, Akron, married, electrician, son of Joseph J. and Geneva Vickery, entered service June 5, 1917 at Cleveland, Ohio, trained at Camp Sherman, promoted to corporal, 30th Co. 8th Training Battalion, 158th D. B. Mustered out Jan. 1919 at Camp Sherman.

VAN CLEAVE, Jesse Newton, 21, Kewanna, student, son of Sherman and Dora Van Cleave. Entered service Sept. 24, 1917 at Bismarck, N. D. Trained at Jefferson Barracks, Mo., and Ft. Sill, Okla. Promoted from private to Corporal, School of Fire, Motor Transport Detachment. Also served as chauffeur. Mustered out Feb. 15, 1919 at Ft. Dodge, Iowa.

WALTERS, Gerald, 21, Rochester, farmer, son of Henry H. and Sophia M. Walters, entered service June 14, 1918 at Rochester, trained at Camps Humphrey and Forest, private Co. F, 15th Regt. Sailed Sept. 28, 1918 with 401st Engineers and did guard duty overseas. Mustered out Jan. 29, 1919 at Camp Sherman.

WHITACRE, Walter Wilson, 18, Delong, student, son of Mr. and Mrs. C. D. Whitacre, entered service Feb. 28, 1918 at Indianapolis, trained at Kelly and Carlstrom Fields. Private 205th Aero Squadron. Mustered out June 20, 1919 at Camp Taylor.

WAGONER, Amos, 24, Delong, farmer, son of John J. and Mary A. Wagoner, entered service May 21, 1918 at Rochester, trained at Ft. Snelling and Camp Devens, promoted to first Class private, Co. M., 73rd Inf. Mustered out Feb. 10, 1919 at Camp Taylor.

WILFERT, Clyde Edwin, 23, Delong, farmer, son of Wolfgang and Fidella Wilfert, entered service May 25, 1918 at Rochester, trained at Taylor and Greenleaf, promoted to private of first class. Served overseas with Base Hospital 115, A. E. F. Mustered out May 12, 1919 at Camp Sherman.

WALTZ, Jesse James, 22, Rochester, farmer, son of William M. and Cora E. Waltz, entered service April 30, 1918 at Rochester, trained at Ft. Thomas and Camp Forrest, made first class private, Co. A., 52nd Regt. Sailed July 6, 1918 with 6th Div. 1st Army Corps, and took part in fighting on Alsace line and in Meuse-Argonne offensive. Discharged June 18, 1919 at Camp Sherman.

WEIR, James Harold, 29, Rochester, farmer, son of George W. and Sarah Weir, entered service May 21, 1918 at Rochester, trained at Columbus Barracks and Camp Custer. 1st Class Private, Co. E, 10th Inf., 14th Div. Discharged Jan. 17, 1917 at Camp Custer.

WRIGHT, Ralph, 21, Tiosa, farmer, son of George and Lura Wright, entered service July 12, 1918, trained at Ft. Wayne, Mich., and Ft. Benj. Harrison, private 3rd Aerial Squadron. Mustered out Jan. 30, 1919 at Ft. Wayne, Mich.

WYNN, William, 22, Rochester, farmer, son of William and Martha Wynn, entered service Sept. 3, 1918 at Rochester, trained at Camp Knox, private 72nd F. A., Battery C. Mustered out Jan. 30, 1919 at Camp Knox.

WADE, Claude, 24, Akron, baker, son of Mr. and Mrs. Canada Wade, entered service July 7, 1918 at Rochester. Sailed Sept. 1, 1918 with Co. K, 21st Engineers, L. R. Mustered out July 12, 1919 at Camp Sherman.

WHALLON, Evan A., 23, Akron, veterinary, son of Henry A. and Viola B. Whallon, entered service Aug. 15, 1917 at Chicago. Made 2nd Lt., and served in purchase of government animals. Discharged Feb. 8, 1919 at Camp Custer.

WRIGHT, Odis Jay, 29, Kewanna, laborer, son of Thomas and Ada Wright. Entered service April 2, 1918 at Rochester. Trained at Forts Hamilton and Tilden. Promoted to First Class Private and served as Sergeant Fireman of C. A. C. and as mine layer. Still in service.

WHARTON, Harmon, 34, Kewanna, mechanic, son of William M. and Nettie Wharton. Entered service April 30, 1917 at DeKalb, Ill. Trained at Camp Logan, Texas. Promoted from private to Corporal, Co. A., 129th Inf. Sailed May 10, 1918. Mustered out July 15, 1919 at Camp Grant.

WEST, Neal Moore, 19, Kewanna, student, son of Mrs. Pearl West. Entered service August 9, 1917 at Indianapolis, trained at Camp Shelby. Sailed May 12, 1918, Battery A, 321st, F. A., 82nd Div. In the St. Mihiel and Meuse-Argonne battles. In service at Calvary, Texas.

WARFIELD, George E., 21, Kewanna, farmer, son of Mr. and Mrs. John T. Warfield, entered service Sept. 4, 1917, trained at Camps Shelby and Taylor, private Supply Co., 18th Inf., 1st Div. Sailed June 12, 1918. In St. Mihiel offensive Sept. 12, Argonne Forest Sept. 30 to Oct. 12, Sedan front Oct 19. Near Metz when armistice was signed and with Army of Occupation in Germany. Mustered out Oct. 4, 1919 at Camp Taylor.

WARE, James M., 29, Kewanna, farmer, son of Henry and Anna Ware, entered service Oct. 4, 1917 at Rochester, trained at Camp Taylor, promoted from Private to Corporal, Battery B., 325th F. A. Sailed Sept. 8, 1918, did Radio work. Mustered out Feb. 13, 1919 at Camp Taylor.

WAITE, Earl Leo, 32, Rochester, physician and surgeon, son of Joseph H. and Marietta H. Waite, entered service August 2, 1917, trained at Ft. Benjamin Harrison and Camp Upton, made 1st Lt., Medical Corps, Regular Army. Mustered out March 22, 1918.

WYLIE, George Henry, 18, Rochester, student, son of Robert and Etta Wylie, entered service Oct. 11, 1918 at Purdue University. Private Naval Reserve Co. S. A. T. C. Discharged Dec. 20, 1918 at Purdue.

WRIGHT, Marcus, 20, Rochester, radio operator, son of Jacob and Malinda Wright, entered service, April 13, 1917 at Ft. Thomas Ky., trained at Ft. Leavenworth, Kelly Field, Aviation Depot, L. I., School of Military Aeronautics, N. Y., Ellington Field, promoted from private to 2nd Lt., as flying instructor Ellington Field, and Squadron Commander, Sergeant Major of Post, Aviation Depot, L. I. Still in service.

WISE, Clyde L., 31, Rochester, pharmacist, son of John F. and Amaretta E. Wise, entered service Dec. 6, 1917 at Ft. Thomas, Ky., trained there and promoted to first class private, instructed class in pharmacy, 42nd Field Hospital, also served in Dispensary. Mustered out Feb. 26, 1919 at Jacksonville, Florida.

WILLARD, Daniel, 19, Rochester, vulcanizer, son of Charles and Bertha Willard, entered service March 22, 1917 at Ft. Thomas, Ky., trained at Brownsville, Texas, promoted from private to corporal to sergeant, served as platoon commander, 37th machine guns, Hdqrs. Co. 58th Inf. Sailed May 10, 1918, served as machine gun instructor. Participated in battles in Meaux sector, July 12 to 17; Aisne-Marne offensive July 18 to Aug. 6; St. Mihiel Sept. 12 to 16; Meuse-Argonne Sept. 6 to Oct. 19. Cited for distinguished services by General Order No. 41, 44th Div. Hdqrs. for "courage and coolness in placing his 37 mm. guns in position despite constant fire from enemy. His work was of utmost value and a fine example for his men." Received machine gun bullet in hip in Aisne-Marne offensive, Aug. 4, 1918, and shrapnel in left foot and slightly gassed, Sept. 27, 1918 in Meuse-Argonne offensive. Still in service.

WILE, Lee M., 37, Rochester, clothier, son of Myer and Amelia Wile, entered service May 11, 1917 at Ft. Benj. Harrison, commissioned 2nd Lt., after training. Promoted to 1st Lt., June 1918. In charge of boat supplies.

WALTERS, J. Bryan, 21, Rochester, clerk, son of Lovell B. and Ina Walters, entered service June 14, 1918 at Rochester, trained at Paris Island, S. C., private, marines. Promoted to radio work. Still in service.

WILHOIT, Joseph H., 22, Akron, butcher, married, son of William A. and Anna M. Wilhoit, entered service July 22, 1918 at Rochester, trained at Taylor, Great Lakes and Johnston. Private, 6th A. R. D. Mustered out Dec. 24, 1918 at Camp Grant.

WHITCOMB, Paul J., 21, Akron, laborer, son of Delno M. and Bessie E. Whitcomb, entered service Sept. 21, 1917 at Rochester, trained at Camps Taylor, Stanley and Arthur, promoted to 1st Cl. Private, Battery B, 21st F. A. Sailed May 22, 1918 with Battery B, 5th Div., and in actions of Frapelle, Parnille and St. Mihiel. Mustered out July 30, 1919 at Camp Sherman.

YEAZEL, Clinton Howard, 24, Rochester, machinist, entered service March 28, 1918 at Rochester, trained at Camp Taylor. Sailed from Newport, N. Y., as private with Co. A, 11th Inf. Gassed June 21, 1918 and treated in Base Hospital 44. Discharged May 5, 1919 at Camp Sherman.

ZARTMAN, Voris D., 22, Fulton, farmer, son of Charles and Mary Zartman, entered service Sept. 3, 1918 at Rochester, trained at Camp Knox, private with 13th Co. 159th D. B. Bat. E. 72nd F. A. Mustered out Feb. 1, 1919.

ZIMPLEMAN, Edward, 26, Kewanna, farmer, son of Valentine and Catherine Zimpleman, entered service at Rochester, July 27, 1918, trained at Camp Taylor and West Point, private Battery F, 326th F. A. Sailed Sept. 9, 1918 and trained at Camp DeSouge, France. Mustered out March 3, 1919 at Camp Sherman.

ZOLMAN, Harley E., 24, Rochester, manufacturer, son of John and Adeline Zolman, entered service April 3, 1918, trained at Ft. Hamilton, made First Class Private. Sailed July 14, 1918 with 54th C. A. C., Bat. B, and 52nd Bn., A. R. R. Art. Participated in Ballencourt-Meuse drive Aug. 28 to 29, St. Mihiel and Meuse-Argonne offensives. Helped on French 13 inch guns firing projectiles weighing 800 pounds. Served in poison gas squad. Gassed Oct. 13 at Death Valley, France. Discharged Feb. 21, 1919 at Camp Sherman.

ZOLMAN, Levi Thornton, 22, Rochester, farmer, son of James C. and Elizabeth Zolman, entered service July 26, 1918 at Rochester. Private Bat. B, 321st F. A. Sailed June 14, 1918 and served as assistant cook with 82nd Div. Discharged May 29, 1919 at Camp Sherman.

MAUDE SPANGLER

RUTH WRIGHT
ORPHA BELLE MIKESELL

EVA GRASS

Fulton County Nurses

CONDON, Ethel, (Mrs. William V. Young, Pottsville, Pa.) daughter of Clark and Martha Condon, Rochester, entered Army Nurse Corps at Chicago, April 7, 1918, assigned to Ft. McPherson, Atlanta, Ga. Sailed from New York, Sept. 14, 1918, and stationed at Verdun-Meuse Evacuation Hospital, No. 15, from Sept. 29, 1918 to May 6, 1919. Discharged Aug. 3, 1919. Accompanying the snap shots Mrs. Young writes a note which reads: "These were taken the other day in dug-outs just outside Verdun. These are just the 'front porches.' They extend way back into the rock. Some are stables and some are billets for the men. The hills around here are alive with them. Saw an immense German plane yesterday with black crosses. I guess it is true that we are homeward bound. Everyone is glad to go. The French want us out."

GRASS, Eva, 21, Tiosa, Ind., teacher, daughter of Chris and Esther Grass, entered service at Rochester Oct. 19, 1918, entered at Camp Jackson as student nurse. Now at Walter Reid Hospital, Washington, D. C.

HOFFMAN, Clare Edna, 31, Chicago, graduate nurse, former resident of Rochester, entered service May 16, 1917 at Chicago, as reserve nurse, Army Nurse Corps, assigned to U. S. Base Hospital Unit 12. Sailed from New York May 19, 1917, and assigned to Hospital at Canniers, France, June 11, 1917. Served as nurse until April 16, 1919 when she sailed for home.

KING, Catherine M., Liberty township, born in Miami county June 9, 1881. Joined the Red Cross at Seattle, Wash., Dec. 31, 1916 and enrolled with University of Washington Base Hospital No. 50, for overseas duty. On Feb. 16, 1917 was called to cantonment duty at Camp Sherman, O., for six months' training. Base Hospital No. 50. Was called to New York, July 19, 1918 for equipment, drill and French study. Sailed Aug. 26, 1918 S. S. LaFrance to Brest, thence to Base Hospital Center Mesves-Bulsy Sept. 6, and to Hospital Headquarters on Sept. 10. Base Hospital opened to wounded soldiers August 1 with only the officers and chore boys to care for them, pending arrival of nurses. After armistice hospital began to evacuate the wounded soldiers back to the U. S. April 19, 1919 to Embarkation Hospital 136 at Vannes. Sailed for U. S. June 9, 1919 and discharged from duty Sept. 7, 1919.

ETHEL GORDON AND FRIEND IN DISGUISE, E. E. ERVIN

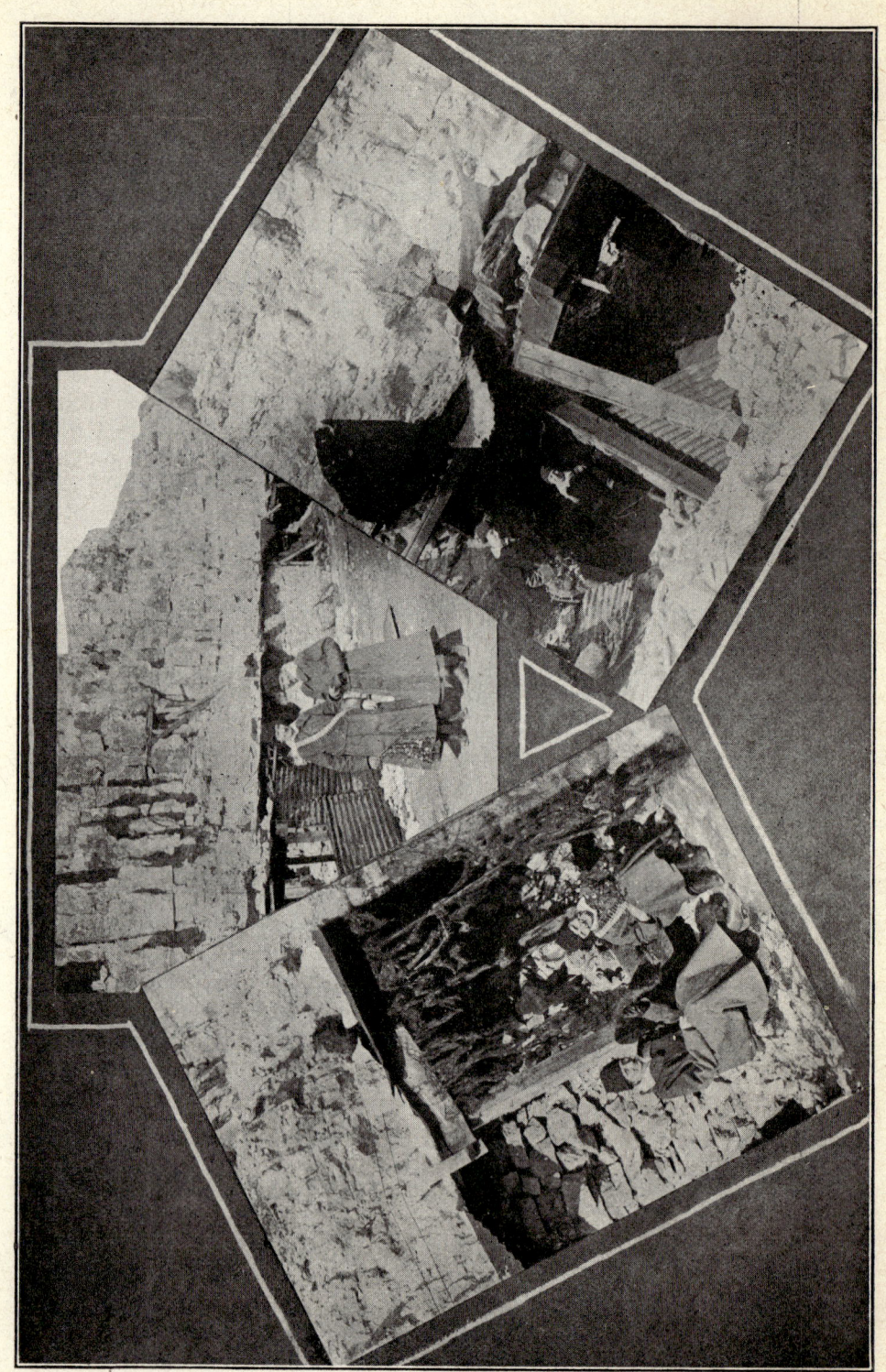

MIKESELL, Orpha Belle, 23, Rochester, daughter of Enoch H. and Lucy Mikesell, enlisted as nurse Aug. 3, 1918. Not called.

SPANGLER, Maude Ann, 24, Kewanna, institutional nursing, daughter of A. R. and L. A. Spangler, entered service as Red Cross Nurse at Ft. Rosencrans, Cal. Discharged April 21, 1919.

WRIGHT, Ruth, daughter of Mr. and Mrs. Wm. Wright, born at Tiosa, Fulton county, Indiana, on January 3, 1893, graduated from Rochester High School in 1912, entered Methodist Hospital Training School for Nurses in September, 1912, graduating in 1915, took post-graduate course at Chicago, Illinois, and did public health nursing at Indianapolis, where she enlisted on September 7, 1917, left Indianapolis for New York City on September 9, 1917, with Lilly Base Hospital No. 32, composed of Indiana doctors, nurses and enlisted men. While in New York was located in Camp Hospital No. 1, and left Hoboken on the S. S. George Washington on December 4, 1917, arriving at Brest, France, on December 24, 1917. Base Hospital No. 32 was located at Contrexeville, France, in the Vosges Mountains, at which place was on duty until June 26, 1918. On the 26th of June, 1918, was sent on detached service to Baccarat, France, (Luneville Sector) on duty with Field Hospital No. 307 and Field Hospital No. 147, where the 77th and 37th divisions were located. On Sept. 14, 1917 left Baccarat going to Toul where she was located only twelve days, in Evacuation Hospital No. 14, following the St. Mihiel drive. Evacuation Hospital No. 14 followed closely behind the American boys, and for a short period of time was at Villers Daucourt, Les Islets and following the Meuse-Argonne drive which started on September 26, 1918, and said hospital was located at Varennes on November 11, 1918, when the armistice was signed. On December 7, 1918, went with Army of Occupation to Trier and Coblenz, where Evacuation Hospital No. 14 was located in a German hospital taken over by the Americans for that purpose. Was at Coblenz until April 14, 1919, and then started to port of embarkation, leaving Brest, France, on June 12, 1919, on S. S. Imperator, arriving in United States on June 20, 1919.

Fulton County's Sacrifice

☆

The faults of these boys we write upon the sands; their deeds upon the tablets of love and memory.

☆

Requiescat in Peace

BENGE, Clarence Oren, 24, Akron, farmer, son of Manley V. and Marietta Little Benge, entered service August 12, 1913 at Denver, Colo., trained at Camp Baker, Cal., private and mechanic 148th C. A. C. and 62nd Replt. Art. Sailed July 11, 1918. Participated in American actions. Died Sept. 19, 1918 of pneumonia in France.

BLACK, John W., 24, Rochester, civil engineer, son of George and Mary C. Black, entered service Oct. 21, 1918 at Chicago, as private American Red Cross, trained at Camp Scott, Chicago, in the Automobile and Mechanical section. Contracted influenza at camp and sent home on sick leave. Died Nov. 25, 1918 from cerebro spinal meningitis following influenza. Made numerous attempts to get into service but was rejected for Officers Training Camp, for conscription and for Y. M. C. A. service on account of physical shortcomings, but was finally admitted as Red Cross Ambulance driver. Buried at Rochester.

BURNS, Ernest V., 20, Grass Creek, farmer, son of Isaac R. and Rhoda Burns, entered service July 14, 1918 at Great Lakes Naval Training Station, served as fireman of the U. S. S. Delaware. Killed. No information as to cause or date.

CLYMER, Claud Everett, 21, Talma, Ind., farmer, son of Harrison C. and Margaret E. Clymer, entered service Sept. 4, 1918 at Rochester, trained at Camp Taylor, 1st Cl. Private 13th Co., 4th Tr. Bn., 159th Depot Brigade. Died Oct. 7, 1918 at Base Hospital, Camp Taylor, Ky.

GOLUB, Jacob, 25, Rochester, junk dealer, born in Russia and son of Harry and Fanny Golub, entered service in 1917 at Rochester. Private, Co. F., 26th Infantry. Killed in action.

Little is known as to the particulars of Golub's death. His sister, Mrs. Jake Polay, Rochester, received the following memorial signed by Gen. John J. Pershing, Commander in Chief of the A. E. F.: "Private Jacob Golub, Co. F, 26th Infantry, was killed in battle, July 18th, 1918. He bravely laid down his life for the cause of his country. His name will ever remain fresh in the hearts of his friends and comrades. The record of his Honorable Service will be preserved in the archives of the American Expeditionary Forces."

HARTZ, Fred, 21, Delong, railroader, son of Nicholas and Eliza Hartz, entered service Sept. 3, 1918 at Rochester, trained at Camp Taylor and Ft. Benj. Harrison, private Co. M, 5th Prov. Bn., E. H. P. Died at Ft. Benj. Harrison from pneumonia following influenza, Oct. 23, 1918. Buried at Leiters Ford, Ind.

HARTZ, Benjamin Joe, 28, Delong, railroader, son of Nicholas and Eliza Hartz, entered service May 24, 1918, trained at Camps Taylor, Beauregard and Newport News, private Co. H, 126th Inf. Sailed Aug. 6, 1918, wounded in action Oct. 14, 1918 and died next day. Buried "somewhere in France."

HUFFMAN, Frank William, son of Mrs. Susan C. Huffman, of Grass Creek, born March 20, 1897, was a private in Battery E, 70th F. A. Engineers. Died Oct. 1, 1918 of pneumonia. No other information available.

IRVINE, Martin Augustine, 24, Rochester, son of Martin A. and Elizabeth Irvine, entered service Dec. 12, 1917 at Rochester, trained at Jefferson Barracks, Custer, Meigs and Ft. Wood. Private, Q. M. Corps and placed in charge of Officers' Launch at Ft. Wood, New York Harbor. Died at Ft. Wood from pneumonia following influenza, Oct. 18, 1918. Burial at Rochester.

KOESTER, Earl C., 21, Wayne Tp., son of Rev. and Mrs. S. P. Koester, entered service March 5, 1918, trained at Kelly Field, private Squadron B. Stricken with appendicitis in May 1919 and died at Camp Sheridan Hospital May 11, 1919 following operation.

MIKESELL, Deane Wilbur, 21, Rochester, teacher, son of Enoch H. and Lucy P. Mikesell, entered service May 30, 1918 at Chicago, trained at Great Lakes at Radio work with Co. O, Radio Depot, Navy. Stricken with influenza Sept. 15, 1918 which later developed into pneumonia which caused his death on Sept. 22. Burial at Rochester.

MEDARY, Otto. Born in Fulton county Jan. 13, 1890, son of Albert and Susan Zabst Medary. Was employed as fireman on the Wabash railway with headquarters at Toledo, O., where he entered service with Co. L, 148th U. S. Inf. Oct. 5, 1917. Trained at Camps Sherman, Sheridan, Lee, promoted private to corporal. He sailed with his company June 25, 1918 and was but a short time getting to the front and was in constant active service for four months. On November 5 in the Argonne offensive he was struck in the abdomen by shrapnel and died ten minutes afterward. He was buried on the east bank of the Escant river, near Heume, Belgium. Letters from Corporal Medary's superior officers praise his loyalty, bravery and devotion to duty.

MADARY, Clarence Verl, 22, Rochester, son of William and Gertrude Madary, entered service March 6, 1918 at Rochester, trained at Newport News, 1st Cl. Private Medical Detachment, 60th R. A. Sailed May 1, 1918, served as assistant dentist. Killed in action.

MERELY, Adolph R., 21, Akron, farmer, son of Charles and Sarah E. Merley, entered service June 5, 1917 at Warsaw, trained at Ft. Harrison and Camp Shelby, private Co. H, 3rd Regt. Sailed June 14, 1918 with Bat. A, 18th F. A., 3rd Div. Operated machine gun. In Meuse-Argonne offensive. Died from bronchial pneumonia, following influenza, at hospital Toul, France, Dec. 25, 1918. Buried in France.

MURPHY, Raymond George, 20, Rochester, farmer, son of Alpheus and Clara Murphy, entered service April 17, 1918 at Rochester and trained at Columbus, O., and Ft. Sam Houston, Tex., private 5th Aero Squadron. Died at Ft. Sam Houston, May 21, 1917.

NICODEMUS, John A., 17, Rochester, student, son of William and Agnes Nicodemus, entered service Jan. 4, 1917 at Columbus, O., trained there and at Ft. Sam Houston. Private Co. B, 3rd Inf., transferred to Co. F, 26th Inf., 1st Div. with which he sailed for France. Wounded in both hands July 19, 1918, taken to hospital at Rouen, erroneously reported killed. In St. Mihiel drive and received gun wound in leg. Returned to duty Sept. 27, 1918 in battle of Argonne between Oct. 1 and 11 and reported killed in action.

PARRISH, George L. D., 22, Rochester, hotel clerk, son of George and Katie Nolan Parrish, entered service July 11, 1917 at Ft. Wayne, Ind., trained at Oswego and Syracuse, N. Y., and Charlotte, N. C., promoted to private 1st Cl., served as nurse on medical staff, overseer of Army Canteen and did banking and bookkeeping for Ambulance Co. 28. Sailed May 1918 with Ambulance Co. 28, 4th Div. R. A. Was in action at Chateau Thierry and killed while giving medical aid to wounded, Oct. 15, 1918, northeast of Montfancon.

REISH, Omer Guy, 30, married, railroad signal man, Leiters Ford, son of Calvin W. and Lizzie E. Reish, entered service June 14, 1918 at Rochester, Indiana, trained Chamber of Commerce, Camp Jackson, S. C., private Co. C, Battery A, 12th Regt. F. A. R. D. Died of pneumonia at Camp Jackson, Oct. 27, 1918, and was buried at Leiters Ford. Widow resides at Georgetown, Indiana.

SNYDER, Jesse LeRoy, 21, Rochester, farmer, son of William and Elizabeth H. Snyder, entered service June 4, 1918 at Rochester. Trained at Camp Taylor with 13th F. H. Co., 4th T. R. Bn., 159th D. B. Died at Camp Taylor.

SHELTON, Leroy C., 32, Rochester, clerk, son of P. Eugene and Aletha Shelton, entered service March 29, 1918 at Rochester, trained at Camp Taylor, private Co. A, 111th Inf., 28th Div. Sailed May 5, 1918, in action at Chateau Thierry and on Vesle River front. Killed in action at Fismette on Vesle river on the night of August 10, 1918.

VAN METER, Frank, 20, Kewanna, farmer, son of Hugh and Rosa Van Meter, entered service Nov. 4, 1915 at Logansport, Ind., trained at Columbus, O., and Ft. Robinson, promoted private to corporal to sergeant. Attended Officers Training School at Camp Stanley, Texas, and was sent to Columbus, New Mexico, where he trained recruits, acted as librarian for his troop and for a time as telegraph operator. Died of influenza, 1918 at Columbus, N. M.

VAN VALER, William Russell, 21, St. Louis, Mo., salesman. son of Charles and Anna Walden Van Valer, of Akron, entered service May 31, 1917 at St. Louis, trained at Camp Maxwell, St. Louis; Camp Clark, Nevada, Mo.; Camp Doniphan, Ft. Sill, Okla. Promoted private to Corporal Co. A, 1st Regt. Inf., National Guards of Missouri, afterwards assigned to Co. A, 138th Inf., 35th Div. U. S. Inf. Sailed May 2, 1918 and participated in battles of Vosges Mts., Hilsenfirst, St. Mihiel, Argonne-Meuse, Vauquis, Cheppy, Straits. Montrebeau Woods and Sommedieu sector. Taken to Hospital Base 45, Mesves, Nevres, France, for treatment for slight wound on arm by hornet, of Sept. 26, the same day his company went into the Argonne fight. Reported dead of pneumonia on Sunday, Sept. 29, 1918, and report confirmed. Messages received five days previous to the 29th made no mention of his being wounded or sick, several of these messages being written on trench cards.

Honor Roll of Fulton County

A

Adams, Capt. Otis
Adamson, A. E.
Adamson, Arthur
Adamson, Edgar H.
Alber, Garrett
Alexander, Fred

Allen, Geo. Edwin
Anders, Arthur
Anderson, Dale
Anderson, Harley
Anderson, James
Anderson, Lloyd W.

Anderson, Louie
Anderson, Max
Armstrong, Max
Ault, Howard

B

Babcock, Charles Clark
Babcock, Dean
Babcock, Otto
Baber, Earl
Bacon, Fred B.
Bacon, Kennith
Baggerly, Clifford
Bailey, Carl
Bailey, G. F.
Baird, Reed
Baker, Ermil
Barber, David Edward
Bare, Carl
Barker, Lee
Barkman, Irvin
Barkman, John
Barnes, Harvey P.
Barnhart, Hugh A.
Barr, Fred L.
Bartik, Joe
Batt, Joseph
Bazmore, Wm.
Beattie, Harry
Beck, Chas. A.
Beck, Thomas
Becker, Carl Reed

Becker, Ernest
Becker, Ed
Becker, Omar
Beery Otto
Bennet, Forrest
Best, Clarence
Biddinger, Chas.
Biddinger, Don
Biggs, Dee
Biggs, Geo.
Black, Albert
Black, Thomas
Blacketor, Paul Shryock
Blacketor, Virgil R.
Blausser, Vern
Boelter, Rudolph G.
Bowen, Ray
Bowman, Sam R.
Bowman, Sidney L.
Buchanan, James
Buchanan, Ruben
Buchtel, George
Bumbarger, Charles
Burge Roy
Burns, Cecil R.
Burns, Ernest

Burns, Ivan R.
Burns, Robert R.
Burns, Vernon L.
Butler, Alfred
Butler, John Leroy
Butler, William J.
Butts, Bailis O.
Brackett, Lyman
Bradway, Lee
Brickle, Harry
Bridegroom, Hugh
Briles, Dale M.
Brouillett, Ralph
Brower, Elmer
Brower, Geo. L.
Bruce, G. Franklin
Brugh, Dean
Bryant, Ernest
Bryant, Harvey
Bryant, Roy Herman
Bryant, W. A. (Bert)
Bryant, Will
Bryant, William
Bryer, Fred
Beyer, Earle

C

Caffyn, Walter Wolf
Cain, Cecil
Cain, Jas. Homer.
Calentine, Clarence
Camerer, Fred D.
Carpenter, Seth C.

Carr, Stanley B.
Carter, Ralph
Caton, Ernest
Caton, Howard
Caton, Wilbur
Chamberlain, Chester

Chamberlain, Clarence
Chandler, Harvey West
Charters, Graham
Churchill, Ruel
Clark, Ora
Clary, Harvey Foy

198

HONOR ROLL

Clay, Roland
Claybourne, Fred
Claybourne, James
Clayton, Bernard
Clayton, Jay
Clemens, Leo R.
Clevenger, William, C.
Clingenpeel, Ralph R.
Clymer, Claud
Collin, Robert Wm.

Colwell, James Albert
Cook, Avon J.
Cook, Ray
Cook, Willis W.
Cooper, Russell B.
Condon, Joseph
Coplan, Geo. Wm.
Coplen, Arthur G.
Coplen, Don
Coplen, Oscar O.

Cornell, Wm. Lloyd
Costello, John W.
Costello, Joseph P.
Coffel, Chas. E.
Crabb, Don
Crabb, Fred T.
Craig, Herbert
Craig, Herbert Hackett
Crownover, Leroy A.

D

Daniel, Earl
Davis, Edwin A.
Davis, Harvey
Davis, Warren
Davidson, Harold Bell
Day, Fred
Decker, Arthur
Delehanty, R. Emmet
Denny, Clyde

Dillon, Clarence Allen
Dillon, Talmadge O.
Ditmire, Jean
Ditmire, Ralph
Diveley, Russell
Dixon, Chas.
Dixon, Joe
Douglass, Albert
Douglass, John

Dovichi, Wm. J.
Downs, Warren
Dudgeon, Dewey
DuBois, John
Dukes, Amos
Dukes, Lawsen
Dukes, Paul
Drake, Fred
Drudge, Omar

E

Easterday, Fred
Easterday, Loris
Eastwood, Wm. Oscar
Eber, Lester A.
Eber, Vern
Eddington, Clarence

Eddington, William
Eiserman, Fred
Eiserman, Glen
Elmerick, Elmer C.
Emeric, Rosco
Emmons, Aubry

Emmons, Grover
Emmons, Lester
Emmons, Wm.
Ericson, Axel Leonard

F

Falls, Guy
Farry, Chas. F.
Faulstick, Chas.
Fansler, ———
Felty, Fred Wilson
Fennimore, Omar
Field, Earnest
Fields, Guy
Fields, Leonard

Filton, Floyd
Flynn, Ray
Foglesong, Harry
Folker, Elmer M.
Foore, James
Foor, Dee E.
Foor, Ossa
Foor, Ferman
Fore, Abbott

Foster, Ora
Foster, Herbert
Fowler, Bernard
Freece, Guy
Freidner, Arthur
Fry, Willard
Fuller, Abbott
Fultz, Dee

G

Garman, Perry
Garman, Reed
Garner, Clarence
Gault, Robert

Geiger, Floyd
Geyer, Buel J.
Gilispie, Warren
Ginn, Harland H.

Ginn, Ivan
Ginther, Herbert
Ginther, Merle
Ginther, Silas

Gocking, Grant Cecil
Gohn, Chas. E.
Golub, Jacob
Goodrich, Daniel
Gorsline, Donald
Goss, Byron
Goss, Raymond
Gould, Francis B.
Gould, Herbert
Graeber, Harry John
Graham, Earl
Graham, Everett
Graham, Frank P.
Graham, Paul
Grass, Eva A.
Green, Dwight
Green, Raymond
Green, Sidney
Greenwood Robert
Greer, James
Grove, Arch
Grove, Oliver

H

Hagan, Lloyd
Hall, Evert Lee
Hall, Justin
Hall, Thomas D.
Hamilton, Ralph
Hammond, Everett
Hand, Floyd F.
Hardin, Guy Max
Harding, John
Harding, Phon, Jr.
Harrold, Gordon D.
Harsh, Vance K.
Harter, Leo S.
Hartz, Benjamin
Haslett, Peter
Hatfield, Arthur
Hatfield, Ralph
Hayward, Richard
Hemminger, Whitfield
Henderson, Earl
Henderson, Hugh
Henderson, Paul
Hendrickson, Arthur
Hendrickson, Florence
Hendrickson, Milan
Hendrickson, Minder
Hendrickson, Robert
Hetzner, Harry
Hiatt, J. E.
Higgins, Forrest. N
Hill, Clarence F.
Hill, Floyd A.
Hizer, Milo
Hoffman, Orval M.
Hoffman, Ralph
Hoffman, Vance E.
Hoffman, William F.
Hogan, Elva
Hogan, Ernest
Holloway, Donald V.
Holman, Hugh
Hoover, Don
Hoover, Ernest
Hoover, Max J.
Hoover, Tom
Horn, Robert M.
Hudkins, Alphonzo A.
Hudson, Emmit
Hudtwalcker, Rudolph
Hulse, Paul
Hunter, Fred
Hunter, Otto
Hunter, Rex

I

Ingram, Milo O.
Irvine, Chas. G.
Irvine, Martin A.
Ivey, Chas.

J

Jamison, Claude
Jenkins, Hugh
Jocking, Grant C.
Johnson, Alvin E.
Johnson, Howard
Johnson, Harry
Johnson, James F.
Johnston, Francis
Jones, Herman
Judd, Howard

K

Kamp, Estil
Kamp, Orville
Karn, Harry D.
Karn, Russell
Kebus, Steven
Keel, Carl Byron
Kepler, Quimby
Kern, Franklin W.
Kesler, Guy
Kestner, Geo. Wm.
Kinder, Ner.
Kindig, Claude
Kindig, Roy
Kindig, Vernon
King, Joseph V.
King, Kenneth N.
King, Milo S.
King, Raymond E.
King, Roy W.
Kissinger, Herschel
Kistler, Chas S.
Krothwell, Ross
Kulp, Daniel, Jr.
Kulp, Ernest

L

Lackey, Hiram Silas
Lantz, Ernest
Larew, Horace
Large, Andrew
Lawson, Earl James
Leininger, Lewis Dale
Ley, Leo Edmond
Long, Ernest M.
Long, Worth W.
Lowden, Claude
Louderback, R. L. V.
Lowe, Clarence S.
Lowman, Jesse
Luey, Walter

Mc

McCarter, Harry
McCarty, Murray
McClung, Fred Garrick
McCoy, Walter
McIntyre, Lovell
McIntyre, Oval L.
McKee, Brant R.
McMahan, Edwin Love
McMahan, James J.
McMahan, John L.
McMahan, Pat
McLung, Arthur

M

Madary, Clarence Verle
Madlem, Harland T.
Mahoney, Dennis
Maroney, Frank
Marriott, Virgil
Marsh, Marion
Marshall, Claud
Martin, Claude
Martin, Harvey
Masterson, Alvin
Masterson, Orange Lee
Masters, Oscar
Mathews, Leroy
Meek, Herold
Meredith, Donald D.
Meridith, Russell S.
Merley, Adolph R.
Messenger, Wm.
Metz, Jack
Meyers, Charles E.
Meyer, Herman A.
Meyer, Omer John
Mezger, Wm. H.
Mikesell, Deane
Miksell, Omer E.
Mills, Earl
Mills, Russell
Miller, Calvert
Miller, Chas. A.
Miller, Earl
Miller, Hanford
Miller, Jacob
Miller, Lucius C. E.
Miller, Raymond
Miller, Robert V.
Miller, Walter W.
Miller, Willhelm
Mitchell, Robert C.
Mogle, Hubert Elden
Moore, Benjamin F.
Moore, Charley J.
Moore, Daniel M.
Moore, Earl
Moore, Fred J.
Moore, Norman C.
Moore, Robert P.
Morphet, Edgar
Mow, Clyde
Mowe, Lee
Murphy, Benjamin
Murphy, Jesse
Murphy, Raymond
Murphy, Russell
Murray, George
Murtha, George
Murtha, Joseph
Musselman, Sherl
Myer, Tom

N

Nehere, Russell
Nehere, Truman
Nellans, Chas.
Nelson, Kenneth R.
Nelson, Phillip
Newell, Manford
Nichol, Frank
Nichodemus, John
Nickles, George
Noftsger, Chas.
Norman, Cleo R.
Norton, Paul B.
Noyes, Vernon
Nye, Clifford V.
Nye, Robert Cleon

O.

O'Blenis, Clem
O'Blenis, Ray
O'Connell, Clarence
O'Dell, Gilbert
O'Dell, Samuel
O'Hare, Earl
O'Hare, John
Osborn, Jay
Overmyer, Howard
Overmyer, Roy
Overmyer, Wm.
Owens, Robert

P

Painter, Paul
Palmer, Oswald
Parrish, Geo. L. D.
Passwater, Geo.
Patton, Harrison
Paul, Ralph R.
Paul, Walter
Pensinger, James
Perry, Ralph
Perry, Walter John
Personett, Mur.
Peterson, Boyd
Peterson, Clarence
Peterson, Earl
Peterson, Elbert R.
Peterson, Guy
Pfeiffer, Edward
Pfeiffer, Lucius
Phillips, Thomas
Picken, Omar
Polen, Vance
Polen, Wm., Jr.
Polly, Lloyd
Pontius, Guy
Pontius, Verl E.
Poorman, Omar
Poorman, Willie
Powell, Harrold N.
Pressnall, Earl H.
Putman, Claude

R

Rans, Edgar Wilson
Redmond, Walter
Rees, Myron
Reese, Loyd
Reish, Donald Carlton
Reish, Omer Guy
Reish, William H.
Reiter, David L.
Rhodes, Ralph
Rhodes, Sumner Jefferson
Richards, Russell
Richmond, Charles
Richmond, Roy D.
Richter, David
Riddle, Geo.
Robbins, Alfred R.
Robbins, Fred
Robinson, Fred
Roden, Harold
Rodgers, Harley Grover
Rogers, Hobart L.
Rogers, Lester Clement
Rolland, Ezra Wm.
Ross, Harold T.
Ross, Walter David
Rouch, ———
Rouch S. Earl
Rouch, Vernie
Ruh, Donald O.
Ruh, Harold
Royer, Carl Lee

S

Sanns, Chas. Joseph
Sanns, Harrison Vernon
Sanns, James Manuel
Saunders, Charles R.
Sauseman, Clifford G.
Scheets, Joseph A.
Schrim, Charles, Lt.
Schrim, Elson
Schrim, John Edward
Schuler, Edward
Scott, Hiram
Scott, Wm. J.
Sears, Charles
See, Gordon Earl
Seigfried, Paul Atwell
Sewell, Guy E.
Shamp, Harry Kay
Sharp, Russell R.
Shaw, Harlan
Sheets, Ottis I.
Shelton, LeRoy Clarence
Shelton, Ralph
Shelton, Ray
Shine, Ermil Neville
Shipley, Donald
Shipley, Frank
Shively, Noah
Shobe, Rex D.
Shriver, Chas. E.
Sisson, Earl
Slifer, Arthur Orville
Smiley, Glen
Smith, Gernie Elgie
Smith, Grover
Smith, Lowell B.
Smith, Noble
Smith, Percy
Snyder, Arthur
Snyder, Byron
Snyder, Clarence
Snyder, Jesse Leroy
Snyder, Loyd Elmer
Snyder, McKinley
Snyder, Merlin
Snyder, Orville
Sowers, Wm. H.
Sparks, Cecil Ray
Stacy, Russell
Stamm, Charles
Stanley, Geo. Russell
Stanley, John
Staton, Geo.
Steffy, Ernie
Stengly, Clarence Grover
Sterner, Howard
Stetson, Ray
Stinson, Max James
Stinson, Stanley
Stockberger, Dennis Dale
Strong, Paul O.
Strock, Wardell Western
Stubblefield, Thurman A.
Sutherland, Harry

Swango, Frank
Swango, Isaac Jacob
Swartwood, Fred G.

Swihart, Frank, Lt.
Swihart, Mellvin
Swihart, Walter

Swintzer, William
Sylvester, Paul

T

Taylor, Frank
Taylor, Guy Hubert
Taylor, Harley W., M. D.
Taylor, Omer F.
Terry, Lyon
Tester, Riley Clesley

Thomas, Dewey
Thompson, Olos Nathan
Thompson, Jacob F.
Thrush, Lotus
Timbers, Archie Roscoe
Tipton, Raymond

Toner, Albert Worth
Town, Cecil
Tramburger, Emel
Tyrell, Wm.

U

Utter, Frank H.

V

Van Blairican, Edgar
Van Cleave, Jessie
Van Valer, Russell

Van Meter, Charles
Van Meter, Ernest
Van Meter, Frank

Van Meter, John
Vandergrit, Quincy
Vickery, Dean K.

W

Wade, Claud N.
Waddups, Thomas P.
Wagoner, Amos
Walters, Gerald
Walters, J. Bryan
Waltz, Jesse
Ware, James M.
Warfield, George Evertt
Warner, Wm.
Warner, Ray V.

Weir, James Harold
Welcheimer, David
West, Neal
Wilfred, Clyde E.
Wilhoit, Joseph H.
Willard, Daniel
Wise, Clyde L.
Wharton, Harrison
Whitacre, Charles
Whitcomb, Paul J.

White, Wm. F.
Wolf, Leroy Sylvester
Workman, Clarence
Wright, Marcus H.
Wright, Otis J.
Wright, Ralph
Wylie, George Henry
Wynn, Wm. J.

Y

Yarter, Gordon

Yeasel, Clinton Howard

Z

Zartman, Voris

Zimpleman, Edward
Zollman, Levi

Zollman, Harley E.

Record of the 42nd Division
(In which Many Fulton County Boys Served)

August 13th, 1918

To the Officers and Men of the 42nd Division:

A year has elapsed since the formation of your organization. It is therefore fitting to consider what you have accomplished as a combat division and what you should prepare to accomplish in the future.

Your first elements entered the trenches in Lorraine on February 21st. You served on that front for 110 days. You were the first American division to hold a divisional sector and when you left the sector June 21st, you had served continuously as a division in the trenches for a longer time than any other American division. Although you entered the sector without experience in actual warfare, you so conducted yourselves as to win the respect and affection of the French veterans with whom you fought. Under gas and bombardment, in raids, in patrols, in the heat of hand to hand combat and in the long dull hours of trench routine so trying to a soldier's spirit, you bore yourselves in a manner worthy of the traditions of your country.

You were withdrawn from Lorraine and moved immediately to the Champagne front where during the critical days from July 14th to July 18th, you had the honor of being the only American division to fight in General Gouraud's Army which so gloriously obeyed his order, "We will stand or die," and by its iron defense crushed the German assault and made possible the offensive of July 18th to the west of Reims.

From Champagne you were called to take part in exploiting the success north of the Marne. Fresh from the battle front before Chalons, you were thrown against the picked troops of Germany. For eight consecutive days you attacked skillfully prepared positions. You captured great stores of arms and munitions. You forced the crossings of the Ourcq. You took Hill 212, Sergy, Meurcy Ferme and Serings by assault. You drove the enemy, including an imperial Guard Division, before you for a depth of fifteen kilometers.

When your infantry was relieved, it was in full pursuit of the retreating Germans, and your artillery continued to progress and support another American division in the advance to the Vesle.

For your services in Lorraine, your division was formally commended in General Orders by the French Army Corps under which you served. For your services in Champagne, your assembled officers received the personal thanks and commendation of General Gouraud himself. For your services on the Ourcq, your division was officially complimented in a letter from the Commanding General, 1st Army Corps, of July 28th, 1918.

To your success, all ranks and all services have contributed, and I desire to express to every man in the command my appreciation of his devoted and courageous effort.

However, our position places a burden of responsibility upon us which we must strive to bear steadily forward without faltering. To our comrades who have fallen, we owe the sacred obligation of maintaining the reputation which they died to establish. The influence of our performance on our allies and our enemies cannot be over-estimated for we were one of the first divisions sent from our country to France to show the world that Americans can fight.

Hard battles and long campaigns lie before us. Only by ceaseless vigilance and tireless preparation can we fit ourselves for them. I urge you, therefore, to approach the future with confidence, but above all with firm determination that so far as it is in your power you will spare no effort whether in training or in combat to maintain the record of our division and the honor of our country.

          CHARLES T. MENOHER,
            Major General, U. S. Army.

Some War Experiences
By Foster ("Bobbie") Owens

May 25, 1919
Rossbach, Germany.

I begin my diary from the time that President Wilson declared war on Germany, which was April 6, 1917, at which time I was in D. Company, 16th Infantry, at Camp Baker, ElPaso, Texas. On the 6th of May we relieved the 6th Infantry, doing patrol duty along the Mexican Border. My Company was stationed at the International Bridge which connected ElPaso, Texas, with Juarez, Mexico. Our duties were to stop all soldiers—either Mexican or American—from crossing the river; also to stop all suspicious characters and investigate their cases.

On the 25th of May we moved to Fort Bliss, which was on the outskirts of ElPaso, where my Company turned in all our infantry equipment and were issued machine gun equipment. They made three companies of the regiment into machine gun companies.

General Pershing had sailed for France with his staff of about two hundred officers and a few engineers, but before he left he picked a division as a van-guard of the mighty American Army which was to play such an important part in ending the war later on. He looked over his different units and found that the 16th, 18th, 26th and 28th Infantry Regiments were in the best condition to take up arms against an enemy.

On the 5th of June we left ElPaso on a trip, none of us knowing where it would end. On the 11th of June we pulled into Hoboken, New Jersey, in the wee hours of the morning—about one o'clock. We loaded onto the transports which were awaiting us. The loading was done so secretly that not many civilians had known of it. On the 14th of June fifteen transports, one U. S. Cruiser and a submarine destroyer, left New York Harbor to run a gauntlet of lurking death and also to outwit the most brutal and merciless foe the world has ever known. The news of our leaving had by now leaked out to some extent around Wall Street and some were gambling ten to one that we would never reach our ports in Europe, but there was a surprise in store for them. We left New York on a zig-zag course. One hour we were sailing in one direction and the next we were going in just the opposite. We sailed in two columns, with the Cruiser on one side and the Destroyer on the other, always on the watch. If anything was sighted the Destroyer would go at almost race-horse speed and investigate what it was.

Everything went along fine until the 22nd of June. When we got up we saw black objects approaching us from all directions. It made us tighten our life-belts a notch tighter as we watched, for everyone thought that our minutes were numbered. I have often since wondered what thoughts passed through the minds of those men who were watching those specks approach us, but as they came nearer our boats slowed down and waited.

We were all watching our Cruiser and the Destroyer, but they never stirred. Right up to the Cruiser they went and then we saw a strange flag flying from their masts. It was red, white and blue. It was the flag, the one we had run the death gauntlet to give assistance when they needed it most. They stayed with us on the rest of the voyage and on the morning of June 24th we sighted the shores of France. We all took a long breath of relief, as it was a strain on all of our nerves, that trip across.

On the 26th of June we unloaded at St. Nazzaire, France. The French people almost went wild. They knew from that day on that the end of the war was in sight. There was one thing that made them gasp in astonishment; that was our appearing so young to them. The French soldiers, to a man, raise moustaches, and I guess we did look younger to them, being all clean shaven, but that same bunch of young boys were to astonish the world with their deeds a few months later.

We stayed in camp here until July 1st, when the 2d Battalion of the 16th Infantry—composed of E. F. G., and Headquarters Companies—went to Paris to parade on the 4th of July. It surely was a great day in Paris. The men were unable to hold their formation in line of march. The people wanted to touch them to see if they were real. Poor France! With all their losses and misery, from that day on they never doubted the outcome of the struggle which they had been in for three long years.

One incident, which I will jot down here, touched many a strong heart that day and made an everlasting tie of devotion between all who witnessed it. As the line was marching down the Place de la Concorde a small child ran out to the line and handed a big corporal a bunch of flowers. The corporal reached down without losing his step, picked the child up on one arm and kissed it; then gently set his precious burden down again. The crowd went wild at that incident, but that was just one of many.

The greatest of all incidents happened at Lafayette's Monument, where General Pershing and staff, President Poincaire, General Joffre, and a great assemblage had gathered to receive the American fighting men. General Pershing uncovered in front of the tomb, stood with bowed head a moment, then looked up and said: "LaFayette, we are here!" Those words will never be forgotten.

On the 12th of July the Division was in its new training area around Gondecourt (Marne) with headquarters at Gondecourt. I am not going to say much about the next three months, during which time we were put through a very strenuous and muscle-hardening course of training in trench warfare, which I doubt if any other troops ever went through; but I will say that on October 23rd they were as hardy a bunch of men as ever wore shoe-leather and went into the trenches in the Luneville Sector, southeast of Nancy. It was a quiet sector up to the time we went there and our artillery soon began to warm things up for us and on the 4th of November—the same night the 1st Battalion of the 16th, 18th, 26th and 28th Regiments were relieved—the Boches, who had been notified by spies that we were being relieved, about three o'clock in the morning put over a box barrage on one platoon of F. Company, 16th Infantry. They followed that curtain of steel to our line of trenches when the chaos settled and the roll was called. Three men had answered the call with their lives and eight were missing.

The Huns had drawn first blood and also had brought down upon themselves the hatred of a mighty nation. They showed their brutality at the beginning by cutting the throat of one of their victims, from ear to ear, after he had been shot through the head, but then and there the men of the 1st Division vowed to show no quarter to the Huns in the future.

We went back to our training area again and on January 5th we left Demange, France, for the Toul Sector north of Toul and directly opposite Mt. See, a high mountain held by the Germans since 1914. It was a great stronghold with observation posts on top, from which all French territory for miles was under observation. We held this sector through January and on February 20th we were to raid their lines, but owing to some mistake on the part of our engineers (whose duty it was to lay a pipe line to the German lines, to gas their front line) they did not get it all connected, but you must not blame them for you must remember this was our first experience in trench warfare. I will say, however, that our artillery, composed of the 5th, 6th and 7th Field Artillery, which joined us in July, on the night of the 20th of February, at twelve o'clock, put over the most perfect barrage which was ever thrown to the Huns. I happened to be watching the woods in our rear at exactly 12 o'clock when the sky lighted up along our front of about two miles and in a few second things began to happen in front of our wire entanglements. Shells were bursting at an awful rate, tearing everything in their path. The barrage was perfect, but our raiding party had not moved because of a flaw.

It was on this night, about three o'clock that I was struck by a piece of shrapnel on the right shoulder, but I did not need any treatment as the wound was not serious. A few nights later the Huns returned the raid on the 18th Infantry, but the 18th was not to be caught napping. They let the Huns get into our wire; then they gave the artillery a signal for a barrage. For the second time our artillery showed us they were on the job. In just eighteen seconds from the time they were signalled the guns were laying a curtain of steel between the Huns and their front line trenches that no human being could go through. The Huns were caught, but a few of them escaped for the 18th doughboys finished their job in good shape.

We were relieved from this sector on February 22nd but we were still after revenge for the raid on us at Luneville, so after we went back to our training area we left a party of picked men under command of Captain Graves to pull a raid on the night of the 4th of March. Our raiding party went to the Germans' third line trenches, only seeing five Huns who were put out by a hand grenade in quick order. Their trenches were badly torn up by our artillery fire.

It was toward the middle of March that General Pershing reviewed his troops again. They had completed their training. There were four divisions, the 1st, 2nd, 26th and 42nd, who were fit for duty. The General told Marshall Foch that he could give him four divisions to help stem the drive which was about to begin for the capture of Paris. We were now under command of the French. The German offensive began on March 21st along the whole front. We were loaded on a train and sent to the Picardy front. Arriving there in April we were put on a sector in front of Cantigny, where the British had backed up. Then began our real baptism of fire.

I have heard, from good authority, that on an average thirty thousand shells fell on this sector every twenty-four hours, but the question which every one of our allies was asking was "Could we hold them?" Their doubts were soon dispelled for on the morning of May 28, the 28th Infantry went over the top, supported by nine French tanks, and captured Cantigny and we held it through six counter-attacks, to the surprise of our allies. It was a minor offensive, but it showed the world that America was to be depended upon.

It was on the night of the 31st of May, while I was taking food to my company in the front lines, that I was caught in a bombardment and was put out of the game for a time; but you have heard of the Soissons affair, which was another great victory. I was sorry I could not be with my company then.

I came back from the hospital in August and on September 12th we were back in Front—Old Mt. See, on the Toul Front—ready for the ALL American Offensive. On the night of September 11th we crept out onto No Man's Land and no sooner had we got into our position than more artillery than was ever used on one front during the war roared forth a destroying fire. At one o'clock for twenty kilometers behind the Hun lines, we were waiting in the rain for the zero hour. None of us knew when it was to be, but we were soon to find out. We were all taking our last smoke at the break of dawn when a curtain of fire started to fall in front of us. We were off and nothing could stop us. You already know what we did there, but it fell to the 1st Division to take the stronghold of Mt. See, and we did it.

On the 26th of September, the Meuse-Argonne offensive began. The 1st, 2nd, 89th and 90th divisions were in reserve, to be used wherever any other divisions were held up or stopped. We were at Verdun, waiting. We could hear the roar of the guns and were anxious to get in front of them. The time was near. October 4th found us relieving the 35th division which had suffered severely along the Oise River near Scheppy. They could not go on. We went in and went ten kilometers in ten days. A prisoner whom we took told us we were on the worst front of all, where every foot of ground cost blood. We fought sometimes hand to hand, sometimes chasing them until we pushed them to the level ground. When we were relieved by the 42nd we left many of our comrades there.

On October 8th I was knocked unconscious and remained so for a half hour, but caught up to my company a little later.

At one place we left more of our boys than at any other. You all know of Hill 272. The Allies were saying that we couldn't take it, but we did, and now I say that we earned our reputation for always gaining ground, never losing an inch of what we took.

It was a tired, nerve-racked bunch of men who marched back off that front; a mere handful compared to the number who went up, but our ranks were soon filled with new men and we drilled them day and night, so they would be in shape for the test. Some of them hadn't been over here more than two weeks, but we soon taught them.

November 1st found us again at the front. We were told that if we could cut the German line of communication at Muzon, where their standard gauge railroad ran along the Meuse, we could end the war; so that was our objective. The end was in sight. When my regiment ended up on November 9th we were on a high hill overlooking Sedan. The war was won and two days later came the end.

We went five days without our artillery and machine guns and with nothing to eat. We cleared that territory of artillery and machine guns with our rifles, which was a remarkable feat.

Well, my little narrative is finished. You will probably get tired of it, but I will swear that every word is true. There is more which I could tell, but I want to forget it now. The 1st, 2nd, 3rd, 4th and 5th divisions are all that are left here in Germany now, but I guess our time will soon come when we will be out of this country and in God's country once more and if the Statue of Liberty wants to see me again when I get back, she will have to face west.

At the end of the war we were farther within the German lines than any other division and we are still at the farthest occupied point in Germany—"The Old Fighting First Division."

(Signed) "BOBBIE" OWENS.

Experiences of An Army Nurse
By Miss Ruth Wright

Army life, as far as the nurse is concerned, has an interesting and pleasant side as well as the uninteresting and sad features.

While in New York awaiting orders to sail for France we were stationed on Ellis Island, and had about three months in which to drill and go sight-seeing. We sailed Dec. 4, 1917, on the steamship George Washington and were seventeen days in crossing. We had very comfortable quarters, but had to keep our port holes closed most of the time. The first few days on the ocean were calm and we enjoyed it greatly. Finally we had two very severe storms, which made everyone keep to their staterooms, dashed several life boats to pieces, and washed several boys, who were on guard duty, overboard. When we reached the war zone we received orders to stay dressed day and night, and at night had coats, canteens and life belts close at hand ready to pick up on a moment's notice. We had "abandon ship drill" on the boat, so many were assigned to each life boat, and by the time we reached the danger zone had the drill down to a fine system.

As we approached France, airplanes and destroyers came out to meet us. We stayed on the boat four days before landing at Brest, France.

Base Hospital No. 32 was located in the Vosges mountains, at Contrexeville, France, which was a famous summer resort, noted for its beautiful scenery and mineral water, and was called the second Monte Carlo of France. The hospitals were in hotels taken over for that purpose.

I was with Base 32 until June, 1918, when I was sent on detached service to Field Hospital No. 307, located at Baccarat. Here we had ten barracks, seven of which were used for patients, and each barrack holding about forty beds.

While at Baccarat we had air raids almost every moonlight night, and I know I shall never see moonlight again without thinking of those raids. We could tell a German plane by its heavy chugging sound, while the allied planes had more of an even musical sound. In our village the hospital barracks were located between an ammunition factory and the railroad station, and the Boches were trying to hit one or both of these places in their attacks. Some nights the raids would be heavy and other nights light. A siren was sounded whenever a German plane was heard coming across the lines, and then the anti-aircraft guns and the allied planes would be on the lookout and usually got in some pretty good work. It made one have a queer feeling during the raids and most everyone would drop whatever they were doing and sit quietly until the siren was again sounded telling the raid was over. Some went to the dugouts, carrying or wearing their steel hats. It was always interesting to see the different kinds of people in the dugouts and the various things they had brought with them to their place of seeming safety. We had one Italian patient, named Joe, who would always crawl under his bed for protection whenever an enemy plane would come over, and after the raid the other boys would hurry to turn on the lights in order to see Joe crawl out from his "place of safety."

One afternoon I saw a bunch of British planes in combat with three Boche planes. One enemy plane was brought down and as it fell caught fire; the aviator fell out when about 200 feet from the ground. They brought him to our hospital morgue. He was a young man about 23 years of age, well dressed and had the picture of his wife and two children in his pocket.

One night a bomb fell about a square from our hospital; the concussion knocked several patients from their beds and several were hit with pieces of shrapnel. Sometimes the enemy plane would drop what is called a star shell, fastened to a parachute affair, and looked like a mammoth chandelier hanging from the sky. It came down very slowly lighting up the country for miles around. It was usually dropped to get a pointer on moving troops.

While doing temporary duty at Base Hospital No. 51 I had two wards of German prisoners (about seventy in number) about half of which were bed cases and the other half were up. It took myself and another nurse almost the whole day to dress their wounds, and to see them you would think the American boys were getting in some pretty good work. One of the prisoners was a married man and had lived in the United States several years and had gone back to Germany on a visit and was sent to the front. We also had one prisoner, not very badly wounded, who persisted in staying in bed, although able to be up. We tried to persuade him to get up and help wait on the other prisoners, and after questioning him we found that he was afraid if he got up he would be mistreated or killed by the Americans. The prisoners were not kept here very long but sent farther back.

When off duty we nurses would take little hikes to other little villages, also visiting the various places of interest, the old chateaus and cathedrals. Was in the Castle of Ann, climbed the circular stairway (which was very dark and damp) to the top of the castle, looked out the turrets over the beautiful surrounding country, and also went down into the undreground rooms and dungeons. The cathedrals were also very interesting, being very old, damp and musty, and paths worn in the aisles and stairways from the tramping of many feet during the past centuries.

While on our way to our hospital, and waiting for the same to be set up, we nurses were in Red Cross Hospital No. 110, located at Villers Dau Court, for temporary duty. This hospital was about eight miles from the front, which was a very active sector. The first night, being the start of the Meuse-Argonne drive (Sept. 25, 1918) after being asleep about an hour we were awakened by the sound of a bombardment. It was a constant barrage, commencing about midnight and lasted until noon the next day. Just seemed like they were trying to use every bit of ammunition they had on this one sector, that is about the only way I can desccribe it. I had heard bombardments while in the village of Baccarat, but that was comparatively a quiet sector. I could almost imagine I saw the real hades in which our boys were fighting. The next morning we put our wards in their last finishing touches, expecting patients to be brought in soon. Miss Goffinet and I were assigned to the shock ward. Our first patient came in about five o'clock that evening, and had been a patient of mine back in the village of Baccarat. He was a New York division boy and recognized me. We did everything we could, but were unable to save him. Then patients began coming thick and fast, and we had really more than we could do, but all the boys were so patient, never complaining, said they had done their bit and were ready to go, and many had to go "west." As the other patients got better they were moved to other wards and finally evacuated to base hospitals to make more room for the other boys from the front.

Finally we had orders that Evacuation Hospital No. 14, at Les Islets, was ready for us and we left in ambulances, went through various villages and towns very prominently mentioned during the war. Went through St. Mihiel (and it was from this place we received patients while in Toul where only a few weeks before one side was occupied by Americans and Germans on the other) there was not a whole building left in the place; bridges were blown to pieces, and we crossed the river on a bridge made of plank platforms and floated on boats. It took eleven boats to hold the floating bridge, the distance between each boat being about the length of the boat itself. It was some river for France, as most of the rivers would be called a creek in the United States. We saw miles of American and German trenches, and miles of wire entanglements, passed through what had been No Mans Land, and all through this desolated region you could see the scarlet poppies growing, adding a touch of color to the dreary waste of land.

In different places we saw the most comfortable dugouts, almost like the home of a cave dweller, built in the sides of the hills by the Germans. To see them from the outside they looked like modern bungalows, and going inside they were papered and furnished very beautifully. One especially, thought to have been used by a prominent German official, was partitioned on the inside, having living, dining, bedroom and bath, and a small kitchen; the walls were papered and paneled, and the furniture of the most expensive kind. This was in the Argonne forest region and, no doubt, the Germans thought they had a life lease on this location, but soon learned differently when the Americans came in this territory.

After leaving Les Islets at 4 o'clock one day, moving into Varennes, arriving at our destination after night, on getting out of the ambulances we stepped into mud at least ten inches deep, a regular sea of mud; this had been No Man's Land a few days before and was full of shell holes. We had no lights, no water, nor conveniences of any kind. At this place our home as well as the hospital were tents. We had to wear boots most of the time. As the weather was cold we had stoves in our tents and had some very hot fires. Our tent was dotted with holes caused by the sparks from our chimney. Quite frequently we would be in our tents, reading, resting or otherwise enjoying ourselves when through the numerous holes in the tent roof came a bucket of water—a guard spying our tent on fire would throw on it a bucket of water and it seemed as though the most of the water fell on the inhabitants inside.

On July 17, 1918, Miss Bowen and myself took a walk over toward the hill that seemed to protect our little village. We walked to the next village, which was half-way between our hospital and the front lines. Here we asked the guard if we might go a little farther. He called a sergeant, who said we might go on a short distance. We walked along the camouflaged road, noticed the shell holes, barb wire entanglements and came to the second village. Visited the church and saw a large hole in the steeple and on inquiry learned the Germans had shot into the steeple a few days before just after the boys had turned the hands of the clock. We asked the guard how far we were from the front lines, and he said over there on the hill about half a mile. We had passed the third and second line trenches and noticed how the guards stared at us, and were told several times to put our gas masks in alert position. There were no civilians in this little village. We could see the village in which the Germans were billeted and were under observation and shell range of the Boche. On arriving at our hospital we told where we had been. Some doubted it, saying it would have been impossible to get by the guards, but after describing what we had seen the captain said there was no doubt but what we had been to the front. Of course, after our visit the other girls were anxious to make the trip, but the captain gave his orders and they did not get to go.

On hours off one afternoon Miss Bowen and I thought we would visit the little American cemetery near our hospital. There was a long row of wooden crosses with tags tacked on them, and a second line pretty well started. While reading the different names to see if there were any we knew four ambulances stopped, carrying in all thirteen boxes. This was at 5 o'clock in the evening, and there was no one there to attend this little last service except the chaplain, the ambulance drivers and a few Frenchmen. They kept the graves dug so as to have them ready for use. Three boxes were put in each grave, the flag draped over them, a short service read, and that was the end. It surely was the most impressive and saddest sight I ever saw.

An interesting sight was to see changing of two divisions, one going to the front, the other leaving the front for a rest. We certainly wondered where all the boys came from, and thought the whole United States army was in that one sector. For days there was a constant stream of moving troops. When we went to bed at night it seemed we were lulled to sleep by the constant tread of the boys marching all night long, night after night. It was at this time the Boche planes would try to get the troops, ammunition and supply trains. The never-ending string of motor trucks, going to and from the front, looked like ants following one another.

To give you an idea how busy our hospital was during the heavy drive, will say there were over eleven hundred patients passed through our hospital in twenty-four hours, and one night thirty-six ambulances filled with boys came up, and as we had only five hundred beds could only take care of the most seriously wounded and send the rest to the next hospital about twenty-five miles back. My work was in the shock ward; here we received all the bad battle cases, all surgical cases. Boys came in shot to pieces, suffering from loss of blood and exposure. We would do all we could for them; give blood transfusions, and get them in condition for operations, if necessary, or to be evacuated to another tent. The boys were all very brave through it all, never complaining, always wanting to know the news at the front.

As patients came in we received the latest news from the front, and one item was that the armistice was to be signed at St. Menehould, which was not far from our little village. Before the signing of the armistice our little village was very dark and quiet, no lights anywhere, seemed as if there were not another person within miles. In the evening of the day that the armistice was signed lights began to pop up everywhere in the village and on the hillsides, and to the south of us in the village of Cheppy a band began playing, and how good to hear real music once more after having lived in mudland and hearing no sound but the constant bombardment at the front, and in the same evening such a wonderful display of fireworks as we did see.

One of the happiest moments, after the signing of the armistice, was receiving the orders that we girls were to go into Germany with the Army of Occupation. On Dec. 7, 1918, we left Varennes, France (in the Argonne forest region) for Germany. We passed over battle-fields, crossed the Meuse, through the lower corner of Belgium, through Luxemburg City, following the Moselle river to Trier, where we stayed several days, until the Germans had evacuated Coblenz. Arrived in Coblenz on Dec. 14, 1918, and on our way passed division after division of American boys marching into Germany, and it kept us busy nodding and waving to them from our ambulances.

We arrived in Coblenz before many of the American boys came in, and one of the greatest and most thrilling sights was to see our boys marching into the enemy's city. We got up early one morning, especially, to see this great event. First would come the bands playing very lively and thrilling music, then division after division, troops after troops, ammunition and supply trucks, cavalry; in fact, all different branches of the army. And the greatest part of it was, there was no disorder, shouting or noise, just marching in the straight, quiet dignified way that characterized the American boys all through the war.

Our hospital in France was located in a former Catholic hospital of the Germans, and we had all conveniences, and surgeries, but here we were to take care of only emergency and sick boys, and not battle cases.

Left Germany for port of sailing on April 14, 1919, stayed at Vannes, France, about seven weeks; finally left Brest, France, for good old U. S. A. on June 12, 1919, on the S. S. Imperator, which was some big boat, carrying about 14,000 passengers. We were about four days' journey on the water when our boat picked up a wireless message that the boat of the president of Brazil was having engine trouble, and we were to go back east about a twenty-four hours' journey to pick up the president and his party, which they did about 2 o'clock the next morning. We were eight days in crossing, and as we neared New York harbor several destroyers came out to meet us, bringing prominent persons to meet the president and his party, and before landing he was given the usual salute accorded rulers of nations, twenty-one guns, but, oh, how grand to see the old U. S. A. once again. I would not take anything for my experiences in the great world war, if it has added anything of peace for future generations.

Brief History of the 4th Division
In Which Were Many Fulton County Soldiers.

The 4th Division was organized in December, 1917, at Camp Greene, North Carolina, Major George H. Cameron commanding. It is a regular army division. The units of the division originally had an enlisted personnel, but were brought up to strength by the inclusion of drafted men. Intensive training of units of all arms was carried out during the winter in the unforgettable mud of Camp Greene.

The division received orders to embark for Europe in the spring. Accordingly the departure for the port of embarkation began in April, 1918, the various units going either to Camp Mills or to Camp Merritt. Some units landed directly in France, but many went through England. With the exception of the artillery, which trained at Camp de Souge, the division was concentrated in the Samer area for training during the latter part of May and received instruction from the British. The division was then in the 11 Army Corps (American).

When the German drive from the Aisne to the Marne threatened Paris in June the 4th Division was one of the American divisions hurriedly brought down from the British area and placed in immediate reserve behind the new French front. The 4th Division went first to Meaux and then up the Marne to the vicinity of La Ferte-sous-Jouarre. While the infantry regiments were disposed about the area and were put under training with the French, the engineers were given the task of constructing a secondary system of defenses along the hills above Crouttes. Later the division was moved up to the vicinity of Lizy-sur-Ourcq and the engineers took up the construction of defensive works in that sector. The artillery during this time was still in training at Camp de Souge, near Bordeaux.

Second Battle of the Marne.

This brings us to the crisis of the war, the second battle of the Marne. Once before at the Marne the Germans had been beaten and had lost their opportunity of winning a short decisive war. This second battle of the Marne was the first big defeat suffered by the German army in many months, and it proved to be the beginning of the end, for it marked the first of a series of retreats that finally developed almost into a rout and from which the Boche could not recover. It fell to the lot of the 4th Division to play no small part in this, its first battle.

What proved to be the last German offensive started July 15. Three days later the Allies counter-attacked. The units of the 4th Division were brigaded with French troops, the 7th Brigade with the 2nd French Corps and the balance of the division with 7th French Corps, both corps being in the VI French Army. During the period in which the division was brigaded with the French, no organization larger than a regiment functioned as a tactical unit and in most cases battalions were sent into action with French regiments.

The 39th Infantry attacked at 8 a. m., July 18, and by 3 p. m. had taken all objectives as ordered, including Buisson de Cresnes. Thereafter Noroy was taken, which, according to plans, was to have been taken by the French. At 4 a. m., July 19, the regiment again advanced and took all objectives. The troops were relieved during the night of July 19-20. Two companies of the 11th Machine Gun Battalion operated with the 39th Infantry during this period. A battery, a great number of minnenwerfer and machine guns and over 100 prisoners were captured.

The 47th Infantry was held in reserve during this phase of the battle, supported by two companies of the 11th Machine Gun Battalion and two companies of the 4th Engineers.

The 58th Infantry, 59th Infantry, 12th Machine Gun Battalion, 10th Machine Gun Battalion and the balance of the 4th Engineers operated with the 7th Corps, the battalions functioning separately. The French and American troops advanced at 4:35 a. m., July 18, without artillery support and took Hautevesnes and Courchamps. The Aericans "in a splendid dash" (to quote the words of General Gaucher, commanding the 164th Division) took the village of Chevillon, then advanced to the Sept Bois southwest of MontMenjon and passed through it. Here these troops came under violent artillery and machine gun fire and were compelled to retire to the west edge of the woods.

The French and American troops took Priez and La Grenouiliere Farm July 19 and Sommelans on the 20th. Petret Farm was taken July 21 and Bois de Bonnes taken and Bois du Chatelet entered on the 22nd.

Upon the completion of this first phase of the battle, the division was regrouped as a reserve for the VI French Army, from July 22 to 24, in the area Marizy St. Mard-Bonnes-Hautevesnes-Brumetz-St. Quentin-Marizy St. Genevieve.

The 47th Infantry was then assigned the task of mopping up the Bois du Chatelet. Later two battalions of the 47th were put at the disposal of the commanding general, 42nd Division, and beginning with July 29 they participated in the offensive of the 42nd Division, crossing the Ourcq and attacking Sergy. Sergy had changed hands a number of times, but the two battalions of the 47th Infantry, acting under the orders of the commanding general, 42nd Division, finally took and held it. The losses were extremely heavy. On July 31 the battalions were relieved by the 39th Infantry, which operated until August 2.

For the first time the 4th Division entered the line as a unit when it relieved the 42nd Division in the Foret de Nesles on the night of August 2-3. The division had been assigned to the I Army Corps (American), which in turn was a part of the VI French Army. The two brigades advanced side by side, the 8th Brigade on the right and the 7th Brigade on the left, without opposition. The enemy had retired across the Vesle. During the night of August 3-4 and the day of the 4th the Division advanced to the south bank of the Vesle, where it was held up by intense artillery and machine gun fire. During the following night and day small groups crossed to the northern bank of the Vesle.

Artillery support was being furnished by the artillery of the 42nd and 26th Divisions. The 4th Artillery Brigade came into action at this time, however, and entered the line on the nights of August 5-6 and 6-7 by taking up filial positions with the units of the 67th Field Artillery Brigade, 42nd Division. The 51st Field Artillery Brigade of the 26th Division had just been relieved.

During the days following the advance to the Vesle, little ground was gained, for the enemy was strongly entrenched on the heights immediately north of the river. From these commanding eminences his artillery could bring practically direct fire to bear on the river.

Furthermore, the heights furnished excellent starting point for counter-attacks. Hence, the result was that every attempt to cross the river in force was met by violent artillery and machine gun fire and by well organized counter-attacks. In spite of this, however, the front line was placed definitely beyond the river on the right of the sector before the division was relieved. One counter-attack, on August 6, was broken up by a machine gun barrage fired by the 10th Machine Gun Battalion from a position on the heights south of the Vesle.

After a week of stubborn fighting in the valley of the Vesle the 4th Division was relieved by the 153rd Brigade, 77th Division, on the night of August 11-12, and retired to the Foret de Dole and Foret de Nesles. The 4th Field Artillery Brigade, after having taken over the entire division sector on relief of the 67th Field Artillery Brigade, August 10 and 11, was finally relieved from the line on the nights of August 15-16 and 16-17.

During this campaign the 4th Division advanced to a total depth of 17 kilometers. No record was kept of prisoners and material captured, but the list was large, especially during the few days when the regiments were brigaded with the French. The total losses during the operataion were 752 killed, 4,812 wounded and 590 missing, a total of 6,154.

Thus the 4th Division had made good as a combat division. Before the counter-offensive of July 18, the division had not been under fire and the mettle of its troops was as yet untried. Yet their conduct met all expectations, for it won the unstinted praise of the French commanders with whose units the regiments were brigaded. Having thus been proven, the division, a few days later, was sent into the fight as a tactical unit and added to its reputation by driving the enemy from the Foret de Nesles to the heights beyond the Vesle.

All units of all arms proved their worth—the infantry and machine gun units in attacking and in withstanding counter-attacks; the artillery regiments, which had never been in a fight before; the engineers, who built roads and who bridged the Vesle; the signal units, who performed the difficult task of maintaining communication with rapidly advancing troops; the divisional trains, which functioned in a highly satisfactory manner, and all the small units whose work contributed to the results achieved.

Training Period.

After the Vesle fighting the division was withdrawn to the Reynel for training. General Cameron had been placed in commands of the V Army Corps and Brigadier General B. A. Poore, commanding the 7th Brigade, was temporarily in command of the division. Then on August 27 Major General John L. Hines took command of the 4th division. The division was assigned to the V Corps, First American Army, and prepared for participation in the approaching St. Mihiel drive. On September 1 all units were moved up to the Vavincourt area for further training.

St. Mihiel Drive.

On the night of September 6-7 troops of the 59th Infantry began the relief of French troops in the Toulon sector southeast of Verdun. This was a very quiet sector at that time. Activities started September 12, however, when the First American Army attacked the St. Mihiel salient. The 4th Division was not called upon to play an extensive part in this operation. The division held on the extreme left of the salient, with the 59th Infantry in the line, the balance of the 8th Brigade in support, and the 7th Brigade and 10th Machine Gun Battalion in reserve. The 4th Engineers worked on divisional roads.

The 4th Division was ordered not to attack without express orders from the Corps. Consequently no attack was made on the 12th or 13th, but patrols were kept out constantly. On the 14th the 8th Brigade took the towns of Fresnes-en-Woevre and Manheulles and thus advanced the line of outposts by several kilometers. The 7th Brigade and 10th Machine Gun Battalion went into immediate reserve behind the 15th D. I. C. on September 13, but were relieved on the 14th.

The 4th Field Artillery Brigade did not function with the division during this operation, but the artillery regiments were in action with the 26th Division and the 15th D. I. C. throughout the entire drive.

On the 15th of September the 59th Infantry was relieved from the line. The entire division was moved to the woods near Lemmes on the night of September 19-20.

Meuse-Argonne Operation.

On the morning of September 26 the 4th Division, as a member of the III Corps, First American Army, attacked northward from Rau de Forges, above Esnes, northwest of Verdun. This was the first blow in this last great battle of the war, the battle that extended all the way from Metz to the North Sea and that may be classed as one of the greatest battles in the history of the world.

The attack was made at 5:30 a. m., September 26. Artillery preparation had started at 2:30 a. m. with a burst of fire that had not been equalled in volume or intensity in this sector since the battles of

Verdun. Three hours later the infantry "went over the top with a great yell" behind a terrific barrage that was strengthened by 155's and supported by the corps and army artillery. Everything fell before this advance, and little resistance was encountered before the attacking troops reached and halted on the corps' objective at 12:40 p. m., to await the arrival at the corps' objective of the division on the left. The advance of the 79th division on the left was much delayed by resistance from Montfaucon, so that the 4th Division was compelled to remain inactive during the afternoon. This gave the enemy an opportunity to reorganize his defense and to place his artillery, so that when the advance was resumed at 5:30 p..m., without waiting for the 79th to take Montfaucon little ground was covered by nightfall.

This attack was made in column of brigades—7th Brigade in advance and the 8th Brigade in reserve. The two regiments attacked side by side, the 47th Infantry on the right and the 39th on the left. The brigade machine gun battalions accompanied their own infantry regiments and the 10th Machine Gun Battalion was with the attacking brigade. The 4th Engineers started work at 9:30 p. m., September 25, on a trail across No Man's Land that had been nothing more than a trail since the beginning of the war. By 1:35 p. m. the following day this trail had been expanded into a complete road with two artillery bridges and traffic was moving over it.

On the second and third days of the attack the line was advanced as far as the northern edge of Bois de Brieulles on the right and the Nantillois-Brieulles road on the left. On the 29th of September the 8th Brigade relieved the 7th Brigade in the line, the 59th taking over the right and the 58th the left. The Bois de Brieulles was entirely cleared of machine gun nests and this place was held against continued and violent artillery and machine gun fire.

The second phase of the campaign opened October 4 when the division attacked and took the Bois de Fays, on the left of the division sector. For the purpose of this attack the 47th Infantry relieved the 59th Infantry on the right of the sector and thus took over the Bois de Brieulles. The 59th thus released followed the 58th Infantry in support . The 39th remained in reserve in the Bois de Septsarges.

The 58th Infantry advanced behind a rolling barrage through the Bois de Fays, Bois de Malaumont, and Bois de Peut de Faux and approached the Bois de Foret. Again the advance of the 4th Division was impeded by the division on its left, this time the 80th Division. The Bois des Ogons proved the stumbling block of the 80th Division. With the left flank of the 4th Division thus exposed for a distance of some three kilometers, and with its right similarly open to attack from the east and north, it was necessary to withdraw to the Bois de Fays and establish a line around the three sides of this wood. This in itself was a salient of considerable magnitude, but it was held stubbornly against repeated counter-attacks from in front and on both flanks, not to speak of numerous attempts at infiltration by the enemy and all in the face of most terrific and harrowing shell fire. The enemy batteries across the Meuse, particularly, were active in shelling the front lines and rear areas. All of the woods, towns and open spaces in the sector received their share, but, of course, the severest shelling was in the forward areas.

The third phase of the operation consisted of an assault on the woods north of Bois de Fays and culminated in the capture of the western part of Bois de Foret and reaching of the army objective in that place. This attack was made by the 39th Infantry. The first attack on the evening of October 9 did not succeed, owing to heavy concentration of gas, the necessity of wearing gas masks, and the resulting difficulty of seeing anything in the underbrush in the gathering darkness. But when the attack was renewed on the following morning the Bois de Malaumont and Bois de Faux were both taken. And on the next succeeding day, October 11, the attack was carried through to the northern part of the Bois de Foret as far east as the 312th Meridian, the eastern part of Bois de Peut de Faux also being occupied. Patrols were pushed out on Hill 299.

On the 11th of October General Hines was ordered to command the III Corps and General Cameron resumed command of the 4th Division.

No further attacks were made by the Division. The troops in the Bois de Foret were relieved by the 3rd Division, October 13, but the 47th Infantry continued to hold the division sector, from the northern part of Bois de Fays to the river Meuse, until the division was relieved by the 3rd Division on October 19 and withdrawn to the Foret de Hesse for rest.

The 4th Field Artillery Brigade and Ammunition Train were not relieved from the line with the balance of the division. They were withdrawn from the line for a few days in the latter part of October, but were sent in again and remained constantly in action until the day the armistice was signed.

In this brief history there is not space to review the work during this operation of all units of the division—infantry, artillery, engineers, machine gun units, signal units, trains, etc.—but it may be stated conclusively that each performed its part with unflinching determination and whole-hearted devotion to duty. The division was fighting over a most difficult terrain and against an enemy whose determination to resist every advance is shown by the fact that he employed all or parts of eight different divisions against the 4th Division in this time. The weather was unfavorable, roads were in bad shape, and the terrain lent itself readily to the machine gun type of resistance employed so effectively by the Germans. The Division was kept in action constantly for twenty-four days and 6,000 men were lost. Yet the division penetrated the enemy defenses to a depth of thirteen kilometers, captured 2,731 prisoners, and took fifty-seven field pieces, four minnenwerfer, 228 machine guns, two tanks and a vast quantity of ammunition of all types. Surely the work of the 4th Division in this last battle is a source of pride to every man concerned.

Rest Period.

Upon being withdrawn from the Meuse-Argonne battle General Cameron was ordered to return to the United States, Brigadier General Poore temporarily taking command of the division. On the 31st of October the present commander, Major General Mark L. Hersey, arrived at Lucey to take command of the 4th Division.

The 4th Division was concentrated first in the Foret de Hesse near Jouy-en-Argonne, and then moved to the Second Army area about Lucey. While resting and in training, the division was a part of the Second Army reserve. On November 4 it was again assigned to the First Army and started moving to the Blercourt area November 6. However, the division was reassigned to the Second Army November 8 and started to return to that area before all units had actually left for Blercourt. The division was attached to the IV Corps, Second Army, and the various units were in the Bois de la Belle Oziere when the armistice was signed, November 11. With the cessation of hostilities, however, all units were concentrated about Boucq and were joined there by the Artillery Brigade, which had been released from the line November 11.

Army of Occupation.

The 4th Division, together with the IV Corps, was relieved from duty with the Second Army and placed at the disposal of the Third American Army on November 17.

Thus, after participating in the three great battles of the American Army, the 4th Division was now to march into Germany as a part of the Army of Occupation. The divisions selected for this army were the 1st, 2nd, 3rd, 4th, 32nd and 42nd, all of which had acquitted themselves conspicuously. Later the 89th and 90th Divisions were also included.

The 4th Division began its march from the vicinity of Boucq November 20. The route lay through Thiacourt, Conflans, Briey, to Hayingen, Lorraine, in which area a halt was made for about a week. Thence the march was to Remich, Luxembourg, and across the Moselle into Germany, the first units touching German soil on the third of December. The march then proceeded down the valley of the Moselle to the Kreises of Cochem and Adenau, in the Province of the Rhine, with division headquarters at Bad Bertrich. The march was completed Dec. 17, 1918. In this, its area of occupation, the units of the division then engaged upon a systematic course of training.

Summary.

During the six months that elapsed from the time the 4th Division arrived in Europe until the signing of the armistice, the division functioned in all three of the great battles that will always be associated with the achievements of the American Army in the war, viz: the second battle of the Marne, the St. Mihiel drive and the Meuse-Argonne battle.

The period of the great Allied offensive, July 18 to November 11, consisted of 117 days. Of this time, all or parts of the division were in action eighty-three days and in immediate reserve four days.

The total losses of the division in all operations were 492 officers and 12,456 men, a total of 12,948.

The advances made by the 4th Division in all operations netted thirty-two kilometers.

Prisoners captured numbered 2,856, which figure does not include an unknown number taken in July.

Material captured in July included, according to General Tenant's citation, "a great number of minnenwerfer and machine guns" turned over to the French. The known material captured in all operations comprised sixty-one field guns, ten minnenwerfer, two tanks, 239 machine guns and many thousands of rounds of artillery ammunition as well as other munitions of all kinds.

Citations.

In closing, it is fitting to state that the gallant conduct of the 4th Division has not gone unrecognized in official citations. General Massenet, commanding the 7th French Corps, highly commended the 8th Brigade, 4th Engineers, 8th Field Signal Battalion, and Motor

Supply Trains, which had been brigaded with his troops when the Allied counter-attack was made July 18. And General Tenant, commanding the 33rd Division (French) cited the 39th Infantry for its work while attached to that division. During the Meuse-Argonne operation Major General Robert L. Bullard, commanding the III Corps, cited the division in General Order No. 29, III Corps for its conduct in the Bois de Fays fighting. And the 4th Division was one of the divisions cited by the Commander-in-Chief in G. O. 143, G. H. Q., for the achievements of the Americans in the second battle of the Marne; in G. O. 238, G. H. Q., for the taking of the St. Mihiel salient, and in G. O. 232, G. H. Q., for the bitterly contested victory won in the Meuse-Argonne battle

Clerical Work in the Army
By Charles G. Irvine

I enlisted in the Regular Army of the United States on the 4th day of December, 1917, for the duration of the emergency. I was at that time twenty-one years of age; and had only a few months before been admitted to the Fulton County Bar and was at the time of my enlistment in the act of opening an office in Akron, Indiana, for the purpose of entering into the active practise of my profession.

I enlisted in Indianapolis, Indiana, as a private and was sent to Ft. Thomas, Kentucky. Here I received my first taste of army life, being immediately sent through Military channels until I emerged therefrom, a properly constituted "Recruit". After this there was nothing to do but spend the time waiting until you were sent to a training camp.

My army life in Ft. Thomas was of short duration, for a few days after Christmas I was sent to Camp J. E. Johnston, at Jacksonville, Florida, arriving there on the last of December, 1917. Here I was assigned to a receiving Company, where I became a cook, but was shortly transferred and assigned to a Clerical Company. While in this Company I attended a six weeks course in Quartermaster work and was given military training. In March I was again transferred and assigned to another company where I was trained and equipped for foreign service. I left Camp Johnston on the second day of May with my organization, which was then known as Training Company No. 3, for Camp Merritt, N. J. From here I went to New York City on the tenth of May; sailed for France on board the Rijndam.

I arrived in Brest, France, on the twenty-third and after a few days, during which time I was billeted in the Pontanezzan Barracks, a debarkation camp at that place. From here I was sent to Gievres, an intermediate supply depot and quartermaster headquarters. I remained here for four days, doing the hardest work of my life and was again transferred to Angers, France, in which city was located an organization and training center for the American army.

This was my first assignment to duty, in that I was put in the Finance Division. I arrived in this place on the first of June, and as the camp had just been opened a couple of months previous to this, the work was not hard. In this capacity I was shifted from one department to another as circumstances required. In this way I soon acquired a working knowledge of each position in the office and could take care of either man's job during such time as they were absent, either through sickness or by reason of their being on leave of absence.

However, this place immediately began to grow and after a couple of months I was put in the pay-roll department, where I remained with the exception of such times when I was substituting in someone's place in one of the other departments. Here in September I received my first promotion since being in the army, being appointed a corporal.

About this time we were paying from our office between twenty-five and forty thousand soldiers and two thousand officers, which, together with the leases then running with the French people and all the other bills payable through an army disbursing office kept us very busy. This necessitated our working every day, Sundays included, and a good many nights, so that a working day with us consisted of from fifteen to eighteen hours.

Up until now I had not had what could be called a really responsible position, but I was soon put in charge of the pay-roll department. Here I found that I had even more work to do than had before, for new duties fell to me which had never entered my day's work. Besides keeping twenty men busy where each would accomplish the most, some of whom had never seen an office before, I had to check every man's pay and every pay-roll before it went to the disbursing officer for payment. Although I was not financially accountable for these I was responsible for their corrections and this was no small job when you are paying thirty-five thousand men, amounting to over a half a million dollars in American money and three million francs, the unit of French money with which the men were paid.

In February I received my second promotion, when I was made a sergeant. Our work in Angers continued until in March, when the city was abandoned as an American center and on the last day of the month I was transferred to St. Nazaire, one of the principal ports of embarkation. Here I was again placed in the Finance Division, but in a less responsible position, as a commissioned officer here held the same responsibility as I had held in Angers.

I was in Angers just ten months and although we experienced no shell shock, I think that if the "s" were taken off the "shell" it would explain very appropriately what we did experience most of the time. During this time I received two seven-day leaves, and on each occasion spent twelve days "seeing France." On my first trip I went to St. Malo, a resort just across the Channel from England, and on the second one I went to the Pyrenees on the Spanish border. Besides seeing these places I traveled across the western part of France and visited a number of cities, the most important of which were, Le Mans, Rennes, Tours, Toulouse, Bordeaux and Paris.

At this time I have been in France over eleven months and expect to be here three or four months longer, perhaps more.

Some Impressions of France
By Charlss F. Farry

Every one has had more or less the same experience in the American Army at home. Perhaps the same is true of the A. E. F. If so it is not repeated in such a manner as to give uniformity of opinion to our home folks. I believe that no other writer will give the majority of the things which I shall mention for I represent a group of Indianians not represented by any other Fulton county soldier.

I was at home on a pass of the spring of 1918, when on April 23 I received telegraphic instruction to return to Camp Taylor immediately. This day shall ever be impressed on my memory. I was enjoying the annual fish banquet with relatives and friends. Only the evening before I had received a five day extension on my pass.

Early in the morning of the 24th of April, I returned to Camp Taylor, well believing that I would not return home until I had set foot on foreign soil. I had no reason to believe such, as the immediate movements indicated the contrary. I was contented but yet I had a certain uneasy feeling, because I had seen home for the last time for an indefinite period, and also I was to leave my original unit, Battery B., 325th F. A., which was home to me with Capt. Rees and other Fulton county men.

On May 5, 1917 a number of us reported for duty at Camp Jackson, South Carolina. Here it was that a prank was played by fate or some one. A call was made for volunteer Military Police. I was quick to grasp the opportunity for I scented excitement. Much to my surprise, I was accepted. To those who know me, on whom was the joke? I had been on duty with the M. P.'s for twelve hours when information came to me that soon five hundred of the four thousand camp personals were to be selected to go overseas within a few days. I was the busiest soldier in camp—hunting the source of the rumor in an endeavor to find the least small particle of truth in it.

For once in my army career a rumor was not a rumor! There were to be five hundred selected. After two processes of elimination I was happy to see my name on the lists. Many thought I was foolish; if I waited a while longer I would go across as an officer. Some of those chaps who gave such advice, could have gone with me. Yes, they received their commission but they never set foot on foreign soil—neither did they have the satisfaction of giving a God-speed to a transport, which was setting out with troops to face first the German U-boat and later the German gas and shell. They took the chance— that I was willing to take—and lost.

After receiving the overseas assignment we had practically nothing to do but wait transportation to Camp Merritt, which was received on May 15th. On May 16th the four hundred eighty of us reported at Camp Merritt. During our six days stay here I was indebted to the Hostess House of the Y. W. C. A. for entertainment and employment of my naturally nervous disposition. On May 23 we boarded the good ship "Chicago," leaving behind a number of our comrades who were quarantined for small-pox. At 3:30 p. m. the "Chicago" pulled anchor. Our detachment together with another composed of twelve hundred Polish troops took a farewell glimpse of good old U. S. A. The port holes were closed as we left the harbor— we were unnoticed and without any advice; alone on our good ship "Chicago," with the protection of a three-inch gun fore and two five-inch guns aft, manned by splendid French gunners, to brave the Atlantic with its hidden U-boats.

For eleven days we zigzagged across the waters under the ever watchful eye of our skipper, creeping along during the day and plowing ahead at night. On numerous occasions submarine alarms were given; we were alert. Occasionly wireless reports of U-boat activities along the Atlantic coast reached us; calmness reigned, no one seemed to take the situation as other than ordinary. For ten days and ten nights we saw neither of friend or foe, excepting the occasional smoke of a very distant tanker or freighter.

On the morning of June 2, we sighted several sea-going crafts and immediately knew that we were nearing some foreign port. At 2:30 p. m. we disembarked at Bordeaux, France, at which place we rested for a week before going to Saumur to attend the American Artillery School. This trip gave us our first impression of the French railway system and accommodation. I am not able to testify the ease and comfort the folks had who were assigned eight to each compartment, including all packs. I was very fortunate in getting an assignment as baggage guard, which usually was distasteful, but this time it was a luxury for I had a comfortable place to sleep and all I cared to eat.

Before continuing I shall mention my first impression, which was received while I was on 3 days pass into Bordeaux. According to the French custom many people had gathered in Garden Pullique for their afternoon promenade. The gathering in such a common way drew my attention but the deep print was made by the mourning of all ages and classes, both men and women, boys and girls. The person who did not wear black was rare and very hard to pick out. Evidently every home had suffered the loss of family blood in the Great War. Many wounded were to be seen; blinded veterans; maimed and crippled; and those people suffering and fighting, as never before, for their France, that she should not be conquered as long as there was a drop of blood in their veins! America awake! You have sacrificed nothing as yet in our cause! And America did awake.

Arriving at Samur on a bright Sabbath morning, June 9, we spent the day getting our location and arranging ourselves for twelve weeks of hard work. We were anxious to know what our cause would be like, so we busied ourselves to counsel one or other of the two thousand soldiers and officers already there and satisfaction was ours to the end.

On our journey we did not realize that we were going to such an illustrious school—the famous Saumur Ecole de Cavalrie, the most noted of its kind in the world. At this time the school was American —the Fort Sill of the A. E. F. The grand old walls bearing the names of the famous French military men and historical battles made one feel so insignificant and realize the task before him.

Although the new life was very much different to all of us—with dining room and chamber service, leaving nothing for us to do in the way of police except personal upkeep—the life would have grown very monotonous I fear if it had not been for our friend, the Y. M. C. A. The Y. M. home was an old chateau which, along with all the furnishings, the owner had turned over for an indefinite period. The building reminded one of an American Club, with its canteen supplies, reading material, music and writing rooms. Perhaps the most appreciated were the two hut angels that were ever ready to give service and advice to the boys. In addition to the Y. M. home the town theatre was operated under the auspices of the Y. M. C. A. where movies and concerts were given fortnightly. The appreciation of the fellows was shown by the continual large patronage and gentlemanly conduct at all times.

The most interesting landmark from a historical point of view, after the school itself, is the Chateau de Cheveaux. Although it was built in the eleventh century, it stands to-day as a master mark of master masonry with its perfectly straight walls of stone running to a height of fifty feet; and extending beyond for a distance of eighty feet are the four towers. Yet to look at it one would recognize that it was built to withstand siege; to pass through its structure one would know that it could do so very successfully in its day. From the main floor there is a man hole that drops down a distance of 210 feet to a number of tunnels which lead out for several kilometers to out lying smaller chateaux. The usefulness of these secret passageways can readily be seen. During the reign of Napoleon this Chateau was used as a political prison.

This Chateau is but one of a great number which are to be found in this section of France. To have seen one is not have seen all, however it gives me a knowledge rather than a conception. The modern attractions of the Chateau de Cheveaux is its museum, which is a collection of stones, rocks, ores, shells, etc., which would furnish days of pleasure to a geologist. Here also are found fine paintings and tapestries of the olden days. The second floor is the home of the zoologist, with its collection of bugs, beetles, animals, fowls and oddities of various descriptions. The third floor was my personal delight—the home of the horse—pictures and reproduction in sculpture of famous mounts, saddles of world renown, riders and horsemen, all sorts of equipment for equitation. In addition is to be found a fine array of battle-axes, spears, weapons, of various kinds of medieval days and a few of the more modern.

Of the many courtesies and favors of the French people I can not speak in detail. Although it is a matter of common understanding as to their pleasant attitude toward the Americans, I cannot fail to mention an experience of mine which illustrates this disposition. I arrived in France June 2, 1918, at which time my financial assets were very small—in other words I was—broke. I had not drawn April pay before leaving the states, neither had I drawn May or June pay up to the middle of July and there were not even any prospects of any pay for days or even months to come. About the middle of July I heard the rumor that we were to be commissioned soon. I had no money and my pals had just as much. There was one chance and that was worth trying since a franc was a million to us at that time. I visited the Credit de Louest of Saumur, from whose officials I received credit of several hundred francs for which they accepted draft on my father's account in dear old U. S. A. Their only security was my word that the draft would be honored by my home bank. What more courtesy or favor could one expect? This sort of treatment I received at all times.

I finished at Saumur late in August and was assigned to the 336th F. A. at Camp de Souge near Bordeaux. I was on duty with them only a short time when it was assigned to dock duty and Stevedoure work at the Bassons docks. I was very fortunate in getting a new assignment immediately but within the few days at Bassons I learned to appreciate the dreary work of these boys who so seldom received the praise and appreciation of the public. Working ten hours a day, rain or shine, day and night seven days a week, unloading heavy cargoes destined to the great fighting machines at the front. These boys worked steadily without complaint, taking their lives into their own hands, for it was a dangerous work as it was no uncommon event to have one of their number taken away in a serious or even in a dying condition.

The latter part of September I was transferred to the 8th F. A. located at Camp Meucon, near Yannes, France. It was raining when I arrived and it was raining when I left, as I know it is still raining. Raining describes my stay at Meucon. It is claimed that in the bright summer time the country is very beautiful. At any rate the peasantry are very clever with needlecraft, I believe such is because they can not get out doors during the larger part of the year. To those who may know the country better than I the foregoing would be a very silly reason.

While at this point life was only more or less interesting, as our intensive work was spiced with Y. M. C. A. activities so much was our morale increased. Too much praise cannot be spoken of their untiring effort to bring more or less cheer into a camp of rain and mud. In the camp they had large barracks and buildings where they kept canteen supplies and held their entertainment. In town French hotels were operated for benefit of the visiting and shopping soldier. The appreciation of the men was noticed. For it was seldom that any other organization had a representive in camp—and never long enough to do any good.

It was during my stay at Camp Meucon that I was given my first opportunity to see Paris when I was detailed for a week's schooling at Chaumont. My visit to Paris came the week after the re-capture of Lille which was an occasion of the reawakening of the French spirit and Paris held its first celebration since the beginning of the war. For three days and nights war booty was hauled into the city, which resulted in a breaking forth of a convulsion of joy on the following Saturday night. Gay street lights were seen in full glow for the first time since 1914 and Paris was no longer a city of darkness. The following day, Sunday, brought the climax when thousands of allied troops and civilians paraded the boulevards and were the centers of patriotic demonstrations. It was a great clebration of the beginning of the end which was to continue along with the steadily increasing success of the allied armies, reaching a climax during the arrival of President Wilson in December.

On December I started on my leave of absence and I had my opportunity of visiting Paris during President Wilson's first arrival. I never saw such insanity of joy and enthusiasm, not so particularly for Wilson but for any one on whom there was an American uniform. This is one topic which was not exaggerated by George Creel and his Publicity bureau.

My first main stop was at Bordeaux to see Captain Rees and Battery B once again, but I was unfortunate in locating any of the boys outside of the Captain from Rochester. Another whom I was very glad to se was "Daddy" Ruch, formerly Lieutenant in Battery B, but now Captain and commanding Battery E. The hours I had to spend at Bordeaux were limited and I had to continue on my way to Marseilles.

During my short stay at Marseilles I was entertained at the American Red Cross Hotel. The city was typically French with its many beautiful drives and boulevards. There were many places of interest—among which were the museum, the zoological and botanical gardens and Notre Dame Cathedral, the sailor's shrine.

From Marseilles I journeyed along the Mediterranean towards the Italian border into the famous Riviera, the scenes of early Roman settlements and Napoleanic conquest. At Cannes, the resort of European aristocracy and nobility, I visited many pottery and stoneware works and old relics of medieval times. The most fascinating side trip was one through Grasse, where are located the famous perfumies, and the Gourge de Gourdon, which will hold one's interest and admiration indefinitely.

The next Mediterranean city is Nice, the headquarters of a great many American soldiers on leave. It is an ideal city for such as it has splendid accommodations and from here radiate any number of routes leading to places of historical interest. In addition to the natural qualification of these various leave centers, the boys had a big asset in the Y. M. C. A. for without the Y, these leave areas would have been impossible.

I did not tarry long at Nice for there were too many places to be visited—besides there were too many Americans at Nice out of whose way I could not keep. I was attracted to the famous Monte Carlo but I was not permitted to play—because I suppose I had no fortune to loose.

The scenery along the Mediterranean does not vary so much except from a historical standpoint. The sea itself flanks you on one side and the foothills of the Alps flank you on the other, from Cannes through Nice, Monte Carlo, Mentone, across the Italian border and on. As impressive as the coast trip may be, the return via the upper road makes one feel as if they were in a new world. The view of the all masterful snow capped Alps on the right, and on the left the shining Mediterranean with the blooming cities of Mentone, Monte Carlo, Nice and Cannes.

These few remarks cover in general my experiences in France. I returned from leave on Christmas Day to receive from Santa orders to return to America. I set sail January 20, on the S. S. Samarinda, landing at Hoboken, February 3, 1919 and received my discharge February 6 at Camp Meade, Maryland.

A Chauffeur's Experience
By Walter I. Redmond

I enlisted in Company C, Third Indiana Infantry, National Guard, on June 1, 1915, at Monticello, Indiana. Upon moving to Indianapolis I was transferred to Battery A, First Indiana Field Artillery. At the outbreak of the Mexican trouble in 1916 we were mustered into the Federal Service and on July 6, 1916, we entrained for the Mexican border.

We were stationed at Camp Llano Grande, Texas, for seven months and through hard drilling and efficient officers we were able to capture first place in practically all of the drilling and target firing contests. We were ordered back to Fort Benjamin Harrison in January, 1917, and we were mustered out of the Federal Service early in February, 1917.

We were again called into the Federal Service on June 25, 1917, due to the United States entering into the war with Germany. Upon entering the service this time we were given a federal number and were known as the 150th Field Artillery. We were later assigned to the 42nd Division, the first complete National Guard Division to be organized and ordered to prepare for immediate service overseas.

The division was to mobilize at Camp Mills, L. I., and the 150th received its orders to proceed there in the early part of September, 1917. Upon leaving Fort Harrison the regiment received orders to send its horses and a detail of men to handle them to Newport News, Va., and I was selected as one of the men to accompany this detail. We arrived in Newport News on the ninth day of September, fully expecting to receive immediate orders to proceed overseas, but our expectations were far from being fulfilled, as we remained in Newport News until February 3, 1918, when we sailed for France aboard the U. S. S. Mexican, with a cargo of 1,057 head of horses and a miscellaneous shipment of army supplies and 109 enlisted men of the 42nd Division aboard. Our trip across the Atlantic was a very pleasant one as the weather was fine and the accommodations were excellent.

My first misfortune of the war happened three days before we landed at St. Nazaire, France, when I took the "mumps." Upon landing at St. Nazaire I, with three others, was sent to Base Hospital No. 101 and we remained there for twenty-five days. Upon

Truck in Armenia, Driven by Walter Redmond.

leaving the hospital we were sent to the Casual Depot at Blois, France, and from there to the Field Artillery Replacement Regiment at La Courtine. Here we were informed that it would be impossible for us to get gack to the 42nd Division, so we decided to join the first organization that would assure us of seeing action. So I was among fifty others that were sent to Army Artillery Headquarters, First Army, then stationed at Bar-sur-Aube. Upon my arrival here I was assigned to duty as a chauffeur on the General Staff of the Headquarters. I remained on this duty until after the armistice was signed.

As a chauffeur I covered all of the American fronts and saw action in Chateau Thierry, St. Mihiel and in the Meuse-Argonne. The life of a staff car driver was not one of ease nor was it considered a "bomb proof' one as we were on the go for 18 to 20 hours every day and during most of this time we were under the German artillery fire. During the time that I was a driver I had several little thrills, the best one being having the back of end of my car blown out by shrapnel from a Boche 77 while I was in the front seat. I was fortunate enough to come out of the war unscratched except for a slight gassing which I received in the Chateau Thierry drive.

Shortly after the armistice was signed I was transferred to the General Headquarters of the American Expeditionary Forces, then stationed at Chaumont, France, and later at Paris. I remained on duty with this organization until the middle of August, 1919, when I was transferred to the American Military Mission to Armenia, a states department organization formed for the purpose of going to Armenia and Turkey and investigating as to the advisability of the United States taking a mandate for those countries.

The mission was formed in Paris with Major General J. G. Harbord as its chief and a personnel of fifty officers and enlisted men. We sailed from Brest, France, on August 24, on board the U. S. S. Martha Washington for Constantinople, Turkey. The officers of the mission were established on board the boat and plans were made to take an overland trip from Constantinople through Turkey and Armenia and rejoining the boat at Batum at the extreme east end of the Black Sea.

Upon our arrival at Constantinople this plan was put into effect and after getting our motor equipment and such other equipment as was necessary for the trip, we left Constantinople on the morning of September 7. The first lap of the trip was made by train, going south from Constantinople on the Bagdad railway through the cities

A CHAUFFEUR'S EXPERIENCE

of Ismid, Eskishehir, Ak-Shehr, Koria, Adana and Aleppo. At Aleppo we turned almost due east, traveling along the northern border of the plains of Mesopotamia to the ancient city of Mardin. At Mardin we left the train and started for Tiflis, Republic of Georgia, by automobile. At the start of the automobile trip I was assigned to duty as driver on a two-ton truck carrying gasoline and rations for the trip. After leaving Mardin we passed through the towns of Diarbekir, Karput, Sivas, Erzinjan, Erzerum, Kars, Erivan, the new capitol of the Republic of Armenia, going from Erivan to the Republic of Azarbaijan and from there into the Republic of Georgia and on into Tiflis where we took the train for Batum, after covering over 3,100 miles by train and auto in less than five weeks. All of the automobile trip was over extremely dangerous country, as there were many dangerous mountain passes on the road, some of them as high as 8,600 feet above sea level, and practically all of the country was infested with bandits.

While going from Kars to Erivan I was overtaken and captured by a band of bandits and in company with the two other men that were on the truck with me was held prisoner until we were able to prove that we were Americans, as none of the papers that we carried were sufficient proof. We were held until the General sent back to see what had become of us. With the assistance of the officer sent back by the General we were able to prove our identity and were released.

At all points on our trip through Turkey and Armenia we came in contact with suffering of the most severe sort, due to the lack of food. Except for the aid furnished by the various American Relief Missions the suffering would have been many times greater than what it was at that time, for in one town alone the American Commission for the Relief of the Near East was feeding over 30,000 women and children. It was no uncommon sight to see women and children gathering the refuse off the streets and eating it, and in one place I saw a mother and three little children whose only food for over three weeks had been green acorns gathered in the woods.

The 89th Division
By Charles Kistler

The 89th Division was composed of troops from the Middle Western states and was commanded by Major General Leonard Wood. It was assembled at Camp Funston, Kansas, in September, 1917, and was trained there until the spring of 1918, when it received orders to embark for France. It sailed under the command of Brigadier General Frank L. Winn, landing at Liverpool early in June and crossing immediately to France and took up intensive training until the first of August, when it was ordered to the front. It took its position on the Lucey sector, northwest of Toul, where it received as its first experience a severe strafing of mustard gas.

On the 6th of September Major General William E. Wright assumed command. Then came St. Mihiel. Through the thick woods and four years' accumulation of German barbed wire, in the face of rifle fire, shrapnel and high explosive shells, this division fought its way to the banks of the Rupt de Mad.

On September 20 the division moved over to the Argonne and without rest kept operating on this offensive until the signing of the armistice. On the morning of November 1, the 89th went over the top and took all objectives on scheduled time, and by afternoon the Heights of Barrimore were in their possession. When Marshal Foch heard the news, it is said, he stated that the war was over.

In the St. Mihiel sector the division was in the line continuously for thirty-five days, and they continued as a front line division for twenty days more. They were in line for twelve days' steady fighting in the Argonne, and then participated in the big drive during the last eleven days of the war.

In all, the 89th captured 194 German officers, 4,867 men, 127 pieces of artillery and 455 machine guns. They advanced over 38 kilometers, including the penetration of two strongly defended positions.

The casualties of this division were 48 officers and 1,081 men killed, 201 officers and 5,560 men wounded, one officer and 57 men missing in action, one officer and four men taken prisoners.

After the armistice I marched with these Middle Westerners through Belgium and Luxembourg into Germany, doing guard duty there until relieved by sailing orders.

Some Notes From a Soldier's Diary
By Lester E. Emmons

June 30—We left New York at 3:15 p. m. on the U. S. S. Henderson with about 750 bluejackets and 800 marines aboard. Seven transports are in convoy and two destroyers.

July 1, 7 p. m.—Our first "sub" scare. One of the destroyers drops several depth bombs, but I never found out whether they got the "sub," or if there was one. About 11 o'clock eleven more ships join us.

July 2—Fire alarm is sounded. We all go to our places and await orders. The fire is a bad one, so a destroyer comes alongside and begins taking the men off. The marines are taken off first. Ropes are made fast to the ship and the men climb down to the destroyers. It rains torrents. I got off about 1 o'clock in the night and was put on the U. S. S. Von Steuben, formerly a German raider. It was sure some crowd on that boat; she was loaded to the guards and put 1,700 more on her. When night came we laid on the decks. I lost all the clothes I had except those I had on. The ship was a fast one and we left the convoy and came on alone.

July 6—They claim a torpedo missed us about 200 feet. I guess it is so, for two of my roommates claim they were on deck and saw the wake of it.

July 8.—Three U. S. destroyers met us about 5:30 a. m. At 11 o'clock one of the destroyers sights a "sub" and drops four depth bombs. We had to sleep with our clothes and life preservers on, and wear life preservers all the time.

July 9—We sight land about 5 a. m. A welcome sight. We get into the harbor at Brest, France, about 8 o'clock.

July 11—We leave the Von Steuben and go ashore. I guess no one is sorry.

July 12—About sixty of us leave Brest at 6 a. m. and arrive at Louent about 1 o'clock, and we are still here. That will give you some idea of a trip over.

With the French Fighters
By Milo S. King

I sailed for France March 22, 1917, and enlisted with the French Army at Paris April 1, 1917, and trained with the French Officers' School for Auto Service at Meaux, France. Made sergeant first class, and was with the 6th French Division from June 6 to 16 on the Chemin des Dames, and again from June 22 to July 4. With the 66th Division Chasseurs in the attack and counter-attack, which lasted eleven days, and then again around the 30th of July on the same fighting ground. With the same company Oct. 17 to 26 on the attack on Malmaison front.

From 1 to September 30, 1918, was with reserves of French Army working with all units in the retreats and advances in the second battle of the Marne. With the 2nd Division, Marocaine, from October 18 to 31 in the Champaigne.

My unit was the first American unit to be awarded the fourragere of colors of Croix de Guerre, and the only American unit to be awarded the Fourragene—colors of the Medaille Militaire—ribbon. The section flag carried, beside the Medaille Militaire Fourraere, six Croix de Guerre. Four of the Ordre de l'Armee; one, Ordre Corps D'Armee; one, Ordre de la Division.

My unit enlisted in the U. S. Army October 3, 1917, but we continued to serve with the French, making no change, only that we were paid and equipped by the United States. The United States enlarged on the service and at the end of the war had fifty sections serving with French Army, each section consisting of one officer, thiry-five men and twenty ambulances.

First Impressions of First Line Trenches
By Lieut. Frank Swihart

I have just returned from my first experience in the front line, and now that I have had a bath, a shave and a chance to go to bed without wearing my boots, respirator, etc., I am feeling quite like myself once more.

My first trip in was without a doubt a wonderful experience and one to be long remembered. As we got near the front and could see the area which had been fought over, one realized for the first time what the horrors of war really meant. To see the towns and woods which had been mowed down by artillery fire until nothing was left standing higher than three of four feet, gave you some idea as to the effectiveness of the means of modern warfare. Of course, your thoughts were soon taken from this by an occasional shell bursting near you, and as you went still nearer the front, these shells were more numerous, and seemingly your chances of ever getting back more slim, but after seeing what a large percentage of the shots fired were misses then you began to think that it wasn't such a bad game after all and that you had a chance to play as well as the other fellow. Well, we arrived at the front line, took a peep at No Man's Land, and then grew anxious to see what was on the other side, so taking advantage of a quiet moment, I raised up a little higher to take a look, but when a machine gun began to sweep the parapet, I found out that it didn't take long to duck below the top, and my curiosity had been satisfied. The first few days in, the ground was frozen and the trenches were quite comfortable to move about in, but then we had a thaw, followed by a rain, and before we left the mud was knee deep. On coming out it was a hard, tiresome job to wade back to the safety zone. You don't get a chance to take much sleep at the front, and during the first few days you don't care for much, but after that when you get a chance for a few hours' rest you can sleep right through the noise and excitement, and it almost takes a gas alarm to wake you. Of course, you are quite willing to leave your clothes and boots on as well as the respirator and the automatic so as not to be taken by surprise, which is quite common.

It was quite evident that Fritz was getting the worst of the bargain for every time he sends a shell over he usually gets an iron ration of five in return.

In the unit I was with there was only one killed and three wounded during the tour of duty, and this was considered very small. We know Fritz had more than that, and we hope to cause him many more in the future.

Byron C. Goss Prominent in Gas Service

Byron C. Goss, of this city, son of the late Jonas Goss, left a professorship at Princeton University and enlisted in the service, as detailed elsewhere in this history.

Brigadier General A. A. Frion, chief of the Chemical Warfare Service, in a letter to Col. Cornwallis De Witt Wilcox, has the following to say of Col. Goss' service to his country:

"With further reference to Colonel Goss, to whom I introduced you when you were here, I desire to state that he is one of the best and ablest men Chemical Warfare Service produced in France. While a trained chemist, who has done considerable work in teaching along these lines, he adapted himself with tremendous rapidity to war conditions and in a remarkably short time mastered the tactical use of gas in the field.

"Joining the First Army Corps in France in March, 1918, he was with it in all the fights in which it took part to the end of the war, at which time he had been promoted to Chief Gas Officer, Second Army. He was in every big battle in which Americans took part, from Chateau Thierry to the attack of the Second Army on the morning of the 10th of November, 1918. As Chief Gas Officer, First Corps, he drew up the plan for gas and smoke operation for that corps and largely for the First Army in the Argonne fight.

"He did more than any other man to get the army in the field to understand gas, its dangers and what was still more important to victory, its use. Prior to America's participation in battle, he visited English and French fronts, where he was under fire many times and saw gas as used by those people and as used by the Germans against them.

"As one of the oldest officers in the Chemical Warfare Service he has seen more fighting, more of the effects of gas, both offensive and defensive, than any other American officer. I feel that he is a particularly capable man to write on field experiences with gas and smoke and any other matters which he came in contact with in that work."

The Thirty-Seventh Division
By Earl Sisson.

The 37th division, a former Ohio National Guard division composed of Division Headquarters—Headquarters troop, 134th Machine Gun Battalion; 73rd Infantry Brigade—145th Infantry, 146th Infantry, 135th N. G. Battalion; 74th Infantry Brigade—147 Infantry, 148th Infantry, 136th M. G. Battalion; 62nd Artillery Brigade—134th, 135th and 136th, Field Artillery 112th, Trench Mortar Battery, 112th Engineers, 112th Engineer train, 112th Ammunition train, 112th Supply train, 112th Sanitary train, 112th, Field Signal Battalion, 112th Military Police and 114th Mobile Veterinary Unit was mobilized at Camp Sheridan, Montgomery, Alabama during the early fall of 1917.

Many of the troops of the division had seen more or less service on the Mexican border during the campaign of 1916 and with but few exceptions, none had been mustered out of service between the close of that campaign and the declaration of war with Germany, April 6, 1917.

Immediately following the declaration of war, the troops of the division were used at different points over the state where patrol duty was necessary, during which time, an active recruiting campaign was being carried on which ultimately filled the depleted ranks of the various units with volunteer soldiers.

Following an eight months intensive training program at Camp Sheridan, under the supervision of Maj. Gen. Chas. G. Treat, the division departed by train on May 20, 1918 for Camp Lee, Va., Maj. Gen C. S. Farnsworth relieving General Treat shortly previous to the move eastward.

During the three weeks stay at Camp Lee, the division was required to bend every effort in order to complete equipment for oversea service.

This completed, the division received orders to embark and in consequence, on June 11, the 73rd Brigade moved by rail to Hoboken, embarking on the Steamship Leviathan, while the artillery batteries set sail on the Nestor, Plassey, Saxon, Titan, Horatio, Phesus and Victoria. The 74th Brigade with Engineers, Signal Corps, Medical and supply units embarked at Newport News, Va., on the transports

Pocahontas, Susquehanna, Castera and Duca D'Aosta, all arriving at Brest, France about July 4th.

A short stay at Pontanezen barracks and a rail trip inland, landed the division intact in the Bourmont, Haute Marne area, where another wait of three weeks was wedged into the schedule while cleaning and refurnishing equipment was completed, when on July 28th, the division received orders to proceed to Baccarat, there to take over their first sector under fire of the enemy.

BACCARAT SECTOR

The Baccarat Sector in the Vosges Mountains, taken over by the troops of the division, extended for a distance of fifteen kilometers from the Forest dex Elieux, north of the village of Badonviller, through the Bois Communal de la Woevre, Bois des Haies, the villages of Merviller, Ancerviller and Neuf Maisons along the edge of the Bois des Pretres. While this sector, in the beautiful wooded hills and mountains of the Vosges, was considered inactive, it was a position of responsibility and just as much effort and hard work was expended in its preservation, as if it were the most vital part of the entire battle line from the North Sea to Switzerland.

Here the men of the division, had their initial training under fire and although interrupted by continuous enemy shelling and aerial bombardments, as well as enemy observation, the training continued. During the six weeks the Division held this sector, men of the division were required by the Commanding General to dominate No Man's Land at all times and under all conditions. Thus it was that when the division was ordered to move and enter the zone of real activity, General Duport, commanding the sixth French Army issued the following commendatory order:

"6th Army French, General Staff,   Sept. 14, 1918
1st Section No. 823-1   Special Order No. 66

"The 37th U. S. Division is leaving the zone of Lunneville at a time when the American Army has achieved great victory and has added new laurels to those already gathered by the first American divisions on the Somme, on the Marne and on the Vestle.

"I am pleased at having the honor of commanding for several weeks the young troops of Ohio, having seen them each day, become more soldier-like and more conscious of their power. I know now that they will come up to the standard in the hardest and noblest deeds they are called upon to perform when they are engaged upon a new battle front.

"The method, the spirit, the discipline which they have shown all the time, when hardly landed on the shores of France, they were called upon to hold a sector, are the best guarantees of future success.

"I wish to express my thanks to General Farnsworth, whose sense of duty and good military qualities make him worthy of the highest confidence, and to the officers and staff and also, to all the unit commanders, officers and men of the 37th Division.

"My best wishes accompany the Buckeye Division in its future battles, in which it will distinguish itself to the honor of its flag and to the triumph of its righteous cause."

Prisoners captured—officers 1, men 6, deserters 7, total 14.

Casualities—killed 16, wounded 80, missing 6, total 102.

Upon the relief of the division in the Baccarat sector on Sept. 16, 1918, movement was made by rail to the area of Revigny, Bar le Duc and Robert Espange. After a rest of four days, another move, this time by bus and truck train, landed at Recicourt. Two days, after, the advance Echelon was moved to a dugout on the Verriers-en Hese Farm, a few kilometers from the ruined village of Avacourt, with historic Verdun within sight to the southeast. In fact the division was on the battlefield of Verdun, where countless thousands of brave soldiers had fallen, and which was soon to be made famous again as the chosen field for the great American drive along the Meuse to the battle famed city of Sedan. So the 37th division was one of the American divisions that gave the initial impetus to that big offensive, that contributed so great a part towards final victory.

During the cold rainy nights of Sept. 24th and 25th, the Division relieved the 79th division along a front of slightly over three kilometers in width. The ruined village of Avacourt lying in the center of the front and just within the lines.

At 10:25 o'clock on the night of Sept. 25th, the artillery preparation commenced and each hour added to the intensity, until guns of all caliber were contributing their part to one of the mightiest artillery offensives ever attempted in this war. This preparation reached its maximum at 5:30 A. M., Sept. 26th, when it rolled off over the enemy trenches in a barrage which enabled infantrymen, following closely and quickly, to overcome any resistance left by the enemy.

The sun rose bright and clear September 26th and for that one day, conditions were ideal for the task of the infantry men. The battle-traced, map road from Avacourt across No Man's Land, was an outline only, and immediately, difficulties began to arise in bringing forward artillery. The ground, soft underneath the dry crust, and pox marked with shell holes, formed quagmires through which, it was almost hopeless to pull the heavy limbers. During that night showers which continued unceasingly, for the next five days added to the burden and the freshly constructed dirt roads soon became a knee-deep trail of mud. Next morning, the infantry took up the attack and pushed on, over terrain torn by bursting shells and through forest tangled with shattered trees and barbed wire. The town of Iviory on the left, was captured. A little later the little town of Montfaucon, slightly off the division sector to the right, entered by patrols the night before, and cleared of the enemy during the early morning hours of the following day, fell to the men of the division. Montfaucon, considered by the Great German General Staff as impregnable, fell during the early morning of Sept. 28th. It was here on this heighth that the German Crown Prince had constructed an observation tower, from which he viewed the battle of Verdun, and on the second day of the great offensive it had fallen and with its fall, the Hindenburg line had again been broken.

Lack of Artillery support, added hourly to the difficulties of the advance and during the days of Sept. 28-29, progress was made and contested for, foot by foot, through fields of mud, through gas filled woodlands through the Bois Emont, Bois de Beuge and on to the Communal de Cierges.

The Division was relieved October 1st, after having fought and advanced for four days against all the weapons of war at the command of the enemy. The front line at that time, ran along a ridge, one and one-half kilometers west and slightly north of Cierges, to a few hundred meters south of that city, thence to the Bois Communal de Cierges.

Still under fire, remnants of companies started for the rear relieved by fresh troops of the 32nd—Michigan division.

It was a hungry, tired, wet, sleepy remnant of a proud division that returned. Many had seen their comrades and officers fall wounded, some severely, some to pay the price supreme. So the part of the 37th division was played in that great offensive, to which it gave the momentum that carried on and on, until on November 11th, the day of the armistice, it had reached the city of Sedan.

The total number of prisoners captured by the division during that offensive, was 13 officers and 1107 men, among which were represented some of the finest divisions of the German Army. The

THE THIRTY-SEVENTH DIVISION

37th German Division, 117 Division, 1st and 5th Guard Divisions, the latter two, among the elite of the Prussian Guard divisions. Large quantities of materials of all kinds were captured, including:

12-77 m-m cannon; 1, 105 m-m cannon; 10, 155 m-m cannon; 4, 77 m-m anti-aircraft guns; 5, Granatenwerfers; engineering material, ammunition of all kinds; 1 Daimler 3 ton truck; railway material; 2000 rifles and over 250 machine guns.

Casualties—officers killed 17, wounded 110; total 127.

Enlisted men killed 410; wounded 2462; missing 137; total 3009; total officers and men 3,136.

Total advance—9.8 kilometers.

Following the relief of the division from the Muese-Argonne offensive, movement was effected by trucks, driven by Chinese coolies. These in the course of twenty-four hours, landed various units at Pagney-sur-Meuse, where a stay of four days permitted troops getting some much needed rest, along with several replacements, although upon receipt of orders to move, depleted ranks were noticeable in every organization.

THE ST. MIHIEL SALIENT

On the night of Oct. 6th, 1918, orders to proceed to the Pannes Sector, a part of the recaptured St. Mihiel salient, resulted in a movement by truck train to Euvezin, where division headquarters were established and the 89th Division relieved. Less than one month previous, this salient which had projected out of the line, continually menacing the Allied communications around Verdun, had been cut off by the first American drive, which had brought Metz within range of big guns.

In the St. Mihiel sector, the division lines extended from the Bois de Jualny de Hailbot along the northern edges of Etang de la Chaussee. Across the way were the villages of Rembercourt-sur-Mad, Dommartin, Dampvitoux and La Chaussee which formed the enemy line. The village of Haumont was in No Man's Land.

Here the division found plenty of activity, although no offensive was in progress. The enemy shelled all parts of the sector with untiring regularity. Aeroplanes paid nightly visits dropping bombs upon every sign of life. The thick deep valleys gave particular advantage to the use of gas and the division was subjected to one of the heaviest concentrated gas barrages the enemy had ever attempted. Active raiding and patrolling were energetically pushed by our men as well as by enemy forces. Day and night from both sides of the line, the incessant clatter of machine guns, the screech of projectiles and the low buzz of the German rotary motor, kept all vigilant to the liklihood of an attack. Even here, training was resumed and every available man, not absolutely needed at the front was further drilled in some branch of warfare.

On October 17th, replacements having been received, equipment again gotten into shape, the division relieved by the 28th, Pennyslvania troops, again took trucks and retraced their steps to Pagney-sur-Meuse.

Casualties—killed 11; wounded 180; missing 6; total 197.

BELGIUM—FIRST PHASE

Two bustling days were spent at Pagney-sur-Meuse in gathering together and preparing for shipment, quantities of provisions and supplies of all kinds. Oct. 18th, French box cars crowded with 40 men, each, slipped away and rattled north through an air of whispered secrecy and surmise. Little by little, as Paris, Amiens, Arrat slipped by and other towns loomed out of obscurity, the mystery cleared and after three days, the trains came to a stop at St. Jean and Wieltje, Belgium, in the shadow of the ruins of the Cathedral of Ypres.

Hesitatingly, the men crawled out of their cars, to gaze with awe upon the desolation which spread as far as the eye could see in every direction. There on the famous battlefield of Ypres, where British and German had fought bitterly for four years, was depicted a sight which pen of man will never describe. There where once had stood flourishing towns, now held their identity only by signboards, with no sign of life visible; where even grass, or vegetation of any kind died in a struggle for existence against the tear of shrapnel and the bursting of explosives, where gas had so polluted the shell hole water that drinking water was at a premium.

On foot, the troops of the division marched across twenty kilometers of this barren waste, to the nearest semblance of shelter. Division headquarters were opened Oct. 22 in the ruined village of Hooglede and from there the division moved in short stages to Lichterveldt, Mulebeke and Dentreghem.

On Oct. 22nd, the division was attached to the French army in Belgium and placed at the disposition of King Albert of the Belgians. This was an honor and a confidence that later events proved not to have been misplaced. During the nights of Oct. 29th and 30th, the division took over three kilometers of front extending along the Courtrai-Ghent railroad, just across the Lys river, with Olsene directly in front of the center.

At 5:30 a. m., October 31st, after an artillery preparation of five minutes and with troops of the 91st American Division on their left, the infantry again went over the top. The enemy answered with gas and vigorous artillery and machine gun fire. So sharp and quick was the attack however, that all counter attempts by the enemy were futile and fighting a rear-guard action, he withdrew his forces to Cruyshautem Ridge. Here on a slight raise, midway between the Lys and the Escaut (Scheldt) Rivers, he reorganized and prepared to stop the advancing khaki line. The French artillery, attached to this division for the operation, worked like trojans. Scarcely had the panting horses been pulled away from the guns, before they spit their whirring shells upon the enemy. In the meantime, other batteries were being rushed forward, each in turn keeping up the tune, while others advanced. All calibers were finally firing on Cruyshautem Ridge and concentrating there for a few moments, lifted barely in time for the on rushing infantry. The Boche were routed and the American troops, gaining momentum, scarcely paused on the ridge, but drove on to the Escaut across which the Boche retreated.

All roads leading forward and all villages were heavily shelled by the enemy batteries. The town of Olsene being completely destroyed, division headquarters moved up to Cruyshautem and on Nov. 1st, plans were laid to force a crossing of the Escaut.

Early on the morning of Nov. 1st, soldiers of the 37th Division swam the river and working from both banks, under a continual hail of machine bullets, shrapnel and high explosive shells, constructed a foot bridge from two trees, fastened end to end. Over this frail structure, infantrymen crossed, some safely, while other slipping off the wet, unstable footing, disappeared beneath the icy waters. Late that afternoon 52 men had succeeded in gaining the east bank. At Heurne, efforts were made to construct a pontoon bridge, but enemy artillery shelled the position so effectually, that the attempt had to be abandoned. An attempt to construct a bridge farther to the south was successful however, although costly in life, but at 7:00 p. m. a completed bridge was established across the river.

All through the night the fight continued. Vengeful Boche planes raided the towns of Meulbeke, Dentreghem and Cruyshautem. The whir of his planes seemed always there and from twenty-five to seventy bombs of different size, ranging from the small "baby bomb" to the giant ton projectile, were dropped on each of the villages. Belgian refugees, driven before the fleeing Germans, had in some instances succeeded in breaking away from their captors and returning to the demolished homes. Others were forced by the Huns to return through the American barrage. When upon instructions from General Farnsworth, the barrage was lifted from the roads to allow them an opening through which they might pass, German airmen followed the roads bombing, killing and maiming as they went.

During the night of Nov. 1, an enemy shell pierced the room occupied by the commanding General, throwing brick, tile and shattered furnishings in its path, but by some turn of fate, the commander escaped unharmed. The intensity continued Nov. 3rd. In desperation, enemy planes flying low over the disputed river, dropped bombs or turned into a nose dive, churning the water and combing the banks with a scathing machine gun fire. By 6:30 that evening nine companies of infantry had filtered across the Escaut. Here they held on, repelling all enemy counter attacks, gradually securing their bridgehead. Food and ammunition were carried over during the night and American infantry had established themselves there, never to be driven back.

On November 4th and 5th, the division was relieved by the French units and returned to Thielt for a hard earned, few days rest. Proudly they marched back, for they were the first and only Allied Division to cross and establish a bridgehead on the east bank of the Scheldt. Again part of the elite of the German army opposed them and failed, for among the prisoners taken, were represented the 6th and 7th German Guard Infantry.

Total prisoners taken—officers 12; enlisted men 316; total 328.

Wounded, taken prisoner 38. Total 366.

Partial list of material captured—3,105 m-m cannon; 3, 77 m-m cannon; 7 Caissons; 5 Limbers; 3, 2-inch Trench Mortars; 11 machine guns; 7 horses; quantities of ammunition of all calibers.

Total advance—14.56 kilometers.

Casualties—officers killed 4; wounded 33; total 37. Enlisted men 218; wounded 1,223; missing 134; total 1,575. Total officers and enlisted men 1,612.

Upon relief, the following General Order was issued by General Penet, commanding the 30th, French Corps:

"30th Corps-Etat Major,   Headquarters, Nov. 9th, 1918.
3rd Bureau, Nn 250-3.   Order No. 57.

"Upon the occasion of the relief of the 37th Division from duty with the 30th C. A., the Commanding General of this Corps takes pleasure in expressing his entire satisfaction with the energy, the bravery and the fighting which took place between October 31 and Nov. 4.

"After having overcome the enemy's resistance, the Division made a vigorous pursuit; then after having been the first division to force a passage of the Escaut (Scheldt) River, it established bridgeheads on the right bank of the river, which it held in spite of repeated counter attacks launched by the enemy.

The Commanding General of the C. A. congratulates the 37th D. I. U. S. warmly upon its brilliant conduct.

"The General Commanding the 30th Corps: H. Penet."

BELGIUM—SECOND PHASE

November 4th to 8th was spent in Thielt, Belgium, cleaning up, requipping and replacing the depleted ranks. During this time the division was transfered from the 30th French corps to the 34th corps, then engaged a few kilometers to the north of the territory liberated during the first Belgian offensive. On November 9th, the Division Post Command, moved to Chateau de Huysse, Belgium, between the villages of Lozer and Huysse, and preparations were imediately made to force another crossing of the Escaut. This time the crossing was to be made about 15 kilometers (9 miles) south of Ghent, between the villages of Klein Meersch and Heuvel.

Rumors of Germany's acceptance of the terms of the armistice began to abound, following closely the collapse of Bulgaria, Turkey and Austria, gave increased morale to the Allied troops. All plans were speeded up and every preparation made to keep the Boche running and to press hard the advantages gained with every day's fighting. The proposed action was set ahead one day and plans so modified, that the French units made the initial attack. At 8:00 a. m., Nov. 10th, the leading troops arrived in the advanced area. On their way to the river, at the village of Syngem, they were greeted by volley after volley of machine gun bullets, high explosive shells and aerial bombs, and again the men were in the hottest kind of fighting.

The Escaut river, for the length of the Division sector, formed a "U" shaped bend with the bottom of the "U" toward the enemy. The ground leading to the river, from the Allied side, was low and marshy and its flooded condition, brought on by recent rains, made the approach for a distance of two or three hundred meters a very difficult matter. The enemy on this side of the river, had a big advantage, the high bluffs of the right bank permitting his overlooking without interruption, the American advance. Taking advantage of his position he had built a veritable thicket of machine gun nests. Crawling and slipping through the mud, taking advantage of any irregularities of the terrain, the men of the division worked their way up to the river edge and held on.

The town of Syngem was heavily shelled and all traffic along the road leading into the town blocked. A bridge was constructed across the river at the town of Heuvel, on the extreme south end of the division sector, and infantry crossing there worked north, gradually clearing the east bank of the enemy. The entire night was spent in feverish activity, in obtaining a foothold across the river and, on the morning of November 11th, with Armistice rumors thick in the air, found the right bank securely held by American soldiers.

The Armistice was signed, going into effect at 11 o'clock on the morning of that day. The fight was pushed up until the last moment and so fast did our troops advance that at the eventful hour, when the advance was ordered stopped, the 37th division was holding the line as far east as the little villages of Dickele, Zwartenbrock, Keerkem and Hundlegem.

The war was over and the afternoon of November 11th, the very stillness, so recently rent by the shriek of artillery shells and the whistle of machine gun bullets, was oppressing. A strange and curious thing, but from some secret nook, the American baseball rolled out and there was being tossed about, where three hours before, no living thing could be exposed.

Total advance: 7 kilometers.

Casualties—officers killed 0, wounded 1, total 1.

Enlisted men killed 9, wounded 56, missing 1, total 66. Total of officers and men 67.

Upon the termination of the Belgian offensive, the following general order 6th French Army, commanded by General Degoutte, was issued:

"VI Army French: Headquarters, Dec. 11, 1918.
General Order No. 31

"In addressing myself to the division of the United States of

America, who had covered themselves with glory in the Chateau Thierry offensive, I said that the orders given by the chief were always carried out, in spite of the difficulties and the sacrifices necessary to win.

"In the 37th and 91st Divisions U. S., I found the same spirit of duty and willing submission to discipline which makes gallant soldiers and victorious armies.

"The enemy was to hold the heights between the Lys and the Escaut ' to the death.' American troops of these divisions, acting in concert with the French divisions of the Group of Armies of Flanders, broke through the enemy line on the 31st, October, 1918, and after severe fighting threw him on the Escaut.

"Then attempting an operation of war, of unheard of audacity, the American units crossed the overflooded Escaut, under fire of the enemy and maintained themselves on the opposite bank of the river, in spite of his counter attacks.

"Glory to such troops and their chiefs. They have valiantly contributed to the liberation of a part of Belgian territory and to final victory.

"Their great nation may be proud of them.

"The General commanding the army.

DEGOUTTE."

HOMEWARD BOUND

The 37th division was selected as one of the divisions to follow the German army in its retreat to the Rhine. It started on its way and in easy stages followed on towards Brussels. Thirty-three kilometers (21 miles) west of that city, at the village of Leeuwergum, the Division received orders to halt and retrace its steps westward from whence it came. Detachments from the Divisions were, however detailed to form the Guard of Honor upon the return to Brussels of the King and Queen of the Belgians, after four years of exile, following the great German advance of 1914.

For its work in Belgium, it had gained the admiration and respect of that noble little kingdom. One hundred and fifty Belgian war crosses are proudly worn by the members of the division, as a reminder of the short, but decisive, campaign in that country. Two hundred and twenty-nine French medals of all degrees are also represented in the 37th Division besides several American Distinguished Service Crosses.

For the recognition received, the Division occupied six active sectors, participated in four major offensives, advanced during offensives, a total of more than 30 kilometers in the face of all kinds of conditions, captured 1475 prisoners of war and suffered, in all, 5,113 casualties in killed and wounded.

Leaving the area of Brussels, the division moved in easy stages to Oost Roosbeke, where, on Thanksgiving day, the men were treated to a "turkey dinner" which consisted of corned beef and Belgian turnips. Leaving the vicinity of Oost Roosbeke on December 4, the march westward continued with halts at Rous Brugge, a beautiful little city on the banks of the famous Yser canal. Then on Dec. 7th, the Division again crossed the France-Belgian border and established their headquarters in Hondschoote, France, where a stay of 10 days brought an order to again move, this time to Wormhoudt, in the Dunquerque area. Here the division remained over the Christmas holidays and on Jan. 13th the division entrained, a short hike to Esquelbecq and again the men were crowded in French box cars bound for the Le Mans district. Two days later the divisional trains arrived at Alencon, where during the following thirty days, a feverish campaign was waged in equipping the troops for their return to the United States, which had then narrowed down to a question of days.

It was at Alencon that General Pershing reviewed the division on January 27th. On February 17th the division effected another lap in the long journey by a thirty-five kilometer hike which landed it in St. Mars-sous-Ballon. In the shadow of one of the oldest of the remaining French castles, in the presence of many French military men of all ranks, General Cardre of the French Army conferred the French Croix de Guerre upon two hundred and twenty-nine men of the Division.

Actual indicitations of a move to the port of embarkation were taking form and on March 1, the Division entrained for the last lap of their journey homeward on French trains. A three day trip and the men detrained at Brest, where a stay of eight days, filled with preparation and expectation elapsed and on March 12th, units hiked from Camp Pontanezen to the docks and embarked on the Transports Geo. Washington, Von Steuben and Leviathan and the Battleships Kansas and Missouri. After an average voyage they again set foot on American soil at Hoboken, N. J., from whence they went to Camp Merritt, N. J., and were finally mustered out of service at Camp Sherman, Ohio, between April 10th and 15th, proud of their part and satisfied that they had done it well.

Death of Verle Madary

How Private Verle Madary met death from a piece of high explosive shell, while at his post of duty, is described in a letter written Oct. 20, 1918, to his mother, Mrs. Gertrude Madary, from Major Edward M. Colis, Medical Corps, 60th Artillery C. A. C. The dead Fulton county boy's officer speaks highly of him. The letter follows:

"My Dear Mrs. Madary:

"By the time that this note of appreciation arrives at your home, you will have had notice through official channels that you have at once lost and won a boy. I put it this way because as surgeon in this regiment, I am in contact with the men who made up the regiment and particularly with the medical department men, of whom Verle was one.

"He was, as his mother should know, a real man, young in years, of which all of the men who have spoken to me have remarked. He made himself felt, that is what I meant by winning—men of that type are not permanently lost. That thought would be unsupportable. The sense of loss is all too recent for any word of mine, however appreciative, to mitigate it. But please feel that you have given and given fully and freely that those things which we at home hold most dear and sacred may be preserved.

"He was killed by a scrap of a high explosive shell which entered the house where he was working. He was at his post of duty at the moment. He was, you know, assistant to one of our dentists. His grave lies under my window in a small flower garden and there are with him ten others, one of whom was struck down in the same way. The other day I saw one of the boys gathering a bunch of such flowers as still bloom. He reverently placed them upon the mound which covers not Verle, but that which was Verle's body.

"If you are as certain as I am, that there is nothing wasted in this world and I believe it in spite of what I have to see here, then feel very proud that you have given so largely for that end which we cannot clearly see, but which our faith tells us is surely there."

Recollections of the Civil War

By Al J. Kitt, Editor Fowler (Ind.) Tribune.

My most vivid recollection of the beginning of the Civil War is associated with the first call for troops. Mrs. Isaiah Hoover, who lived in the old Walker residence east of Jesse Shields' place, came to our home rather early one morning in a very excited state. Throwing off her sun-bonnet she turned to my mother and said: "Well, it has come at last; the war bills are up all over town." The "war bills" proved to be President Lincoln's first call for 75,000 men. I remember seeing one of the bills tacked up on the front of Jesse Shield's old store, while a great crowd of men surrounded it discussing the coming war. Doubtless the experience of Rochester at the beginning and during the Civil War was that of all similar communities. It was not only the sons that went then, but the fathers, and exceptions were not made for tillers of the soil or supporters of families. It was a war in which the home and fireside and the life of a great Republic were at stake. The scenes of those early days can be easily recalled. The recruiting office, the fife and the drum, and the fever of interest and excitement that subjected everything else to its force; the company of gallant boys as they marched down the street to embark for the front, many of them never to return, the sidewalks and streets crowded with weeping women and children and cheering men. The old town was twenty miles from the nearest railroad, no telegraph and the telephone secret was yet in the bosom of the future, and the enlisted men were transported to Logansport and other points by wagons. Then the days of waiting, but few daily papers taken and those uncertain, the suspense can be easily imagined. Us boys met on the commons and the banks of the lake and discussed the great war, telling over and over again of the many virtuous and generous deeds of the men who had gone to the battlefields. News had been received that a great fight (Chickamauga) was imminent, and there were days of tense waiting when tearful and drawn faces kept present the mighty tragedy that followed. Then came the news of a great battle in which thousands were slain and wounded, but no list of the victims. The old 87th was known to be in the thick of the fight and to this belonged many of the brave boys who marched through our streets but a few months before. Nearly every man, woman and child was represented by ties of blood or heart. Days of waiting in which the atmosphere and fear of impending tragedy filled every home. It finally came—the list of Union losses; it embraced the names of husbands, fathers, sons and sweethearts; a number killed, many wounded, other prisoners, some missing. Scarcely a home but that was directly or indirectly afflicted through this mighty struggle for the preservation of the Union. With this picture in mind, as it is with older ones, it is easy to realize something of the tragedy recently enacted in Europe, and of the part not of the battlefields or trenches; but of the tears, heartaches and heroism of those at home, many of whom must bear the burden not only of the present but in the years to come. The Civil War counted its sufferers by the thousands; in the record of the titanic struggle just closed they were counted by the millions.

Little Glimpses of Soldier Life

Gleaned from Letters, Newspaper Stories and Other Sources, all of Which Concern Fulton County Service Men.

"Cooties" are Fierce

"I have seen thousands of German prisoners with the P. G. on their backs. I think they are most ignorant looking, and the way they stare at a person it's a pity all of them hadn't been shot. The negro soldiers were great convoys for them. It was their delight to shoot one.

"The lieutenant announced tonight that there would be a collection taken up for the orphans' fund. The 62nd is going to adopt several orphans. We have one with us now whose father was killed in 1914.

"How is everything at home? Winter will soon be here—are you prepared? I have been receiving the papers, now and then, but I suppose some of them have been lost in transit. Influenza seems to have been doing some awful work at home. This company has been lucky so far. There were only a few who went to the hospital. But there are lot of boys who get 'cooties,' and they are fierce."

PVT. ROSS D. EMRICK,
Co. A, 62nd Regt., T. C., A. E. F., France.

Chasing the Huns.

"I am just about fifteen miles west of Metz. You can find it on the map. I was in the Toul drive, St. Mihiel drive and the Argonne drive. The last was a burning hell on earth. It was fearful, but we never yielded a foot of ground—always advancing. I saw men lying in piles, dead, hit by shells and machine gun fire, but the majority of them were Huns. It is all over now, and glad of it. The people back in the States don't know what war is. For nine days and nights we marched to get at the Huns after our first drive, then went into action and began to pound away. Now I am riding a motorcycle for a Major, with a sidecar. It is an easy job. France has some very good roads. It has been pretty cold here, but has not snowed. I have a rubber suit to ride in and a long leather coat that Uncle Sam puts out. Can't get cold or wet.

"No Frenchman ever drinks water—all drink wine. We can get beer and light wine and lots of other junk to drink if we want it. We captured two barrels of beer from the Germans, and it was fine, for we were cold, tired and hungry and it didn't last long.

"Since the war has been over I have been in Germany. Our shells were beginning to drop on their country and hit their towns, and they could not stand for that. A German will give us anything, almost, for a cake of soap or a little handful of sugar."

PVT. ROY OVERMYER,
Hdq. Co. 115 F. A., A. E. F.

Last Farewell to Brother.

"Old Man Censor is going to be good to us this once; has removed a few of his whiskers for the time being, so we can tell you more about our part in history making since landing in France.

"I hardly know where to begin, now that I have the chance to tell it.

"Our date of sailing, you know. We came over on one of the biggest ships afloat, the Olympic, and reached port in Southern England Nov. 24, disembarking on the following day and taking a train across old England.

"This was a grand trip through English country. The trees were leafing out and everything looked beautiful.

"We passed through many towns and villages, suburban to London, and reached Dover, a city of darkness, at 10 p. m. From there we took another boat across the channel, being convoyed across, reaching Calais, France, in the evening of May 14.

"Here we remained in a rest camp three days, turning extra equipment and drawing English gas masks and rifles. We left there by train, which, according to the inscription on the side, held '36 hommes or eight chevaux,' but they were good to us and only put twenty-four soldiers in each car, which was enough, at that.

"That was my first experience on a troop train in France, but by no means my last. We expected a long ride, but got a short one instead, with a five-mile hike at the end, reaching a small French village not many miles from St. Omar. There we spent the rest of May and the first days of June training under the direction of the English. Those were days of hard work but of good fellowship, for it was my first opportunity to get acquainted with the boys of my company, aside from those from home.

"One Saturday we were ordered to turn in our English rifles

for those of the U. S. A., then we knew that we were due to go to an American sector. We left the next day, Sunday, and hiked for three days, took a day's rest and then got on another troop train which took us near Paris. After a week in billets, we moved out again, this time by trucks, reaching our stopping place late in the evening.

"Roy and I pitched our tent together and went to bed, not waiting for supper. A week was spent here in gas and bayonet drill, and then we moved up Marne valley toward Chateau Thierry, the division going into service along the Marne.

"A model platoon was selected from our company to go up with the French for an attack. Three Rochester boys were among those selected, and all three were wounded in the attack which, however, was successful. One of them, I understand, is now on his way back home—there, I expect by this time.

"When the Germans started their attacks in July and the big offensive on the 14th, we were lying in the woods below Chateau Thierry, with the Marne below us. Then the Germans started through and we moved up part of the division, going into the lines about the 18th. On Saturday afternoon, July 20, I was gassed, but at that time I did not know it, not until about daylight on Sunday, when, along with some other fellows, I was taken to the hospital. Here it was that I bid Roy good-bye. Both realized that it might be our last good-bye, without admitting it. I did not want to go, for I knew what was coming, but they took me, anyway.

"That day will long be remembered by me. What Roy went through with from Chateau Thierry to the Vesle, he alone could tell. We can rest assured that he did his full duty and did it bravely, but why he should have been taken we must leave to Him who knows better than we.

" From the gas hospital I went to Base Hospital No. 32, at Contrexville. This was a beautiful location for a hospital and we were treated fine. My nurse was a personal friend of Miss Ruth Wright, who did not happen to be there, as she was on duty up at a field hospital. My nurse promised to remember me to Miss Wright, but whether she did or not I do not know. They used to kid me at the hospital for sleeping so much. But I did not care, for I had a good bed and was sleepy.

" When I left the hospital I went to a replacement camp, expecting to get back to my company. This camp was in a village not far from Paris and near the Marne river.

"August was spent here, the replacement battalion moving out the last of the month.

"On this trip we went through Chateau Thierry, which had been taken by the Germans a month before, going through Metz, Epremay and Toul. During September and October we were at camp not far from Toul. This is one of the old fortified towns of France, the old part being surrounded by a stone wall and moat.

"The first of November we moved again, this time landing near Clermont on Argonne, about 27 kilometers southwest of Verdun, and here we still remain out in the woods, seemingly miles from nowhere as far as going anywhere or seeing anything is concerned.

"I have seen about all of France I care to see, unless it is Paris. France is all right for the French, but not for me—I'll take my chance back in old Indiana and the sooner I get there the better."

RAY SHELTON.

A Glimpse of Germany.

"I have not seen any Fulton boys at all since I have been over here and that has been since June 28, 1917, the longest any troops have been in Europe. The First Division has taken part in every battle that the Americans ever gave or received and never yielded an inch in retreat, they always went forward. If we did not we would not be where we are today. We took part in the Cantigney, Soissions, St. Mihiel, Argonne and Sedan drives. The last battle the Americans gave the Dutch we made them all pay very highly in land and troops for the Yanks were headed for Berlin, and would have reached there only for the armistice. We were on our way when we received news that Kaiser Bill had signed the note for his men to cease firing at 11 o'clock. It was the eleventh day, eleventh hour, and eleventh month that the armistice was signed. We are now stationed near the Rhine river doing guard duty and looking out for the Dutch farther up the Rhine so they do not start their dirty work again. We are in the state called Unter Westerwald and this is where the grape wine is made. Everywhere there is a valley. It is nothing but a large mass of grape vines. They have them growing in the shape of a corn stalk and supported by driving a stake by the side of the stalk and tieing them together. Even the high hills running up from the south side are grape yards. Hills that look so steep no person could climb them, but there are grapes there for wine. I have often heard talk of the mighty Rhine and Moselle rivers, but I can not see anything great about them. We crossed the Moselle river in Luxemberg in five minutes on a bridge, and the Rhine we crossed into Coblenz on a pontoon bridge in the same length of time. It is not so wide as I have been told or so swift. It is not as wide as the Mississippi river. The Moselle joins the Rhine at Coblenz. A small river here is a collection of words joined together during spare time. Here Father Rhine awaits for fair Mother Moselle, who comes hurrying through the valley of the Moselle with her vineclad colors and embracing her with his mighty arms, carries her away to meet their lordly king, the sea.

"Since we have been in Germany we have been treated fine, having nice warm beds to sleep in and all that we can eat. The people were not so bad off as we heard they were. At night you are welcome in their best room or any place you wish to go. The father sits and reads while the mother spins wool or flax, which is something we never see in the states. We have electric lights and street car lines near our town, but one thing we do not see and that is horses, as they were all killed in the war. The people milk one and sometimes two cows, they then take them and hitch them to a buggy or wagon and drive them like horses."

BENJAMIN WESTWOOD,
Supply Sergeant, Co. E, 18th Inf.

Some Impressions of England and France

Of course I worked and worked some in the army for I was a blacksmith, but what I am going to tell here is of places I have been and things I have done along with my work. I entered the service of the U. S. A. on the 4th day of Oct., 1917, at Rochester. I went into training at Camp Taylor, Ky., on the 5th day of Oct., 1917, and remained in training until the 1st day of May, 1918. Was then transferred to the Field Rifle Range at West Point, Ky. I remained here until Sept. 3rd and we then boarded the train for Hoboken, N. J. At Hoboken I received my overseas equipment along with the other men of the company and the 8th day of Sept., 1918, we sailed on the White Steam Line, the ship "Canada," manned by an English crew, with a convoy of 14 transports, 8 sub chasers or cruisers and 1 battleship. We were twelve days on the water and we all thought that food for the fishes was never so plentiful. How the old boat did rock! We ate fish, moldy cheese and drank black English tea on the hop, run and jump, some times hanging onto a post but more often lying where we fell. The first sign of land over there was Estle Crege, standing 215 feet above sea level, just off the coast of Ireland in the Irish Sea. Then Hurrah, land, and welcome, too. The rolling dipping green of Ireland. We sailed up the river Clyde, receiving shouts of welcome from far and near, while the band played "We're Coming Over and We Wont Go Back Till It's Over, Over Here." It sure made a man feel that he was doing his duty. We docked at Glasgow, Scotland on the 21st of Sept., 1918, at 2 a. m. At 4 p. m. the same day we left for Winchester, England. Leaving the rails we hiked five miles to Camp Windledown, an English rest camp, where we were permitted to visit the oldest cathedral in England. Construction started in 885 and the building was finished in 1300. It is 56 feet long, 220 feet wide and 120 feet high and overlooks the whole city of Winchester. It is known as the place where the most wonderful and beautiful statuary in England is kept on exhibition. In this Cathedral King Charles the 1st was beheaded and here also is the tomb of Queen Victoria, marked by a Bronze Monument that cost $30,000. We visited English College, built in 1300, a school only for the rich, where tuition is paid previous to birth. From Camp Windledown we hiked 21 miles under full pack to South Hampton and there took a boat across the English Channel to La Havre, France. There we left the boat to board dainty little French trains, with the cars marked—40 hommes, 8 cheveaux—meaning 40 men or 8 horses. In this way we traveled to Camp Desauge, a camp 16 miles from Bordeaux, France There we were in constant training on the firing range from Sept. 30 to Oct. 28. While at Camp Desauge we were privileged to visit Bordeaux. Visited St. Andrews and St. Mary's Cathedral, built in 1300. There we saw 39 preserved people, who had been buried in the ground for 300 years and on exhibition for the last 100 years. Their skin was like leather but perfect in form. From Camp Desauge I, along with a number of other men, was transferred to St. Nazaire and then came more hard work, Sunday as well as Saturday. Finally came rest and a permit for furlough to visit the ruins of Belgium, all historical points in Paris, the underground city at Verdun, Dead Man's Hill, Belleau Wood, Chateau Thierry, Soissons and a U. S. Army cemetery where lie 1800 soldiers, with only a small wood monument to mark each grave. We visited all points of interest along the Rhine, also Metz, Germany and another underground city.

On the eighteenth day of June, 1919 we left St. Nazaire on the good old ship "Powatan" for the U. S. A. and home. Landed at Charleston, S. C., on June 30th. From the boat we went to Camp Jackson and a week later were transferred to Camp Taylor, Ky. After two days we left here for home, Rochester, Ind., with an honorable discharge certificate and a smile on my face to see my seven months old daughter, wife, parents and friends. Once more at home and happy. All's well.

CLARENCE K. GARNER.

From a "Y" Worker's Letters

On our way to Paris we saw two places where they were threshing. It was some sight, too. I had often seen many round stacks out in the fields that were as near perfect as possible, but never knew what was in them, but now I know they are wheat stacks and goodness only knows when they were made. Four of these were close to the road we were on, where they were threshing with their crude machine. The engine had two very large flywheels that ran rather slowly; a smokestack about twelve feet high, and stood about thirty feet from the separator, or beater, as they called it. Two men stood on the stack pitching the large, long bundles to a woman on the top of the separator, who cut the bands and passed them to a man standing on a platform at the side of the separator, feeding it very slowly. I did not see just how it was arranged on the inside, but the wheat was cleaned excellently. The straw came out of the rear looking as though it had not been touched. The heads looked full, but upon examining several of them I did not find a grain. Several men worked there putting the straw in large bundles and tying them with straw, then stacking them in large stacks again. Some were weighing the grain which came out very slowly. Their water tank was a two-wheeled cart with a barrel upon it.

As we had to go through Versailles we decided to stop there a few hours to see the wonderful sights. One of the things that attracted our attention was the magnificent park, which, I should judge, is the largest in France. Many beautiful walks, fountains, statues and flower beds were to be seen in all directions. I was informed by a soldier that it was twenty-seven miles around it. We soon fell in with a French guide and a couple of other soldiers who were going through the place. We visited many of the wonderful rooms. Among them was the chamber which contained the bed in which Louis XIV died, who seemed to be the principal character in the history of the palace, as he was the one that completed it during his reign there. In front of the bed was a large banister that was formerly of solid gold and silver, but now of stone. The former being removed long ago when the country was in need of its gold and silver for other purposes more important. Callers would often come in this room up to the banister to see the king arise in the morning, which they considered quite an honor in those days. We passed through the Hall of Mirrors, which is no doubt the large room in which the Germans made the French sign the treaty of peace in 1871, and the one in which the Germans will have to swallow their own pill by signing the treaty of 1919. We also saw the table on which the treaty is to be signed. This room was the ball room of Louis XIV. The walls are full of large mirrors. The ceiling is covered with paintings that took one artist ten years to complete. Another room that was of interest to me was the one that contained nothing but large paintings of war scenes. One picture in this room I was very much suprised to see was that of the siege of Yorktown, showing as the prominent figures, Washington, LaFayette and Rochambeau.

After leaving the palace we went out to see where the German delegates were stationed. Here the street fence was blockaded by a small picket fence which was the marking line for out-of-bounds regions for them. From here we went on into Paris. On Sunday we took a metro to the old part of the city to visit the catacombs. Here we went down, down a very long flight of winding stairs till we came to the bottom, then passed on through a long tunnel till we came to a place where there were many large rooms. Here was the most peculiar sight that I have ever seen. Thousands upon thousands of human skulls and other bones, mostly bones of the legs and arms, were piled up like cordwood, but arranged in a very artistic style. One place a cross was made out of skulls alone; another the skull and cross bones were shown in reality. In one of the many rooms there was a little cave back in the solid rock that had iron bars in front. Upon looking in here we saw a full grown skeleton standing upright. No doubt we would have felt a little "creepy," way down there with our little candle if it had not been for the company we had, as we fell in with a party of about one hundred Americans whom the Y. M. C. A. man was conducting through. When we came out we were about a half-mile from the place where we went in. I do not know much about the history of these catacombs, other than that they were the burying places of the notables in the early days. People do not think anything about finding human bones when they come across them in their diggings, as we saw where some Frenchmen were repairing a broken gas pipe. They had to dig down in the street to make the necessary repair. In doing so they came across some human bones which they threw out as unconcerned as if they were dirt clods.

I saw something in Paris this time that I hadn't seen in France before. Guess! Well, it was a rocking chair, but it had been brought from America, and was in the Soldiers' and Sailors' Club. I had something while there, too, that I hadn't had since I have been here. It was real for sure ice cream. When we got to Verdome, one of the outposts of the Tours division, we learned the sad news of one of the Y camionetts turning over and killing a Belgian girl. We came across the wrecked car about two kilometers out from Verdome on the road to Tours. The car was a complete wreck. The soldier detailed to the Y as chauffeur was placed under arrest and is in the guard house to await court martial.

Tours, France, May 30, 1919.

To-day was Memorial Day, the greatest I have spent for many days. It was one I hope I never will forget. Throughout France, as well as in the States, it was a holiday for the people of my country; not a holiday for pleasure alone, but for the purpose of decorating the graves of those who paid the highest price for the honor of their country and the welfare of mankind. At ten o'clock a parade started from the headquarters here, led by the Eleventh Marine Band followed by two companies of our gallant Marines with their rifles on their shoulders, their arms and bodies swinging in rhythm, their feet giving out that measured tread which they got through their good training. Next came a group of the French poilu. There were about a hundred of them. They made a striking contrast to the Yankee boys, as they were not in step and their lines were very crooked. Following them were about fifteen automobiles, hauling some of our distinguished officers and some of the French also, Field Marshal Petain being among the latter. Last in the parade, but not the least important by any means, were hundreds of doughboys unarmed. The column, in all, was nearly a half-mile long.

A short, solemn program was rendered at the cemetery. The graves were all decorated with beautiful flowers and a little U. S. flag. Old Glory was waving leisurely in the breeze at half mast. No fewer than three hundred of America's best men lay here in sweet repose side by side in three rows clear across the cemetery. Each has a white cross at his head, with his name, rank and the day he died painted artistically in black letters. I wish every mother who has a boy buried there could have seen that beautiful sight after the decoration was done. No doubt tears would have come to her eyes for sorrow, but at the same time her heart could not but have thrilled with the feeling that would make her proud to know that she was the mother of so gallant a son, one who had given the highest price any man could give—dying for his country. Close by, but a little to one side, were two graves that were also decorated with beautiful flowers, but with a flag of a different nation. They were sons of England and had little British flags waving over them. At the far end of the cemetery were about fifty graves decorated with flowers. Each had the white cross at the head with the name, rank and date of death, the same as those of the Americans and the two British, but there were no flags on their graves. These were the graves of some of our conquered foes. These German prisoners of war whom our men had captured, died before the time had come for them to be released to go back to the fatherland. A striking example of American patriotism, honor, friendship and brotherly love was shown here, not only to her own dead sons, but to the sons of her foe and friend as well. Three volleys were fired over the graves of our fallen heroes; taps were then blown; our national hymn and that of France was played by the band; the dear old flag was then swung at the top of the mast, ending the first ceremony of its kind on foreign soil.

Yet, at the same time the graves of our honored dead were being decorated at home and abroad, there were others who died for us whose graves were not decorated at all, the graves of those buried at sea while on their way to the scene of war. No flowers, no flags, no white crosses mark their last resting places. No one will even know the exact location of their graves. The sun, moon and stars will send their radiant rays over them, imitating the cross, flowers and flags and while gazing at them we can have the satisfaction of knowing that God decorates the graves of those buried in the sea as well as those buried in the ground, and the waves and winds will furnish the music for the beautiful ceremony, while we stand with our heads bowed, our thoughts will be with them the same as the others.

FREDERICK K. DEARDORF.

An Engineer's Life

First we went on the Chateau Thierry drive, that being one of the hardest drives, I think, outside of the last one. We were putting in a bridge, or I was—with a company of 250 men—across the Meuse river and it was a pontoon bridge and it took me three hours to build the bridge with my men. Every time I was ready to connect it with the other bank the Huns would shoot it out. I tried it five times before I made it, but I finally made it across. As soon as our artillery found the big guns that were shooting our bridge to pieces one shot finished their game. When I got it done and counted my men I was short 14 men, all killed.

Well you might think I was done but I was not for the whole

division was waiting to cross. We grabbed our guns and went right after the Germans hot and heavy for each man's blood was boiling, ready to fight anything. Next day they shelled hell out of a road we were using and we had to fix it so they could get supplies to the boys at the front.

Our company had nothing to eat for 24 hours and no sleep. This will be all about this drive but in the meantime we buried lots of dead. Americans, and dead Germans. Both sure lost lots of good men on this drive.

Our second drive was on front St. Mihiel. We started this drive right behind the doughboys building roads and were the first engineers on "No Man's Land." About all we did on this drive was build roads and build barbed wire cages for German prisoners and there sure were a lot of them. We had pretty good eats and got quite a lot of sleep. But I worked more than anyone in our outfit for anything special they wanted done they always called on Master Eng. Houser to do it.

Third drive on front Argonne or Verdun. Here is where I had hell. I never think I will go to hell for I have been through it once. Where we first started there was a woods and in this wood four years ago the French fought 100 days and lost 100,000 men and couldn't budge them. We got through over a seven hour barrage and had them running. Then over the top after them. That day we got 3,000 prisoners. The Germans had dugouts 50 feet deep with electric lights, steam heat and everything just like they never intended to leave, but believe me the Yanks made them go. You can just about picture that field when they got through shelling, shellholes 20 feet deep and we had to have light artillery going over in two hours— that was my orders—and believe me orders are orders over here. I started in to make a road where there was not a sign of a road. In less than two hours we had traffic going over and sometimes we were ahead of the doughboys, and all the time we were doing this rebuilding work the Huns were trying to shell our road and throwing gas shells at us. Believe me you couldn't hear yourself talk because of the noise the guns were making.

This drive started about one and-half miles from Avacourt. I guess you can find it on the map; if you can, you can do more than I can do here, for I can't find it here for there isn't a stone left of it and about the same as all the rest of the towns in the war zone. I never will forget Sept. 25 and 26, 1918. The night of the 25th was the worst for I wouldn't have given a cent for my life. I was in charge of 29 trucks all loaded with bridge and road material and the Germans were trying to get us, trying to blow up the trucks and there were shells flying all around us and all at once one hit a truck and that was all I ever saw of it—men and all. There were four men on the truck and after the shell hit it you couldn't find a piece of them. I was within 10 feet of it, but I am still alive and feeling fine. Then it was our move so we moved right up within 300 yds. of the Huns first front line trench and started to unload and we got some more hell. I hadn't any sleep for 48 hours and nothing to eat only what I picked up along the road and that was damn little.

We drove them about 15 kilometers the first day and never left them stop until they quit. I was still right behind them and now we are at Stenay, France; just about where they quit. We are going into Germany on the border and watch them until they get all their troops out and see that we get all our men back. I guess now that peace will be signed by the time you get this letter.

A. W. HOUSER,
Master Engr., Co. A., 602 Engr., A. E. F., France.

Praises War Workers

Had the big pleasure of getting away from a rationed mess and of resting in a real bed last night. It was glorious. Yesterday I also ran into a shell hole occupied by some of the faithful Salvation Army. There I found quantities of chocolate cookies made in the United States. I purchased my allotment and then munched away the choice food, feeling like a king in luxury. Such an adventure as we are going through makes one a lover of each little comforting thing. As to hardships, they are part of the adventure, which we revel in rather than growl about. It is part of the game and is expected. Usually the bark is worse than the bite.

We are the best fed of all the armies. Today I had some peaches from California, beef from Chicago, and so on. The faithful Red Cross, the Y. M. C. A. and the Salvation Army are doing excellent work. It is through the Y. M. C. A. that we get the daily papers and such luxuries as cakes and candies. We get such articles from the Y. M. C. A. at about cost. The Red Cross does not sell anything, but gives! The Salvation Army has become famous for its home-made doughnuts. All three of these organizations risk the dangers of shell fire to get such things to the soldiers.

The people at home are doing their part to win this war and I wish you to know that we realize the sacrifices the entire country is making to help the A. E. F. win out.

The work that is being done for us is sure producing results, and the appreciation is beyond expression.

HOWARD STERNER.

Little Glimpses of War

I have seen some of the most striking features of warfare as it is today, and will give them to you in an impersonal way, as I have seen them.

A call for all the men to the guns at some hour of the night—a few scattered artillery shots which soon become intense firing and continues until one is relieved of the pitch-like darkness and can see ones way through the difficult places by light of the steady gun flashes, fire continues until there is an order to advance, we go forward, over a road made almost impassable by our previous shell fire. We cross the enemies old front line, "The Hindenburg" which is nothing but shelled craters. What was once barbed wire entanglements galore, are now but short pieces of wire and bits of stakes, only a few good stakes are scattered here and there. As we advance we meet lines of prisoners coming in under guard, now and then four of the latter carry one of the boys on a stretcher. We set our guns, fire—await orders and advance again—such is war without the details.

Details—A German sits beside the road shot in the face, breast, arms, legs, still able to speak but unable to walk—my first glimpse of the wounded.

I once talked with an Australian, when I first came to France. Of course I asked him about the war. He had been on the front, had been gassed and was returning. He was a fine, intelligent looking fellow, and in response to my question he said, "Oh Boy, it will break your heart."

"It will break your heart." I did not appreciate those words as much when I saw that German, nor yet when I saw the wounded boys go by; one with his arms strapped to his chest and one leg pulled along behind stiff at the knee, the same fellow who said with a smile "Oh, I am one of the lucky ones," but when I had seen dead Germans day after day and the above sights repeated time and time again, there came another day. I was close behind the guns, was walking away from them, was stopped by the noise of a falling limb, looking back at the guns I saw a big smoke, I went back. A gun had blown up and two of the best boys in the battery had "gone over" blown to bits. When I had helped to get them out and straightened things up a bit, I felt a little sick and I remembered those words—"It will break your heart."

I see you have been guessing where I am located—you missed locating me on Sept. 16, by about four miles if you remember where that was, but Uncle Sam's soldiers are like the Irishman's flea—you may not agree with me, but I know the Kaiser will. The first night I was on the front, that has been a long time ago, I was in a little woods, the Sergeant in charge of our detail was scared of gas and shut the dugout up so tight that I decided to lay out under a tin shelter. I had hardly stretched out when Fritz put a high explosive three-inch in the edge of the woods 200 yards off, it was followed by others—he combed the woods for fair, moving his fire down towards my shack—I hated to be chased out, and thought I had better not run too soon, but when the fragments of shell and pieces of dirt and rock commenced to cut the leaves on the trees around me I decided it was time to sell out. I have been moved by shells since, but am not going to forget that first night.

In addition to the other experiences which I have told and have one yet to tell. I prize this one. I have laid down beside a muddy road on a cold rainy night and have gone to sleep time after time on a night march and haven't caught cold. I now have a little house to stay in, large enough for six, we have a stove and think we are in a keen place.

FRED L. SAFFORD,
Battery F., 114 Field Art., France.

Chasing the Enemy

We put over a barrage on the morning of Nov. 1st and it sure was a fierce one. It lasted for about six hours and our doughboys went over the top and got lots of prisoners, guns and material. They got the Dutch on the run and could not keep up with them, so our doughboys got in trucks and followed them. Just got word that they cannot find a Dutchman. We have moved up 25 kilometers and are going to go up 20 more tonight, so you see they sure went some. We went through five towns that were completely destroyed and I never saw so many trucks, guns and a little of everything in my life as was on the road and it has been straight going for two days; it never stops. The last position we had was the limit; we got in it about 10 o'clock at night and dark as pitch. It was in a valley at the edge of a town and the first thing we did was to get our lines out. It is hell after night for you cannot have any light and shell holes are very thick. I just got started and the Boche commenced to shell us and I thought they had my number for they were very close. My back was sore from dropping to the ground. We got some gas but not enough to hurt us; only make us sneeze. After we got the lines out we put up the tent for our central and was very tired, so laid down for a little snooze and over came one and lit about five or six feet from the tent and believe me it shook us up some and put several holes through the tent. That one just got settled down when they sent one over with gas that was hell for we had to put on our masks and it is very hard for me to wear one, so we put in a bad night, but that is only one. We had lots of them. The next morning over came their planes and I knew there was going to be something doing. I did not think that there ever was a 6-in. outfit as close to the Dutch line as we were—one and one-half kilometers. The machine guns were behind us, yet we got several wounded but not seriously. Last night there were several planes over and believe me they dropped some bombs. I think that they raised the end gate and kicked them out as they did no damage that I heard of. Yesterday we were grazing the horses and saw an air battle. They brought down one Boche plane; they got pretty low and shot at us with machine guns. I have only been in the hospital once and was only wounded once; that was on the Chateau Thierry front. I have been in some pretty close places but have been lucky so far and think that it is about all over the way it looks now for we seem to take anything we want and the prisoners say it is all over and they are tired of war, but they are no more tired than I am. Sleeping on the ground in a pup tent for so long at a time has about got me. You know I am no chicken any more.

HARRY (Mike) BRICKEL,
Bat. A., 150th F. A.

Germans and "Cooties"

The things you read in the papers you can partly believe, because the Jerrys (Germans) sure have done some awful things. I have been in towns where there is nothing left but a mass of ruins. We go to water every day where there used to be a town, but there isn't anything left of it now.

I suppose you read about the front where we are now. I dare not tell you any names of the towns. But you can believe me our division is sure doing its bit. I don't suppose you would believe me if I told you of the prisoners I have seen at different times. It wasn't hundreds, but thousands.

I have been over lots of country where Jerry has been. At one place I saw one of Jerry's graveyards. They have a cross at each head with the name on it.

I just had to stop and scratch myself. If you were here I would give you a job helping me kill the cooties. I sure have lot of 'em.

When Jerry sends over a shell we always say, "There comes one." I don't supose you will believe it, but when we hear a shell coming we can tell what kind it is by the sound of it. There are lots of different kinds of shells.

I am not corporal anymore. I asked to be reduced, so they made me wagoner again. So I and Buddy have four horses on one wagon. I let Buddy drive all four so I can look around.

ARCH FLORA

Glimpse at Camp Life

Every one on the Post here has been examined for overseas service and practically all in our company passed the exam. In letters received from some of the boys at Camp Eustis they said that they were in mud up to their ankles, grubbing stumps and working like blazes. It is just a new camp. I like it better here every day. Those daily dips in the old Atlantic and Uncle Sam's beef and beans are making me fat. I now weigh 185 and feel like I will just have to keep on getting fatter—I don't know what the end will be.

There are a lot of new buildings being erected here, right along; new barracks, hospital, Y. M. C. A. and buildings for various other purposes. So you see we are right up with the times down here in Dixie. We have had two lectures on "Gas" and have some more coming. The talks were very interesting, dealing principally with the history of gas, the various kinds used in Europe today, the way it travels and methods of defense. An illustration of the varoius masks and the ways in which they are used was also given. About a week ago our company all attended a moving picture show at the "canteen" during one of our regular drill periods. The pictures were produced by various medical, physiological and hygenic organizations working in cooperation with the government and illustrated very vividly and distinctly the bad effects and results of contracting some of the diseases incident to camp life. Some of the pictures of these unfortunate victims almost made me shudder. I think the show impressed the seriousness of these diseases on our minds more than a hundred lectures would have done. But I will say this for Uncle Sam if any of his soldiers get this affliction it is nobody's fault but their own. They sure get plenty of warning before hand. We have instructions and drill work on machine guns every day now. We are using the Colt's gun. The Captain said we would soon be having target practice with them.

Yesterday a bunch of us from our company went to Charleston to load a barge with various provisions and supplies for Ft. Moultrie. I enjoy these trips and the work fine. We get lots of it to do.

CLAUDE MARSHALL.

From a Flying Field

Believe me, this isn't exactly a home for feeble-minded kittens. This is the first day of real rest I've had since I've been down here. A fellow flies all day and then goes to school after supper and works until 9:30. At 9:30, the lights go out and then you shave, take a bath and go to bed. One is generally too tired to sleep right away, so he thinks over things and makes plans for his flying the next day.

Yesterday was a rotten day for air work. It was hot and gusty as the devil. The land here is mostly clay loam and the farmers are starting their spring plowing. Now the land that isn't plowed is a brilliant yellow and gives off lots of heat rays and upward air currents; and the land that is plowed is black and the air currents over it go downward. So the land is alternately black and yellow and the air is in banks and pockets, and the plane—!

To top it off I had a "ship" that wouldn't go over 50 an hour and the tail kept wanting to get round in front. Diverting, to say the least.

Am to be promoted tomorrow. An instructor will observe six or seven of my landings, give me a grade and then I go over to another sector to do loops and spirals. Lots of fun in spirals.

MARCUS WRIGHT.

They Also Helped.

On the following pages appear the names of men, women and children of Fulton county who did their part in the winning of the war. They put over the Liberty Loan Drives, bought War Savings Stamps, contributed to the United War Work drive, helped the Red Cross and did all that was asked of them to back up the boys in the service.

The names were secured through square mile men and women, and other war working agencies of the county, and it is probable that the list is not complete in spite of the effort made to have it so. For that reason it must not be inferred that a person whose name is missing lacked in patriotism or loyalty.

Aubeenaubbee Schools

Archer, Willard.
Ball, Wilma.
Baldwin, Albert.
Baldwin, Bessie.
Baldwin, Homer.
Baldwin, Ralph.
Beerwart, Robert.
Best, Norman.
Biddinger, Carroll.
Biddinger, Kermit.
Biddinger, Mae.
Book, Altie.
Book, Lucy.
Bowersox, Chester.
Bowersox, Herbert.
Bridegroom, Bernard.
Brooker, Mildred.
Brugh, Albert.
Brugh, Francis.
Brugh, Helen.
Burns, Audrey.
Burns, Kathleen.
Burns, Oral.
Butt, Berneice.
Butts, Oren.
Butt, Orville.
Calhoun, Charles.
Calhoun, Margaret.
Campbell, Claribel.
Campbell, Grace.
Campbell, Garnet.
Campbell, Rosemary.
Campbell, Theodore.
Cavender, Chester.
Cavander, Florence.
Champ, Muriel.
Coughenour, Fred.
Cowen, Clifford.
Cowen, Marie.
Davis, Dale.
Davis, Emery.
Davis, Norman.
Davison, Dennis.
Davison, Francis.
Davison, Frank.
Decker, Addie.
Decker, Anna.
Decker, Paul.
Denny, Jordon.
Denny, Joseph.
Ditmire, Virginia.
Edgington, Harry.
Edgington, Louimay.
Engle, Bernis.
Engel, Julah.
Engel, Robert.
Ewing, Alvin.
Faulstick, Bertha.
Faulstick, Dortha.
Faulstick, Fred.
Faulstick, Harvey.
Faulstick, Hermy.
Faulstick, Jennie.
Faulstick, Joseph.
Faulstick, Walter.
Fernbaugh, Carl.

Fernbaugh, Grace.
Fernbaugh, Herald.
Fisher, Alvah.
Fisher, Dora.
Fisher, Elnora.
Fisher, Orvil.
Fisher, Virgil.
Folk, Carl.
Fox, Bernice.
Fox, Geneva.
Fox, James.
Freese, Annabell.
Freese, Florence.
Freese, Francis.
Freese, Gladys.
Freese, Marguerite.
Freese, Mary.
Frye, Alton.
Frye, Raymond.
Funnell, Alvie.
Funnell, Harley.
Funnell, Telford.
Funnell, Woodrow.
Gibson, Harold.
Gibson, Ralph.
Ginther, Herman.
Goodman, Everett.
Goodman, Vernon.
Graham, Charles.
Guise, Olive.
Guise, Wilson.
Hackett, Annabelle.
Hall, Clara.
Hall, Donna.
Hall, Lonnie.
Hall, Lorene.
Harned, Jesse.
Harpster, Bessie.
Harpster, Naomi.
Hartle, O. C.
Hartle, Neoma.
Hartle, Vernard.
Hartz, Clora.
Hartz, Ethel.
Hartz, Harry.
Hartz, Lena.
Hartz, Nettie.
Hauser, Arthur.
Hauser, Cecil.
Hauser, Clifford.

Hauser, Willard.
Heeter, Howard.
Hrueischer, Eugene.
Hoesel, Everett.
Hollaway, Deverl.
Hosimer, Ruth.
Johnson, Ethel.
Johnson, Mabel.
Kaley, Chester.
Kelly, Clara.
Kelly, Francis.
Kelly, Robert.
Keeler, Fern.
Keller, Ruth.
Kistler, Betty.
Kistler, Ralph.
Kistler, Sidney.
Kistler, Wayne.
Klein, Evelyn.
Klein, Frances.
Klein, Robert.
Kreischer, Edna.
Kreischer, Estie.
Kreischer, Ethlyn.
Kurtz, Avanelle.
Kurtz, Marguerite.
Lahman, Clifford.
Lahman, Oscar.
Large, Alfred.
Large, Chester.
Large, Juanuta.
Large, Lester.
Laughenbahn, Edward.
Laughenbahn, Frances.
Laughenbahn, Gertrude.
Laughenbahn, Henry.
Laughenbahn, Loretta.
Laughenbahn, Marie.
Leese, Vera.
Leiter, Robert.
Lewis, Florence.
Lewis, Hazel.
Lewis, Retha.
Lucas, Clara.
McCarter, Edith.
McConkey, Carl.
McKee, Ermal.
McKee, Helen.
McKee, Sarah.
Mahler, Alma.

CONTRIBUTORS

Mahler, Bert.
Mahler, Bernice.
Mahler, Byron.
Mahler, Charlotte.
Mahler, Elmer.
Mahler, Goldie.
Mahler, Hazel.
Mahler, Helen.
Mahler, Ivyl.
Mahler, Olive.
Mahler, Milo.
Mahler, Mable.
Miller, Harold.
Miller, Robert.
Milliser, Alonzo.
Milliser, Ethel.
Milliser, Russel.
Milliser, Verna.
Monesmith, Pauline.
Monesmith, Vera.
Moon, Marguerite.
Mosher, Cleo.
Mosher, Nelson.
Mosher, Ruth.
Muhrling, Everett.
Murray, Agnes.
Myers, Boyd.
Myers, Margaret.
O'Blenis, Agnes.
O'Blenis, Dorthy.
Overmyer, Eugene.
Overmyer, Everett.
Overmyer, Louise.
Overmyer, Theodore.
Passwater, George.
Pickins, Cecil.
Pickens, Dorthy.
Pickens, Jessie.
Pickens, Loyd.
Pickens, Naomi.
Pickens, Walter.
Reinholt, Donald.
Reinholt, Earl.
Reinholt, Eva.
Reinholt, Hattie.
Reinholt, Mabel.
Reinholt, Ray.
Reish, Audrey.
Rhodes, Howard.
Rhodes, Lewis.
Rhodes, Samuel.
Rhodes, Walter.
Rinehart, Leona.
Rinehart, Lucile.
Ribinson, Cecil
Robinson, Geraldine.
Robinson, Gladys.
Robinson, June.
Robinson, Letcher.
Robinson, Mildred.
Robinson, Olive.
Robinson, Thelma.
Rouch, Clela.
Rouch, Joe.
Rouch, Madonna.
Rouch, Victor.
Sanns, Ralph.
Schuyer, Charles.
Schuyer, Jonas.
Schuyer, John.
Schuyer, Michael.
Schuyer, William.
Shadle, Frances.
Shidaker, Harry.
Shidaker, Joseph.
Shidaker, Rufus.
Shidaker, Russel.
Slonaker, Ethel.
Slonaker, Hope.
Stahl, Kennith.
Stahl, Lester.
Stayton, Ethel.
Stubbs, Gwendolyn.
Stubbs, Vernie.
Swartzel, Mary.
Swartzel, Robert.
Stevens, Ella.
Taylor, Helen.
Thomas, Beulah.
Ullom, Chas.
Vankirk, Helen.
Vankirk, Eveline.
Vankirk, Robert.
Votaw, Gladys.
Votaw, Mildred.
Wagoner, Aaron.
Wagoner, Byron.
Wagoner, Emma.
Wagoner, Frank.
Wagoner, Florence.

Wagoner, Louise.
Wagoner, William.
Warner, Ruth.
Wentzel, Charles.
Wentzel, Eveline.
Wentzel, Marie.
Whitacre, Arnot.
Whitacre, Bertha.
Whitacre, Clarence.
Whitacre, Dortha.
Whitacre, Louisa.
Widman, Anna.
Widman, Charles.
Widman, Elnora.
Widman, Rose.
Widner, Harley.
Widner, Mayme.
Wilson, Everett.
Woodcox, Annabell.
Woodcox, Benny.
Woodcox, Mary.
Woodcox, Ulrich.
Yelton, Maurice.
Young, Cecil.
Young, Everett.
Young, Wilma.

Aubbeenaubbee Township

Adams, Mrs. E. M.
Agster, Mr. and Mrs. Fred.
Babcock, Miss Alice.
Bailey, Mr. and Mrs. Lewis.
Bailey, Mr. and Mrs. W. J.
Baker, Mr. and Mrs. T. H.
Baker, Wm.
Ball, Mr. and Mrs. David E.
Ball, Mr. and Mrs. Joseph H.
Balwin, Mr. and Mrs. Wm.
Baldwin, Mr. and Mrs. Wilber A.
Barger, Mr. and Mrs. John W.
Batz, Gans.
Beerwart, Mr. and Mrs. John B.
Berry, Mr. and Mrs. F. L.
Berry, Kathleen.
Biddinger, Mr. and Mrs. Albert.
Biddinger, Mr. and Mrs. Cleve.
Biddinger, Lizzie.
Biddinger, Mr. and Mrs. S. L.
Bisher, John.
Bitterling, Mr. and Mrs. George.
Blackburn, Nora.
Blair, Mr. and Mrs. H. N.
Blair, Olive.
Bowersox, Mr. and Mrs. Jefferson.
Bowersox, Mr. and Mrs. Roy.
Bridegroom, Mr. and Mrs. T. J.
Brucker, Mr. and Mrs. A. P.
Bruce, Mr. and Mrs. Benjamin.
Bruce, Mr. and Mrs. Francis.
Brugh, Mr. and Mrs. Anthony.
Brugh, Elmer.
Brugh, Fred.
Brugh, Mr. and Mrs. George. W.
Brugh, Mr. and Mrs. Harry.
Brugh, Lillie.
Brugh, James B.
Brugh, O. J.
Brugh, Wilson.
Bryan, Mrs. Clarence.
Bryan, Mr. and Mrs. Frank.
Bryan, Mr. and Mrs. Walter.
Bunn, Mrs. Amanda.
Bunn, Crete.
Burns, Mr. and Mrs. James B.
Campbell, Mr. and Mrs. B. B.
Campbell, J. M.
Castleman, Eliza.
Cavander, Mr. aand Mrs. Edward.
Cavender, Mr. and Mrs. Wm.
Clover Leaf Reb. Lodge.
Coughenour, Clark.
Coughenour, Mr. and Mrs. William.
Cook, Mr. and Mrs. J. H.
Cook, L. M.
Cook, Mr. and Mrs. W. H.
Costello, Miss Clara.
Cowen, Mr. and Mrs. George.
Cunningham, Mr. and Mrs. Otis.
Curtis, Mr. and Mrs. Oliver.
Davis, Mr. and Mrs. A. B.
Davis, Mr. and Mrs. Bert.
Davis, Mr. aand Mrsr. C. C.
Davis, Mr. and Mrs. Guy.
Davis, Mr. and Mrs. L. E.

Deck, Mr. and Mrs. C. E.
Deck, J. E.
Decker, Mr. and Mrs. John E.
Denny, Mr. and Mrs. Ransome.
Ditmire, E.
Ditmire, Mr. and Mrs. S. F.
Edgington, Mr. and Mrs. Ellsworth.
Faulstick, Mr. and Mrs. Albert.
Faulstick, Charles P.
Faulstick, Walter.
Feece, Mr. and Mrs. Wesley.
Fernbaugh, Mr. and Mrs. Wm.
Fisher, Mr. and Mrs. I. A.
Fox, Mr. and Mrs. Henry.
Friece, Mr. and Mrs. Henry.
Friece, Mr. and Mrs. Frank S.
Frye, Mr. and Mrs. Richard N.
Gausch, Mr. and Mrs. Chas.
Gausch, Mr. and Mrs. Paul.
Garner, Mr. and Mrs. Clyde.
Gibson, M. L.
Gibson, Mr. and Mrs. Milton.
Ginther, Mr. and Mrs. Abraham.
Ginther, Mr. and Mrs. A. J.
Ginther, Albert Fredrick.
Ginther, Mr. and Mrs. A. R.
Ginther, Mr. and Mrs. Dean.
Ginther, Mr. and Mrs. J. K.
Ginther, Mr. and Mrs. J. O.
Graham, Mr. and Mrs. Charley.
Greer, Mr. and Mrs. Wm.
Guise, Mr. and Mrs. Frank.
Guise, Mr. and Mrs. George.
Guise, Mr. and Mrs. Harley C.
Guise, Mr. and Mrs. Perry.
Guise, Mr. and Mrs. Tabor W.
Guisinger, Mrs. Melinda J.
Hackett, Mr. and Mrs. L. B.
Hall, Mr. and Mrs. E.
Hamed, Mr. and Mrs. L. B.
Hamir, Geo.
Harpster, Mr. and Mrs. Wm.
Harris, Rev. J. B.
Hartle, Mr. and Mrs. Fredrick,
Hartle, Walter.
Hartz, Eliza.
Hartz, Mr. and Mrs. N. F.
Hawkins, Mrs. O. W.
Hay, Mr. and Mrs. Carl.
Hay, Mr. and Mrs. James H.

Heeter, Mr. and Mrs. Wm.
Heeter, Mr. and Mrs. W. H.
Hetter, Mrs. Susanna.
Hiatt, Doc.
Hoesel, J. L.
Hoff, Mr. and Mrs. Leroy.
Holzbauer, Joe L.
Home Lumber Co.
Howard, Mrs. Claude.
Hudkins, Daniel.
Hudkins, Mr. and Mrs. Dee.
Hudleson, Mr. and Mrs. Garl.
Johnson, Mr. and Mrs. S. D.
Johnston, Wm.
Kaley, Mr. and Mrs. Arthur.
Kaley, Christena.
Kaley, Mr. and Mrs. Isaac R.
Kaley, Mr. and Mrs. Simon C.
Kaley, Mr. and Mrs. Wm.
Keya, Mr. and Mrs. Carl.
Keeler, Mr. and Mrs. Edd
Keitzer, Mr. and Mrs. Wm.
Kelley, Clarence D.
Kelly, Mr. and Mrs. Samuel L.
Keller, Margaret.
King, Mr. and Mrs. Robert.
Kistler, Mr. and Mrs. Milton.
Kline, Mr. and Mrs. Frank M.
Kline, Mr. and Mrs. Grover C.
Kline, Mr. and Mrs. Lewis.
Kreighbaum, C. E.
Kurtz, Mr. and Mrs. F. H.
Lahman, Mr. and Mrs. Simon P.
Large, Mr. and Mrs. E.
Laugenbohn, Mr. and Mrs. Peter.
Leiters Ford M. E. S. S.
Lewis, Lucinda.
Lewis, Mr. and Mrs. Omer.
Lough, Mrs. Lewis M.
Lucas, Mr. and Mrs. Wm.
Luckenbell, L.
McIntyre, Mr. and Mrs. A. M.
McKee, Mr. and Mrs. Samuel.
McKoney, Mrs. Atch.
Mahler, Clara.
Mahler, Esta.
Mahler, Harley
Mahler, Mr. and Mrs. Joseph.
Mahler, Mr. and Mrs. John.
Mahler, Lester.

Mahler, Martha A.
Meiser, Mr. and Mrs. Fred.
M. E. S. S., Class No. 6.
Mikesell, Mr. and Mrs. Lester.
Miller, Mr. and Mrs. Fred.
Milliser, Mr. and Mrs. George.
Milliser, Mr. and Mrs. R. J.
Milliser, Mr. and Mrs. Stephen.
Monn, Mr. and Mrs. Frank B.
Monesmith, Mr. and Mrs. Oscar.
Monesmith, Mr. and Mrs. Wm.
Moore, Mr. and Mrs. Henry.
Moon, Frank.
Mosher, O. L.
Mossman, Mr. and Mrs. Charley.
Murfitt, Mr. and Mrs. Charley.
Murry, Mr. and Mrs. J. H.
Myers, John.
Myers, Mrs. John.
Myers, Samuel.
Myers, Mr. and Mrs. W. H.
Newcomer, Edward.
Overmyer, Mr. and Mrs. Amos.
Overmyer, B. F.
Overmyer, Mr. and Mrs. Ben.
Overmyer, Mr. and Mrs. Clyde.
Overmyer, Mr. and Mrs. Dan.
Overmyer, Mr. and Mrs. Howard.
Overmyer, Mr. and Mrs. S.
O'Keefe, Wm.
Patsel, Mr. and Mrs. Douglas.
Patsel, Mr. and Mrs. Raymond.
Paulson, Hans.
Pickens, Mr. and Mrs. Wm. C.
Polly, Mrs. George.
Powell, Mr. and Mrs. Freeman O. B.
Reed, Mr. and Mrs. Fred.
Reichard, Mr. and Mrs. A. K.
Reichard, Mr. and Mrs. E.
Reichard, Mr. and Mrs. Omer.
Reichard, Mr. and Mrs. Paul.
Reish, Adam.
Reish, Forest Bud.
Reish, Florence.
Reish, Merle.
Reish, Mrs. O. G.
Robinson, L. A.
Robinson, Mr. and Mrs. L. V.
Robinson, Mr. and Mrs. Wm.
Rouch, Mrs. Martha.
Sales, Mr. and Mrs. Charles.
Sales, J. O.
Sales, Mrs. Nancy.
Sanns, Mr. and Mrs. Peter.
Schadle, Mr. and Mrs. C. W.
Schadle, Edward.
Schadle, Mr. and Mrs. Henry.
Schewer, Frank P.
See, Earl.
Seistle, Mrs. Ed.
Shewer, Mr. and Mrs. Peter.
Shidaker, Mr. and Mrs. Jonas.
Shidaker, Milton.
Slayton & Hackett.
Slonaker, Dr. and Mrs. C. L.
Slonaker, Mrs. L. B.
Southall, Mr. and Mrs. Omer.
Staddon, Mr. and Mrs. John.
Stahl, Mr. and Mrs. B. F.
Starkey, Mr. and Mrs. B. F.
Stinehiser, Della.
Stubbs, Mr. and Mrs. Dora.
Stubbs, Mr. and Mrs. Lester.
Swartzel, Mr. and Mrs. John.
Taylor, Geo. C.
Toner, Mr. and Mrs. A. D.
Ullom, Mr. and Mrs. E. S.
Vankirk, Mr. and Mrs. John.
Wagoner, Mr. and Mrs. J. J.
Wagner, Madge Bunn.
Wagner, Mr. and Mrs. Noah H.
Walters, Vaughn H.
Washburn, B. F.
Wentzel, Mr. and Mrs. Charles.
Wentzel, Mr. and Mrs. Edward.
Wentzel, Mr. and Mrs. Harry J.
Whitacre, Mr. and Mrs. O. D.
Widman, Mr. and Mrs. Ambrose.
Wilfert, Mr. and Mrs. W.
Williams, Mr. and Mrs. Ira C.
Wilson, Mr. and Mrs. George.
Woodcox, Mr. and Mrs. Harley A.
Woodcox, Mr. and Mrs. Samuel.
Wolf, Mr. and Mrs. L. E.
Wrentmore, Marjorie.
Yetton, Mr. and Mrs. Wm. H.
Young, Mr. and Mrs. Bert.
Young, Mr. and Mrs. E. S.
Young, Mr. and Mrs. Jessie.
Young, Mrs. Leota.

CONTRIBUTORS

Henry Township

Adamson, A. L.
Alspaugh, S. S.
Applegate, E. J.
Arter, Earl.
Arter, E. S.
Arter, Ethel.
Arter, Glen.
Arter, H.
Arter, J. A.
Arter, N.
Arter, Mr. and Mrs. Phillip.
Arter, Ralph.
Ashelman, Mr. and Mrs. A. K.
Babcock, J. R.
Ball, Cass.
Ball, Vera.
Ballinger, Mr. and Mrs. Harvey.
Ballinger, Marvin.
Ballinger, Mr. and Mrs. Wm.
Bally, George.
Barber, Minerva.
Barns, Mr. and Mrs. Albert; Arvada, Fred, Catherine, Jeanette,
Barns, Mr. and Mrs. George A.
Barns, Isaac.
Barnes, Mr. and Mrs. Isaac.
Barnett, Mr. and Mrs. J. B.; Edwin, Roscoe, Dean, Carl.
Barnhisel, Anna.
Barr, Mr. and Mrs. Earl; John.
Barrett, Ethel.
Bemenderfer, Berthaa.
Bemenderfer, Mr. and Mrs. F. P.
Bemenderfer, Mr. and Mrs. Gerald.
Bemenderfer, Mr. and Mrs. W. J.
Blackburn, Fred.
Blasdel, Mr. aand Mrs. Ambrose.
Bowen, Albert.
Bowman, Mr. and Mrs. Benj.
Bowen, Mr. and Mrs. Ed; two children.
Bowen, Mr. and Mrs. Joseph; Bernice, Willis, Pauline.
Bowen, Kinsman.
Bowen, Milo; Agnes, Fern.
Bowen, Nancy.
Bowen, Nelson.
Bucher, Mr. and Mrs. John.
Burch, Mr. and Mrs. Clyde; Lawrence.
Burch, Don.
Burch, Mrs. Elizabeth.
Burckholder, Mr. and Mrs. Ernest.
Burkett, R. J.
Burkett, T. J.
Burns, Mr. and Mrs. Hiram.
Burns, James.
Burns, Mr. and Mrs. R. G.; family.
Buss, Mr. and Mrs. Hiram; Bertha, Lena, Mary, Willimena, John, Anna.
Buse, Lee.
Bradway, Chester.
Bradway, Cliff.
Bradway, Frank.
Brady, Mrs. E.
Bright, Mrs. D.
Bright, Mr. and Mrs. E. L.; family.
Bright, Mrs. W. H.
Broulette, Celestia.
Brown, Mr. and Mrs. David.
Bryant, Glen.
Bryant, Mrs. Ida; Donald, Edith, Olive, Cleo.
Bryant, Mr. and Mrs. J. E.
Bryant, Mr. and Mrs. John; Tedie.
Bryant, Loyd.
Carpenter, Mr. and Mrs. Elbridge.
Carr, John.
Carr, R. R.
Carter, Mr. and Mrs. William.
Case, Dr. A.

Case, Ed.
Case, Gennett.
Chestnut, Mrs. Robert; Robert.
Churchill, Mr. aand Mrs. Abner; family.
Clayton, Bernard.
Clemans, Mr. and Mrs. D. O.
Clemmens, Mr. and Mrs. James.
Clevenger, Mr. and Mrs. David; Wm. C.
Clevenger, Ella.
Clevenger, Frank.
Clinker, Mr. and Mrs. Alvin; Gerald, Lura.
Clinker, Mr. and Mrs. Wm.
Clinton, John.
Coffin, Mr. and Mrs. L. J.; Ivan.
Cook, Mrs. F.
Cook, H. A.
Coplen, Mr. and Mrs. Willard.
Correll, Mr. and Mrs. M.
Craft, Mr. and Mrs. Albert A.; Howard, Jene, Charles, Delight, Bert.
Cuffel, Wm.
Craig, Virgil.
Culver, H.
Curtis, Mr. and Mrs. Ed.
Curtis, Mr. and Mrs. James.
Curtis, Mr. and Mrs. Justin.
Cutschall, M.
Daniels, C. A.
Daub, Mr. and Mrs. Otto.
Davenport, Mr. and Mrs. Sylvester; Earl.
Davis, C.
Davis, Mr. and Mrs. Chas. M.
Davis, John.
Daivs, Mr. and Mrs. Voras.
Davis, Mr. and Mrs. Walter; Edward, Herbert.
Dawson, Ina.
Dawson, Frank.
Dawson, Mrs. Martha.
Day, Chas.
Day, J. H.
Day, Ralph.
Dickerhoff, Mr. and Mrs. A.
Dickerhoff, Mr. and Mrs. Dan.
Dickerhoff, Mr. and Mrs. Fred.
Dickerhoff, Jacob.

Dickerhoff, Mr. and Mrs. John, Dosha.
Dickerhoff, Mr. and Mrs. L.
Dillman, Mr. and Mrs. Frank.
Dillman, Mr. and Mrs. Franklin; Audra, Aubrey.
Dillon, Mr. and Mrs. Morgan.
Dixon, Blanche.
Dowman, Mr. and Mrs. S. D.
Drudge, Mary.
Drudge, R. R.
Eaton, Mr. and Mrs. W. A.; Albert.
Eber, Mr. and Mrs. John.
Ellis, Mr. and Mrs. Edward.
Elwell, J.
Emahiser, A. C.
Engle, Mr. and Mrs. Isaac.
Engel, Mr. and Mrs. Lloyd.
Erb, J.
Eshelman, Alvin, J.
Eshelman, George.
Eshelman, Mr. and Mrs. J. P.
Exchange Bank.
Euler, Mrs.
Feec, Mrs. Eliza.
Fellers, Mr. and Mrs. Eron.
Fennemore, F. R.
Ferree, Mr. and Mrs. Emory; John. Alfred.
Ferry, Mr. and Mrs. P. L.
Fleck, J.
Flohr, Mr. and Mrs. Chas.
Foor, Mr. and Mrs. A. H.
Foor, Mr. and Mrs. Wm. E.
Fultz, Mrs. India.
Fultz, Marion.
Funk, Mr. and Mrs. John.
Gast, A. A.
Gast, Fay.
Gast, Karl.
Gast, Mr. and Mrs. R. M.
Gearhart, Mr. and Mrs. Earl.
Gerard, Fred.
Gerard, Mr. and Mrs. Will.
Gerard, Mr. and Mrs. Wm.
Ginn, Mrs. C.
Ginn, Gussie.
Godwin, Esther.
Godwin, I. R.
Godwin, Wendel.

CONTRIBUTORS

Graham, Clyde.
Graham, Lenora.
Grogg, Mr. and Mrs. Mason H.
Groninger, D. L.
Groninger, Mr. and Mrs. R. L.
Groves, Albert.
Groves, Lydia.
Haldeman, C. H.
Haldeman, Frank.
Haldeman, Mr. and Mrs. Henry; Vernon, Delta, Loyd.
Haldeman, Jennie.
Hammond, Clem.
Hammond, Wilber.
Hand, Noah.
Harsh, B.
Harsh, G.
Harsh, Mr. and Mrs. J. B.
Hart, Mr. and Mrs. J. R.
Harter, Mr. and Mrs. Clem.
Harter, Mr. and Mrs. C. W.; Wilber.
Harter, Mrs. Eva.
Harter, Mr. and Mrs. John R.
Harter, Mr. and Mrs. Herbert.
Harter, William.
Hartman, Mr. and Mrs. Arthur.
Hartman, Mr. and Mrs. Henry; Floyd.
Hattery, Ralph.
Hattery, Warren.
Heddinger, Mr. and Mrs.; children.
Heeter, Francis.
Heeter, Mr. and Mrs. Hollis.
Heeter, Mr. and Mrs. O. H.
Heighway, E. A.
Heighway, John.
Helser, A. H.
Helvey, Frank.
Henderson, Ed.
Herendeen, Mr. and Mrs. C. B.
Herendeen, Mr. and Mrs. John.
Herrold, Mr. and Mrs. Arthur.
Hickey, Mr. and Mrs. J. F.; Elmer, Mabel Mary.
Hickey, Mr. and Mrs. W. E.
Higgens, Mr. and Mrs. Thos.; three children.
Hoddman, Mr. and Mrs. Chas.
Hoffman, C. L.
Hoffman, Mr. and Mrs. Ezra.
Hoffman, Mr. and Mrs. John.
Hoffman, Joe.
Hoffman, Mr. and Mrs. P. P.
Hoover, Mr. and Mrs. C. F.
Hoover, Mrs. C. M.
Hoover, J.
Hosman, W. C.
Hosman, W. E.
Howard, H.
Huling, Glen.
Huling, Mrs. Viola; Helen.
Hutchinson, Elva.
Hutchinson, James H.
Johnson, Eliza.
Johnson, Mr. and Mrs. Olaf.
Johnson, Mr. and Mrs. Sam.
Johnson, Theo.
Jones, Mr. and Mrs. Charles.
Jones, Chas. H.
Jones, Mary E.
Jones, Maud.
Jontz, Max.
Jordan, R. H.
Kamp, Mr. and Mrs. Reuben; Estil, Guy, Ada, Faye, Robert, Walter.
Kamp, Una.
Karn, J.
Keesey, Elnor; May, two children.
Keesey, Odie M.
Keever, Joseph.
Kern, Mr. and Mrs. J .W.; Frank, Ruth.
Kesler, Mr. and Mrs. Max.
Kiley, Mr. and Mrs. Lloyd.
Kime, Mr. and Mrs. Charles; Marie, Orma, Donald.
Kinder, Mr. and Mrs. George; Ner.
Kinder, Mr. and Mrs. John.
Kinder, Mrs. P. M.
Kindig, Mr. and Mrs. B. F.
Kindig, Estel.
Kindig, Mr. and Mrs. John; Byron, Pauline, Herman, Gerald, Nellie.
Kindig, Lou.
Kindig, Mr. and Mrs. Ray.
King, Mr. and Mrs. Geo. W.; Clem.
King, Mr. and Mrs. Howard; Donald, William.
King, Mr. and Mrs. J. J.
King, Mr. and Mrs. Josiah.

Kistler, A. A.
Klise, Mr. and Mrs. Jesse.
Knott, Joshua.
Kreamer, Mr. and Mrs. John W.; Ruth, Wilber, Dean.
Kreigh, Mr. and Mrs. Chas.
Kreig, Mr. and Mrs. Francis; Dorthy.
Kreig, Mr. and Mrs. Geo.
Kreig, Mr. and Mrs. George; Thelma, Gladys.
Kreig, Mr. and Mrs. Harvey; Joanna, Trilla.
Kreig, Mrs. L. A.
Kreg, Mr. and Mrs. Walter.
Kuhn, A. J.
Kuhn, Mr. and Mrs. Alvin; Max.
Kuhn, Mr. and Mrs. Arthur.
Kuhn, C. L.
Kuhn, Mr. and Mrs. Clyde.
Kuhn, Mrs. Sophia.
Kuhn, Mrs. Wm.
Lamar, Mrs. Faye.
Lamoree, Nile.
Lamoree, Vora.
Landis, Roy.
Lantz, John.
Lantz, Mr. and Mrs. Joseph.
Lattimer, Dr.
Lawshe, J. E.
Lee, Mrs. Venton.
Leech, Mr. and Mrs. Ora; Mary.
Lehner, R. W.
Leininger & Sons.
Leininger, Claud.
Leininger, Mr. and Mrs. David.
Leininger, Earl; Roy.
Leininger, Oliver.
Leininger, Mr. and Mrs. Oliver; Marie, Carl, Jessie, Omar.
Leininger, Mr. and Mrs. Wm.; Kennith, Marion.
Leisure, Sarah A.
Little, James.
Lidecker, V. L.
Long, Harvey.
Love & Secor.
Love, J. H.
Lowman, Samuel.
Lynch, Mrs. Sarah; Jesse.
Lynch, Mr. and Mrs. Will; Lowell, Elizabeth.
McClain, Mr. and Mrs. Wm.
McCollough, John.
McCallough, Ruth.
McIntyre, Mr. and Mrs. Wm.; Herman, Russel, Don.
McIntyre, Mr. and Mrs. Dan; Orval.
McMahan, Mr. and Mrs. Chas. W.
Maby, Mr. and Mrs. S. P.
Maddox, Mr. and Mrs. R. D.
Madeford, Frank.
Madlem, Jacob.
Martin, Mr.
Masteller, Mr. and Mrs. Clarence.
Masteller, Mr. aand Mrs. Harry.
Masteller, Mr. and Mrs. Justin; Helen, Robert, Claud.
Mechlin, Mr. and Mrs. Guy; William, Grace.
Merideth, Mr. and Mrs. Charlie.
Meridith, H. L.
Meridith, Willis.
Merley, Mr. and Mrs. L. F.
Merley, Mr. and Mrs. L. F.; Sarah, Don.
Merley, Mr. and Mrs. Nyle.
Merley, Ralph.
Merly, Mrs. Chas.
Merly, Mr. and Mrs. Dewey.
Merly, Mr. and Mrs. Wm.
Miller, Mrs. A.
Miller, Mrs. Adam.
Miller, Mr. and Mrs. Chas.
Miller, Mr. and Mrs. Chas. M.
Miller, Cora.
Miller, Edna.
Miller, F. E.
Miller, H. W.; Gladys, Helen, Mabel, Ethel, Ralph, Blanche.
Miller, Sarah J.
Miller, Joseph.
Miller, Otto O.
Miksell, Mr. and Mrs. P. A.
Miller, Ruby.
Miller, Mrs. Sarah; Fred, Jacob.
Miller, Mr. and Mrs. Vern; Esther, Irene, Erma.
Miller, W. C.
Moonshower, Henry.

CONTRIBUTORS

Moonshower, Jim.
Moore, David L.
Moore, Mr. and Mrs. Eldridge.
Moore, Mr. and Mrs. J. Marion.
Moore, Laura.
Moore, Lee.
Moore, Mr. and Mrs. M. D.
Moore, Mr. and Mrs. Ora.
Moore, Mr. and Mrs. Orville.
Morett, Elizabeth.
Morris, Roy.
Myers, Chas.
Nelson, Mr. and Mrs. Clarence; Vern, Mabel.
Nelson, Clarence.
Nelson, Mrs. Sadie.
Nicodemus, Mr. and Mrs. Jo.
Nicodemus, L.
Nicodemus, Mary.
Noftzger, Mr. and Mrs. Naaman.
Norris, Mr. and Mrs. Chester.
Nowell, R. R.
Noyer, Ella.
Nye, Arthur.
Nye, Mr. and Mrs. Clifford; Clifford, Jr.
Nye, Mr. and Mrs. G. S.
Nye, Isaiah.
Oliver, Kennith.
Orr, Edna E.
Orr, J. N.; sisters.
Patterson, M. L.
Patterson, W. A.
Perry, Mr. and Mrs. Allen.
Perry, Mr. and Mrs. Estel.
Perry, Mrs. H. A.
Perry, N.
Persnet, Richard.
Peterson, Mr. and Mrs. F. E. Deverl.
Pontius, Mr. and Mrs. Ambros; Verl, Clyde, Russel, Myrtle, Edith.
Pontius, Mr. and Mrs. C. W.; Grace.
Pontius, Rachel; Lillian, Walter.
Pontius, Mr. and Mrs. W. A.
Powell, Mr. and Mrs. Benjamin; Boyd.
Pressnall, F.
Prill, Bert.
Prill, Mrs. Mabel.
Putman, Allen.
Putman, Mr. and Mrs. Ira; Arvid.
Quick, Herbert.
Rader, Mr. and Mrs. C. E.; Rex, Ralph Eugene.
Rader, Mr. and Mrs. S. C.
Rader, Mr. and Mrs. Wm. N.
Rames, John.
Ramsey, Mr. and Mrs. Ivan.
Reed, Mr. and Mrs. Ivan; Ruth.
Reed, Mrs. J.
Rehard, Russel.
Rhoads, Mr. and Mrs. Charles.
Rhodes, Mr. and Mrs. S. C.; Sumner.
Richardson, Mrs. John.
Richter, Mr. and Mrs. L. R.
Riggle, H. M.
Riley, Mr. and Mrs. Dora.
Riley, Ellis.
Riley, Mrs. James.
Riley, T. J.
Rogers, Mr. and Mrs. Harley.
Roger, Mr. and Mrs. Reuben.
Roger, Mr. and Mrs. Reuben; Robert, Vernon.
Roger, Mr. and Mrs. Samuel; Carl, Edna.
Rogers, Walter.
Rookstool, Mr. and Mrs. Sam; family.
Ross, Mrs. Retta.
Rowe, Mr. and Mrs. Fred.
Rowe, Mr. and Mrs. George.
Rowe, Wm.
Royer, Mr. and Mrs. Jesse.
Runkle, Edgar.
Runkle, Mrs. Ida.
Sands, R.
Sands, Wm.
Sausaman, Florence.
Sausaman, Mr. and Mrs. William.
Scott, A. E.
Scott, Brothers.
Scott, El.
Secor, Dan.
Siffert, Daniel P.
Sippy, Louis.
Sippy, Mr. and Mrs. Sherman.
Simon, Charley.
Shafer, Mrs. Alice; family.

Shaffer, Josephine.
Shields, Fannie.
Shesler, Mildred.
Shesler, S. N.
Shewman, Mrs. and Mrs. Roy.
Shewman, Worthy.
Shimer, Grant.
Shipley, Mrs. Anna; Carl, Chas., Mildred, Raymond, Louisa.
Shipley, Mrs. Mary; Elsie, Ethel.
Shipley, Mr. and Mrs. R. L.; Dale.
Shipley, Mr. and Mrs. W. V.
Shively, Mr. and Mrs. Evest; baby.
Shively, Mr. and Mrs. Wm. Noah; Ala.
Shoemaker, Mr. and Mrs. C. S.
Shoup, Mr. and Mrs. John.
Shriver, Mr. and Mrs. Chester; Wilbur, Mary Jane.
Shriver, Clarence.
Shriver, David.
Shriver, Mr. and Mrs. Elias.
Shriver, Frank.
Shriver, Mr. and Mrs. Frank.
Shriver, Mr. and Mrs. Jno.
Shriver, Mr. and Mrs. Samuel.
Shriver, Mr. and Mrs. Walter.
Shriver, Wilson.
Shuman, Mr. and Mrs. Meryl.
Shuman, W. D.
Slaybaugh, Mr. and Mrs. Arthur; two children.
Slaybaugh, D.
Slaybaugh, J.
Smith, Mr. and Mrs. Cary; family.
Smith, Chas.
Smith, Mr. and Mrs. Chas.
Smith, Mr. and Mrs. Dorcy.
Smith, E. J.
Smith, Frank.
Smith, Mrs. Eliza; Frank, James.
Smith, Mr. and Mrs. F. D.; Ralph, Hazel, Blanche.
Smith, Mr. and Mrs. Frank P.
Smith, Mr. and Mrs. Jesse; Gladys, Irene, Harold.
Smith, Jessie.
Smith, John.
Smith, Mura.
Smith, Ross L.
Smoker, Mr. and Mrs. Albert; Fred, Opal, Ernest.
Smoker, Mr. and Mrs. Chas.
Smoker, Mr. and Mrs. Frank; Lela.
Snyder, Bert.
Sofferm, Mr. and Mrs. Dan; Kenneth, Robert.
Snyder, Mr. and Mrs. O. O.; family.
Snoke, S. K.
Sowers, Mr. and Mrs. Peter; sons.
Sparks, Ed.
Stahl, J.
State Bank.
Stauffer, W. W.
Steel, Thos.
Stinson, Dr. and Mrs. A. E.
Stoner, F.
Stoner, H.
Stout, Wm.
Strong, E. O.
Strong, Mary.
Strong, S. A.
Strong, Sidney.
Stultz, Joe.
Sullivan, Mr. and Mrs. D. Marcella.
Swartzlander, Mrs. A.
Swartzlander, Mr. and Mrs. Chas.
Swartzlander, Frank.
Swihart, Mrs. A.
Swihart, Elias.
Swill, Mr. and Mrs. Jesse L.; family.
Tait, Mr. and Mrs. Warren; Helen, Doris, Elsie, Lester, Howard, Ira.
Tatman, Chas.
Thompson, C. C.
Thompson, Frank.
Thompson, Wesly.
Thompson, Mr. and Mrs. W. O.
Townsend, Mr. and Mrs. Lawson.
Tracy, Mr. and Mrs. D. M.
Tracy, Mr. and Mrs. J. H.
Trinebrink, Jesse.
Trout, Mr. and Mrs. Ralph.
Troutman, Mr. and Mrs. Earl.
Tucker, Mr. and Mrs. Una.
Tullis, Glen.
Utter, Frank.
Utter, Mr. and Mrs. H. A.; Alfred, Ethel, Henry, Norman.

CONTRIBUTORS

Utter, Mr. and Mrs. H. R.
Utter, James.
Utter, Mr. and Mrs. J. B.
Utter, Mr. and Mrs. Oliver.
Vanlue, Mark.
Vanlue, Mr. and Mrs. Milo.
Vanlue, O. H.
Vickery, Chas.
Vickory, Edith.
Wade, Ruby.
Wakely, Manford.
Walton, E. J.
Ward, W. H.
Ward, W. R.
Weachter, Cornelius.
Weachter, J. R.
Weachter, Ruth.
Weaver, Frank.
Weidman, Elmer.
Weirick, F. J.
Weller, Mr. and Mrs. Charles.
Wells, Chas.
Welton, Mr. and Mrs. L. G.
Whitcomb, Del.
Whitcomb, Dwight.
Whittengill, Mr. and Mrs. Sol.
Whitsell, Grace.
Whittenberger, D.
Whittenberger, Mr. and Mrs. Daniel.
Whittenberger, Mr. and Mrs. George.
Whittenberger, Mr. and Mrs. Merrill; two children.
Whittenberger, Miller.
Whittenberger, Scott.
Wideman, Bros.
Wideman, Mr. and Mrs. A.
Wideman, Mr. and Mrs. Elmer.
Wideman, Mr. and Mrs. W. H.
Wildermuth, S. R.
Wilhoit, & Hoffman.
Wilhoit, Mr. and Mrs. A. J.
Wilhoit, Mr. and Mrs. A. L.
Wilhoit, Mr. and Mrs. C. V.
Wilhoit, S.
Wilhoit, Wm.
Willis, Daniel.
Wines, Geo.
Wise, Mr. and Mrs. Charles.
Wolpert, Eugene.
Worthington, T. J.
Yarian, Mr. and Mrs. Henry; Maxine.
Young, Mr. and Mrs. C. L.
Young, Mr. and Mrs. Clarence; children.
Young, Laura.
Zahner, Mr. and Mrs. John.
Zartman, Mr. aand Mrs. Ferdie.
Zartman, Mr. and Mrs. J. E.
Zartman, Mr. and Mrs. Perry.
Zeibart, Mr. and Mrs. Ernest M.; family.
Zimmerman, Elmer.
Zimmerman, Mr. and Mrs. Frank.
Zimmerman, Mr. and Mrs. J.
Zimmerman, Walter.
Zollman, J.

Liberty Township

Aaron, Mrs. and Mrs. Joe.
Agle, Mr. and Mrs. David; Truman.
Allen, Mr. and Mrs. Jess; Howard.
Apt, Mr. and Mrs. C. G.; Dalem, Bernice, Olive, Erma, John, Margaret.
Apt, Mr. and Mrs. Elmer.
Armstrong, Hugh, William.
Aryen, Mr. and Mrs. Orval; Claude, Earl Dean.
Ausman, Mr. and Mrs. Ben.
Baird, Mr. and Mrs. Chas.; Bernice,
Fairbanks, Edith, Walter.
Baird, Mr. and Mrs. Wm.; Reed, Lawrence, Ernest, Ruth.
Baker, Mr. and Mrs. Levi; Ethel.
Baker, Mr. and Mrs. Samuel; Edgar, Lyman.
Baker, Mr. and Mrs. Virgil; Lewis, Dortha, Richard.
Baldwin, Mr. and Mrs. Ross E.; Wayne, Carol.
Beattie, Mr. and Mrs. Mark; Grace, Donald.

Becker, Mr. and Mrs. Chas.; Omer, Ruth, Mary, Hershel, Sylvester.
Becker, Miss Emma.
Bennett, Mrs. Stella.
Bevelhimer, Mr. and Mrs. Jesse; Katherine.
Black, Mr. and Mrs. Andrew.
Black, Mr. and Mrs. Gale.
Black, Mr. and Mrs. George; Eugene, Albert.
Blacketor, Mr. and Mrs. Fred; Eveland.
Books, Mr. and Mrs. Mont; Harry, George.
Bowen, Mr. and Mrs. S. F.
Briles, Mr. and Mrs. Chas.; Dee.
Brookshire, Mr. and Mrs. Wm. H.; Rena, Ruth.
Bushawn, Mr. and Mrs. Sarah.
Bussart, Mr. and Mrs. Albert.
Calloway, Mr. anad Mrs. Otto.
Chalk, Mr. and Mrs. Harry.
Chalk, Chas.; Libbey.
Chambers, Mr. and Mrs. John.
Chambers, Mrs. Mollie.
Champ, Mr. and Mrs. Clyde; Estel.
Chizum, Mr. and Mrs. George.
Clemans, Mr. and Mrs. Newton.
Cline, Mr. and Mrs. Finley.
Coal, Mr. and Mrs. Len; Milo, baby.
Collens, Mr. and Mrs. Newton; Christel, Homer, Laren.
Colins, Tommy.
Conn, Mr. and Mrs. Joseph H.; Floyd.
Cooper, Mr. and Mrs. George, Josephine.
Cooper, Mr. and Mrs. Jud.
Cornell, Mr. and Mrs. C. E.; Perry, Marie, Claude, May, Ruth, Fern, Mary.
Cox, Mr. and Mrs. Loyd; Helen.
Cunningham, Mr. and Mrs. Jacob.
Cunningham, Mr. and Mrs. Lester.
Cunningham, Mr. and Mrs. Rolla; Marcell, Gerald, Victoria, Goodrich, Gresham, Gilbert.
Cunningham, Mr. and Mrs. Roy.
Cunningham, Mr. and Mrs. Will; Lola, John.

Dague, Mr. and Mrs. Samuel; Dortha.
Daly, John P.
Davidson, Mr. and Mrs. Harry; Francis, Thelma, Garnet, Panzy.
Davidson, Lee, Celia.
Deo, Cecil, Robert.
Dice, Mr. and Mrs. James; Cecelia.
Dill, Mrs. Fannie.
Doud, Mr. and Mrs. Lucien.
Easterday, Mr. and Mrs. George.
Easterday, Mr. and Mrs. William; Edward, Carrie.
Eber, Mr. and Mrs. Chas.; John, Paul, Carl.
Edington, Mr. and Mrs. Robert.
Elkens, Chas.
Ellis, Mr. and Mrs. John.
Emerson, Mr. and Mrs. Charles.
Emerson, Mr. and Mrs. Ralph.
Emery, Mr. and Mrs. Carl; babe.
Evans, Mr. and Mrs. Elzie; Ora, Russell, Gladys, Ines, Francis.
Ewer, Mr. and Mrs. Ben.; Ersel.
Eyetcheson, Mr. and Mrs. Isaac.
Eyetcheson, Mr. and Mrs. Otha; Marie.
Eyetcheson, Mr. and Mrs. Ralph Donald.
Fair, Mr. and Mrs. Joe; children.
Fall, Mr. and Mrs. Cecil.
Felder, Mr. and Mrs. Emerson; Emerson R.
Felder, Mr. and Mrs. Lewis W.; Verra.
Felty, P. W.; Lucile, Irene, Emerson, Iverson, Roy, Helen.
Fenstemaker, Mr. and Mrs. Fred; Louise, Harold, Raymond, Ellen.
Fenstemaker, Mr. and Mrs. Ivan; Rethel.
Fenters, Frank, Elvira M., Minnie., Harold E., Maude L.
Fisher, Mr. and Mrs. Charles.
Fisher, Mr. and Mrs. Fred.
Fisher, Mr. and Mrs. Homer.
Fred, Mr. and Mrs. C. H.
Fred, Mr. and Mrs. Claude C.; Alice.
Fry, Mr. and Mrs. Arthur; Opal, Chester.

CONTRIBUTORS

Fry, Charles L.
Fry, Mr. and Mrs. Ross L.; Marnet.
Gilbert, Mr. and Mrs. Lamont; Cleon, babe.
Goodner, Mrs. Catherine.
Goodner, Mr. and Mrs. Noble.
Goss, Mr. and Mrs. Edd; Herschel.
Gott, Mr. and Mrs. W. M.; Zelma, Walter, Murray.
Gottschaalk, Wm. A.; Martha A., May, Bertha, Alice, Laura, Charley, Fred.
Gray, Mr. and Mrs. Wm. H.; Letha, Floyd, Ester, Florence.
Gregery, Mr. and Mrs. Richard.
Grimes, Mr. and Mrs. Van.
Harding, Mr. and Mrs. Wm.; John.
Heckathorne, Mr. and Mrs. Henry; Golda, Kirsch, Lester, Kenneth.
Heckathorne, Mrs. Mary E.
Hendrixson, Mrs. Mary O.
Hendrickson, Mr. and Mrs. Jacob.
Hendrickson, Mr. and Mrs. L. W.; Ray, Ruth.
Hicks, Mrs. Rosa.
Hoover, Mr. and Mrs. Sidney; Glen, Robert, Ethel.
Horton, Chas. G.; Emma.
Horton, Glen; Nellie E.
Horton, Ray, Velma.
House, Mr. and Mrs. Joseph.
Jackson, Mrs. Mary.
Jewell, Mr. and Mrs. Harry; Corlas.
Johnston, Mr. and Mrs. Frank; Carl, Francis.
Jones, Mr. and Mrs. John.
Julian, Mr. and Mrs. Nathan; Paul, Faye, Mable.
Kachendifer, Frank; Casa.
Keub, Mr. and Mrs. Bert; son.
King, Mr. and Mrs. Virgil; Anna.
Lane, Mr. and Mrs. Vinton.
Large, Mr. and Mrs. John A.; Andrew, John, Annabelle, Kourt, Lena.
Linder, Mr. and Mrs. John.
Lisey, Mrs. Mary Jane.
Leonhart, Mr. and Mrs. Lee; Mary, Irene, Edna.
Lochhart, Mr. and Mrs. William;
Belle, Ralph, baby.
Loman, Mr. and Mrs. Silas.
Lovatt, Mr. and Mrs. William.
Lowe, Mr. and Mrs. John; Isaac.
Lucas, Mr. and Mrs.; Pearl, Lloyd, Edith.
Ludwig, Mr. and Mrs. Phillip.
Ludwig, Mr. and Mrs. Sidney, Ida.
McCrosky, Cecil; Elizabeth.
McCrosky, Mr. and Mrs. Harley; Gerrald.
McCroskey, Mrs. Nancy; Con, Clarence.
McCroskey, Mr. and Mrs. V. P.; Clifford, Lester, Carl, Arlow.
McGrew, Mr. and Mrs. Christopher; Glen, Anna, Sylvia.
McLoughan, Mr. and Mrs. Leo.
Maroney, Mr. and Mrs. Sylvester; children.
Martendale, Mr. and Mrs. Oliver; Cleo, Edna.
Martin, Mr. and Mrs. Ruba; Roland, Mary J.
Martin, Mr. and Mrs. S. L.
Mathias, Mr. and Mrs. Chas. W.; Hugh Z., Herman V., Ernest L., Noble D.
Messinger, Mr. and Mrs. Henry; Helen.
Miller, Mr. and Mrs. C.; Francis, Cecil.
Miller, Mr. and Mrs. Curtis.
Miller, Mr. and Mrs. Gary E.; Kennith, Mildred, Fren.
Mogle, Mr. and Mrs. Floyd E.; Eugene, Fayme.
Moon, Mr. and Mrs. Jacob.
Moor, Mr. and Mrs. James.
Musselman, Mr. and Mrs. Joe; Grace.
Nichols, Mr. and Mrs. Wm. J.; Genevive.
Norris, Mr. and Mrs. Vern.
Norris, Mr. and Mrs. W. V. S.; Dewey, Cleo, Lola.
Oliver, Mr. and Mrs. Irvin; Shirley, Marjorie, Lola Grace.
Oliver, Mr. and Mrs. J. A.; Gail, Mrs. Lucy.
Olmstead, Mr. and Mrs. Elza; Lee.

Packard, Mr. and Mrs. Oscar; children.
Pownall, Mr. and Mrs. L. M.; Roy, Don.
Pownall, Mr. and Mrs. V. J.; Mabel, Ruth.
Pownall, Mr. and Mrs. Wm.
Rans, Mr. and Mrs. Cary.
Reeser, Mrs. Hatty.
Reed, Mr. and Mrs. Chas.; Zilphia, Minnie.
Reed, Mr. and Mrs. J. C.; Clarence, E., Emmor D.
Reed, Mr. and Mrs. Otto; Gwendolyn.
Reed, Mr. and Mrs. Richard.
Reed, Mr. and Mrs. Robinson B.
Reed, Mr. and Mrs. Samuel.
Reed, Mr. and Mrs. Sherman.
Reed, Mr. and Mrs. Thomas; Thelma, Blanche, Dale.
Rhemenschneider, Mr. and Mrs. Harley.
Robbins, Mr. and Mrs. Chester; Dona, Betty.
Robinson, Mr. and Mrs. John; Lela.
Rouch, Mr. and Mrs. Emanuel; Vuel.
Rouch, Mr. and Mrs. H. W.; Goldie.
Rouch, Mr. and Mrs. Jonah.
Rouch, Mr. and Mrs. Levi.
Rouch, Mr. and Mrs. Schuyler.
Rouch, Mr. and Mrs. Wm.
Sanders, Josephine; Lucy, Bessie, Thomas D., Albert.
Sears, Mr. and Mrs. Russel; Wilfred.
Sheets, Mr. and Mrs. Clinton; Mamay, Emery, Harry.
Sheets, Mr. and Mrs. Elmer; Dale.
Shelton, Miller.
Shoemaker, Mr. and Mrs. Elmer; Alvah.
Showley, Mr. and Mrs. Alfred; Lloyd, Elsie, Cleo, Edna.
Skinner, Mr. and Mrs. Walter.
Staley, Mr. and Mrs. Russell; baby.
Stanley, Mr. and Mrs. Frank; Nathan, Edna, Lucile.
Stanley, Mr. and Mrs. Samuel.
Steudebaker, Mr. and Mrs. Claude; Byron.
Steudabaker, Mrs. Emma.
Stith, Rev. and Mrs. Allie; Roy, Marie.
Stookey, Mr. and Mrs. Harry; Opal, Orville, Margaret.
Stubblefield, Mrs.
Thorp, Mr. and Mrs. Luther; Ora S., William.
Townsend, Mr. and Mrs. Ancil B.; Ruth.
Townsend, Mr. and Mrs. Earl; Mildred.
Trout, Mr. and Mrs. Wilson; Russel, Murriel, Harold.
Ulch, Mr. and Mrs. Edd.
Ulch, Mr. and Mrs. G. W.
Van Nice, William; Harry.
Wade, Mr. and Mrs. H. F.
Walters, William.
Ward, Mr. and Mrs. Truman H.; Mary, Robert, Emerson, Glen.
Weller, Mr. and Mrs. Clint; Belva, Lena.
Werner, Mr. and Mrs. Levi; Charles.
Wheadon, Mr. and Mrs. Albert; Mary, Paul.
Whybrew, Mr. and Mrs. James.
Wildermuth, Mr. and Mrs. Floyd F.
Wildermuth, St. Clair.
Williams, Mr. and Mrs. Willard.
Wilson, Mr. and Mrs. Earl.
Yankee, Mr. and Mrs. Chas.; Ray, Grace, Nettie, Alberta, Gail, Gilbert.
Zabst, Ben.
Zabst, Mr. and Mrs. Joe; Eldon.
Zartman, Mr. and Mrs. Irvin; Omer, Ray, Hazel.

Fulton and Liberty Township Red Cross Auxiliary

Chairman—Mrs. Roy Johnson.
Secretary-Treasurer—Mrs. Lillie Redmond.
Sewing Committee—Mrs. Frank Bowen. Mrs. Ida Ditmire. Mrs. Ethel Studebaker.
Knitting Committee—Mrs. W. I. Rannells. Mrs. Ida Dielman. Mrs. Lillie Redmond.
Buying Committee—Mrs. Lillie Redmond. Mrs. Frank Bowen. Mrs. W. I. Rannells.
Committee on Ways and Means—Mrs. James Moore. Mrs. Dora Ewer. Mrs. Chas. Meyer. Mrs. Carl Blackburn. Miss Emma Becker.
Charter Members—Mrs. Roy Johnson. Mrs. Lillie Redmond. Mrs. James Moore. Mrs. Ida Ditmire. Mrs. Ida Dielman. Mrs. W. I. Rannells. Mrs. Frank Bowen. Mrs. Ethel Studebaker. Miss Emma Becker.
Red Cross Nurse—Miss Katherine King.
Special Contributors—Fulton U. B. Ladies Aid Society, $5.00. Fulton U. B. Sunday School Class, No. 2, yr. 1918 linen shower, Fulton U. B. Sunday School class, No. 5, yr. 1918, linen shower. K. O. T. G. Club, auxiliary fund, $5.00. Fulton U. B. Sunday School, class No. 2, yr. 1918, ½ day sewing per week. Mt. Olive School, yr. 1918-19, old clothing. Fulton O. E. S., No. 376 and Fulton F. and A. M., No. 665, 75 yds. flannel.
Liberty Township by Square Mile Organization to Auxiliary, $221.05
Liberty Township Red Cross Membership Organization
Membership Director—Mrs. W. E. Redmond.
Solicitors, Fulton—Mrs. James Snepp. Mrs. Dora Ewer. Mrs. W. E. Redmond. Miss Vera Rouch. Miss Marie Richards.

Liberty Township
MEMBERS

Allen, Jess
Allen, Rex
Apt, Mr. and Mrs. Elmer
Apt, Mr. and Mrs. C. G.
Armstrong, William
Armstrong, Mr. and Mrs. L. G.
Arvin, Orval
Bacon, Mrs. Clarisa
Baird, Mrs. Chas.
Baird, Mr. and Mrs. Will
Baker, Mrs. Geo.
Baker, Ray
Baker, Mrs. Daisy
Baker, Mrs. Virgil
Baker, Mrs. Jacob
Baker, Sam
Barker, Verd
Barker, Mrs. Eva
Battenburg, Mr. and Mrs. Conn
Beattie, Miss Grace
Beattie, Mr. and Mrs. Mark
Becker, Mrs. Mary
Becker, Miss Emma
Bennett, Stella
Berry, Mrs. Jennie
Berger, Wilfred
Berry, Mrs. Glen
Bevelhiemer, Mrs. Katherine
Bevelhiemer, Mr. and Mrs. Jess
Bish, Mr. and Mrs. Ray
Black, Grace
Black, Frank G.
Black, Mr. and Mrs. George A.
Black, Mrs. Andy
Blackburn, Mrs. Carl
Books, Mont
Bowen, Mr. and Mrs. S. F.
Briles, Mr. and Mrs. Chas.
Brown, Chas.
Brown, Walter
Brown, William
Brookshire, Mrs. Emma
Buckingham, Mrs. Hazel
Buckingham, Frank
Buchanan, Ed
Cain, Mr. and Mrs. Gilbert
Calaway, Clarence G.
Calaway, Mr. and Mrs. Dell

Calaway, S. C.
Campbell, Chas.
Campbell, Elmer
Carr, Ray
Carr, Ruth
Caton, Mrs. Pearl
Chalk, Miss Libbie
Champ, Clyde
Champ, Osa
Chizum, Mr. and Mrs. George
Clevenger, William
Clevenger, Mr. and Mrs. Elmer
Clevenger, Orol
Clevenger, Mrs. Mable
Clemans, Walter
Cline, Jas. F.
Cline, Mrs. Eva
Cline, Chas.
Coffing, Edgar E.
Coleman, Mrs. Nat
Coleman, Mr. and Mrs. William
Collins, G. R.
Collins, Newton
Collins, Mr. and Mrs. Dora
Conn, Mr. and Mrs. George
Conn, J. A.
Conn, Jessie
Conn, A. C.
Conrad, Madison
Conrad, Mrs. Ella
Cornell, Chas.
Cornell, Perry
Cornwell, Joe H.
Cook, Mrs. Amanda
Cooper, George
Cornwell, Miss Dora
Cox, Mrs. Lydia
Cox, Loyde
Cripe, Elmer
Cunningham, Mr. and Mrs. R. L.
Cunningham, Mr. and Mrs. Jacob
Cunningham, Will
Cunningham, Rolla
Cunningham, Orrie
Dague, Sam
Davis, Ed
Davidson, Mr. and Mrs. Lee
Dawald, John H.
Dawald, Mrs. Estie
Dawald, Lula
Dawald, Benjamin F.

Day, Arthur
Dice, Mrs. Kitty
Dielman, Mr. and Mrs. Frank
Dill, Mrs. Anna
Ditmire, Mrs. Ida
Ditmire, Frank
Doud, Mr. and Mrs. Lucien
Doud, Brenton
Doud, Mrs. E. J.
Durbin, Mr. and Mrs. Thomas
Durbin, Miss Opal
Easterday, William
Easterday, G. W.
Easterday, Miss Mable
Eber, Mr. and Mrs. Charles
Edington, Mr. and Mrs. Robert
Elkins, Mrs. Pearl
Emerson, Mrs. Mae
English, Mr. and Mrs. W. V.
Enyart, Chas. F.
Enyart, Mr. and Mrs. Morton
Evans, Elzie
Ewer, Mrs. Dora
Eytcheson, Otha
Eytcheson, Isaac
Etycheson, Mrs. Len
Eytcheson, Elmer
Fall, Cecil
Fall, Olive
Felder, Mrs. Lottie
Felder, Mrs. Ruth
Felder, Louis
Felty, P. W.
Fenstermaker, Mrs. Ivan
Fenstermaker, Mr. and Mrs. Fred
Fenters, Elvira M.
Fenters, Frank
Fenters, Maud
Fisher, Eliza
Fisher, Ora
Fisher, Frank
Fisher, Homer
Fissel, Mary A.
Fissel, Mary C.
Flenner, Fayne
Flenner, Edna
Fred, Claude
Fry, Daniel
Fry, Chas.
Fouts, Joe
Fouts, Mrs. Joe

CONTRIBUTORS

Fowler, J. S.
Fultz, Mr. and Mrs. John
Frain, Mr. and Mrs. Howard
Geier, Chas.
Gott, Mr. and Mrs. Wm.
Gott, Miss Zelma
Gottschalk, Mrs. William
Goodner, Mr. and Mrs. Noble
Goodner, Mrs. Catherine
Gordon, S. V.
Goss, Mr. and Mrs. Ed
Gray, Mr. and Mrs. William S.
Gray, Ancil C.
Gray, Mrs. Lola M.
Gray, Mr. and Mrs. Wm. H.
Green, J. E.
Gregg, Miss Vera
Gregg, Lewis
Gregory, Mrs. Frank
Halterman, Ernest
Hanson, Mrs. John
Hartman, Irvin
Heath, Mr. and Mrs. Robert
Hendrickson, Mr. and Mrs. L. M.
Hendrickson, Mr. and Mrs. Jacob
Henderson, Metta M.
Henderson, Mrs. Sophia
Hicks, Mrs. Rose
Hudleson, Al
Hudson, O. A.
Hudson, Mary
Horton, C. G.
Horton, Emma
House, Mrs. Joseph
Jewell, Harvey
Johnson, Mr. and Mrs. Roy
Johnston, Mr. and Mrs. Frank
Johnston, Carl
Johnston, Francis
Johnston, Richard
Johnson, Miss Helen
Kessingler, Rev.
King, Mr. and Mrs. Chas.
Koffel, A. E.
Lane, Mr. and Mrs. Vinton
Large, John F.
Large, Mr. and Mrs. J. A.
Leavell, Mr. and Mrs. Clyde
Leavell, John
Leavell, Miss Garnett
Lemon, Mrs. Mary E.

Linder, John
Linder, Nora
Lisey, Mary Jane
Locke, Mrs. Daisy
Locke, William
Lovett, Mr. and Mrs. Wm.
Lowe, Mrs. Neal
Lowman, Mrs. Silas
Lucas, Pearl
Ludwig, Miss Lillie
Ludwig, Miss Mary
Ludwig, Sidney
Ludwig, Kate
Ludwig, Philip
Madary, Mrs. Susan
Martin, Mrs. Hulda
Martin, Mrs. Edward
Martin, Mr. and Mrs. S. L.
Martin, Crissie
Marsh, Mr. and Mrs. John
Masterson, Cassel
Mathias, Chas. W.
Matthews, Robert M.
Matthews, Mrs. Ella
Maxwell, William
Maxwell, May
Maxwell, Chas.
Messinger, Henry
Meyer, Mrs. Chas.
Meyers, Henry
Meyers, Mrs. Henry
Mills, Mr. and Mrs. Fred
Mills, Mr. and Mrs. Mell
Miller, Mr. and Mrs. Clinton
Minter, P. O.
Mogle, Mrs. Floyd
Morts, Mrs. Emma
Morts, Laura
Morts, Ray
Moss, John
Moss, Mrs. Dillie
Moon, Mr. and Mrs. Jacob
Moore, James
Moore, Mrs. James
Musselman, Joseph
Musselman, Mrs. Joseph
Myers, Mrs. John
McFadden, Mr. and Mrs. F. P.
McDougle, Mrs. Mary
McFadden, Miss Lulu
McDougle, Mrs. Ed

McDougle, Ed
McDougle, Joshua
McDougle, Frank M.
McDougle, Miss Bessie
McCrosky, Mr. and Mrs. Earl
McCrosky, Mrs. Nancy
McGrew, C. C.
McGrew, Mrs. Clara
McMillen, Ida
McCarter, Pearl
McCarter, Edgar
McCarter, Mary E.
McCrosky, Delbert
Martin, Mr. and Mrs. George
Martindale, Ella
McCrosky, Cecil
McLoughlin, Mr. and Mrs. Leo
McCrosky, Mr. and Mrs. Harley
Nellans, William
Nickols, Wm. J.
Nichols, Mrs. Ella A.
Nordloh, Mr. and Mrs. Henry
Norris, Hugh
Norris, O. V.
Norris, Mr. and Mrs. W. V. S.
Norris, Miss Cleo
Odell, Delmer
Ogle, Mrs. Jane
Olmstead, Mr. and Mrs. Elza
Oliver, Mr. and Mrs. Irwin
Oliver, Mr. and Mrs. J. A.
Oliver, Miss Gail V.
Packard, Oscar
Painter, John
Patterson, Mr. and Mrs. William
Peppers, Mrs. Betsy
Peffers, Erbert
Peffers, Samuel
Phoenix, Russel
Poorman, Mr. and Mrs. Dave
Poorman, James M.
Poorman, Mr. and Mrs. Earl
Pownall, Mr. and Mrs. William
Pownall, Frank
Pownall, Mrs. Hazel
Pownell, Lee
Pownell, Mrs. Lulu
Pownell, Ivan
Pownall, V. J.
Pownall, Clara
Quick, Philo M.

Quick, Hannah
Rannells, Mr. and Mrs. W. I.
Rannells, Mrs. Mae
Rannells, D. G.
Redmond, Mr. and Mrs. W. E.
Reed, Mrs. Agnes
Reed, Mr. and Mrs. Pearl
Reed, Richard
Reed, Charles
Reed, Mrs. Nona
Reed, Mr. and Mrs. J. C.
Reed, Clarence
Reed, Mr. and Mrs. Otto
Reed, Calvin
Rentschler, George, Jr.
Rentschler, Robert
Rentschler, Andrew F.
Rentschler, Mr. and Mrs. George, Sr.
Rentschler, Mr. and Mrs. Henry
Rhemenschneider, Harley
Rhemenschneider, Mrs. Silvia
Richards, Miss Marie
Richart, Rev. O. L.
Rickison, George
Robinson, Mr. and Mrs. John
Robbins, John
Robbins, Sarah A.
Robbins, Mr. and Mrs. Chester
Rose, Harvey
Rouch, Mrs. Leonie
Rouch, Mrs. Maggie
Rouch, Hiram
Rouch, S. C.
Rouch, Mr. and Mrs. Omer
Rouch, Emanuel
Rouch, Nelson
Rouch, Mrs. Maude
Rouch, Miss Goldie
Rouch, Mr. and Mrs. Jonah
Sanders, Albert
Sanders, Josephus
Sanders, Mrs. Lucy A.
Sanders, Miss Bessie
Schindler, Jacob
Sears, Russel
Sears, Mrs.
Sedam, Mrs. Alex
Severns, Amos
Severns, Mrs. Amos
Shaver, Anna A.
Shaw, Clayton

CONTRIBUTORS

Shaw, Mrs. Emma
Sheets, Clint
Sheets, Harry
Sheetz, Elmer
Shelton, Miller
Shelton, Mrs. Ross
Shoemaker, Elmer
Showley, Mr. and Mrs. Alfred
Showley, Lloyd Alfred
Slifer, Susie
Smith, Russel H.
Smith, John F.
Smith, Ira
Snepp, Mrs. James
Snyder, Mrs. Lillie
Sparks, Mrs. Newton
Staley, Mrs. Earl
Staley, Will
Stingley, Jacob
Stingley, Mrs. Sadie A.
Stingley, I. E.
Stingley, Miss Essie
Stooky, Mr. and Mrs. Harry
Stooky, Miss Opal
Strouss, Aim
Studebaker, Mr. and Mrs. Claude
Surface, Mr. and Mrs. George
Surface, Miss Edna
Surface, Miss Isabelle
Swank, Geo.
Swank, W. S.
Swank, Tieta
Tharp, Luther
Thomen, Mrs. Fred
Thurston, Mrs. Chas.
Townsend, Earl
Townsend, Mrs. A. B.
True, Mrs. Walter
Trout, James
Tyrell, Mr. and Mrs. James
Tyrell, Miss Agnes
Tyrell, Wm.
Tyrell, Mike
Ulch, Mr. and Mrs. Ed
Ulch, Mr. and Mrs. G. W.
Wade, Frank
Walters, William
Ward, Truman
Warner, Mrs. Martin
Weller, Clint
Whybrew, Mrs. Joseph
Whybrew, Mrs. Goldie
Whybrew, Colonel
Whybrew, Chester
Wheaclose, Mell
Wildermuth, St. C.
Wildermuth, Mr. and Mrs. Floyd
Williams, Chas.
Wilson, Mr. and Mrs. Carl
Wolford, Mrs. G. W.
Yankee, Mr. and Mrs. Chas.
Zanger, Mrs. B. F.
Zanger, B. F.
Zartman, Omar
Zartman, Chas.
Zartman, Cloyd
Zartman, Vern
Zartman, Samuel
Zartman, Virl
Zigafuse, Miss Tena
Zook, John
Zook, Mrs. John

Newcastle Township

Alber, Mr. and Mrs. E. H.; Florence, Novanah, John, Frank, Herman, Ella, Helen, Thyel.
Alderfer, Mr. and Mrs.
Alderfer, Roy.
Alderfer, Dorothy.
Alspaach, Mr. and Mrs. Henry.
Alspach, Mr. and Mrs. John.
Alspach, Mr. and Mrs. Neal.
Arter, Mr. and Mrs. Frank; Fern, Lois.
Anderson, Mr. and Mrs. O. C.; Bernice, Ernest.
Barr, Mr. and Mrs. Burr; Fred, Blanche, Earl.
Barr, Charles.
Barr, Mrs. Daisey.
Barrett, Mr. and Mrs. Donald.
Barrett, Mr. and Mrs. Steve.
Barkman, Mr. and Mrs. Alonzo; Gertrude, Boyd, Floyd.

Barkman, Mr. and Mrs. B. F.; Mary Ruth.
Barkman, Mrs. Ellen.
Barkman, Mr. and Mrs. George.
Barkman, Mr. and Mrs. I. N.; Fay, Clyde, Dan, Cloa, Herman, Mary.
Barkman, Mr. and Mrs. Mondo.
Batz, Mr. and Mrs. Henry.
Batz, Mr. and Mrs. I. A.; Carl, Mildred.
Baugher, Mr. and Mrs. W. H.; Mary.
Bellward, Mr. and Mrs. Frank.
Bidleman, Mr. and Mrs. Earl.
Boganwright, Mr. and Mrs. Lawrence; John, Ruth, Mary.
Bowman, Mr. and Mrs. Albert; Wonda.
Bowen, Mr. and Mrs. Henry.
Brecktle, Amiel.
Bright, Mr. and Mrs. Bert.
Bright, Mr. and Mrs. Geo.
Brockey, Mr. and Mrs. Abe.
Brockey, Mr. and Mrs. Ben; Lloyd, Opal.
Brockey, Mr. and Mrs. Verdie.
Bryant, Mr. and Mrs. Ancil; Eva, Golda.
Bryant, Mr. and Mrs. Estil; David.
Bryant, Mr. and Mrs. Geo.
Bryant, Mr. and Mrs. John; Teddy.
Bryant, Mr. and Mrs. Phillip.
Bunch, Miss Katherine.
Busenberg, Bert.
Busenberg, Mr. and Mrs. David; Esco, Ernest, Mable, Reatha, Opal, Everett.
Busenburg, Mr. and Mrs. Fred; Rosella, Beulah.
Busenburg, Mr. and Mrs. Loren; Dale.
Bybee, Elmer, Etta, Mary.
Bybee, Mr. and Mrs. Joseph.
Bybee, Mr. and Mrs. Lawson.
Bybee, Mr. and Mrs. Wm. L. Halbert.
Chapman, Mr. and Mrs. Earl.
Clingenpeel, Mr. and Mrs. Wm.; Mary, Willie, Lenden, Aurist.
Clymer, Mr. and Mrs. Harry; Claud, Hazel, Forrest.
Collins, Mr. and Mrs. Francis, Almira, Lucile.
Conklin, Edward.
Conrad, Mr. and Mrs. Bert.
Cooper, Mr. and Mrs. Harry.
Coplen, Mr. and Mrs. Alonzo.
Coplen, Mr. and Mrs. Chas.; Lucy, Jessie, Josephine, Francis, Page, Hope.
Coplen, Mr. and Mrs. Chauncy.
Coplen, Mr. and Mrs. Elmer; Floyd, Grace, Fern, Frank.
Coplen, Mr. and Mrs. Frank; George, Olive, Artemus.
Coplen, Mr. and Mrs. Lee.
Coplen, Lyman.
Craft, Mr. and Mrs. Ira.
Cuiler, Mr. and Mrs. Clem; Audrey, Kenly, Herbert.
Culer, Mr. and Mrs. Roy; Russell, Rethal, Ignota.
Cox, Mr. and Mrs. Alvah; Wilber, Omar, Roy, Geo. R., Elsie, Marion Harold.
Dalton, Charley.
Darr, Oat; Marie, Katherine.
Daulton, Charles B.; Lucia, Goldie, Velma, Joe, Bennie, Dail.
Dawson, Mr. and Mrs. John.
Deamer, Mr. and Mrs. M. F.; David, Dorthy.
Deamer, Mr. and Mrs. Geo. W.; George.
Deamer, Mr. and Mrs. Wm.
Dewall, Mr. and Mrs. James; Eva.
Dick, Mr. and Mrs. Willard; June, Carl, Sidney.
Drudge, Mr. and Mrs. Amos; Cleo, Cena, Lorena.
Drudge, Mr. and Mrs. Chas.; Wilson.
Drudge, Mr. and Mrs. Francis; Edith.
Drudge, Mr. and Mrs. Frank; Isabelle.
Dunlap, Mr. and Mrs. Jasper.
Duvalt, Mr. and Mrs. Bert.
Eaton, Mr. and Mrs. Artie; Devon.
Eheranman, Mr. and Mrs. Albert.
Eherenman, Mr. and Mrs. Loyd.
Emmons, Mr. and Mrs. Geo.
Emmons, Mr. and Mrs. Glen.

CONTRIBUTORS

Emmons, Harley.
Emmons, Mr. and Mrs. Jesse.
Emmons, Mr. and Mrs. Loren.
Emmons, Mr. and Mrs. Otis; Alene.
Emmons, Mr. and Mrs. Tom.
Entsminger, Mr. and Mrs. Warren.
Erwin, Mr. and Mrs. John.
Essig, Mrs. Kissy; Charles, Ermal.
Farry, Mr. and Mrs. A. O.; Charles, Isabella, Creamer.
Finney, Mr. and Mrs. J. D.; Helen, Alvin.
Fisher, Mr. and Mrs. S. M.
Foor, Mr. and Mrs. Fred.
Fore, Mr. and Mrs. Will; Turl, Thelma, Verl.
Gladdis, Evert R.
Good, Louisa.
Gordon, Mr. and Mrs. John; Charles.
Grass, Mrs. Esther; Eva, Russell, Zoa.
Grass, Mr. and Mrs. Jacob; Emerson, Mary.
Grass, Mr. and Mrs. Joseph J.
Green, Mr. and Mrs. Sidney L.; Rudolph, Addie, Charles, Carrie.
Griffiths, Mr. and Mrs. Milo; Gilbert.
Grove. Mr. and Mrs. Lou.
Grove, Mr. and Mrs. Symon; Archie, Oliver.
Haimbaugh, H. J.
Haimbaugh, Mrs. Henry.
Haimbaugh, J. B.
Haimbaugh, Mr. and Mrs. John; Edith, Ethel, Roland, Devon, Omer.
Haimbaugh, Mr. and Mrs. Lon.
Haimbaugh, Mr. and Mrs. Mack; Geraldine, Alonzo.
Haimbaugh, Mr. and Mrs. Meade; Wilma, George, Anna, Doris.
Haimbaugh, Mr. and Mrs. Obe; Rex, Edna.
Halderman, Mr. and Mrs. Fred; Kennith, Darl.
Hamlet, Mrs. Emma.
Hart, Mr. and Mrs. Elmer; Willis, Mildred, Donald.
Hatfield, Mr. and Mrs. Loren; Ralph, Arthur.
Haynes, Mr. and Mrs. John; Carrie, Nora, Alice, Howard, Herman.
Heighway, Mr. and Mrs. Albert.
Heighway, Mr. and Mrs. Albert H.; Franklin, F., Henry, John, Sarah.
Heighway, Mr. and Mrs. Dilly.
Heighway, Mr. and Mrs. H. C.; Margaret.
Hedrick, Amos; Amy, Thelma, Emil, Estil, Lorine.
Horn, Mr. and Mrs. Ora; Robert.
Hudkins, Mrs. Lucetta; Okel, Meriam, Thelma
Huffman, Mr. and Mrs. Charles; Laviy, Donald.
Jefferies, Mr. and Mrs. Ancil; Donald, Maurine.
Jefferies, Mrs. H. E.
Jones, Mr. and Mrs. Charles T.; Eva, Aaron, Charles, Herman.
Jurgensmeyer, Mr. and Mrs. William; Ralph.
Kalmbacher, Mr. and Mrs. John; Oliver, Reathel.
Karns, Mr. and Mrs. Elza; Marjorie, Willa.
Katherman, Mr. and Mrs. Boyd.
Keler, Mrs. Geo.; Anna M., Malita.
Kelly, Mr. and Mrs. James; Bernice, Wayne, Ancil, Audrey.
Kenedy, Mrs. Elizabeth.
Kessler, Everett.
Kesler, Mr. and Mrs. Lloyd; Mary Marjory.
Kessler, Mrs. Mary E.
Kesler, Mr. and Mrs. Milton; Bernice.
Kepler, Mr. and Mrs. Fred.
King, Mr. and Mrs. Chas.; Clara Eve.
King, Henry.
King, Mr. and Mrs. John; Edna, Raymond.
Kistler, Mrs. Margaret; Loren.
Kochenderfer, Doc; Ethel, Farrel, Van.
Kochenderfer, Joseph.
Large, George.
Leininger, Mr. and Mrs. David.
Linch, Dian; Beverly.

Long, Mr. and Mrs. Alonzo; Robert, Jessie.
Long, Mr. and Mrs. Allen A.; Charles, Sarah, David, Virgil, Gilford, Lester.
Long, Mr. and Mrs. Jay.
Long, Mr. and Mrs. John D.
Long, Wilvan; Fay.
McGarvan, Mr. and Mrs. Melville; John, Howard, Tressie.
McGee, Mr. and Mrs. F. M.
Mahoney, John; Emma.
Marsh, Clarence; Emma, Burl, Hazel, Lee, Armetta.
Markley, Mr. and Mrs. Chauncy.
Mathewes, Mr. aand Mrs. Harley; Mary, Martha, Ernest.
Mathewes, Lon; Bessie.
Mathewes, Mr. and Mrs. Steve; Roy, Gail, Howard.
Meridith, Slias; Ruth, Edwin, Francis.
Meridith, Mr. and Mrs. Vinson; Grace, Maude, Herbert.
Metzler, Mr. and Mrs. Herman; Emaline, Jerry.
Mickey, Mr. and Mrs. F. V.
Mickey, Howard.
Mikesel, Mr. and Mrs. Alva; Herold.
Mikesel, Mr. and Mrs. Asa; Earl, Russell.
Mikesel, Clifford.
Mikesel, Mr. and Mrs. John; Clarence, Irvin.
Mikesell, Philip.
Miller, Mr. and Mrs. Charles.
Miller, Mr. and Mrs. Chas.
Morrett, Mr. and Mrs. Bruce; Olive Louise, Lulu May.
Montgomery, Mr. and Mrs. Francis C.; Bella.
Montgomery, Mr. and Mrs. Omer; Levoy.
Murray, Mr. and Mrs. Lew.
Myers, Frank.
Myers, Mr. and Mrs. J. K.
Nelson, Mr. and Mrs. Allen; Don.
Nelson, Mr. and Mrs. Samuel; Mary.
Nichols, Mr. and Mrs. Laura; Mattie, Don, Ernest, Edna.
Noonan, Mr. and Mrs. Robert; George, Eleanor.
Norris, Mr. and Mrs. John.
Norris, Mr. aand Mrs. Wm.; Mary, Mildred, Grace.
North, Mr. and Mrs. Christian; Mable.
Nye, Mr. and Mrs. Esly.
Nye, Mr. and Mrs. O. E.
Othniel, Leo.
Partridge, Mr. and Mrs. Earl; Lavoy.
Partridge, Mr. and Mrs. Frank; Ruth, Ruby, Thomas.
Ffund, Mr. and Mrs. Will.
Pfund, Mr. and Mrs. Will.
Phillips, Mr. and Mrs. Bert.
Phoebus, Mr. and Mrs. Howard.
Perschbacher Alice.
Perschbacher, M. W.; Meridith, Miles, Jr.
Peterson, Mr. and Mrs. Chas.; Boyd, Joe, Walter.
Peterson, Mr. and Mrs. Ransford.
Rahfeldt, Mr. and Mrs. Fred.
Ralston, Mr. and Mrs. Clint.
Ratlifon, Mr. and Mrs. Elmer; Helen, Everet.
Roger, Mr. and Mrs. F. A.
Rogers, Herbert; Susia.
Rouch, Mr. and Mrs. John L.
Rogers, Mr. and Mrs. N. O.; Bernice, Georgia, Bernard, Morris, Lester.
Rogers, Mr. and Mrs. Raymond.
Rubley, Mr. and Mrs. Lewis, John, Rethel, Mary, Fred, Harold, Herbert.
Russel, Zane
Sensibaugh, Mr. and Mrs. Kenedy.
Severns, Mr. and Mrs. Lewis.
Severns, William.
Sherman, Mr. and Mrs. Charles; Doris.
Shoemaker, Mr. and Mrs. Floyd.
Shoemaker, Mr. and Mrs. Levi.
Shock, Chas., Della.
Shutz, Mr. and Mrs. Will; Estle, Lloyd.
Smith, Mr. and Mrs. C.; Retha, Pearl.
Smith, Mr. and Mrs. Daniel.
Smith, Dorris, Della.
Smith, Mr. and Mrs. Foy.

CONTRIBUTORS

Smith, Mr. and Mrs. L. D.
Starner, Mr. and Mrs. Polk; Eva.
Stockberger, Mr. and Mrs. Alva M.
Stockberger, Geo. A.; Martha, Frances, Loren, Otis, Dwight, Eddie.
Stuckey, Mr. and Mrs. Geo.; Rudy.
Sullivan, Mrs. Angeline.
Sullivan, Mr. and Mrs. Walter; Gerald.
Surguy, Dr. A. B.; Dewey, Fred.
Sutherlin, Mr. and Mrs. John.
Swonger, Mr. and Mrs. David.
Taylor, Mr. and Mrs. Charles; Elva, Verl, Delford, Ily, Ima.
Taylor, Mr. and Mrs. Oscar; Ruth, Carl.
Teel, Mr. and Mrs. Thedore.
Teeter, Mr. and Mrs. F.
Teeter, Mr. and Mrs. Vincent.
Thompson, Mr. and Mrs. Samuel; Elza, Frank.
Thornburg, Mr. and Mrs. Geo.
Tipton, Schuyler.
Tippy, Mr. and Mrs. Levi; Robert, Raymond.
Tippy, Mr. and Mrs. E. B.
Truman, Jacob.
Umbaugh, Mr. and Mrs. Geo.
Umbaugh, Mr. and Mrs. John; Reda, Edna.
Umbauagh, Mr. and Mrs. Loy; Francis, Esther.
Wagoner, James.
Walburn, Mr. aand Mrs. Clinton L.
Walburn, Mr. and Mrs. H. Keith.
Walters, Mr. and Mrs. Abe.
Walters, Alonzo; Earl, Harold.
Walters, Mr. and Mrs. Russell.
Waltz, Mr. and Mrs. Geo.; Luez.
Welker, Mr. and Mrs. Emery; Zelda.
Wenger, Harry.
Weygandt, Mr. and Mrs. Jay.
Williams, Roy H.; Ethel, Laura, Hugh.
Wilson, Mr. and Mrs. Orville; Mary.
Zent, Mr. and Mrs. Lloyd; Earl, Orton.
Zolman, Carrie, Grace, Berneice, Guy.
Zolman, Mr. and Mrs. C. C.
Zolman, Mr. and Mrs. S. P.

Richland Township

Adams, Mr. and Mrs. Geo.
Alderfer, Mr. and Mrs. Amos.
Alderfer, Mr. and Mrs. Clinton and children.
Alderfer, Mr. and Mrs. Henry.
Alexander, Mr. and Mrs. W. R.
Anderson, Mr. and Mrs. Geo. R.
Anderson, Mr. and Mrs. H. L.
Anderson, Mr. and Mrs. Milo.
Anderson, Mr. and Mrs. Oren.
Andrews, Mr. and Mrs. Wm.
Arnold, Mr. and Mrs. Sam.
Babcock, Mr. and Mrs. Edward.
Bailey, Mr. and Mrs. Thomas.
Bair, E. S.
Bair, P.
Baldwin, Mr. and Mrs. James.
Ball, Mr. and Mrs. Clyde.
Ball, Mr. and Mrs. Frank.
Ball, Mrs. Maggie.
Ball, Mr. and Mrs. Vernon; Marjorie.
Barkman, Mr. and Mrs. Charles; children.
Beck, Mr. and Mrs. John.
Beck, Mr. and Mrs. Thomas, Sr.; Helen.
Beck, Mr. and Mrs. Valorous.
Beehler, Mr. and Mrs. David; Bessie.
Beehler, Mrs. William; Clyde, Ruth, Alta, Reo, Reathel.
Biddinger, Mr. and Mrs. William.
Bordin, Mr. and Mrs. A. C.
Bower, Mr. and Mrs. John.
Buehler, Mr. and Mrs. Charley.
Buehler, Mrs. P. H.
Bunn, Mr. and Mrs. Frank.
Burkett, Mr. and Mrs. Austin.
Bush, Mrs. Margaret.
Calhoun, Mr. and Mrs. Tom; Donald.
Calvert, Mr. aand Mrs.; children.
Carey, Mr. and Mrs. D. L.; Vera, Vida.

Caslow, Mr. and Mrs. Arthur.
Caslow, Mr. and Mrs. Dan.
Castleman, Mr. and Mrs. Clarence; Verneice.
Cime, Mr. and Mrs. Ell.
Coflen, Alonzo.
Cole, Mr. and Mrs. Claude.
Cole, Mr. and Mrs. Emmet.
Conaway, Mr. and Mrs. Geo. E.; Ralph, Joe.
Conrad, Mr. and Mrs. Kit; Zella.
Cook, Mr. and Mrs. Daniel.
Corry, Mr. and Mrs. Oscar.
Cowan, Mr. and Mrs. Wm.; Dewey.
Crable, Festulis.
Day, Carl.
Dillon, Mr. and Mrs. G. A.
Drew, Mr. and Mrs. John; Ora, Elton, Flavilla.
Dudgeon, Mr. and Mrs. James.
Dudgeon, Mr. and Mrs. Albertus; Dewey.
Eash, Mr. and Mrs. Edward.
Eash, Mrs. Elizabeth.
Edington, Jerry.
Fieser, Mr. and Mrs. A. C.
Fisher, Alva.
Fisher, Mr. and Mrs. O. P.
Fletcher, Elihu.
Fletcher, Mr. and Mrs. Martin.
Flora, Mr. and Mrs. Ira; Ralph, Ruth.
Florence, Mr. and Mrs. Abednego.
Foor, Mr. and Mrs. Parlee; Harold.
Foster, Wm.
Fultz, Mr. and Mrs. Geo. W.; Ruth.
Gaby, Mr. and Mrs. Daniel.
Gelbaugh, Mr. and Mrs. Leslie.
Gorden, Anna.
Gordon, Mr. and Mrs. Joseph; George, Alexander.
Gordon, Mr. and Mrs. Roy; Lillian, Margaret.
Guise, Hugh.
Guise, Mr. and Mrs. J. H.
Hallermans, Mr. and Mrs. Leroy; children.
Halterman, Mr. and Mrs. Ben.
Harpester, Mrs. Jane.
Hassenplug, Mr. and Mrs. Elby; Mable, Obid, Aletta Ruth.
Hiatt, Mr. and Mrs. Alvin.
Hiatt, Chauncy.
Hiatt, Estella.
Higgens, John Henry.
Hisey, Mrs. A.
Hisey, Mr. and Mrs. Creighton; Rosa, Elmer.
Hubbard, Mr. and Mrs. James.
Hubert, Hettie, L'zzie, Lilly, Caldie.
Jackson, Mr. and Mrs. Charles.
Jackson, Mr. and Mrs. Mark; Geneive.
Johnson, Mr. and Mrs. Dan.
Jordan, Mrs. Jane.
Kale, Mr. and Mrs. Alva.
Kanouse, Mr. and Mrs. Elmer; Donald, Dean.
Kerle, Anna, Dollie.
Kewney, Mrs. Sarah.
Kindig, Mr. and Mrs. Cleabe.
Kindig, Mr. and Mrs. Lan.
Krouse, Earl.
Leedy, Mr. and Mrs. Bert; Margaret.
Leedy, Mr. and Mrs. Chas.; Oren.
Lunsford, Mr. and Mrs. Frank; Loyd, Harry.
McGriff, Mr. and Mrs. Ben; Oren, Lors.
McGriff, Mr. and Mrs. John.
McPherron, Mrs. Minnie; Emil, Clarence, Mary, Florence, May, Carl, Wilma, Harry Edwin.
McQueeney, Miss Ella.
Martin, Mr. and Mrs. Chas.; Gearold.
Martin, Mr. and Mrs. F. E.; Mildred.
Matchett, Mrs. Ella.
Means, Charles.
Mechling, Henry.
Mechling, Mr. and Mrs. Henry.
Mechling, Mr. and Mrs. Isaac.
Meek, Dr. L. C.
Metzger, Mr. and Mrs. John.
Metzger, Mr. and Mrs. Sue.
Miller, Mrs. Catherine.
Miller, Mr. and Mrs. Fred.
Miller, Mr. and Mrs. Orville F.; Mildred.
Miller, Wm.
Moore, Mr. and Mrs. Charles.
Moore, Mrs. Pendleton.

Mow, Mrs. Catherine.
Mow, Mr. and Mrs. Clate; children.
Mow, Clyde.
Mow, Mr. and Mrs. Dean; Evelyn.
Mow, Mr. and Mrs. Lee; Edward Lee.
Mow, Marion.
Mow, Mr. and Mrs. R. D.
Mow, See.
Munn, Mr. and Mrs. Charles; Georgia, Ethel, Lola.
Nellans, Mr. and Mrs. Dean.
Newcomb, Mrs. Alice.
Newcomb, Mr. and Mrs. Willard; Ruth.
Norris, Mr. and Mrs. George.
Nutt, Mr. and Mrs. Oliver; Kennith, Bonnie, Cloyd, Ebert, Virginia.
O'Blenis, Mr. and Mrs. Sanford.
O'Blenis, Mr. and Mrs. Wm. C.; Clem, Ray, Dean.
O'Connell, Mr. and Mrs. J. P.
O'Dell, Mr. and Mrs. Frank; Samuel, John G., Thomas, Isaac.
Olds, Mr. and Mrs. George.
O'Neal, Mr. and Mrs. John; Hazel.
Ormsbee, Fred.
Ormsbee, Mr. and Mrs. Los.
Overmyer, Mr. and Mrs. A. B.; Alpha, Clarence.
Overmyer, Mr. and Mrs. Bennie.
Overmyer, Mr. and Mrs. Boyde.
Overmyer, Mr. and Mrs. Carrie; Georgia.
Overmyer, Nelson.
Overmyer, Mr. and Mrs. Walter.
Overmyer, Mr. and Mrs. W. S.; Bessie, Hazel, Arthur.
Pally, Mr. and Mrs. Tuck; Edward, Richard.
Reed, Mr. and Mrs. J. Howard; Donald T., Joseph F.
Reed, Mr. and Mrs. Robert R.; John H.
Rhinesmith, Mr. and Mrs. C. E.; Leon.
Rhodes, Mr. and Mrs. Riley; Beecher, Dean.
Ridder, Mr. aand Mrs. A. J.
Rinker, Mrs. Bessie.
Ritter, Mr. and Mrs. Frank; Goldie, Fern, Lolo, Dolan.
Rodgers, Mr. and Mrs. Wm.; Crystal, Mildred.
Rogers, Mr. and Mrs.
Rohrer, Mr. and Mrs. Frank; Mable.
Rohrer, Mr. and Mrs. Jesse; Jacob.
Runnels, Mr. and Mrs. James H.
Runnels, Mr. and Mrs. Thomas A.
Rush, Mr. and Mrs. Frank; Helen, Nellie.
Safford, Mr. and Mrs. Charles.
Salts, Mr. and Mrs. Chas.
Sanders, Mr. and Mrs. Charles; Carl, Loyd, Irene, Irvin, Delta.
Sanders, Mr. and Mrs. Henry.
Sanders, Mr. and Mrs. Thomas; Daniel.
Sausaman, Mr. and Mrs. Bert.
Schaul, Mr. and Mrs. Emerson.
Scott, Mr. and Mrs. Q. E.
Shafer, Mr. and Mrs. R. W.
Sissel, Mr. and Mrs. Charles; Weldon Robert, Joe.
Smith, Mr. and Mrs. Byron O.; Irene.
Smith, Mr. and Mrs. Del; Ted, Donald.
Stichler, Mrs. Maine.
Stockberger, Clyde.
Stockberger, Mr. and Mrs. Delbert J.; Kenneth, Harold, Margie.
Strawderman, Wm.
Swihart, Mr. and Mrs. Dave; Melvin, Fred, Velma, Ruth.
Thorp, Mr. and Mrs. Al.
Thorp, Mr. and Mrs. J. O.
Towne, Mr. and Mrs. Charles; Gilford, Ronald, Demoine.
Towne, Mr. and Mrs. Chas. E.; Oyis, Mildred.
Towne, Mr. and Mrs. G. W.
Trimble, Mrs. Lydia; Clinton D.
Vanatta, Mr. and Mrs. Arnett.
Walters, Mr. and Mrs. Charles.
Walters, Mr. nd Mrs. Ervine.
Walters, Mr. and Mrs. Ervine.
Walters, Mr. and Mrs. Perry.
Walters, Mr. and Mrs. Robert.
Warner, Mr. and Mrs. Riley; Von.
Weir, Mr. and Mrs. George; Harold, Howard.

Widup, Mr. and Mrs. M. V.
Williams, Mr. and Mrs. J. R.; Ruth.
Wolferman, Johnnie.
Wright, D. E.
Wynn, Earl.
Wynn, Mr. and Mrs. Eli.
Wynn, H.
Wynn, Mrs. Martha; Catherine, Blanche.
Wynn, Mr. and Mrs. Milo.
Young, Mr. and Mrs. Perry.

Rochester Township

Adams, A.
Adamson, Mr. and Mrs. Wm.
Albright, Mr. and Mrs. George.
Allen, Mr. and Mrs. Alfred; Frances, Pauline, Cleo, Robert.
Alspach, Mr. and Mrs. Calder; Ola, Phelisha.
Alspach, Mr. and Mrs. Claud; Edith, Myra.
Alspach, Mr. and Mrs. Ezra.
Anderson, Mrs. Mary; Madge, Roscoe.
Anderson, Mr. and Mrs. Wm.; Dale, Dee, Guy.
Arnold, Clara.
Aughinbaugh, Mr. and Mrs. Chas.; Ruth, Dorthy, Byron, Billy.
Ault, Mr. and Mrs. Fred; Ruth, Everett, Guy, Milo.
Ault, Mr. and Mrs. Clyde; one child.
Bailey, Mr. and Mrs. Max, Lavona, Bettie Jane, Max.
Baker, Mr. and Mrs. Wm.
Ball, Mr. and Mrs. Jesse.
Barkman, Mr. and Mrs. Vernon; Mildred M.
Beall, Mr. and Mrs. John W.; Avonelle.
Becker, Mr. and Mrs. Henry L.; Mable, Lucy, Lee, Walter.
Becker, Mr. and Mrs. Virgil; Margaret.
Beel, Mr. and Mrs. J. A.
Beghtel, Russell.
Berrier, Mr. and Mrs. Dee.
Berrier, Mr. and Mrs. Newton.
Berry, Mr. and Mrs. J. C.
Bick, Mr. and Mrs. Clyde; Leroy, Lola, Bernice, Andrew, Alvada, Robert.
Bixler, Mr. and Mrs. Sidney; Dorthy.
Black, Mr. and Mrs. Alex.
Black, Mr. and Mrs. Dal.
Blackburn, Mr. and Mrs. Elza; Wm.
Blackburn, Glen.
Blackburn, Mr. and Mrs. H. O.; Lyman.
Blackburn, Mr. and Mrs. Wm.; Anna, Lucy.
Blackburn, Mrs. Susan.
Blacketor, Mr. and Mrs. Abe; Etta, Percilla.
Blacketor, Mr. and Mrs. S.
Bligh, Mr. and Mrs. Martin; Thomas, Edgar, Bonita, Almyrta, George.
Boothel, Mr. and Mrs. O. E.; Russel, Mabel.
Bouch, Claude, Fred.
Bour, Mr. and Mrs. J. F.; Florence, Frank, Robert.
Bowman, Mrs. Amanda; Alice, Charles.
Bradley, Mr. and Mrs. C. E.; Elizabeth, Johnnie.
Braman, Mr. and Mrs. John.
Brockman, John; Eugene.
Brouilette, Mrs. Elsie.
Brown, Mr. and Mrs. Eugene; Orlo, Carl, Pauline, Ruth, Elsie.
Brown, Mr. and Mrs. George; Georgia.
Brubaker, Mr. and Mrs. Joel; Eugene.
Brubaker, Mr. and Mrs. Wm. H.; Isabelle.
Brunson, Mr. and Mrs. John; Irene, Bernice.
Bryan, Mr. and Mrs. Sydney.
Bryan, Mr. and Mrs. T. J.
Buck, Mr. and Mrs.
Bumbarger, John.

CONTRIBUTORS

Bumbarger, Wm.
Burdge, Mr. and Mrs. A. W.; Roy.
Burkett, Mrs. Ford; Annabelle, Lyman.
Butler, Mr. and Mrs. Barney; Helen, Claude, Jessie, Theodore, Belle.
Callaway, Mr. and Mrs. Howard; Kermit.
Camerer, Mr. and Mrs. Omer G.; Luther, Marjory Manning.
Carr, Mr. and Mrs. B. F.; Louise.
Carr, Mr. and Mrs. Fred; Clarence, Ruth, Madge, Clarabel, Ida Catherine.
Carr, Mr. and Mrs. Harley; Howard, Robert, Bernice, Weldon, Byron.
Carr, Mr. and Mrs. Rube; George, John, DeVerl.
Carruthers, Mr. and Mrs. Lon; Mary, Harold, Margaret, Ruth, Morris, Jennie.
Carter, Mr. and Mrs. Gene.
Carter, Mr. and Mrs. John R.
Castleman, Mr. and Mrs. C. C.; Vernon.
Castleman, Lloyd; family.
Cessna, Mrs. Hattie; Otto, Minnie, Dale, Lorine, Doris, Keith.
Cessna, Mr. and Mrs. Jno. L.
Chamberlain, Mr. and Mrs. Jesse.
Charters, Mr. and Mrs. Albert; Ardith, Cecil, Albert.
Charters, Mr. and Mrs. James V.
Charters, Mr. and Mrs. Jesse.
Charters, Mr. and Mrs. John B.; Gretchen, Carl, Earl, Alice, Ruth.
Charters, Mary C.
Charters, Samuel.
Circle, Mr. and Mrs. I. W.
Clark, Mr. and Mrs. Joseph; Ernest.
Clay, Mr. and Mrs. Roy.
Clay, Wm.; Ida, Hazel.
Clelend, Mr. and Mrs. Herman; Belva, Louis, George, Joe.
Clinger, Mr. and Mrs. Charles.
Cole, Mr. and Mrs. Bert; Harold, Leona.
Collins, Mr. and Mrs. Chas.
Conrad, Mr. and Mrs. Dave.
Conrad, Mr. and Mrs. John; Eva.
Conrad, Mr. and Mrs. Russel; Rachael.
Corbin, Mrs.
Crabbs, Fanny; Carl.
Crabbs, Mr. and Mrs. J .N.
Crabbs, Mr. and Mrs. L. E.; C'Dale, Lester, Leora.
Curran, Mr. and Mrs. Thomas J.
Curtis, Mr. and Mrs. M.
Czapansky, Mr. and Mrs.
Darr, Mr. and Mrs. Chas.; Cleo, Helen, Howard, Pauline, Evelyn, Marjory, Barbara.
Darr, Mr. and Mrs. I. N.
Davidson, Mr. and Mrs. Frank; Rebecca, Samuel.
Davidson, Mr. and Mrs. Turp; Harriet.
Davisson, Mr. and Mrs. C. S.
Davisson, Mr. and Mrs. O. E.; Patricia.
Dawson, Mr. and Mrs. Merley; Wesley, Liman, Loyd.
Day, Mr. and Mrs. Ed.; Cecil, Zinda, Levora, Jessie, Raymond.
Deardoff, Mr. and Mrs. Floyd; James.
Deardoff, Mr. and Mrs. Fred; Fredrick.
Deardoff, Mr. and Mrs. Wm.
DeVore, Mr. and Mrs. John.
Dixson, Mrs. Alia.
Dixson, Mr. and Mrs. Charles.
Dixson, Mrs. Minnie; Joe, Thomas, Henry, John.
Downs, Mr. and Mrs.; children.
Downs, Mr. and Mrs. Jake.
Downs, Mr. and Mrs. James; Warren, Ruth, Clifford, Leah, Marjorie, Morton.
Downs, O. B.
DuBois, Mr. and Mrs. George; Rex.
DuBois, Henry; Jonathan, Mary, Catherine.
DuBois, Mr. and Mrs. John.
Eash, Mr. and Mrs. Leo.
Eddington, Mr. and Mrs. Simeon, Lawrence, Emory.
Eiseman, Mr. and Mrs. John.

Emmons, Mr. and Mrs. Wm.; Harly, James, Clara.
Emmons, Mr. and Mrs. Orlando; Etta.
Engquist, Mr. and Mrs. Chas.; Walter, Esther.
Essick, Mr. and Mrs. Viv.
Estabrook, Mr. and Mrs. J. J.; Sadie, Warren, Hamilton.
Evans, Mr. and Mrs. W. J.; Frances, Evans.
Ewing, Mr. and Mrs. Oliver S.; W. Steele, Bula, Grace.
Eysberg, M. and Mrs. Eyric; Peter Herman, Helen.
Fairchild, Mrs. J. E.
Faroute, Charles.
Fenstemacker, Mr. and Mrs. Roy; Mrs. Etta.
Finney, Mr. and Mrs. Chas. E.; Hortense, Curtis.
Finney, Mr. and Mrs. Geo. E.
Fisher, Mr. and Mrs. Frank; Forrest, Elva, Paul, Opal.
Foor, Mr. and Mrs. Wesley; Alta, Lesle.
Freeman, Charles.
Fultz, Mrs. Emma; Mildred.
Fultz, Mr. and Mrs. John; Dee, Ray.
Fultz, Mrs. Norah; Mildred.
Garner, Mr. and Mrs. Milo.
Gaumer, Mr. and Mrs.; Helen, Leonard, Floyd, Doris, Madge.
Garner, Mr. and Mrs. Wm.; Gladys.
Good, Alvin.
Good, Mr. and Mrs. Fred O.
Good, Mr. and Mrs. Willard.
Gohn, Mrs. Charles; Ernest, Raymond, Eva.
Gohn, Mr. and Mrs. D. W.; Florence, Vera, Hazel, Marion.
Gohn, Raymond.
Gorden, Mr. and Mrs. Eugene; Emerson, Dorma, Forest.
Gottschalk, Mr. and Mrs. George.
Graffis, Mr. and Mrs. Clarence; Homer, Lorene.
Green, Mr. and Mrs. Wm.
Greer, Mr. and Mrs. Chas.
Greer, Mr. and Mrs. Clay; Ellis, Odessa, Glen, Frank, Dorthy.
Greer, Harry.
Greer, John.
Greer, Mrs. John.
Gurdes, Mr. and Mrs. Theodore.
Habich, Gus.
Hagan, Mr. and Mrs. Ed.
Hagan, Mr. and Mrs. John; Lloyd, Ruth.
Hannah, Mr. and Mrs. Jerry.
Hannah, Mr. and Mrs. Robert.
Harter, Mr. and Mrs. David; Trella, Otis.
Haslett, Mr. and Mrs. George.
Hayward, Mr. and Mrs. Boyd; Richard, Lee.
Hedges, Oscar.
Henderson, Mr. and Mrs. E. E.; Howard.
Herbaugh, Thomas; America.
Herlick, Mr. and Mrs. John.
Heeter, Mr. and Mrs. Dick.
Hetzner, Mr. and Mrs. Wm.; Carl, Tessie.
Hiat, Mr. and Mrs. Chas.
Hoffman, Mrs. Mary, Robert, Ruth.
Holden, Mr. and Mrs. Chas.
Hoover, Mr. and Mrs. Frank.
Hoover, Mr. and Mrs. John.
Hoover, Wm.
Horn, S. N.
Howard, Mrs. Cornelius.
Hudkins, Wm.; family.
Huffman, Mr. and Mrs. Biglowe.
Hunter, Al.
Hunter, Mr. and Mrs. Cassius; Irene.
Hunter, Guy.
Jay, Mrs. Ida; Opal, Bertha.
Keel, Mr. and Mrs. Omer; Burl, Claud,
Keim, Mr. and Mrs. Israel.
Kennell, Mr. and Mrs. John.
Kennel, Mr. and Mrs. Wm. L.; Blanche, Marian.
Kersey, Mr. and Mrs. Edward.
Kersey, Mrs. Electra.
King, Fred.
King, W. Harold.
King, Mr. and Mrs. Wm.; Ethel, Lester.

CONTRIBUTORS

Klepinger, Mr. and Mrs. Oliver.
Koch, Mr. and Mrs. Frank; Wm. Russell, Isabelle, Alta.
Koffel, Mr. and Mrs. James F.
Krom, Mr. and Mrs. George W.; Norabelle, Mary, George, Abe.
Lear, Mr. and Mrs. Louis.
Leiter, Mr. and Mrs. Levi.
Lewis, Mr. and Mrs. Lee; Harvey, Raymond, Louise, Evelyn.
Lowe, Mr. and Mrs. Ben.
Lowe, Mr. and Mrs. Peter; Alice, Helen.
McClung, Mr. and Mrs. John L.; Marjory.
McClung, Mr. and Mrs. N. A.; Ralph, Arthur, Paul.
McCurdy, Mr. and Mrs. Henry.
McGriff, Mr. and Mrs.
McKee, Mr. and Mrs. Herbert.
McKinney, Mr. and Mrs. John; Mabel, James, Fred.
McKinney, Mr. and Mrs. John W.
McMahn, Clara.
McMahan, Mr. and Mrs. Hugh.
McMahan, Mr. and Mrs. Pat.
McMillen, Mr. and Mrs. Guy; Gerald, Francis.
McMillen, Mr. and Mrs. Henry.
McTavish, Mrs. E. D.
Magriff, Mr. and Mrs. Alzonzo.
Marriott, Mr. and Mrs. Frank; Virgil, Orpha, Marion, Bessie, Loren, Archie.
Martin, Alex.
Marsh, Mr. and Mrs. J.; Pearl, Lloyd, Marion.
Mathias, Wesley; Paul, Helen.
Mathias, Mr. and Mrs. John; Earl.
Mathias, Mr. and Mrs. Wm.; Harry, Oren, Floyd.
Meiser, Mr. and Mrs. Charles; Roland.
Mercer, Mr. and Mrs. Fred.
Mikesell, Mr. and Mrs. E. H.; Von, Orpha Belle, Victor C., Kennith L., Arthur D.
Miller, Mr. and Mrs. Carl; Agnes, Ester, Ruth.
Miller, Mr. and Mrs. Clem R.; Russell, Virgil, Donald.
Miller, Mr. and Mrs. G.; Charles, Pearl, Lillian, Dee.
Miller, Mr. and Mrs. J. W.; Mary.
Miller, Mary.
Miller, O. M.; Alida, Hugh, James, Donald.
Miller, Mr. and Mrs. Robert.
Miller, Mr. and Mrs. Tona.
Morgan, Mr. and Mrs. High; Pauline, Donald.
Moore, Mr. and Mrs. Fred; Lee, Ida C.
Moore, Mr. and Mrs. Henry H.; Clarice, Maxine, Cecil.
Moore, Mr. and Mrs. John.
Moore, Mr. and Mrs. Ross; Harriet, Florence, Dale.
Moore, Mrs. Mahala, Homer.
Myers, Mr. and Mrs. Bert; Arthur, Paul, Elna, Catherine, Herbert, Clarabelle.
Nafe, Mr. and Mrs. Earl.
Nafe, Mr. and Mrs. E. P.; Mildred, Emerson, Lucile.
Nafe, Mrs. James.
Neff, Mrs. Harriet.
Neff, Mr. and Mrs. Hiram; Florence, Cletus.
Neher, Mr. and Mrs. John.
Nelson, Mr. and Mrs. Lee, Marjory, Geraldine, Eldora.
Newman, Mr. and Mrs. George; Maurice, Donald, Oren.
Nixon, Mr. and Mrs. Alfred.
Norris, Mr. and Mrs. Leo; Nelson, Lucille.
Norris, Mr. and Mrs. Lewis; Charles.
Nungesser, Mr. and Mrs. John; Layton.
Oliver, Mr. and Mrs. B. C.
Oliver, Mr. and Mrs. Elmer; Mabel.
Oliver, Mr. and Mrs. John; Larue.
Olson, Mr. and Mrs. Howard.
Olson, Mr. and Mrs. Theodore.
Overmyer, Mr. and Mrs. Frank; Opal, Irene.
Overmyer, Mr. and Mrs. Roy.
Overmyer, Mr. and Mrs. George; Russel.

Palmer, Mr. and Mrs. D. S.
Palmer, Mr. and Mrs. James.
Peeples, Mr. and Mrs. George.
Perkins, Mr. and Mrs. Ed.
Personette, Mr. and Mrs. U. S.; Katherine.
Phebus, Mr. and Mrs. Sam.
Piper, Mr. and Mrs. Chas.; Thurl, Anna Ruth.
Poenix, Mr. and Mrs. D. A.
Poffenberger, Mr. and Mrs. Milton.
Pontius, Mr. and Mrs. Periece; Harry.
Pownell, Mr. and Mrs. Henry.
Preist, Mr. and Mrs. Arnold.
Putman, Mr. and Mrs. Audry; Helen, Marjory, Mary, David.
Putman, Mr. and Mrs. David.
Pyle, Mr. and Mrs. Steve.
Rans, Mr. and Mrs. H. O.; Blanche, Isabelle, Donald, Forrest.
Ravencroft, Mr. and Mrs. Ralph J.; Holden, John Edward.
Ream, Mr. and Mrs. John.
Reinhart, Mr. and Mrs. J. H.; Freedona, Rovene, Lucille, Leona.
Rhodes, Mr. and Mrs. Frank B.; Gorden, Cecil, Gladwin.
Rhodes, Orville.
Rice, Mr. and Mrs. Elmer.
Rice, Mr. and Mrs. Perry; Lester.
Riffax, Claude; family.
Rogers, Mr. and Mrs. Tola; Richard, Jessie.
Rouch, Mr. and Mrs. Claude; Donald.
Roudebush, Mr. and Mrs. Harvy.
Roules, Mr. and Mrs. Frank; Milda, Estel, Janet.
Sanders, Mr. and Mrs. Amos; Thelma, Ralph.
Sanders, Mr. and Mrs. M.; John.
Seibert, Mr. and Mrs. Kent B.; Alfred, Porter, Frances, Clara.
Severns, Mr. and Mrs. Frank; children.
Sewell, Hugh.
Sheets, Mr. and Mrs. Frank; Marie, Mude, Donald.
Shelton, Mr. and Mrs. Eugene.
Sheets, Mr. and Mrs. Lon; Jack, Anonidas, Faye, Lora.
Shinn, Mr. and Mrs. Francis.
Sixby, Mark.
Smiley, Mr. and Mrs. Milton; LaVern, Jewell, Gladys, Russel, Frank, Dorthy.
Smith, Mr. and Mrs. Marion.
Smith, Mr. and Mrs. Marshall.
Smith, Mr. and Mrs. Omer.
Snyder, Mr. and Mrs. Wm.
Snyder, Mr. and Mrs. Wm.; Louise, Janet, Bernice, James.
Spurlock, Mr. and Mrs. Maley.
Spurlock, Mr. and Mrs. T. H.
Staley, Mr. and Mrs. Carl.
Staton, Mrs. George.
Steininger, Mr. and Mrs. Milo.
Stinson, Mrs. Amelia; Glue.
Struckman, Mr. and Mrs. Wm.
Sturkin, Mr. and Mrs. Charles; Maude, Mary.
Tatman, Mr. and Mrs. J. W.
Tatman, O. T.; Kennith, Omer, Lucy.
Thomas, Mr. and Mrs. David; Robert, Hubert, Harry, Harold.
Tilden, Mr. and Mrs. Jack.
Tobey, Mr. and Mrs. George; Mildred, Hugh, Mary, Helen.
Tobey, Mrs. Mary, Stacy, Minnie.
Toughman, Mr. and Mrs. Thomas A.; Chlae.
Touhy, Mrs. Lulu May.
Tranberger, Mr. and Mrs. Doris; Emmett.
Utter, Chester; family.
Vandergrift, Mr. and Mrs. C. H.
Vandergrift, Mrs. John; Harold, Bertha, Albert.
Vanduine, Elias.
VanDuyne, Mr. and Mrs. Frank; Fred, Joe, Dan, Mildred, Bobby, Mary.
Vanlue, Mr. and Mrs. J. W.; Anna, Orval, Leonard, Hubert, Baby.
Wagoner, Mr. and Mrs. Charles.
Wagoner, Mr. and Mrs. Edward C.; Russell, Melvin, Omer, Stella.
Wagoner, Mr. and Mrs. I. Irma.

Wagoner, Mr. and Mrs. Harry A., Ruth, Dale.
Wagoner, Mr. and Mrs. Harvey, Pauline.
Wagoner, Mr. and Mrs. Wm.; Robert, Franklin, Herman, William Edward.
Wales, Mr. and Mrs. Frank; Carrie, Ernest, Ora, Jennie, Ada.
Walters, Mr. and Mrs. Henry; Robert.
Weber, Mr. and Mrs. Ralph; Margaret, Arthur.
Weirick, Mr. and Mrs. Henry; Maude.
Werner, Mr. and Mrs. Martin; Lloyd, Clarebelle, Gertrude, Pearl, Charles.
West, Mr. and Mrs. John.
White, Mr. and Mrs. John F.
Whittenberger, Mr. and Mrs. Milton; Milton, John, Hubert, Mary.
Wilson, Mr. and Mrs. N. C.; Alta, Howard, David.
Winegardner, Mr. and Mrs. Chas.; Delta, Nellie, Esta, Donald.
Wiser, Mr. and Mrs. Finley C.
Wisley, Mr. and Mrs. Clifford.
Wolf, Mr. and Mrs. David.
Wolf, Mr. and Mrs. David; Bertha, Lloyd, Dorthy, Claretta, Ruth.
Wolf, Mr. and Mrs. John M.; Thelma, Eva, Helen.
Woodcox, Mr. and Mrs. Eli; family.
Young, Mr. and Mrs. Theodore.
Zartman, Mr. and Mrs. Al.
Zegafuse, Mr. and Mrs. Francis, Donald, Margeret.
Zegafuse, Mr. and Mrs. John; Adam.
Zellars, Mr. and Mrs. Wm.; Robert.

City of Rochester

Abbott, Mr. and Mrs. C. B.; Leo, Harold, Arthur.
Abbott, Mr. and Mrs. James.
Adams, Mr. and Mrs. Earl; Nadine.
Adamson, Mr. and Mrs. H. L.
Agnew, Mr. and Mrs. Daniel.
Agster, Mr. and Mrs. Fred.
Alexander, Mr. and Mrs. A.; Fred, Frank.
Alexander, Mr. and Mrs. Vern.
Allison, Mr. and Mrs. John; Harry, James.
Allman, Mr. and Mrs. Sol.
Alspauch, Mr. and Mrs. Charles.
Alspach, Mr. and Mrs. Guy; Mary Jane.
Alspach, Mr. and Mrs. Milton; William.
Alspach, Mr. and Mrs. Sylvester.
Anderson, Mrs. Mary J.
Appleman, Mr. and Mrs. C. H.; Mabel, Ruth, Audrey.
Apt, Mr. and Mrs. John.
Armstrong, Mrs. Blanche; Louise, Fredrick.
Arnold, Mrs.
Arnold, Mr. and Mrs. Ralph.
Arter, Mr. and Mrs. Samuel; Lester.
Arven, Mr. and Mrs. Elmer.
Aukinbaugh, Mrs. Elizabeth.
Ault, Mr. and Mrs. Joseph.
Austin, Mrs. Pearl.
Babcock, Mr. and Mrs. A. E.
Babcock, Mr. and Mrs. A. O.; Leon, Harold, Grace, Ruth.
Babcock, Mr. and Mrs. Fred.
Babcock, Mr. and Mrs. Ira.
Babcock, Mrs. Laura; Alice, Lawrence.
Babcock, Dr. and Mrs. L. J.
Babcock, Mr. and Mrs. Pete.
Babcock, Mr. and Mrs. Ray; Hertha, James Albert.
Babcock, Mrs. Winfred; Charles.
Bachelor, Mrs. Myrtle; Wm., Hattie, Dorthy.
Bacon, Mrs. M. E.
Bailey, Ethel.
Bailey, Mr. and Mrs. S. P.; Louise, Elliott, Byron, William Bailey Wagner.
Bair, Mr. and Mrs. Nelson.

Baker, Mr. and Mrs. Alvah; Dean.
Baker, Peter; Bertha, Bess.
Baker, Mrs. Tamer.
Baldwin, Mr. and Mrs. Oscar.
Ball, Mr. and Mrs. Nooval; Barton, Wilidine.
Ballinger, Mr. and Mrs. Frank; Sarah, Oliver, Margaret, Thomas.
Barcus, Mr. and Mrs. Frank.
Barger, Mr. and Mrs. Guy; Virginia.
Barger, Mrs. Vida.
Barker, Mr. and Mrs.
Barkman, Mr. and Mrs. Henry; Ray, John.
Barkman, Mr. and Mrs. Martin; Mary.
Barnhart, Mr. and Mrs. Dean; Mary Louisee.
Barnhart, H. A.
Barr, Mr. and Mrs. Guy.
Barr, Mr. and Mrs. John.
Barrett, Mr. and Mrs. A.; Pearl.
Batt, Mr. and Mrs. Martin.
Baum, Mrs. Sadie.
Beattie, Mr. and Mrs. Mark; Grace, Donald.
Beattie, Mr. and Mrs. Wm.; Margarete.
Becker, Mr. and Mrs. Cal; Alice, Carl.
Beeber, Belle.
Beeber, Mr. and Mrs. G.
Belt, Mr. and Mrs. B.; Minnie, Charles, Melissa.
Bemenderfer, Mr. and Mrs. John.
Bernetha, Belle.
Bernetha, Harry.
Bernero, Mr. and Mrs. L.; Johnnie, Celia, Gus.
Berry, Mr. and Mrs. Thomas; Kathelyn.
Beuhler, Mrs. Emma; James.
Bibler, Letha.
Biddinger, Mr. and Mrs. Carl B.
Biddinger, Mr. and Mrs. Peter.
Biddinger, Mr. and Mrs. Will; family.
Binding, Mr. and Mrs. L. R.
Bingham, Mr. and Mrs.
Bitters, Mr. and Mrs. Albert; Margaret.
Bitters, Mr. and Mrs. A. T.
Bitters, Mr. and Mrs. C. K.; Edna, Edith.
Bitters, Mr. and Mrs. Harry.
Bitters, Mrs. M.
Black, Mr. and Mrs. George.
Blacketor, Mr. and Mrs.
Blacktor, Mr. and Mrs. Paul; Paulanna.
Blacktor, Mr. and Mrs. T. B.
Boelter, Mr. and Mrs. Otto; Katherine, Otto, Jr.
Bonine, Mr. and Mrs. J. D.
Bonine, Mr. and Mrs. Wyle; Wyle G., Ernest.
Borden, Mr. and Mrs. E.
Boring, Mr. and Mrs.; two children.
Bowell, Mr. and Mrs. James; Glen, James, Jr., Hope.
Bowers, Mr. and Mrs. A. F.
Bowles, Mrs. Mary.
Bozarth, Frances.
Bozarth, Mr. and Mrs. Jap.
Brackett, Mr. and Mrs. Charles.
Brackett, Mrs. Effie; Jimmie.
Brackett, Mr. and Mrs. L. M.; Lyman.
Brausford, Mr. and Mrs. Carl.
Bresee, Mr. and Mrs. B. W.; Marjory, Audrey.
Brewer, Mr. and Mrs. George.
Brickel, Glen.
Brickel, Oscar; Maurice, Bernice.
Briles, Mr. and Mrs. Dale.
Briney, Mr. and Mrs.
Briney, Mrs. Erma; Frank.
Brinkman, Mr. and Mrs. Wm.; Ruth.
Brookins, Mr. and Mrs. Claud; Leah, Wade.
Brower, Mr. and Mrs. Harry; Donald, Meredith, Fredrick.
Brower, Mr. and Mrs. L. K.; Walter, George.
Brown, Dr. and Mrs. Arch; Mary Ruth, Edna, Martha Alice.
Brown, Mr. and Mrs. James D.
Brown, Mrs. Mary; Hattie, Bessie, Mamie.
Brown, Mr. and Mrs. Seldon.
Brown, W. K.
Brubaker, Mr. and Mrs. Arthur.

CONTRIBUTORS

Brubaker, Mr. and Mrs. Claude.
Brubaker, Mr. and Mrs. Jackson; Mabel.
Brubaker, Mr. and Mrs. Joel; Eugene.
Brubaker, Mr. and Mrs. Roy.
Bruce, Mr. and Mrs. Elza; Iretta, Goldie, Arthur, Freida, Gale.
Bruce, Mr. and Mrs. Richard; George.
Bryant, Mr. and Mrs. Frank E.; Margaret, Frances.
Bryant, Mr. and Mrs. Guy; Wilma.
Bryant, Mrs. Hannah.
Bryant, Mr. and Mrs. H. L.; Pauline, D'Von.
Bryant, Mr. and Mrs. Ruby; Evelyn, Faye.
Buchanan, Mr. and Mrs. P. M.; Geo.
Bundy, Mr. and Mrs. Noah; Eva, Ellen, Charles.
Burns, Mr. and Mrs. Furel.
Burns, Mr. and Mrs. Jake.
Burns, Mr. and Mrs. J. C.; Deveda, Albert, Robert, Charles Lee.
Burns, Mrs. Mellissa.
Busenberg, Mrs. Sarah.
Bussert, Mr. and Mrs. B.
Bussert, Mr. and Mrs. Dan; Palmer, William.
Bussert, Mr. and Mrs. Salem.
Butler, Rev. and Mrs.
Butler, Mr. and Mrs. George; Carl.
Buuck, Mr. and Mrs. W. O.; Wayne, Donald.
Byrer, Mr. and Mrs. J. E.
Byrer, Mr. and Mrs. J. W.; Grace, Celia.
Caffyn, Mrs. Emma; Walter.
Campbell, Mr. and Mrs. Charles.
Camerer, Mrs. Emma.
Capp, Mrs. Minnie; Edward.
Cardiamenus, George.
Carithers, Mrs. Sarah; Fanny.
Carlson, Mr. and Mrs. Otto; Christine, Donald Wright.
Carlton, Mr. and Mrs. C. B.; Isabelle, Josephine, Francis, Mary.
Carter, Mr. and Mrs. Alf; Voris.
Castle, Mr. and Mrs. Friday; Lola, Howard.
Chamberlain, Mr. and Mrs. B.; Helen.

Chamberlain, Mr. and Mrs. Harry.
Chamberlain, Mr. and Mrs. Jack.
Chamberlain, Mr. and Mrs. Jesse; Bernice, Clude, Lenly, Willard, Sara.
Chandler, Mr. and Mrs. S. F.; Robert.
Chestnut, Mrs. A.
Chestnut, Edith.
Chestnut, Mrs. Esther; Myrtle Jane.
Cissel, Mr. and Mrs. C. C.
Clarke, Miss Lenora.
Clary, Mr. and Mrs. Elbert; Harvey.
Clayton, Mr. and Mrs. Bernard.
Clayton, Mr. and Mrs. Sampson; Ruth.
Clinger, Mr. and Mrs. Joe.
Collins, Mr. and Mrs. Chas.; Mildred, Milo, Howard.
Combs, Ted, Robert.
Condon, Mr. and Mrs. Clark; Walter.
Conkle, Dr. and Mrs. E. C.; Dortha B., Paul, Ruth.
Conger, Mr. and Mrs. Mildred.
Conger, Mrs. Minnie; Mildred.
Cook, Mr. and Mrs. D. F.; Dr. T. P.
Cook, Mr. and Mrs. Ed.
Cook, Mrs. Elizabeth; Ray.
Cook, E. S.
Cook, Howard; Pauline, Robert.
Cook, Mr. and Mrs. Wm.
Cooper, Mr. and Mrs. Lou; Harold.
Cooper, Mr. and Mrs. Will.
Copeland, A. P.; Ruth, Arthur.
Coplen, Mr. and Mrs. Eugene; James, Maurice.
Coplen, Mr. and Mrs. G.; Kennith.
Coplen, Mr. and Mrs. Herman; Chas., Herman.
Coplen, Mr. and Mrs. J. P.
Coplen, Milo; Porter.
Coplen, Mr. and Mrs. O. M.; George, Grace, Ray Omer.
Corbet, Mrs. Ida.
Cornell, Mr. and Mrs. P. O. William.
Crabbs, Mrs. Bessie.
Crabill, Mrs. Ida; Fern, Zelma.
Craig, Mr. and Mrs. Bert; Hubert, Albert, Mildred, Lucille, Opal.
Craig, Mr. and Mrs. Merle.

Crane, Rev. and Mrs. George.
Creviston, Mr. and Mrs. I. E.; Milo, Pauline, Kenneth, Edna.
Crim, Mr. and Mrs. Jacob.
Crose, Mr. and Mrs. George.
Crownover, Mrs. Roy.
Crownover, Tom.
Cunningham, Mr. and Mrs. J.; James Baker.
Cunningham, Mr. and Mrs. Joe.
Curtis, Mr. and Mrs. Vine; Frances, Junior, Katherine, Percy.
Daggy, Mr. and Mrs. Albert; Elma, Verna, Densie, Nilah, Roy.
Dague, Grant.
Damas, Mr. and Mrs. John; Edna.
Darrah, Mr. and Mrs. James.
Davis, Mr. and Mrs. Anson; Donald, Mary, Everette, Lela.
Davis, Mr. and Mrs. Chas. A.; June.
Davis, Mr. and Mrs. Cy.
Davis, Mrs. John.
Davis, Marcellus.
Davis, Mr. and Mrs. Marion; Faye, Annabelle.
Davidson, Mr. and Mrs. A. C.
Davidson, Mr. and Mrs. Harold.
Dawe, Mr. and Mrs. G. Robert.
Dawson, Mr. and Mrs. Geo. V.
Day, Mrs.
Day, Mr. and Mrs. Albert.
Delp, Flo.
Delp, Mr. and Mrs. Will; Edward, Howard, Helen, Lawrence, Mary, Alice.
Demont, Mr. and Mrs. Wm.
Deniston, Mr. and Mrs. A. L.; Dorthy, W. H., Jr., Barbara.
Deniston, Mr. and Mrs. Wm. H.
Dillon, Mr. and Mrs. A. J.
Dillon, Wm. A.; Grace.
Ditmire, Mr. and Mrs. Henry.
Dosh, Paul.
Downs, Mr. and Mrs. Kenneth.
Downs, Mrs. John.
Dubois, Mr. and Mrs. Howard; Robert, Benny.
Dudgeon, Mr. and Mrs. George.
Dull, Mr. and Mrs. Ransom; Catherine.
Dulmatch, Levi
Dunlap, Mr. and Mrs. Heber; Clair, Floy.
Durkes, Mr. and Mrs. Frank; Arthur, Berdena, Fuller.
Drake, Mr. and Mrs. H. S.
Drudge, Mr. and Mrs. Wilson.
Dysert, Mr. and Mrs. J. F.
Eash, Mr. and Mrs. John.
Easterday, Mr. and Mrs. Elmer.
Eastwood, Mr. and Mrs. Wm.; William, Jr., Charlie, Ethel.
Eiler, Mrs. Martha; Bernice.
Eisenman, Mrs. John.
Elliott, Mrs. Lydia.
Elliott, Mrs. Margaret, Frances.
Emmons, Mr. and Mrs. Chas.
Emmons, Mrs. Ellen.
Emmons, Mr. and Mrs. Ike.
Emmons, Mr. and Mrs. Thomas.
Emrick, Mrs.
Enoch, Mrs. James.
Entsminger, Mr. and Mrs. Clyde; Yetta, Merriam.
Enyart, Mr. and Mrs. C. V.
Erb, Mr. and Mrs. Clarence.
Ernsperger, Mrs. Ida; Belle, Fred.
Ewing, Joe.
Ewing, Mrs. Margaret; Marie.
Feece, Mr. and Mrs. Clinton E.; Donald, Vera.
Fields, Mr. and Mrs. Chas.; family.
Feiser, Mr. and Mrs. Ed.; Arthur.
Felts, Mrs. Kate; DeVanee, Howard, Dale.
Fenstemaker, Mr. and Mrs. Ora; Helen.
Ferree, Mrs. Sabitha.
Flagg, Mr. and Mrs. Chas. E.; Doris.
Foglesong, Mr. and Mrs. Henry; Harry.
Folker, Mr. and Mrs. Elmer.
Freece, Mr. and Mrs. Arthur; Morton.
Fretz, Mr. and Mrs. B. F.
Fretz, Mr. and Mrs. Ray; Byron, Marjorie.
Fristoe, Mr. and Mrs. H. A.; Margaretta, Ericson. Mrs. Eva, Axtel.
Fromm, Mrs. Elsie.

Frushour, Mr. and Mrs. J. F.
Fugate, Mr. and Mrs. G.
Fugate, Mr. and Mrs. James; Orle, Cleo, Elma.
Fugate, Sarah.
Fulkinson, Mr. and Mrs. Chas.
Fuller, Mr. and Mrs. Martin; Frank, Abbott, Carlton, Byrdie, Rovel.
Fultz, Mr. and Mrs. Harley; Irene.
Garner, John.
Geyer, Mr. and Mrs. John L.; Buel. Herchel.
Gibbons, Mr. and Mrs. W. C.
Gibson, Mr. and Mrs. Earl; Lepna, Herschel, Chas.
Gilbaugh, Mr. and Mrs. H. A.
Gilbaugh, Mr. and Mrs. Israel; Elsie, Geneva, Eugene.
Gilbert, Mrs. Lavina; Charles.
Gilliland, Mr. and Mrs. R. K.; Mary, Geiger, Robert, Alice, Wm., James.
Ginther, Mr. and Mrs. Jay.
Ginther, Mr. and Mrs. John.
Ginther, Martha C.
Glick, Mr. and Mrs. E.
Goltry, Mr. and Mrs. B. O.; Voris, Luther, Ferman, Florence, Opal, Grace.
Good, Mr. and Mrs.
Good, Mr. and Mrs. I. N.
Good, Mr. and Mrs. Wesley; Clarice, Max, Leona.
Goodrich, Mr. and Mrs. Alfred.
Goodwin, Mr. and Mrs. A. B.; Helen.
Gordon, Mr. and Mrs. Bill; Dorthy.
Gordon, Mr. and Mrs. R. M.; Elmer.
Gorden, Mr. and Mrs. Roy; Lillian, Margaret.
Goss, Mr. and Mrs. Geo.; Harold.
Goss, Mrs. Mary.
Goss, Mr. and Mrs. O. B.; Edna, Raymond.
Gould, Dr. and Mrs. Chas.
Graber, Mrs. Effie; Merriam.
Graffis, L. M.
Greer, Mr. and Mrs. Bert.
Gregory, Mr. and Mrs. Chas.; Omer, Harry.
Green, Mr. and Mrs. A. B.; Dwight.
Greeen, B. F.; Elsie.
Green, Mrs. Rachel A.
Green, Mrs. W. H.; Georgia.
Gribben, Mr. and Mrs. Chas.; Hester, Dwight.
Grimes, Mr. and Mrs. Hez; Ruth, Ethel.
Gross, Mr. and Mrs. Eugene; Samuel, David, Fredrick, Harriet, Irene.
Grove, Mrs. O. K.
Hagan, Mr. and Mrs. Otis.
Haimbaugh, Dr. and Mrs. D.; George Don.
Hall, Mr. and Mrs. John; Elbert, Pauline, Genivere, Helen.
Harper, Mr. and Mrs. Will; Delta, Blanche, Dorthy.
Hardin, Mr. and Mrs. William H.; Olive, Max.
Haren, Mr. and Mrs.
Harrison, Mrs. Mary.
Hartle, Mr. and Mrs. Arthur.
Hartman, Mr. and Mrs. L. D.; Dale, Walter.
Hartung, Mr. and Mrs. Carl; Robert, Phillip.
Hartung, Mr. and Mrs. Henry; George.
Haslett, Mr. and Mrs. Foster
Hattery, Mr. and Mrs. Frank.
Hawkins, Mr. and Mrs. Percy.
Hay, Mr. and Mrs. Mel, Marjory.
Hayward, Mrs. Mary.
Heath, Mr. and Mrs. Perry; Curtner.
Heck, Katherine.
Hedges, Mr. and Mrs. Sam; Arline, Gilbert.
Heeter, Mr. and Mrs. F. A.
Heeter, Mr. and Mrs. L. W.; Mary, Harold, Fred.
Henderson, Mr. and Mrs. Clyde; Huron, Geneva.
Henderson, Myrtle.
Hendrickson, Mr. and Mrs. John; Donald, Dale.
Hendrickson, Mr. and Mrs. O. M.
Hendrickson, Mr. and Mrs. R. B.; Earnest, Mable, Olive, Joseph, Alice.
Henthorn, Mrs. Ella.

Herbster, Mr. and Mrs. J.; Albert, Luther, Madeline.
Herring, Charles.
Hetzner, Mr. and Mrs. M.
Hill, Mr. and Mrs. George.
Hill, Mrs. J. J.
Hill, John; Clarence.
Hill, Mr. and Mrs. J. P.; Mary, Robert.
Hill, Mr. and Mrs. Marsh.
Hill, Mr. and Mrs. Mel; Margaret, Morton, Byron, Isabelle.
Hilburn, Ferd.
Hisey, Mr. and Mrs. Bert.
Hoffman, Mrs. Anna.
Hoffman, Mr. and Mrs. Sam.
Hoffman, Mrs. Wm.
Hogue, Carrie.
Holloway, Mr. and Mrs. Granvil.
Holman, George.
Holman, Mr. and Mrs. Hugh; Evangeline, Hugh.
Holman, Mr. and Mrs. J. D.
Holman, Mrs. Minta; Nina, Earl.
Holtz, Mr. and Mrs. L. G.; Harry, Irene.
Holzman, Mrs. E.
Holzman, Henry.
Hood, Mr. and Mrs. H. H.; Martha, Mary Jane, Hannah.
Hoover, Mr. and Mrs. Cal.
Hoover, Mrs. Elizabeth.
Hoover, Jake.
Hoover, Mr. and Mrs. John; Tom.
Hoover, Mrs. Margaret; Trude.
House, Mr. and Mrs. Walter; Elsie, Edgar, Helen.
Howard, Mr. and Mrs. Joseph.
Howard, Mr. and Mrs. Will; Ayrton, George.
Hudtwalcker, Mrs.
Hunneshagen, Mr. and Mrs. Chas.; Hazel.
Hunter, Mrs. Effie; Leona, Rex.
Hunter, Mr. and Mrs. Otis.
Hurst, Mrs. Bessie; Jonathan, George, Edith.
Irvin, Mrs. Grace; Barrett.
Irvin, Mr. and Mrs. M. A.; Conrad; Wilbur, Milo, Gilbert, Rose.

Ivey, Mr. and Mrs. I. W.; Charles.
Izzard, Mr. and Mrs. Charles.
Izzard, Mr. and Mrs. Newton.
Jackson, Mrs. Chas.
Jackson, Willis.
Jamison, T. E.
Jenkins, Mrs. Elza; Minnie.
Jewell, Mr. and Mrs. C. R.
Jewell, Mr. and Mrs. W. E.
Johnson, Mr. and Mrs. Albert; Rudolph, Helen, Mildred, Arthur.
Johnson, Mr. and Mrs. Amos; Mabel.
Johnson, J. C.
Johnson, Mrs. Nettie; Frank.
Johnson, Mr. and Mrs. R. C.
Jones, M. C.
Jones, Mr. and Mrs. Perry.
Karn, Mrs. Reuben.
Keel, Mr. and Mrs. Charles; Carl, Luther.
Keel, Mr. and Mrs. J. T.; Estella, Bessie.
Keel, Mr. and Mrs. S. W. Byron; Myron, Chleo, Leo.
Kepler, Mr. and Mrs. C. K.
Kepler, Mr. and Mrs. J. F.; Edna.
Kersey, Noah.
Kessler, Mrs. Del; family.
Kestner, Mrs. Matilda; William.
Kile, Mr. and Mrs. Ray; Letha, Charles, Foster, Stanley, Wayne.
Kilmer, Mr. and Mrs. Chas.; Baker, Lucile.
Kilmer, Mr. and Mrs. W. C.; Robert Lee.
Kimes, Mr. and Mrs. Ed.
Kindig, Douglas.
King, Dr. M. O.
King, Mrs. Samantha.
Kirkendall, Mr. and Mrs. Fred; Raymond, Howard.
Kline, Mr. and Mrs. James; Gladys, Tilman, Roy, Mabel, Wm., Cecil.
Klise, Mr. and Mrs. Harvey.
Knickelbine, Mr. and Mrs. Albert; Howard, Mary, Chester.
Knight, Mr. and Mrs. Thomas; Beatrice.
Koshendefer, Mr. and Mrs. Ben.
Krathwohl, Dave.

CONTRIBUTORS

Kratzer, Mrs. B. F.
Kriegel, Mr. and Mrs. John.
Kuhn, Mr. and Mrs. Elmer; Maurine, Barbara, Eveline, James.
Lacey, Rev. and Mrs. J. H.
Laudaman, Mr. and Mrs. E. Q.; Faye, Fern.
Leavell, Mrs. Allie.
Leiter, Mrs. Caroline.
Leiter, Ethel.
Leiter, Mrs. Lyda; Jane, Mollie, Catherine Hunneshagen,
Leiter, Mr. and Mrs. U.; Hazel, Florence, Robert.
Leiter, W. J.; Della, May, Fred.
Leonard, Mr. and Mrs. Clem; Mildred, Catherine.
Leonard, Mrs. Lucille; George, John.
Levi, Mrs. Bertha; Florence.
Levi, Mr. and Mrs. Joe; Jeanette.
Lewis, Mr. and Mrs. Ephraim.
Lewis, John; Robert, Russel, James.
Lewis, Mr. and Mrs. S. M.
Linkenhelt, Mr. and Mrs. Lou.
Litchenwalter, Dr. and Mrs.; DeVon, Dale, Pauline, Ruth, Alden.
Long, Mrs. H. C.; Horace.
Loring, Dr. and Mrs. Chas.
Lough, Clyde.
Lowden, Mr. and Mrs. Frank.
Lowman, Eva, Treva, Ray, Roy, Moneta.
Lowman, Mr. and Mrs. Frank.
Lowman, Mrs. Jennie; Jessie.
Loy, Mr. and Mrs. William; Lucille.
Lunsford, Mrs. Leota.
McCall, Mr. and Mrs. Walter; Lewis, Herman.
McCance, Mr. and Mrs. Dave.
McCarter, Mr. and Mrs. Frank; Catherine.
McCarter, Mr. and Mrs. Fred; Seretta, Veda.
McCarter, Mr. and Mrs. Harley; Lillian.
McCarter, Mr. and Mrs. Isaac.
McCarty, Murray.
McDowell, Mr. and Mrs. H.; Sadie.
McElwee, Mr. and Mrs. R. J.
McIntyre, Mrs. Lovell.
McIntyre, Mr. and Mrs. Dan; Ernest, Bessie, Millicent, Frances.
McIntyre, Mrs. Mark; Carmen, DeVerl.
McKay, Jasper.
McKee, Mr. and Mrs. Albert; Bessie, Agnes, Gladys, Katherine.
McKee, Frank; Robert, Rhu.
McKee, Mrs. Martha.
McMahan, Edwin.
McMahan, Mr. and Mrs. Otto; Revabelle, Robert, George.
McMahan, Mrs. Rebecca; Jessie, John, James.
McPherson, Mr. and Mrs. Jake.
McVean, Mr. and Mrs. Chas.
McVey, Mr. and Mrs. Luther; Lethia.
Mackey, Mrs. J.; Joe, Luella.
Madary, Mrs. Gertrude; Inez, Roy.
Manley, Mr. and Mrs. Will.
Manning, Lillian.
Manning, Mr. and Mrs. L. L.; Velma, Opal, Mildred.
Marsh, Misses Etta and Nettie.
Marsh, Mr. and Mrs. Frank.
Martin, Mr. and Mrs. Harrison.
Martin, Mr. and Mrs. J. Gordon; John Gordon, Jr.
Mason, Mr. and Mrs. Eddie; George, Robert.
Mason, Mr. and Mrs. James T.
Masteller, Mrs. Tully; Fern.
Masters, Olie.
Masterson, Mr. and Mrs. Harold; Frances.
Masterson, Mr. and Mrs. James.
Masterson, Mrs. William.
Mattice, Mr. and Mrs. E. H.
Metcalf, Mrs.
Metz, Mrs. Versa; Jack Marvin.
Metzler, Mr. and Mrs. Arthur; Marjory, Louise.
Miller, Mr. and Mrs. A. E.; Merriam, Robert.
Miller, Mr. and Mrs. Archie B.
Miller, Mr. and Mrs. Clem; Clarence.
Miller, Mr. and Mrs. Earl.
Miller, Mrs. Elizabeth.
Miller, Mr. and Mrs. Fred; Robert.
Miller, Mr. and Mrs. Harry.

Miller, Mr. and Mrs. H. G.; Marjory, Hiram.
Miller, Mr. and Mrs. John.
Miller, Mr. and Mrs. Lee; Belva.
Miller, Mr. and Mrs. Robert.
Miller, Mr. and Mrs. Vincent; Ray, Sylvia, Harold.
Mills, Mr. and Mrs. Ira; Wessley, Glen.
Minter, Mrs. S.
Mitchell, Mr. and Mrs. Charles; Fred.
Mitchell, Mr. and Mrs. Dora; Phillip, Daisy.
Mitchell, Mr. and Mrs. Wm.; Mary Angeline.
Mogle, Mr. and Mrs. Chas.; Robert, Everett, Hubert.
Mogle, Mrs. Ella.
Mohler, Mr. and Mrs. Ed; Marjorie, Cutis, Hilda West.
Montgomery, Mr. and Mrs. Guy; Frances, Harold Dee.
Montgomery, Mr. and Mrs. Harley; Barr.
Montgomery, Mrs. Madge.
Moore, Mrs. Anna.
Moon, Rev. and Mrs. F. C.
Moore, Mr. and Mrs. Chas.
Moore, Mr. and Mrs. F. F.; Robert.
Moore, Mr. and Mrs. Fred; Helen, Hugh.
Moore, Mr. and Mrs. James; Ralph, Frances, Johan.
Moore, Mrs. Jennie.
Moore, Mr. and Mrs. Lee; Guy.
Moon, Mr. and Mrs. F. C.
Morgan, Mr. and Mrs. John; Burdett, Harold.
Morningstar, Mrs.; Charles.
Mow, Mr. and Mrs. Enoch.
Mow, Mr. and Mrs. Henry.
New, Isom.
Mow, John.
Mow, Mrs. Viola; Lee.
Mullen, Ethel.
Murphy, Mr. and Mrs. Columbus.
Murphy, Mr. and Mrs. E. E.; Robert, Hugh, Mabel Irene Mohler.
Murphy, Mr. and Mrs. T. C.
Musser, Mrs. Sarah; Bertha, William.
Musselman, Mr. and Mrs. Frank; Glen, Lefa, Don, Opal, Lova.
Mutchler, Charles.
Mutchler, Mr. and Mrs. Samuel.
Myers, Mr. and Mrs. Al; Charlie.
Myers, Mr. and Mrs. Enoch.
Meyer, Mr. and Mrs. Henry, Beryl.
Myers, Mr. and Mrs. Jacob; Bertha, Anna.
Myers, Joe.
Myers, Mrs. Jonas.
Myers, Mr. and Mrs. Julian; Julia Anne.
Myers, Mr. and Mrs. Leroy.
Myers, Mrs. Mollie.
Myers, Mrs. Nancy; Rose, Congo.
Myers, Mr. and Mrs. Ray; Jacob.
Neher, Mr. and Mrs. John; Russel.
Newby, Mr. and Mrs. Fred.
Newcomb, Mr. and Mrs. William; Dean, Alida.
Newcomer, Mr. and Mrs. Chas.; Edna, Robert, Annebelle, Milo.
Newcomer, Mr. and Mrs. Ray; Donald, Harold.
Newman, Mrs. Anna M.
Nicodemus, Mr. and Mrs. Wm.; Harry, Fred.
Nichols, Mr. and Mrs. Charles; Hugh, Charlotte, Charles.
Niece, Dal.
Niece, Mark.
Niven, Rev. and Mrs. W. J.; Jimmie.
Noftsger, Mr. and Mrs. Ben.
Norris, Mr. and Mrs. Chas.
Norris, Mrs. Fern; Elizabeth.
Norris, Mrs. Mary.
Norris, Mr. and Mrs. Will; Steele, Wade, Nilah, Rachael, Jane, Billy.
Nutt, Mr. and Mrs. Wm.
O'Blenis, Mr. and Mrs. James; Nellie.
Oliver, Mr. and Mrs. Alvin; Lucy, Lowell, Mark.
Onstott, Mr. and Mrs. Frank.
Onstott, Mr. and Mrs. Ike; family.
Orr, Mr. and Mrs. Eldridge; Thomas, Russel, John, Walter.
Orr, Mrs. Mary; Robert.
Orr, Mr. and Mrs. Wm.; Edna, Wm.
Osborne, Mrs. Jennie.

CONTRIBUTORS

Osborn, Mr. and Mrs. Robert; Jay.
Osgood, Mrs.
Oxley, Mr. and Mrs. Ora; Clara Mae, Ruby.
Overmyer, Mr. and Mrs. C. C.; Henrietta, Florence.
Overmyer, Mr. and Mrs. Harvey; Esther, Thelma, Nettie.
Packer, Mrs. Nissa.
Painter, Mr. and Mrs. Sant; Lucile, Paul, Carrie.
Paremore, Mr. and Mrs. Fred; Myra.
Parcell, Mr. and Mrs. Steve.
Parker, Mr. and Mrs. Emett; Lorena, Henry, Mary Emily Christal.
Parker, Norah.
Parker, Mr. and Mrs. Sam.
Parker, Mr. and Mrs. William.
Paschall, Mr. and Mrs. Carl.
Paschall, Mr. and Mrs. John.
Patton, Mrs. Pearl; Mabel, Josephine, Robert.
Perry, Mr. and Mrs. L. B.; Reva, Walter.
Perschbacher, Mr. and Mrs. Fred; Fredrich, Katherine.
Personette, Arwesta.
Peters, Mr. and Mrs. Sterling.
Peterson, Mrs. Carrie; Raymond.
Peterson, Mrs. Sarah.
Pfeiffer, Mr. and Mrs. H.; Lucius, Edward, Mary.
Phillips, Mr. and Mrs. Sam; Irwin.
Pike, Mr. and Mrs. O.
Plank, Mr. and Mrs. C. K.
Pollay, Mr. and Mrs. Jacob; Esther, Ida, Sylvia.
Pontius, Mrs. Della; Guy.
Pontius, Mr. and Mrs. Roscoe.
Pontius, Mr. and Mrs. Telly; Ruth, Howard.
Porter, Mr. and Mrs. Marion.
Preston, Mr. and Mrs. D. E.
Prill, Mr. and Mrs. Ray; Donald, Devoris, Mildred, Mary, Claud.
Primans, Mrs. Ella.
Pugh, Mrs. Lida.
Pyle, Mr. and Mrs. C. E.; Mary.
Pyle, Mr. and Mrs. John.
Quigg, Mr. and Mrs.

Rannells, Mr. and Mrs. E. A.; Robert, Lucile, Kathleen.
Rannells, Mrs. Emma.
Rannells, Mr. and Mrs. Robert; Jean, John.
Rausch, Mr. and Mrs. Val; Emma.
Ravencroft, Mr. and Mrs. Ralph; John, Holden, Edward. M
Raymer, Mr. and Mrs. Chas.; Kathleen, Claribel.
Rea, Mrs. Sylvia A.; Lucretia.
Reddick, Mr. and Mrs. Oren; Ralph, Amos.
Redinger, Mr. and Mrs. Albert; Gladys, Lloyd, Hilda.
Reed, Mr. and Mrs. Alvin.
Reed, Almetta.
Reed, Mr. and Mrs. Chas.
Reed, Mr. and Mrs. Fred; Floyd.
Reed, Mr. and Mrs. Warren; Edith.
Rees, Mrs. M. O.; Hermie, Mabel.
Reeder, Mr. and Mrs. Martin.
Reiter, Mrs. Anna.
Reiter, Mr. and Mrs. H. A.; Helen.
Reinhart, Mr. and Mrs. Ira; Edyth, Martha.
Reiter, Mr. and Mrs. Samuel.
Reno, Mr. and Mrs. Lawrence; Donald.
Rhodes, Mrs. Clara; Cyril.
Rice, Mr. and Mrs.
Richards, Mr. and Mrs. Chas.
Richardson, Mr. and Mrs. C.; Fairy.
Richardson, Mr. and Mrs. Frank; Frances, Glen.
Richardson, Mr. and Mrs. K. P.
Richter, Mr. and Mrs. Mark.
Richmond, Mr. and Mrs. Chas.; Roy, Ruth, Harry.
Richter, Mr. and Mrs. Leslie; Elizabeth.
Rickman, Mr. and Mrs. Robert.
Robbins, A. D.
Robbins, Mrs. A. F.; Fred.
Robbins, Mr. and Mrs. Chas. E.; Clara, Mae, Fred, Grace, Edith, Howard, Angeline.
Robbins, Mrs. Clara; Fern.
Robins, Mrs. Cyrus.
Robbins, Mrs. Lavina; Sard.

Robinson, Mr. and Mrs. Otto.
Roberts, Mr. and Mrs. David; Kennith, Harold, Helen.
Roberts, Mr. and Mrs. Willie.
Rolls, Mrs. Mallissa.
Roming, Mr. and Mrs. Jesse; Mary Ruth.
Ross, Mr. and Mrs. Albert; Zora, Mildred, Donald.
Ross, Mr. and Mrs. Chas.; Pearl, Ruth.
Ross, Mr. and Mrs. Frank.
Ross, Mr. and Mrs. Geo.
Ross, Mr. and Mrs. Loy; Myrtle.
Ross, Mr. and Mrs. Omar; Harold, Bernice, Emory, Harriet, Leslie.
Roth, Mrs. Mary, Edna.
Rouch, Mr. and Mrs. Glen.
Rouch, Mr. and Mrs. W. H.; Pearl.
Rowley, Mr. and Mrs. Julius.
Rude, Mr. and Mrs. Sylvester.
Ruh, Mr. and Mrs. Alex.
Ruh, Mr. and Mrs. Fred.
Runner, E. E.; Sylvia.
Russel, Mr. and Mrs. Faye; Mildred, Pauline.
Sanders, Mr. and Mrs. Elza; Ellen.
Sanders, Mrs. W. F.; John, Maud, Marion.
Sayger, Mr. and Mrs. John.
Schall, Mr. and Mrs. John.
Schertz, Mr. and Mrs. Henry; Irma.
Schmitt, Mr. and Mrs. Frank; Harley A.
Schuler, Edward.
Scott, Mr. and Mrs. F. K.
Seaman, Mrs. Martha; Anna, Grace.
See, Mr. and Mrs. Chas.; Elsie, Donald.
Seigfred, Mr. and Mrs. Atwell.
Shafer, Dr. and Mrs. Howard; Betty, David, John.
Shafer, Mrs. Laura.
Shafer, Mr. and Mrs. Tommie.
Shafer, Mrs. W. S.
Sheets, Mr. and Mrs. Clay; Mildred, John W., Martha, Dee, Donald, Arthur.
Sheets, Mr. and Mrs. W. H.; Estell, Loy, Leon.
Sheets, Edna.
Sheets, Mr. and Mrs. Wm.
Shelton, Mr. and Mrs. Horace.
Shelton, Mr. and Mrs. John; Louise, Leone.
Shelton, Mrs. Martha.
Shelton, Mr. and Mrs. Maurice; family.
Sherbondy, Mr. and Mrs. Bruce; Laura.
Sheridan, Mr. and Mrs. Michael; Charles, Helen.
Sherrill, Mr. and Mrs. Frank.
Sheward, Mr. and Mrs. B. F.; Lucille.
Shindler, John.
Shiply, Mr. and Mrs. Bryant.
Shiply, Mr. and Mrs. M. O.; Max Frank, John Ross.
Shobe, Mrs. Cy.
Shobe, Mr. and Mrs. Ed; Ruby.
Shobe, Mr. and Mrs. Herb; Mattie, Hattie, Everett.
Shobe, Mr. and Mrs. Samuel.
Shonk, Mrs. Caroline; Eveline.
Shontz, Mr. and Mrs. George; Lena.
Shore, Mr. and Mrs. Arthur; Byron.
Shore, Mr. and Mrs. C. K.
Shore, Mr. and Mrs. Earl B.; Glendon, Wilnetta.
Shore, Mrs. P. M.
Shott, Mr. and Mrs. Gust; Robert, Irene, Margaret, Hubert.
Showalter, Mr. and Mrs. Harry; Maxine, Eveline.
Shuman, Mr. and Mrs. A. M.; Helen, Ruth.
Shriver, Mr. and Mrs. Everett.
Shryer, Mrs. Maude; Lillian.
Slusher, Mr. and Mrs. Wm.
Smiley, Mr. and Mrs. LaVerne.
Smith, Admiral; Arthur, Madeline.
Smith, Mr. and Mrs. Albert; Curtis, Ermil.
Smith, Mrs. Amos.
Smith, Mr. and Mrs. Ernest; Phyllis, Robert, James, Nellie Mae.
Smith, Mr. and Mrs. Ed F.; Josephine, Liston.
Smith, Mr. and Mrs. Frank; Thelma, Frank, Jr.

CONTRIBUTORS

Smith, Mrs. Ella.
Smith, George; Mildred, Wilma.
Smith, Guy.
Smith, Mr. and Mrs. John.
Smith, Mrs. Laura; Amie.
Smith, Mr. and Mrs. Milo; Venus, Grace, Bernice, Victor.
Smith, Mrs. Molly; Celia.
Smith, Mr. and Mrs. O. B.; Percy, Genevive.
Snails, Mrs. A. E.
Snapp, Mr. and Mrs. Cecil.
Snowgrass, Mr. and Mrs. John.
Snyder, Mr. and Mrs. James; Fern.
Snyder, Mr. and Mrs. Jos.; Esta, Lula, Norman, Alfred, Lenora.
Spade, Mr. and Mrs. John.
Spohn, Mr. and Mrs. Francis; Hazel, Charles, Dorthy, Elsie, Ruth, Omer.
Spotts, Mrs.
Spotts, Lewis M.
Squires, Mr. and Mrs. Rube; Arthur.
Stacy, Mr. and Mrs. William H.; Mary, Russel.
Stahl, Mr. and Mrs. Charles; Donald.
Stahl, Mr. and Mrs. J. E.
Stauffer, Mr. and Mrs. C.; Paul.
Stanley, Mr. and Mrs. John.
Stanton, Mrs. E. C.
Steffy, Mr. and Mrs. Frank; Ethel, Earl, Earnest, Elsie, Elsworth, Claude, Carl.
Stegeman, Mr. and Mrs. Carl; Magdeline, Carl, Jr.
Steininger, Mr. and Mrs. Artie; Nettie, Lloyd, Herschel, Paul.
Stengel, Mr. and Mrs. O. W.; George.
Sterner, Mr. and Mrs. Frank.
Stetson, Mr. and Mrs. Frank; Ray.
Stevenson, Mr. and Mrs. W. K.
Stockberger, Mr. and Mrs. Joel; Dennis, Margaret.
Stoner, Mr. and Mrs. N. R.; Rosella, Howard, Francis, Robert.
Stingly, Mr. and Mrs. Peter; Grace.
Stinson, Mr. and Mrs. Webster; Loretta, Bernice.
Stinson, Mrs. L.
Sutherland, Dr. and Mrs. Ruth.

Swabey, Mr. and Mrs. E. C.; Mary, Helen, Laura.
Swabey, Mrs. Mary.
Swartwood, Mr. and Mrs. John; Howard, Donald, Harold.
Swartwood, Mr. and Mrs. Sam.
Swartwood, Mrs. Sarah.
Sweany, Mr. and Mrs. Byron; Roberta.
Sweat, Mr. and Mrs. Ben.
Taylor, Mr. and Mrs. Chas.; Hubert.
Taylor, Mrs. Deliah.
Taylor, Dr. and Mrs. Harley; Marietta.
Taylor, Mr. and Mrs. Orbra.
Terry, Mr. and Mrs. F. H.; Lyon, Sarah.
Thalman, Mrs. Belle; Harry.
Thompson, Mrs. Ed; Everett, Marjorie.
Thornburg, Mrs. Elda; Harold, Catherine.
Thompson, Mr. and Mrs. H. J.; Stella.
Thompson, Mr. and Mrs. Ike.
Thrush, Mrs. Ellen; Rufus.
Thrush, Mr. and Mrs. Harold.
Timbers, Mr. and Mrs. O. R.
Tipton, Mr. and Mrs. Fred.
Tipton, Mrs. Isaac; Raymond.
Townsend, Mr. and Mrs. Joel.
Totman, Mr. and Mrs. F. M.; Marion.
Tracy, Mr. and Mrs. Frank; Flavilla.
Trimble, Mrs. Jennie.
True, Chas.
True, Mr. and Mrs. R. P.; Lucy, Grace.
Troutman, Mr. and Mrs. Olvin; baby.
Turner, Frank, Isabelle, Nona, Marie.
Van Blaricon, Mr. and Mrs. Henry; Nellie.
Van Dien, Mr. and Mrs. Bert; Albertus, Gwendolyn, Mary Ann.
Van Dien, Mr. and Mrs. Burdett.
Van Trump, Mr. and Mrs. Carl.
Van Trump, Mr. and Mrs. Harold; Helen.
Van Trump, Mr. and Mrs. Pete; Elizabeth, Martha.
Vawter, Mr. and Mrs. Alfred; Hope.
Vawters, Mrs. Sarah A.

Vawter, Mr. and Mrs. Ed; Merriam, Alice, Helen.
Veirs, Mr. and Mrs. Clarence; Margaret, Annabelle.
Viverette, Mr. and Mrs. A. J.; Dolores.
Von Ehrnstein, Emily.
Wagner, Mrs. Elizabeth; Margaret.
Wagner, Mr. and Mrs. Wallace; Donald, Helen, Walter, Mary, Merril, Howard.
Wagoner, Mr. and Mrs. Elsworth; Vivian.
Wagoner, Mr. and Mrs. Omer.
Wagoner, Mr. and Mrs. W. D.; Dorthy.
Wallace, Mr. and Mrs. Charles; George, Byron.
Wallace, George H.; Ruth, Harry.
Wallace, Madge.
Wallace, Mr. and Mrs. R. C.
Walters, Mrs. Catherine.
Walters, Mr. and Mrs. S. B.; Robert, Martha Louise.
Walter, Mrs. Vera; George, Harry, Frances.
Ward, Mrs. Blanche; Henrietta.
Ward, Mr. and Mrs. Gus; Robert, Ray, Ralph.
Ward, Stella.
Welch, Leona.
Wenger, Mrs. Catherine.
Wenger, Mr. and Mrs. S. A.
Werner, Mr. and Mrs. Wm.; Marvel, Robert, Florence, Eveline.
Wertz, Mr. and Mrs. L. I.; Forrest, Olive, Margaret.
West, Mr. and Mrs. B. O.
West, Helen O.
Weygandt, Rev. J. B.
Wheadon, Mr. and Mrs. W. H.
White, Mrs. J. C.; Florence, Marie, Frances.
Whitmer, Mr. and Mrs. A. L; Orville.
Wicks, Mr. and Mrs. Earl.
Wicks, Mr. and Mrs. Mark.
Wilder, J. S.; Mary.
Wile, Mrs. M.; Ike, Arthur, Lee, Rose.
Willard, Mr. and Mrs. Charles; Joshua, Daniel.
Williamson, Wm.
Wilmont, Mr. and Mrs. Ed; Hildred, James.
Wilson, Mr. and Mrs. Clyde.
Wilson, Mrs. Emma; Helen, Etta.
Wilson, Mr. and Mrs. Harry.
Wilson, Mr. and Mrs. Harry; Margaret, Dorthy, Marjorie.
Wilson, Dr. M.
Wilson, Mr. and Mrs. Wm.
Wolf, Mrs. Angie; Herma.
Wolf, Mrs. H. E.; Roy, Esther.
Wolf, Dessa.
Woods, Mr. and Mrs.
Woods, Mrs. M.
Wood, Mr. and Mrs. Wm.
Wrentmore, Mr. and Mrs. A.; Lawrence, Marjorie.
Wright, Mr. and Mrs. Wm.; Faye, Lefa, Ruth Rena.
Wynn, Mr. and Mrs. Arlie.
Wylie, Mr. and Mrs. Robert; George, Donald, Ardine, Lucile.
Yike, Mr. and Mrs.; Annabelle, Martha.
Young, Mr. and Mrs. Elliott; Warren.
Young, Mr. and Mrs. H. G.; Carl, Helen.
Young, Mr. and Mrs. Levi.
Young, Mr. and Mrs. U. B.; Thurston, Velma, Charles, Jack.
Young, Mr. and Mrs. Wm.
Zachman, Mr. and Mrs. George.
Zeazel, Mr. and Mrs. Joe; Rebecca, Clinton.
Zimmerman, Mr. and Mrs. Leo; Emerson, Herbert, Leo, Jr., Major, Valentine.
Zimmerman, Mr. and Mrs. Lon; Sarah, J.
Zimmerman, Mr. and Mrs. Val.
Zimmerman, Mr. and Mrs. Wm.; Nina, Dale, Lura, Wilma, Byron, Ralph, Martha.
Zolman, Mrs. Martha.
Zook, Mrs.

Union Township

Adams, Mr. and Mrs. A. A.
Albert, Mr. and Mrs. R. D.
Anderson, Mr. and Mrs. Alfred
Anderson, Mrs. Ruth
Anderson, Mr. and Mrs. W. T.; Keith, Lloyd.
Arnott, John.
Ash, Mr. and Mrs.; Flo, Robert.
Ayers, Mrs. Belle.
Bainter, Ralph.
Baldwin, Olie; Hugh, Ralph, Ruby, Goldie.
Barger, Mr. and Mrs. Samuel J.; William, Edwin, Mary.
Barker, Mrs. Nancie.
Barker, Mr. and Mrs. Wm. A.
Barnett, Mr. and Mrs. John; Enid, Edith, Alex.
Barrie, Mr. and Mrs. A. J.
Barsh, Mr. and Mrs. Henry.
Baxter, Mr. and Mrs. Sam; Ray Gertrude, Bill, Herschel.
Bennett, Amanda.
Bennett, Lee.
Benson, Mr. and Mrs.
Bixler, Mr. and Mrs. Daniel B.; Orville, George.
Bixler, Mr. and Mrs. Jonathan.
Blausser, Mr. and Mrs. Eliza; Lucille.
Blausser, Mr. and Mrs. Roy; Frederick.
Blosser, Mr. and Mrs. J. B.
Bowersox, Mr. and Mrs. Frank.
Brant, Mr. and Mrs. Arnold; Edward, Wm.
Bremon, Mr. and Mrs. John; Margaret.
Brice; Mr. and Mrs. Daniel.
Bringham, Wilber.
Brodsord, Mr. and Mrs. Wm.
Brooker, Mr. and Mrs. David; Edwin, Maud, Mildred, Nobeline, Lois.
Brooker, Edward; Lois.
Brooker, Isaac.
Brooker, Mr. and Mrs. Rudolph.
Brooker, Mr. and Mrs. Walter; Geneva.
Brown, Mr. and Mrs. Frank.
Bruce, Mr. and Mrs. Chas.
Bruce, Mr. and Mrs. Albert; Elvon, Burdell, Ralph.
Bruce, Miss Glen.
Bruce, Mr. and Mrs. Stephen.
Buchanan, Mr. and Mrs. E. J.
Burk, Mrs. Samuel.
Burns, Mr. and Mrs. James; Bernice, Donna, Ruth.
Callahan, Mr. and Mrs. George.
Calvin, Mr. and Mrs. Arthur.
Calvin, Mr. and Mrs. Geo. M.; Edith.
Calvin, Mr. and Mrs. V. W.; Edna.
Calvin, Mr. and Mrs. Vere S.
Campbell, Mr. and Mrs. C. C.; Mildred.
Campbell, Frank; Lester, Doyle, Dortha.
Cannon, Mr. and Mrs. E. C.
Cannon, Mrs. Mollie; Evert.
Cannon, Mr. and Mrs. Wm.; Hugh.
Carr, Mr. and Mrs. J. H.; John, Wilber, Thomas, Catherine, Nancy.
Carter, Mr. and Mrs. Ernest.
Carter, Mrs. John.
Carter, Marian, Sadie, Frederick.
Clark, Mrs. Lizzie.
Clark, Samuel.
Collins, Mr. and Mrs. Cylde; Ruth Alene, Lois Irene.
Collins, Mr. and Mrs. S. S.; Cecil.
Collins, Mr. and Mrs. Wat.
Compton, Mr. and Mrs. Feilder; Ermal, Frances.
Cook, Mr. and Mrs. Elmer; Robert, Lois.
Cook, Mr. and Mrs. O. E.
Cooper, Mr. and Mrs. Melvin.
Corsant, Mr. and Mrs. Chas.; Dortha, Chas. R., Oscar M.
Cox, Bert.
Cummings, Mr. and Mrs. Riley.
Cummings, Mr. and Mrs. Warren; Audra Irene.
Cummon, Mr. and Mrs. Joseph.
Crabb, Mr. and Mrs. Alvah; Ersa, Thelma, Opal.

Crabill, Mr. and Mrs. Harrison; Mabel, Mildred.

Crabill, Mr. and Mrs. Judson; Lucille, Catherine.

Crabill, Mr. and Mrs. Lester; Savilla, Ulysses, Dewey, Carl, Ermal.

Daniel, Mr. and Mrs. L. E.; Ruth.

Davis, Mr. and Mrs. Harry; Opal, Donald.

Davis, Mr. and Mrs. Roy; children.

Dellinger, Mr. and Mrs. John; John Foster.

eMoss, Mrs. Grace; Vera, Velma, Mamie.

Denniston, Mr. and Mrs. J. M.; Mabel.

DeVault, Mr. and Mrs. E. B. and children.

DeWitt, Mr. and Mrs. Allen; Robert, Thurman.

Dukes, N. E.

Eger, Jacob; Ezra, Homer, Ralph, Pearl, Roy, Martha.

Eiseman, Mr. and Mrs. Henry; Blanch.

Elston, Mr. and Mrs. W. C.; Harriet, Ruth.

Emmons, Mr. and Mrs. Chas.; Herald, Annabelle, Thelma, Carl, Donald.

Enyart, Mr. and Mrs. Erve; Foster.

Enyart, Mr. and Mrs. Oscar.

Enyart, Mr. and Mrs. Joseph.

Epler, Mr. and Mrs. James; Aneda.

Epler, Mrs. Mary.

Evans, Mr. and Mrs. Chas.; Hugh.

Evans, Mr. and Mrs. Elmer O.; Carl Hugh.

Evans, Joe; Jake.

Evans, Mr. and Mrs. Wm.

Ewing, Mr. and Mrs. Wilber; Harry, Chloe.

Fairchild, Mr. and Mrs. Newton J.; Jessie, Paul.

Fansler, Mr. and Mrs. Stephen; Bertha, Mary, Arthur, Ann, Gilbert, Earl, Richard, Emma, Lester, Donald.

Farner, Mrs. Minnie; Athene.

Feilds, Mrs.

Feilds, Mr. and Mrs. Wm.; Cesil.

Felder, Mr. and Mrs. A. E.; Grant.

Felder, Mr. and Mrs. Chas.; Mary Ellen, Roseva, Carl.

Felder, Mr. and Mrs. Chris.; Arthur, Frank.

Felder, Mr. and Mrs. Clifford.

Felty, Jonathan.

Foglesong, Mr. and Mrs. Donald.

Foglesong, Mr. and Mrs. Ralph.

Foglesong, Mr. and Mrs. Wm.; Laura.

Franklin, Mr. and Mrs. John E.

Freind, Mr. and Mrs. Mathew; John.

Garman, Mr. and Mrs. Geo. W.; Dola, Trella, Victor, Ralph.

Garman, Mr. and Mrs. Harry; Harry, Jr.

Garman, Mr. and Mrs. Leroy; Louisa.

Gibbs, Mr. and Mrs. Clarence; Walter.

Gilbert, Dr. and Mrs. A. I.

Geiseman, Mr. and Mrs. Forest E.; Opal.

Gillespie, Mr. and Mrs. Bert.

Gillespie, Mrs. Warn.

Gillespie, Mr. and Mrs. Mrs. Vantyle; Frances Lucille.

Gohl, Mr. and Mrs. W. H.; Earnest, Chester.

Gorshine, Mrs. Susan; Bert.

Gorshine, Mr. and Mrs. Wm. M.

Gotschalk, Mr. and Mrs. Edward; Elnora, John.

Gould, Mr. and Mrs. F. P.; Helen, Florence, Mary, Gertrude.

Graffis, Mr. and Mrs. George.

Graffis, Mr. and Mrs. Thomas E.; Fred.

Graffs, Mr. and Mrs. Wm.; Bessie, Edna, Mammie.

Gray, Mr. and Mrs. Wm. F.; Mary.

Guise, Mr. and Mrs. Aden; Leota.

Guise, Daniel.

Guise, Mr. and Mrs. Earl.

Guise, Mr. and Mrs. Harvey.

Guise, Mr. and Mrs. Henry.

Guyer, Mr. and Mrs. A. D. Paul.

CONTRIBUTORS

Haag, Mr. and Mrs. H. D.; Carl, Grace, Edith, Ernest.
Hammilton, Mr. and Mrs. Ralph.
Harding, A. P.; A. P., Jr.
Harris, Mr. and Mrs. Wilfred.
Hartman, Mrs. Sarah.
Harrison, Mr. and Mrs. Thos. H.; Paul.
Hecktor, Mr. and Mrs. Axel; Carl, Ruth, Adolph, Ethel, Edwin.
Heminger, Mr. and Mrs. Amos; Violet.
Heminger, Mr. and Mrs. Lenord; John, Whitfield, Helen.
Henrichs, Mr. and Mrs. Daniel.
Henrichs, Mr. and Mrs. Frank; Cuba, Daniel.
Henrichs, Mr .and Mrs. Wm.; Margaret.
Hensinger, David; Neoma, Lester, Orpha
Henderson, Mr. and Mrs. Bert; Void, Ruby.
Henderson, Mr. and Mrs. Eli.
Henderson, Mrs. Isaac.
Henderson, Mr. and Mrs. Wm.
Hendrickson, Mr. and Mrs. Frank; Robert, Louise, Loretta.
Hendrick, Mr. and Mrs. George; Anna, Virgil.
Herd, Mr. and Mrs. John.
Herman, Mr. and Mrs. David; Morris.
Hern, Harry.
Herr, Mr. and Mrs. John; Cyril, Paul, Catherine.
Hetzner, Charles.
Hiatt, Mr. and Mrs. C. H.; Paul, Nada.
Hickel, Mr. and Mrs. Amos.
Hickle, Mr. and Mrs. Colen; Elmer, Elsie, George.
Hickel, Mr. and Mrs. Geo.
Hickle, Mrs. Rosa; Elsie.
Hiem, Mr. and Mrs. Herman; Marie, Carl.
Hiland, Mr. and Mrs. Milton; Robert, Betty, Arthur.
Hilflicker, Mr. and Mrs. George; Ruth Graham.
Hilflicker, Mr. and Mrs. John; George, Helen, Frances.
Hill, A. G.
Hill, Emma.
Hogan, Mr. and Mrs. Elra; Roy, Nelda.
Hogan, Mrs. Dema.
Holland, Mr. and Mrs. W. F.; Lawrence, Willard.
Holmes, Mr. and Mrs. John; Madge, Doras.
Hoob, Mr. and Mrs. J. W.
Hott, Mr. and Mrs. James; Grace, Milo, Elva, Charlie, Perle Nobeline.
Howell, Mr. and Mrs. Henry D.
Huber, Mr. and Mrs. John.
Hudkins, Adrian.
Hudkins, Mr. and Mrs. Aloin.
Hudkins, Mrs. Arch.
Hudkins, Mr. and Mrs. Basil.
Hudkins, Mr. and Mrs. David.
Hudkins, Mr. and Mrs. D. B.
Hudkins, Mr. and Mrs. Edward; Violet, Retha.
Hudkins, E. V.
Hudkins, Mr. and Mrs. Ezra.
Hudkins, Mr. and Mrs. Frank.
Hudkins, Mr. and Mrs. Frank; Francis.
Hudkins, Mr. and Mrs. L. J.; Jennie, Dorcas, William.
Hughy, Mr. and Mrs. Frank; Ruth.
Hunneshagen, Mr. and Mrs. Adolph.
Hunneshagen, Eugene; Hugh, Ralph, Chester.
Hunneshagen, Mr. and Mrs. Harry; Joseph, Margaret.
Jackson, Mr. and Mrs. J.; Thelma.
Jennings, Mr. and Mrs. W. H.; Glen, Myron, Florence, Lois.
Jewell, Mrs. Nannie.
Judy, Mr. and Mrs. Roy; children.
Keesey, Mr. and Mrs. Frank; child.
Kennard, Mrs. Anna; Mary.
Keney, Mr. and Mrs. Dave; Clide, Pearl, Geraldine, Corlista.
Kile, Mr. and Mrs. P. K.
Kimball, Mr. and Mrs. Nolan; Cleah, Ermal.

Kingrey, Mrs. Bernice.
Kingery, Mr. and Mrs. P. J.; Norah, Delilah.
Kinnear, Mr. and Mrs. John.
Kirchner, Mr. and Mrs. George.
Kissinger, Mr. and Mrs. Thomas; Raymond and Donald.
Koff, Mr. and Mrs. Daniel; Minnie, Hellena, Frederick, Katherine, Alice.
Kough, Mr. and Mrs. J. L.; Katie.
Kough, Mr. and Mrs. Wm.; Ralph, Roy, Donald, Frank.
Kreamrer, Mr. and Mrs. Ed.
Kreamer, Mr. and Mrs. Harry.
Kreamer, Mr. and Mrs. J. H.; Naomi.
Kumler, Mr. and Mrs. H. B.; Margaret, Florence, Charlotte.
Lamb, Mr. and Mrs. Sam; Hazel, Bernice, Marion, Dorthy.
Lambert, Mrs. Esthe.
Lamborn, Mr. and Mrs. Clifford; Margaret.
Lamborn, F. W.; Marjorie, Alice, Opal, Darl, Alleo.
Lamborn, Mr. and Mrs. O. J.
Landis, Fannie.
Leap, Mr. and Mrs. Loren; Bulah Frances and Manson.
Leasure, Mr. and Mrs. John.
Leasure, Mrs. Lewis; Naomi.
Lebo, Mr. and Mrs. Alvah.
Lebo, Mr. and Mrs. Ralph; Raymond, Ruth, Julian, Alice.
Leiter, Mr. and Mrs. John.
Lewis, Cora.
Ley, Rev. E. A.
Ley, Frank.
Limimg, George.
Lindern, Mr. and Mrs. Albert; Hobert.
Litchinall, Mr. and Mrs.
Lisey, Mrs. Jane; Mettie.
Lisey, Jacob.
Lisey, Mr. and Mrs. John; Mary.
Lynch, B. B.
Lord, Mr.
Louden, Mrs. Loura; Tresa, Melba.
Lough, Isabell; Ray.
Mahler, Odella.

Marsh, Mr. and Mrs. Ora; Angdon.
Martin, Mr. and Mrs. John; Reba, Erma, Alice.
Mathews, Mr. and Mrs. Henry.
Mathias, Chas.
Masters, Mr. and Mrs. Johnson; Earnest, Naoma, Margaret, Chester, Lester.
McBeth, Mr. and Mrs. Wm.; Robert, Mary, Josephine, Bertha, Harold, Floyd.
McConaughy, Mr. and Mrs. J. R.; Hugh R., Sarah.
McConnell, Mr. and Mrs. Ralph; Joseph Margaret.
McCoy, Mr. and Mrs. G. B.
McCoy, Mr. and Mrs. Wm.
McKee, Mr. and Mrs. Virgil.
McKee, Mrs.
McKinsey, Harold Byron.
McLain, Mr. and Mrs. D. A.; Bertha, Scott, Walter, Emett, Grace, Vera.
McMurray, Mr. and Mrs. Andy; Annabelle, Martin.
McPherson, Mrs. Wm.
McVay, Mr. and Mrs. Harry; Ray.
Meade, Mr. and Mrs. Wm.
Meridith, Mr. and Mrs. Chas.
Metz, Hazel.
Metzger, Mr. and Mrs. David; Julia.
Metzger, Mr. and Mrs. Homer; Ruba.
Metzger, Jacob; Verda.
Metzger, Wm.; Nellie, Anna, Bertha, Ruth.
Metzger, Mr. and Mrs. Peter; Nellie, Ruby.
Milbren, John; Letha.
Mills, Mr. and Mrs. L. C.
Miller, Mr. and Mrs. Elias.
Miller, John.
Miller, Mr. and Mrs. Mose.
Mishler, Mr. and Mrs. Roy; Johnnie.
Miller, Mr. and Mrs. Stacy.
Miller, Wm.; Donald, Elias, Robert.
Molencapp, Mr. and Mrs.; mother.
Montgomery, Herbert.
Moon, Mr. and Mrs. Harry.
Moon, Henry.
Moon, Mrs. Mary Jane.

Moore, Mr. and Mrs. George; Louis, Helen, Wildamae.
Moore, Mr. and Mrs. Samuel; Margaret, William.
Morris, George; Lyman, Ras, Geneva.
Mott, Mr. and Mrs. George.
Morrow, Mr. and Mrs. Otto; Lorine, Russel, Mary, Norma, Gilbert.
Murphy, Arabelle.
Mutchler, Mr. and Mrs. Howard H.; Josephine, Isabelle Jennett.
Myers, Mr. and Mrs. Clarence.
Myers, Frank.
Myers, Mr. and Mrs. Irwin.
Myers, Mr. and Mrs. Seawell.
Myers, Mr. and Mrs. Wm.
Myers, Mr. and Mrs. Wm. E.
Nafe, Mr. and Mrs. D. O.; Annabelle, Mabel.
Natham, Mr. and Mrs. Francis; Robert.
Neff, Mr. and Mrs. Dean.
Neff, Mr. and Mrs. Thos.; Clyde D.
Nelson, Mr. and Mrs. N. E.
Nickles, Mr. and Mrs. Warren.
Niseley, Mr. and Mrs. Chas. C.
Norris, Mr. and Mrs. Frank.
Nutt, Mr. and Mrs. Roy; Violet, Harold.
Osborn, Mrs. Charles.
Overmyer, Mr. and Mrs. Ed.
Overmyer, Mr. and Mrs. Ernest; Ora Lafaun.
Overmyer, Mr. and Mrs. Ira J.; Edna, Raymond, Burdell, Carl.
Overmyer, Mr. and Mrs. John.
Overmyer, Mr. and Mrs. Lincoln.
Overmyer, Mr. and Mrs. S. C.; Hobart, Charlie, Paul Fred.
Parker, Mr. and Mrs. Hugh; children.
Parker, Mr. and Mrs. J. A.
Parker, Mr. and Mrs. John; Vernon, Arlie, Landreth.
Patter, Lewis.
Penrod, Mr. and Mrs. Daniel; Paul.
Penrod, Mr. and Mrs. J. F.
Peters, Christ; Nellie, George.
Pickins, Mr. and Mrs. Frank; Herma, Helen, Esthe.
Pickens, Mr. and Mrs. Will.
Plaietz, Mr. and Mrs. Fred; Eldona.
Polen, Mr. and Mrs. George.
Polen, Mr. and Mrs. Raliegh.
Polen, Mr. and Mrs. Wm.
Polly, Mr. and Mrs. Frank.
Pratt, Mr. and Mrs. George; Omer, Russel, Freda, Meda.
Rankin, Mr. and Mrs. John; Mabel.
Ranns, Bud; Earl, Donna.
Reedy, Rev. and Mrs. G. S.; Paul.
Reeser, Mr. and Mrs. Carlie; Nettie, Creath, Harry.
Reese, Mrs. Frank; Dottie.
Reno, Mrs. Maria.
Rhinsmith, Mrs. Flora.
Rhodes, Mr. and Mrs.
Rhodes, Mr. and Mrs. Harvey; Loyd, Thelma.
Robbins, Alexander.
Rolston, Mr. and Mrs. G. W.
Roth, Mr. and Mrs. S. B.
Rouch, Mr. and Mrs. J. E.
Russel, Mr. and Mrs. John P.
Sales, Mr. and Mrs.; Robert, Genevieve.
Schirm, George.
Schirm, Samuel.
Scott, Mr. and Mrs. Frank S.
Sears, Mrs. Ellen.
Shere, Mr. and Mrs. John; Sadie.
Sheridan, Mr. and Mrs. Daniel; Michael, Mary.
Shine, Albert.
Shine, Mr. and Mrs. W. M.
Shoemaker, Mr. and Mrs. L. M.; Albert, Ralph.
Showley, Mr. and Mrs. Arthur.
Showley, Mr. and Mrs. Charles; Forest, Doyle, Sanford, Dortha.
Showley, Jacob.
Sibert, Mr. and Mrs. D. W.
Simmons, Mr. and Mrs. Fred Louise.
Singer, Brice.
Singer, Mrs. Ettie.
Singer, Mr. and Mrs. Lester.
Singer, Wm.
Slick, Mr. and Mrs. Herman.
Slick, Joseph.

Slick, Mrs. Lucie; Emma.
Slonaker, Mr. and Mrs. Blake; Isaac, Ethel, Joanna.
Smith, Mr. and Mrs. Arthur; Carl.
Smith, Mr. and Mrs. Boid.
Smith, Mr. and Mrs. B. F.; Ruth.
Smith, Mr. and Mrs. Dan.
Smith, Mr. and Mrs. Elmer; Chester, Thelma.
Smith, George.
Smith, John.
Smith, Mr. and Mrs. John.
Smith, Mr. and Mrs. Joseph.
Smith, Mr. and Mrs. J. K.
Smith, Maud; Oren.
Smith, Mr. and Mrs. M. L.
Smith, Mr. and Mrs. Oliver.
Smith, Mr. anr Mrs. Roy; Beulah, Beuford.
Smith, Mr. and Mrs. Samuel; Margaret, Elizabeth, Georgia, Ralph, Helen.
Smith, Sile.
Snepp, Mr. and Mrs. D. H.
Snepp, Mrs. Fannie.
Snyder, Mr. and Mrs. J. S.; John, Paul, Walter, Hubert.
Spangler, Mr. and Mrs. Adam; Jessie.
Sparks, Mr. and Mrs. C. J.
Sparks, Mr. and Mrs. Justin C.
Staman, Jessie; Charles, Hugh.
Stams, John.
Starr, Mr. and Mrs. Wm. B.; Alta, Wallace, Lewis, Lorena, Kathryn, George, Mildred.
Steele, John; Dilla.
Steinke, Mr. and Mrs.; Carl, Florence.
Stiefenhoefer, Dora.
Stingly, Mr. and Mrs. Amos; Fred, Chloe, Esther.
Stout, Mr. and Mrs. W. H.; Earl.
Stubbs, Mr. and Mrs. Edward.
Stubbs, Mr. and Mrs. Frederick.
Stubbs, Mr. and Mrs. Schuyler.
Taber, Mr.
Talbott, Mr. and Mrs. Arthur; Paul.
Talbott, Mr. and Mrs. J. B.; Maurice, Annabelle, Albert, Harlen, Ralph, May, Charles, Simon.
Teeters, Mrs. Ettie; Mildred, Jessie.
Tomlison, Mr. and Mrs. Robert R.; sons.
Tonily, Mr. and Mrs. Cole.
Troutman, Mr. and Mrs. H. N.
Troutman, Mr. and Mrs. George B.; Arthur, Ester.
Troutman, Mr. and Mrs. Ottis.
Troutman, Mr. and Mrs. Roy; Vearl, Enith, Jean.
Urbin, Mr. and Mrs. Guy.
Urbin, Mr. and Mrs. H.; Bruce.
Vankirk, Belle.
Wagners, Don B.; Frank L., Dona B.
Walle, Wm.; Gertrude, Gerald.
Walsh, Mr. and Mrs. Jas.; Mary.
Walters, Mr. and Mrs. C. N.
Walters, Mrs. Eliza; Lola.
Walter, J. A.
Walters, Mr. and Mrs. John; Wilda, Wilber.
Walters, Wm. Eldon.
Washburn, Dr. and Mrs. J. M.; Helen, Herbert.
Ware, Mrs. Martha.
Weaver, Lizzie.
Weiser, Mr. and Mrs. Weiser, Eri.
Weller, Mr. and Mrs. Claud.
Weller, Mr. and Mrs. Jesse; Helen.
Wentzel, Mr. and Mrs. Charlie; Marie, Harold.
Wentzel, Mr. and Mrs. George; Eva.
Wentzel, Mr. and Mrs. J. S.; Irma.
Wentzel, Mr. and Mrs. Nathaniel; Arthur.
West, Mr. J. M.; Chas.
Wharton, Mr. and Mrs. Orville.
Wharton, Mr. and Mrs. W. B.; Marion, Ruth, Harlan, Esther.
Wharton, Mr. and Mrs. Wm. M.; Roy, Gladys.
Wilckson, Mr. and Mrs. L. C.
Wilckson, Loel.
Williams, Mrs. Mary.
Willoughby, Mr. and Mrs. F. S.; Paul.
Willoughby, Mr. and Mrs. Thos. J.; June, Gail, Doris.

CONTRIBUTORS

Willoughby, Mr. and Mrs. W. N.; children.
Wilson, George.
Wilson, Mr. and Mrs. George.
Wilson, John.
Wilson, Mr. and Mrs. James.
Wilson, Mr. and Mrs. John L.; Darline, Margaret.
Wilson, Mr. and Mrs. John M.; Sarah, Clifford.
Wilson, Mr. and Mrs. John; James.
Wilson, Mr. and Mrs. Thos. R.; Hellen.
Wilson, Mr. and Mrs. Wm. F.
Wolington, Mr. and Mrs. Lloyd.
Wood, Mr. and Mrs. Arthur; Ethel.
Wood, Mr. and Mrs. Samuel.
Worfeild, Mrs. John.
Workings, Mr. and Mrs. Frank.
Working, Mr. and Mrs. Peter; Lester, Dana, Elizabeth.
Wright, Mr. and Mrs. A. C.; Bonnie.
Wright, Mr. and Mrs. Thos.; Glenn.
York, Mr. and Mrs. Ebert; Chester, Tessie.
Zartman, Mrs. Louella; Imogene.
Zea, Mrs. Mary; Charles.
Zellars, Mr. and Mrs. Henry.
Zeller, Mr. and Mrs. Howard; Izola, Arnold, Helen, Bernice.
Zellers, Mr. and Mrs. J. J.
Zellars, Mr. and Mrs. M.
Zellars, Mr. and Mrs. Roy.
Zellars, Mr. and Mrs. Ruddy.
Zellars, Wm.
Zimmerman, Mr. and Mrs. Lewis.
Zimpleman, Mr. and Mrs. Michiel; Martha, Mollie, Dessie.
Zuck, Mr. and Mrs. Jesse; Claude, Irene.

Wayne Township

Alber, Mr. and Mrs. Daniel; Calvin, Garrett, Jauneta, Berdenia, Winnefred, Theadore, Nina, Clifford.
Albro, Mrs. Jane; Sula.
Ashby, Mr. and Mrs. J. C.
Bailey, Mr. and Mrs. James, Sr.; Garl, James, Jr.
Baker, Mr. and Mrs. Earl; Thelma, Forest.
Barker, Mr. and Mrs. Eli; Mae.
Barker, Mr. and Mrs. Ellis; Vern, Edith.
Barnett, Mr. and Mrs. Harry; Helen, Mary Nina, Mack, Bessie.
Beattie, Mr. and Mrs. Ray; Claud, Ruby, Roy, Walter.
Beattie, Warren; Charles.
Bennett, Mr. and Mrs. Harvey.
Brewer, Mr. and Mrs. Carl; Dean H., Audrey May.
Bruce, Mr. and Mrs. Albert; Eldon, Berdilla.
Buchanan, Mr. and Mrs. Chas. F.; Dessie, Martha, Lela, James.
Burns, Mr. and Mrs. Arthur.
Burns, Mr. and Mrs. Isaac; Minnie, Donald.
Burns, Mrs. Josey.
Caldwell, Mr. and Mrs. James; Elenor.
Callahan, Mr. and Mrs. Russell; Dorthy.
Calvin, Mr. and Mrs. E. P.; Mable, Elizabeth, Vincent, George.
Calvin, Frank.
Calvin, John.
Calvin, Mr. and Mrs. V. W.; Bertha, Arthur.
Carr, Mr. and Mrs. C. L.; Oscar, Dorothy.
Carr, Mr. and Mrs. Lonnie; Evelyn Erma.
Carter, Mr. and Mrs. James; Thomas, Walter, Fayette, Merle.
Caton, Mr. and Mrs. C. E.; Lulie, Cornell, Donald.
Caton, Mr. and Mrs. Robert M.; John, Joseph.

Comer, Edna.
Conn, Verl B.
Conner Nancy.
Connery, Mary; Nancy.
Cornell, Mr. and Mrs. Jerry; Ray, Velma, Mary, Irvin.
Costella, Mr. and Mrs. Edward W.; Laura M.
Costello, Mr. and Mrs. John W.; Mary, Ellen, Edward, J. W., Jr., Joseph, Clara, Ada.
Cowell, Mr. and Mrs. B. M.; Mabel, Cornell.
Cummings, Mr. and Mrs. John; Lucile, Cleotis.
Cunningham, Mr. and Mrs. James; Everet.
Daiz, Mr. and Mrs. Doratha.
Denton, John; Harley, George.
Dively, Mr. and Mrs. William; Russel, George, Edgar, Florence, Pauline, Violet.
Douglass, Mr. and Mrs. Frank; Albert, John, Eva, Joseph, Elmer.
Downs, Alfred; Grace.
Eiselman, Mrs. Margaret.
Esterbrook, C.
Foutz, Mr. and Mrs. Harry; Harold, Elmer.
Fredner, Mr. and Mrs. Wm.
Freeman, Mrs. Lillie; Gladys, Maude.
Geier, Mr. and Mrs. Andrew.
Geier, James B.
Geier, Michel F.
Geier, Mr. and Mrs. Roy.
Graffis, Mr. and Mrs. Virgil W.; Warren, George, Sybil, Doris, Blanche Irene.
Graham, Mr. and Mrs. Perry; Frank, James, Wilma, Blanche, Elmer, Fredrick.
Grube, Mrs. Mary; Jennings.
Harrison, Mr. and Mrs. John, Sr.
Harrison, Mr. and Mrs. John, Jr., Minnie.
Harrison, Mr. and Mrs. Thomas.
Henderson, Mr. and Mrs. Richard; Delma.
Herd, Mr. and Mrs. Thomas; John.
Herrold, Mr. and Mrs. Chas.; Luville.

Herrold, Mr. and Mrs. Henry.
Herrold, Mr. and Mrs. John W.; Carl, Don.
Heward, Mrs. Irene.
Heyer, Mr. and Mrs. Joseph, Sr.; Mary.
Hiatt, Mr. and Mrs. Harry.
Hill, Mr. and Mrs. Lyman; Donald, Warren, Marjory, Mildred, David.
Hirch, Henry.
Hirch, Tone.
Hiyer, Mr. and Mrs. Wm. B.; Florence, Violet.
Hizer, Mr. and Mrs. Aaron; Denis.
Hizer, Mr. and Mrs. Daniel F.; Fred, Icel.
Hizer, Mr. and Mrs. Henry; Dave.
Hizer, Mr. and Mrs. Nelson; Franklin.
Horton, Mr. and Mrs. Leon.
Huffman, Mr. and Mrs. Clarence; Everett, Merle, Mildred.
Huffman, Mr. and Mrs. Thurman; Joseph, Donald.
Jenkins, Mr .and Mrs. Robert; Mary.
Jensen, Mr. and Mrs. J.; Ronald, Richard.
Jones, Mr. and Mrs. Dorley; Geraldine, Blanche.
Jones, Mr. and Mrs. Edmond.
Julian, S. W.; Lillie.
Kaenig, Mr. and Mrs. Geo.; Caroline, Ella, Anna, May, Bessie, Floyd, Ruby, Fay, Roy.
Kent, Mr. and Mrs. Wm.; Dessie, Ralph.
Kimble, Mr. and Mrs. Edward; Lena, Lester, Beatrice.
Kines, Mrs. Ellen.
King, Mr. and Mrs. Wm.; Dwight.
Kirk, Mr. and Mrs. Leonard; Blanche, Samuel, Golda.
Kumler, John J.; Mae.
Kumler, Mr. and Mrs. Roy; Loren, Lois, Byron.
Lambert, Mr. and Mrs. H. C.
Leasure, Mr. and Mrs. Floyd; Wayne.
Leedy, Mr. and Mrs. Bert; Harold, Clyde, Dale.
Long, Mr. and Mrs. Clarence; Irene,

CONTRIBUTORS

Everett, Marie.
Lower, Mr. and Mrs. Mose; Alfred, Ida.
Luey, Mr. and Mrs. John; George, Russell.
McClain, Mr. and Mrs. D. A.; Walter, Scott, Vera, Grace, Emmitt.
McCoy, James; Lela.
McDonough, George; Jane.
McLochlin, Mr. and Mrs. John R.; Marie, Omar, Albert, Gurtie, Ralph.
Mangold, Mr. and Mrs. Gustave.
Marsh, Mr. and Mrs. Earl; Annal, Rosalie, Sherrel.
Marsh, Mr. and Mrs. S. C.
Marsh, Mr. and Mrs. Sherman.
Martin, Mr. and Mrs. John.
Maudlin, Mr. and Mrs. Ray.
Meyers, Mr. and Mrs. J. F.; Madge, Jessie, Hazel.
Miller, Mr. and Mrs. Alva.
Miller, Mr. and Mrs. Michael; Ethel, Pearl, Olive, Alva.
Mogle, Mr. and Mrs. Harry; Leah, Marion.
Miller, Mr. and Mrs. Oliver.
Moore, Mrs. Enoch; Ernest, Freida.
Morphet, Mr. and Mrs. John.
Murray, Mr. and Mrs. Asa J.; George, Rex, Flossie, Cloyde.
Nichol, Mr. and Mrs. S. S.; Elma, Elva, Ruth, Paul, Ralph, Ruby.
Nickels, Mr. and Mrs. Chas. E.; Dessie, Fred, Howard, Bertha.
Nickles, Walter, Elsie, George, Phoebe, Ruth, Dan, Florence.
O'Brien, Mr. and Mrs. Patrick A.; Pricilla, James, Allen.
Parcel, Mr. and Mrs. John; Mary, Theodore.
Pensinger, Mr. and Mrs. Warren; Margaret, Helen, James.
Phillips, Freemont, Virgil.
Rans, Mr. and Mrs. Daniel.
Rans, Mr. and Mrs. F. M.; Edgar.
Rans, Mr. and Mrs. Roy; Ethel, Helen, Harold, Hubert.
Rans, Spurgen.
Rans, William.
Rife, Mr. and Mrs. Charley; Marvin, Hewell, Henrietta, Nellie, Lloyd.
Robbins, Mr. and Mrs. Clyde; Kennith.
Robbins, Arthur, Glenn.
Roberts, Mr. and Mrs. T. F.; Ranna Margaret, Fern Fay, Forrest May.
Sadler, Mr. and Mrs. C.; Elvin.
Sadler, Mr. and Mrs. Edward; Nelson, Jack.
Saunders, Mr. and Mrs. E. J.; Eugene, Eva, Marjorie.
Sedan, Mr. and Mrs. Ora; Lottie, Ruth, Clod, Lee, Herold.
Shanley, Mr. and Mrs. Wm.
Smith, Mr. and Mrs. Henry; Laura, Lester.
Smith, Mr. and Mrs. James; Lafayette.
Snyder, Mr. and Mrs. Michael.
Spotts, Mr. and Mrs. Fred; William Perkins.
Stewart, Mr. and Mrs. O. P.; Tressa, Marie, Beaula, Ruby.
Stone, W. C.; Dora, Harvey.
Tatman, Mr. and Mrs. John; Leslie, Jessie, Clarence, Vernie, Roan, Raymon.
Thomas, Mr. and Mrs. Richard M.; Lela, Robert, Floyd.
Thompson, Mr. and Mrs. Kennith; Josephine.
Thrush, Robert; Milo.
Thrush, Mr. and Mrs. Winfield; Ola.
Todd, Mr. and Mrs. Roy W.; Bruce.
Torrence, Mr. and Mrs. John.
Waddups, Mr. and Mrs. George; Ruth, Mary, George E.
Walsh, Mr. and Mrs. F. K.; Dorothy.
Walsh, Mr. and Mrs. Will, Sr.; Joseph, Margaret, Thomas, Arthur, Helen, Lawrence.
Ware, Mr. and Mrs. Greenville; Earl.
Weasner, Mrs. William.
Wilson, Mr. and Mrs. Henry; Chas. Olive.
Wilson, Mr. and Mrs. Roy; Forest, Ruth, Hazel.
Young, Chester.

Illustrations

Soldiers Leaving for Camp _____ 1
Gen. Pershing's Headquarters _____ 26
General Headquarters in France _____ 26
Whippet Tank _____ 66
Liberty Guards _____ 82
Groups of Soldiers _____ Every Other Page
    between _____ 96 and 150
Nurses _____ 186
Dugouts at Verdun _____ 188

Gold Star Men

    Benge, Clarence Oren _____ 191
    Black, John W. _____ 191
    Burns, Ernest V. _____ 191
    Clymer, Claude Everett _____ 192
    Golub, Jacob _____ 192
    Hartz, Fred _____ 192
    Hartz, Benjamin Joe _____ 193
    Irvine, Martin A. _____ 193
    Koester, Earl C. _____ 193
    Mikesell, Deane Wilbur _____ 194
    Madary, Clarence Verle _____ 194
    Merely, Adolph R. _____ 195
    Murphy, Raymond George _____ 195
    Nicodemus, John A. _____ 195
    Parrish, George L. D. _____ 196
    Snyder, Jesse LeRoy _____ 196
    Shelton, Leroy C. _____ 197
    Van Meter, Frank _____ 197

Table of Contents

Aubbeenaubbee Schools ---------------------------------277

Banks -- 94
Boys in Khaki--- 95
Bridge Workers --------------------------------------- 93

Civil War, Recollections -----------------------------258
Committees --- 42
Contributors ---277
Councils of Defense----------------------------------- 54
Conscription Board ----------------------------------- 71

Death of Verle Madary -------------------------------257

Financing the War------------------------------------ 62
Food Administration ---------------------------------- 70
4th Division ---204
42nd Division --218
Fuel Administration ---------------------------------- 79
Fulton County in the War----------------------------- 40
Fulton County's Policy------------------------------- 56

General Pershing's Story ----------------------------- 25
Gold Star Men ---------------------------------------191

Honor Roll ---198

Liberty Guards --------------------------------------- 81
Liberty Red Cross ------------------------------------293
Library Work --- 80

Miscellaneous Statistics ----------------------------- 39

Nurses ---187
Newspapers --- 94

Red Cross Work --------------------------------------- 83
Rochester Workers ------------------------------------ 49

Soldiers' Letters and Experiences

Brickel, Harry ---273
Deardorf, Frederick K. ---266
Emrick, Ross D. ---260
Emons, Lester E. ---241
Flora, Arch ---274
Ferry, Chas. F. ---229
Garner, Clarence K. ---264
Goss, Byron C. ---244
Houser, A. W. ---269
Irvine, Chas. G. ---227
King, Milo S. ---242
Kistler, Chas. ---240
Marshall, Claude ---275
Overmyer, Roy ---260
Owen, Foster ---206
Redmond, Walter I. ---236
Swihart, Frank ---243
Sisson, Earl ---245
Shelton, Ray ---261
Sterner, Howard ---271
Safford, Fred L. ---272
Wright, Marcus ---276
Wright, Miss Ruth ---212
Westwood, Benj. ---263

Township Workers --- 43

Victory Boys and Girls --- 79

War Savings --- 65
Women's Work --- 87
Women's Liberty Loan --- 91
Women's Committees --- 50
Work on Farms --- 67
Work in Schools --- 75

The World War --- 9
    First Battle of the Marne --- 11
    Fighting the East --- 13
    War in Air and Sea --- 16
    The West Front --- 17
    The Russian Collapse --- 19
    United States Enters War --- 21
    Last German Drive --- 24